D1233533

JOHN LYLY

JOHN LYLY

The Humanist as Courtier

by

G. K. HUNTER

Harvard University Press
Cambridge Massachusetts
1962

Printed in Great Britain

CONTENTS

v

PREFACE

CERTAIN FEATURES of this book spring from an original intention to write a short critical account of Lyly's work, concentrating on what was of aesthetic value and leaving scholarly problems and documentation for my Clarendon Press edition of the *Works*. This did not prove possible; I have been obliged (by the nature of Lyly's virtues) to interpose more explanation between the author and the reader than I intended, and in particular to sketch out alternative perspectives in the literary history of the time—alternative, that is, to those most current today. I have persevered in simplification, none the less, for the necessity to *introduce* and *explain* Lyly to the modern world still seems strong. I have translated foreign languages, wherever possible, and I have modernized the spelling and punctuation of old authors; names and titles I have retained in their old form, however, if that seemed sufficiently standard to make the modernization awkward.

In the course of writing I have contracted many debts, not least to the books of predecessors; the works of John Nichols, E. K. Chambers, and R. Warwick Bond have come to seem like a condition of life. Above all I have depended on the massive labours of Albert Feuillerat; I have been able to move quickly through the life of Lyly, because Feuillerat had already uncovered the basic facts and reduced them to order. I have seldom been able to agree with Feuillerat's critical conclusions, but my very disagreement is dependent on his researches.

My debts to the dead cannot be repaid unless I have added a mite to the understanding of the past; the living exact a less terrifying rate of interest; the many personal favours I have met with can find some answer in personal acknowledgement. D. J. Gordon and William Ringler read and criticized an early draft. My colleagues in Liverpool, Kenneth Muir,

D. B. Quinn, Inga-Stina Ewbank and B. F. Nellist read chapters in typescript. Ernest Schanzer read the whole book, and his criticisms made many rough places plain. At proof stage I have received valuable assistance from many persons, notably J. C. Maxwell, Lisa Rauschenbusch and F. W. Sternfeld. Miss Margaret Burton reduced my foul papers to a fair copy. My wife has made space in our home for this demanding visitor out of the past; she has also equipped him with an Index.

To all these my gratitude is great; but I am well aware that no phalanx of friends can protect me from myself, in error or in bias. The former I would correct if I knew how; the latter I must accept. Such books as the present would be intolerable were they not seen as part of the unceasing tug-of-war by which opinion comes to feel like understanding. I cannot pretend to know a better motto for such a book than Lyly's own:

Commend it, or amend it.

G. K. HUNTER

The University, Liverpool
September 1961

ABBREVIATIONS

C.S.P.	Calendar of State Papers
E.E.T.S. e.s.	Early English Text Society: extra series
E.E.T.S. o.s.	Early English Text Society: ordinary series
Feuillerat	Albert Feuillerat, *John Lyly* (1910)
H.M.C.	Historical Manuscripts Commission
J.W.C.I.	*Journal of the Warburg & Courtauld Institutes*
M.L.N.	*Modern Language Notes*
M.L.R.	*Modern Language Review*
M.S.R.	Malone Society Reprints
Nichols	John Nichols, *The Progresses of Queen Elizabeth*
R.E.S.	*Review of English Studies*
S.P.	*Studies in Philology*
S.T.C.	Pollard and Redgrave, *Short title catalogue of English books before 1640*
U.T.Q.	*University of Toronto Quarterly*
V.C.H.	Victoria County History

I

HUMANISM AND COURTSHIP

THE ONLY English work of criticism, written about John Lyly before this present one (I mean John Dover Wilson's Harness Prize essay, *John Lyly* [Cambridge, 1905]), opens with a clear statement that the interest of the subject lies not in his intrinsic merits, but in the influence he exerted and the developments he encouraged. The only other critical book written about Lyly (M. Feuillerat's massive French thesis, *John Lyly: contribution à l'histoire de la Renaissance en Angleterre* [Cambridge, 1910] begins with almost the same sentiments: 'il m'a paru que Lyly avait surtout une valeur historique et philologique, et que vouloir l'offrir au délassement des simples amateurs de belles-lettres c'eût été l'exposer à des affronts'.

This is a depressing unanimity; yet it seems to the present writer to rest on distinctions which allow some play in their interpretation. Of course, to approach the works of Lyly by any kind of 'direct method' would be ridiculous. No modern reader can be expected to enjoy *Euphues* or the plays without some preparation in the modes of thinking and writing which they exemplify. Lyly has left no works which speak directly to the human heart of the twentieth century as do many of the lyrics of the period, for example, Ralegh's 'The Lie' or Wyatt's 'Be still my lute'. Lyly has no personal voice of this kind which can carry across the intervening centuries and stir the responses of the sympathetic but uninstructed reader today.

Yet to say that these works have 'aesthetic' value while Lyly's have only 'historical' interest seems an unnecessarily sharp distinction. For if by 'historical' we mean that they contribute to our understanding of the age in which they

A   I

appeared, I do not know how they do this unless they make us respond to the attitudes they convey; and this *response* seems to me an aesthetic one. What is more, the response seems to work two ways. An appreciation of Lyly sharpens our awareness of what the Elizabethan Age was really like; but it is also true that an understanding of Elizabethan attitudes enables us to see the virtues of Lyly in a sharper focus.

It is along these two lines that I wish to conduct the argument of this book. I wish to approach Lyly from a historical point of view, but to dwell at the same time on his individual merits rather than his influence on others. For concentrating on what Dover Wilson (following Taine) calls his 'dynamical' interest —estimating what he contributed to others, and especially to Shakespeare—seems to me to distort quite basically the qualities he had. For he is not seeking to do the same kind of thing as Shakespeare; he is not appealing to the same responses; he was, in fact, a different kind of writer. Though the gap in time and class between the two men was small, there is a historical gap of some magnitude between the points on which their separate gazes are fixed—Shakespeare looks forward where Lyly looks back.

The approach to the Elizabethan age that begins with Shakespeare is natural and inevitable; but it has its limitations, and at some stage in a closer study it has to be abandoned. Through major authors the historical situations in which they lived become universal; 'any man' we suppose, 'could think thus' discovering High Toryism in Dr Johnson, Christian Pessimism in Swift, Puritanism in Milton or Bunyan. But the modernity of such authors can be as misleading as illuminating, for the supposition that the whole age was really trying to achieve the 'modernity' of its greatest figures often fatally distorts its minor ones. The cultural history of Elizabethan England has suffered especially from this 'Whig'[1] inter-pretation of its tendencies, and from the assumption that its tendencies were also its principles.[2]

This standard view sees the voyages of Drake, the defeat of the Armada, the daring plays of Marlowe, the wild life of Robert Greene as different manifestations of the same central urge towards modern freedom and naturalness, the same impatience with restraints (physical or intellectual) which might impede the vigorous flow of life, released at last from the long sleep of the medieval 'night' preceding—an energy which found its fullest expression in the mature plays of Shakespeare. From this point of view the 'spaciousness' of Elizabeth's reign is a setting for a new-found freedom of the human spirit[3], where (as J. R. Green long ago pointed out):

> The sphere of human interest was widened as it has never been widened before or since, by the revelation of a new heaven and a new earth. It was only in the later years of the sixteenth century that the discoveries of Copernicus were brought home to the general intelligence of the world by Kepler and Galileo, or that the daring of the Buccaneers broke through the veil which the greed of Spain had drawn across the New World of Columbus.
>
> (*Short History* (1886), p. 412)

Green may be brasher in expression than later historians, but the general view he expresses here may be said to remain a popularly accepted line in history (certainly in literary history) up to the present time. The widely influential *History of English Literature* by Legouis and Cazamian (revised edition, 1933) may serve as a convenient example of this, not because it is especially tendentious, but because its views are so coherent and well-organized. Beside Green's statement we may set Legouis' summary:

> The Renascence showed in England almost all the characteristics which it had throughout Europe: thought was liberated and broadened so that it broke its scholastic framework; destiny and morals ceased to be the matter only of dogma and became problematical; a rebellion against the spiritual authority was first incited by the Reformation . . . men looked with a new wonder at the heavens and the earth as they were revealed by the discoveries of the navigators and astronomy; superior beauty was perceived in the literature of classical antiquity. (p. 200)

We may also note his later point:

> By two successive advances [in literary production], the one made in 1578 [*Euphues* and *The Shepheard's Calendar*] while Drake was sailing round the world, the other in 1589 [*Faerie Queene*, I suppose], on the morrow of the Armada, England caught up with her continental rivals, if indeed she did not outpace them . . . The impulse for this production was derived from patriotism. It sprang from England's growing consciousness of strength, her

pride of prosperity, the spirit of adventure which animated her
sons and caused them always to aspire to the first place, and her
faith in her own destiny . . . For most men, the exactions of God
did not go beyond those of patriotism . . . in truth, the country
was . . . eager not for religion but for games and pleasure,
ambitious of the free development which is the very spirit of the
Renascence. The intellectual paganism of humanism rested on
the broad basis of an instinctive paganism scattered wide among
the people. (pp. 250 f.)

Indeed, even though modern (non-literary) historians are
more cautious of committing themselves than was Green, one
may cite a paragraph from the current Oxford History of the
Age of Elizabeth showing the same views:

The outgoings of the spirit are conditioned by its in-takings, and
the imaginative reach of the man of letters keeps pace with the
widening horizon of his experience. The countless adventures on
land and sea that made England respected and feared, and
opened up the world to English enterprise, produced an exaltation of soul which the poet and the philosopher by the alchemy
of their genius transmuted into the unforgettable beauties and
enduring strength of a great literature. Like Drake and Cavendish,
Shakespeare and Bacon circumnavigated the earth and grew rich
on its spoils.

(J. B. Black, *The Reign of Elizabeth* [2nd edn., 1959], p. 280)

Such statements are surrounded, it is true, by qualifications,
but in the absence of any other positive cultural interpretation
of the period this may well be taken as the author's view.
Certainly Black is at one with Legouis in seeing 'the prevailing
tone' of the age as 'markedly secular and worldly' (p. 278)—
taking the words of preachers and satirists as objective truths
(speaking of 'the atmosphere of egoism, paganism, and
epicureanism in which the Elizabethan lived and moved and
had his being') and ignoring the standpoint of piety from which
such statements are made, and which they presuppose in their
readers.

So long as this view of the English Renaissance is accepted,
and with it the coordinate view of the relationship between
England and Italy in the period (see Black, p. 279), Lyly can
only appear as an awful example, the author of a work 'the
style of which is, perhaps, more elaborately and systematically

4

bad than that of any work in the whole extent of literature'⁴. For in so far as he shared in the new freedom of his time Lyly used this only to concoct 'a style modelled on the decadence of Italian prose' (Green's words). His liberty expressed itself as licence and as all good Whigs know, this leads to the abrogation of liberty itself. He is a writer without the hearty vitality that is supposed to be typical of the age, not a sea-dog of a writer but an exquisite miniaturist, a jewel-encrusted Fabergé nightingale, not a genuine English bird in the re-discovered world of natural beauty.

Indeed, even if we abandon the distortions of these literary-history preconceptions altogether, it is not obvious what attitudes to Lyly can take their place. The latest approaches to the literature of the English Renaissance are biassed by their method in favour of the complex lyric expressing indi-vidual soul-state. Such a work as the 'Pelican Guide' volume on *The Age of Shakespeare*, though the arguments against Lyly that I have indicated are dropped, does nothing to bring him into a new focus; and it is worth noting that the eclipse of Lyly is shared by Sidney, while Spenser (too large to be ignored) is given a travesty of treatment as an appendix to Chaucer. It would seem that with the decline of 'lit.-hist.' the sixteenth-century part of 'Elizabethan literature' has vanished.

I have already suggested that the only possible approach to Lyly is through the temper of the time in which he lived; but this can hardly be seen in perspectives which emphasize the incipient 'modernity' of the period, at the expense of its traditions; and these are the commonest perspectives in modern literary history and literary criticism. Fortunately, however, there is also a wealth of specialized scholarship on the period, which can be brought to bear on Lyly's position and which yields a different picture of his situation.

The English Renaissance, it appears, was never, by itself, a movement which could have condemned Lyly as 'artificial'—the word was, of course, at that time a term of praise. The days of Elizabeth may have seemed 'spacious' even to those who lived under the Queen, but the space was seen in very different terms from Green's by those who occupied it. The terms in which the age seems to have been aware of itself and proud of itself were terms which showed it to possess a new power over the moral content of life (morals being taken to include manners); this was coupled to a sense of release from the muddle of the past, from the medieval tendency to spin schemes and dreams and leave the practice to founder in the mud.[5] The age was aware of concentrating its cleverness on *this* world, a world of solid and colourful objects, and of using eloquence to produce a human rather than a theoretical order, by actualizing the moral ideals that God had supplied. But this is very far from supposing that forceful action or liberty from restraint are goods in themselves.

The age sees the historical movement as one out of contemplative *idleness* (pictured as a monk in Spenser, and elsewhere) and into practical utility.[6] Religion, says Sir John Cheke (who taught King Edward and all Cambridge Greek) has two parts, 'the one of which is placed in the searching after *knowledge* and in the tracing out of those things which are grateful and well-pleasing unto God; but the other is employed in *action*, which puts forward into life and performance what she understands to have the divine approbation'. That which is active, Cheke says, 'we may name piety'.[7] There can be little doubt that Cheke himself, and most vocal Elizabethans, supposed that this second was the crucial part of religion;[8] it was obviously so if the scriptures were plain, open, easy and fruitful, as they were often said to be.

It follows that forceful action *of the right kind* could be seen as the highest human activity by many Elizabethan theorists, and here they were at one with continental Humanists. Man was widely admired in the period for his power to remould himself and his destiny.[9] Even the staid Erasmus says that Prometheus is a figure to be admired and imitated.[10] But this ideal of 'Promethean man' is no late nineteenth-century anarchist or even radical vision; rather is it part of a priggish course in self-improvement. C. S. Lewis has amusingly presented the essential difference between Renaissance *humanitas* and medieval *humilitas*;[11] self-consciousness in virtue certainly seems to be a recurrent feature of the Renaissance, as of its idol, Cicero.

The energy that is admired widely and with complete orthodoxy is the energy which is disciplined in the mind by *order*, so as to effect and control an order in the world outside.

The 'Promethean' men of the English Renaissance—Ralegh,[12] Sidney, Burghley—are as devoted to self-conscious moral platitudes as are the 'irregular' dramas of the populace. Both see energy reaching out to touch an immutable set of moral norms; the 'spaciousness' of the Queen's reign was seen as stretching between the little that man had done and the great deal that man could do, but what man could do was not to be determined by the limits of human energy but was everywhere bound in by a divinely appointed frame of order. Discovery of 'those things which are pleasing unto God' will lead from self-conscious probity to action—and this is seen at its highest as the kind of action which will reduce 'divers cities, countries and nations . . . to civil order and politic life' (Starkey's *Dialogue between Pole and Lupset* [ed. Burton], p. 22).

Both the pleasures of self-conscious rectitude and sense of Divine Mission in the power to order secular affairs point to a truth about the Elizabethan court. Elizabeth and her establishment remained at the centre of the national consciousness throughout the 'spacious days' we admire so much, and this would seem enigmatic if we were to suppose that the main national effort of the time was in the direction of freedom and naturalness. For the court of Elizabeth was neither natural nor free. Its ritual was artificial to the last degree, despotic and repetitive. The sovereign was a painted idol rather than a person; the codes of manners it encouraged were exotic, Petrarchan and Italianate. Yet this artificial and insincere world had the power to harness the diverse energies of high and low alike. Its artifice does not seem to have cut off the sovereign from her people, but on the contrary seems to have focussed more clearly what they wanted to see—a manifestation of Divine Order on earth, and a guarantee of the meaning of secular energy, in terms which recalled the ritual of divine service.

The writers of the Elizabethan court show the same characteristics, and for the same reasons. Sidney, Spenser and Lyly are 'artificial' writers, but this hardly means that they were out of touch with their age. As the artificiality of the court was an efficient means of expressing its serious and indeed religious sense of the 'space' that was open to it, so the artifice of these writers was part of a serious attempt to display what were

7

generally taken to be the deepest values of the age. Exquisiteness of form in Lyly, Spenser or Sidney is no more an argument for superficiality of treatment than are the love-locks and silk stockings of the courtiers a sign of effeminateness; one supposition is as crass as the other. The common modern assumption is that the 'real' Elizabethan qualities are found in popular rather than courtly literature of the time. The formality of the court writers is usually seen not as an effort to impose order on the chaos of secular experience but rather as an attempt to emasculate the 'natural' vitality of the Elizabethan spirit. For Green, 'wild, reckless, defiant of all past tradition, of all conventional laws, the English dramatists owned no teacher, no source of poetic inspiration, but the people itself'.[13] If this were true, then Sidney, Lyly, Spenser would indeed be coterie pedants, only coming alive (if ever) when their natural vitality broke through their sense of decorum.

These assumptions, however, seem to distort both the popular and the courtly art of the time. Our ideas of court formality and of the art which is appropriate to that seem, on the whole, to belong to Versailles rather than to Whitehall. The neo-classical pronouncements of Elizabethan critics are so much more intelligible than the art-forms they use that we tend to substitute one for the other, when we wish to discuss ideals; it is much easier to see what Sidney was aiming at in the neo-classical canons of *The Defence of Poesie* than to discover the rationale of the *Arcadia*—that 'pastoral-romantic-heroic-philosophical prose-poem'.[14] If we pursue the 'mixed wit' of the *Arcadia* or *The Faerie Queene*, however, we find a Gothic concern for variety of experience and for the different levels of meaning which links them to the 'art' we discover in Shakespeare, when we cease to see him (in the Green manner) 'warbling his native woodnotes wild'. The popular Elizabethan drama (as Miss Bradbrook has taught us all) was just as 'artful', as dependent on themes and conventions as was the court art of the time. Both kinds of writing use the same 'multiple' modes of presentation; instead of concentrating on a single viewpoint, and subordinating all else, they bring together different attitudes, stories, experiences, situations, and require them to harmonize 'thematically' as best they can. But in the popular work of the time, this may well seem to modern readers an art without art—may even seem to be 'nature'—while in the court works it is intellectual and obviously intentional. We cannot patronize the work of Sidney and Spenser in the same way that critics often patronize that of Greene or Lodge; we must accept it as seriously artful, or not accept it at all.

The difference may be seen in terms of the distinction between the *tendency* of the age and its *self-consciousness*, already touched on. The courtly artists are more obviously self-conscious; in consequence they reflect the sense of the need for order, which I have described, more obtrusively than their popular contemporaries; they appeal to an audience well aware of the abstract implications of their own mode of life. But the popular authors did not have a different creed; they subscribed to the same general assumptions and worked by the same artistic methods. Though we may find it easier to ignore the artfulness of *their* 'Gothic' methods, they were not different in principle. If we are to understand the 'Elizabethan' quality even in Shakespeare we must understand his art as well as his exuberance, his energy; and his art is an unpretentious variant on the formal art of the court. The two aspects are derived from one age and from unified individuals; they point in different directions, but they belong together, and modify one another continuously.

With this sense of the homogeneousness of Elizabethan writing, courtly and popular, in our minds, we may see why contemporaries looked on 'friendly Shakespeare' and other popular writers as all right in their kind, but of a rather lowly kind. Today we may prefer the spontaneous, unfinished sketch or fragment to the laboriously polished masterpiece,[15] but we should see why, in an age which prided itself on its sense of secular Order, this judgment had to be reversed. Looking back on the period with the eyes of Romantics, and through the vistas of neo-classicism, we are liable to talk about its *freedom*; but this is only possible because we are seeing history the wrong way round; what, from our nostalgic point of view, may seem 'vitality and freedom' must have seemed then more like the threat of chaos,[16] to be held in check by whatever formal means were available. And this is the achievement of the court artists of Elizabeth's reign—to have found formal means of containing the experience of the time, and so to pass on to the age following the easier task of humanizing and modifying the formal heritage.

Another way of looking at this achievement is to look at it in terms of *wit*. I have suggested that the Elizabethans modified the attitudes they inherited by concentrating the interest of their art on *this* world, and so turning the complex valuations of spiritual and worldly experiences (as in *Piers Plowman* or poems of the *de contemptu mundi* tradition) into complex valuations of different kinds of worldly experience. The ease with which a man moves among these comparative valuations may be measured by his capacity to play them off, one against the other, and this is obviously a capacity involved in 'witty' writing, such as we find in Lyly's *Euphues*. Indeed I shall argue that Lyly's works are characterized throughout by a remarkable capacity to balance modes of experience against one another. It may be a coincidence, but if so it is an interesting one, that about this time the word *wit* seems to have acquired a new sense.[17] Dr Johnson tells us that 'it was about the time of Cowley that *wit* which had been till then used for *intellection*, in contradistinction to *will*, took the meaning, whatever it be, which it now bears'. (Life of Cowley) Johnson would seem to be wrong about the date. The Oxford Dictionary gives *Euphues* as the first source for the meaning, 'liveliness of fancy'; this is not a final dating, but it is certain that *Euphues, the Anatomy of Wit* is concerned to define *wit* in an unusual way. I may quote here the note of Professor Croll:

> The word as used by Ascham in the passage which suggested Lyly's title [*see below*, p. 49], means simply talent for studies, intellectual capacity. This is the usual meaning in the 16th century. Lyly often places it, however, in antithesis with *wisdom*, much as he contrasts *lust* and *love*. A new turn is thus given to the word (which it also displays in other writers).
>
> (*Euphues*, ed. Croll and Clemons, p. 2)

The extreme formality of the structure and the expression of *Euphues* I am suggesting to be a measure of Lyly's effort to organize the different levels of experience in this life so that they throw light on one another. He reflects and comments on the courtly world of Elizabeth by organizing into witty patterns different responses to its key ideas—'wit', 'honour', 'love', 'royalty', etc. Seeing his work in this way we may see how far Lyly could be himself, and also the entertainer of Elizabeth and other vital creatures, and perhaps the largest single influence on that 'spacious' genre, Shakespearian Comedy.

I have suggested that the formal literature of Elizabeth's court expresses the society we profess to admire in a more exact way than the popular literature that provides our first glimpse of it. It is also worth noticing that modern political enthusiasm for the reign of Elizabeth does not belong even chronologically with modern taste for 'Elizabethan' drama (largely the product of the last ten years of the Queen—'the decline' as Professor Neale sees it[18]—and the reign of James). The literature which we admire most easily belongs to a political set-up that we do not admire. The individualistic soul-searching and suspicion of conventionality which we meet in Bacon, Greville, Jonson, Donne, and in Shakespeare's tragedies is the mirror of a general loss of faith in society; and it speaks directly to our own individualistic suspicions of social good. But the genuinely Elizabethan works cannot make this appeal; their claim is rather to be representative of the milieu in which they first appeared, and they can most conveniently be approached through the social and intellectual presuppositions of their social background. To see the works of Sidney and Lyly only as precursors to the modern novel and drama is, I suggest, to deny them what coherence they have; we are reduced to the position of the learned historian of the novel, who complains that the Elizabethans never managed to approach the novel form, because they never had any inkling of what a novel was like.[19] Likewise to see them only as precursors to the more sympathetic writers at the turn of the century is to destroy their individual quality. Our hope must be that if we can understand an author like Lyly in relation to his original context, his works will acquire meaning in terms of our own very different context. The hope is better founded than it might seem. In their elaboration of style, their virtuoso techniques asking for expert admiration, their attempt to derive an ideal way of life from a set social system, such works are not so remote from us today as they were from the Whig historians of literature at the beginning of this century. The breakdown of belief in the individual life as the resting-place of all real goodness has thrown a corresponding weight upon our view of the institutions and systems which contain individuals. We are in consequence more prepared today to allow the seriousness of works which show ideals of living only to be realized in highly developed and to that extent artificial societies. It has become easier for us to understand that society may seem an immutable good, a divinely appointed organism and to see that flattery can be an activity that is compatible with self-respect, being indeed only the homage that the self-aware individual pays to such a society. In more purely literary terms, we have become correspondingly uncertain of the necessity for an artist to be *original*; and it follows from this that we are more prepared to accept Imitation as a legitimate approach to creative writing. If this is so, then the hope may be justified that Lyly can now be seen as more than a mine for antiquarian research; for Lyly is par excellence both flatterer and imitator. We cannot find a way into Lyly's prose-works and plays by pretending that his worlds are real worlds in which we ourselves might live. His aim is to create a mode of life which is so witty, so poised, so brilliant that we are flattered by being thought refined enough to forget real life and enjoy its ideals of love and honour; of these the characters are only mouthpieces, and these the works assume without argument to be desirable. A modern audience does not bring such assumptions to the work, but the aspiration to a life of witty elegance is sufficiently general to give us at least a point of entry.

I have suggested that the natural approach to Lyly lies through the society for which he wrote, and whose ideals he reflected. I argue also that his works stand at the end of a tradition of courtly entertainment and relate to the general entertainments or literature of Shakespeare or Marlowe only to the extent to which the terms of one tradition can be translated into another. Both of these suggestions depend for their plausibility on an understanding of the traditional notions about art and entertainment which governed the thinking of court artists and of the court itself in Tudor times. If we cannot approach Lyly through the understanding that an appreciation of Shakespeare gives to us, we must try to approach him through the tradition of what is called Humanism.

I am reluctant to use this word since it raises the fearsome question, 'What is Humanism?' a question within whose murky depths whole libraries might be sunk without affording a foothold. If we restrict ourselves to England, however, a basic description is possible: the Humanists were those who promoted and engaged in the study of Greek and of Ciceronian Latin, and, as C. S. Lewis blandly remarks, followed 'the critical principles . . . which ordinarily went with these studies'. Unfortunately (for definition) we cannot limit the Humanist principles to those of literary criticism. Humanism, like any other seriously pursued discipline, was a way of life, defining itself by its violent antipathy to other ways of life; in this case the obvious enemy was the medieval attitude to contemplation, with its accompanying views on the function of study in *this* world, and on the purpose of elegance and order in the mind.

From this point of view the Humanist movement was, it is true, part of a general movement of secularization; but it seems an error, as far as England is concerned, to think of it as anti-religious, or at all like the modern movement of the same name. It sought to turn religious ideals and energies towards the amelioration of life in this world and to achieve an order in this life corresponding to the religious vision of man's worth. The ideals of civility were in most cases based on the civilization of pagan antiquity, but this did not seem to them to require an abandonment of Christian conscience. It is absurd to call English Humanism 'pseudo-humanism—not pagan, but Christian' (as J. A. Gee does in his life of Lupset [p. 29]), not only because the humanism of Pico and Ficino shows the same bias (and if theirs is not the true Humanism, whose is?), but because there was, in fact, no contradiction between the classical literary enthusiasms of Erasmus, Melanchthon or More and their enthusiasm for a renewed and purified Christianity. They saw themselves as freeing religion from a cloistered uselessness, a concentration on theory coupled to an ignorance of practice, and there is a lot to be said on their side. Mighty though their admiration was for Greek clarity and Roman civility they had no doubt that they themselves had a basic advantage over their classical forebears in the revelation of Christian truth.

It is only in the context of this practical Christianity that their untiring pursuit of the faded elegancies of Ciceronian Latin can be seen in correct perspective. The desire for elegance, urbanity and that sophistication which instinctively recognizes the *mot juste* was part of their desire for order in this world as a whole, an order which would show itself in its fulness only when Ciceronian urbanity controlled philosophical senates or philosopher-kings and created a state where the Christian potentialities of man could be realized, where the *vita contemplativa* of the saint could enrich and enlarge the *vita activa* of the statesman. Christ himself, Richard Pace pointed out, could be seen as the type of the Humanist, for He was not only saintly but also practical, using persuasive eloquence to impart his message; this example (together with that of the Evangelists and the Fathers) imposed an obligation to do the like on all Christians:[20] 'to this [end] all men are born and of nature brought forth: to commune such gifts as be to them given, each one to the profit of other (Starkey, p. 22); [for] virtue and learning, not communed to other is like unto riches heaped in corners never applied to the use of other' (ibid. p. 24). Eloquence and Rhetoric are simply the means of carrying out this duty of communication most efficiently;[21] and it was as such it was taught in the grammar schools: 'so as to work in themselves [the pupils] a greater love of the virtue and hatred of the vice, and to be able with soundness of reason to draw others to their opinion' (Brinsley, *Ludus Literarius* [ed. Campagnac], p. 175).

The aim, as can be seen, was high, and the programme coherent; but there was a fatal weakness in the position. Since Humanism was concerned to point spiritual energies and enthusiasms into this world and so to ameliorate its condition, it deprived the scholar of his natural refuge in contempt of the practical world. For this very reason, as English history moves forward, and as the Humanists seem to move nearer to their ideal of a philosophical state, so their involvement in politics becomes more crippling; their natural instinct as scholars is to remain theorists (even if theorists of practical affairs), but the philosophy of scholarship within which they are operating keeps them from retiring altogether. Their position *vis-à-vis* any opportunist politician (like Wolsey or Henry VIII) who wished to use them as official apologists was thus fatally weak, and was ruthlessly exploited; but in spite of this, the possibility of affecting human destiny in a *real* (as against a theoretical) way remained a powerful myth for humanists, from Wolsey to Milton and beyond. Certainly the history of English Humanism can be seen as an exercise in the myth of the political effectiveness of learning: we see Wolsey, Cromwell, Henry, Edward and the young Elizabeth, each for a different purpose, requiring the Humanists to use their talents in the preparation of policy statements and the persuasion of other countries. It is only by the middle of Elizabeth's reign that government becomes sure enough of itself to dispense with their sometimes embarrassing services; by this time, however, the myth of state-service as the natural end of a training in the humanities is so well established that the up-and-coming literati cannot escape from it: it controls the outlook and attitudes of a man like John Lyly, and to understand the course his life took as well as the mode in which he wrote we must trace something of its development in England.

The first generation of Englishmen who studied Greek and Latin in the new Italian manner was, inevitably, a medieval generation. Grey, Gunthorpe, Free, Flemming, Sellyng—that choice band of pioneers one can read about in Professor Roberto Weiss's *Humanism in England during the fifteenth century* (1941)—were all ecclesiastics, and their careers remained ecclesiastical: two became bishops, two became deans and one became a prior, but this can hardly be said to be a direct consequence of their knowledge of Greek. They founded no schools and left no clear tradition, and it has required modern scholarship to unearth their very names. In a tenuous way one may say there was some continuity: Sellyng taught Linacre, and Linacre is the eldest of the next generation of humanists and the 'studiorum praeceptor' of Thomas More; but the demands on humanism were so altered by the historical developments of the sixteenth century that the earlier experience of Greek studies could have little to say to the later.

The next generation—of Linacre, Grocyn, Latimer, Fisher, Fox, More, Colet and William Lily, to which one may annexe the extra-territorial name of Erasmus, is the generation of pedagogues; most of these men seem to have been in orders of some kind, but their lives, and their fame now, centre upon their founding, organizing, establishing instruments of the new learning—Corpus Christi College in Oxford, St Paul's School, The Royal College of Physicians—and their elaboration of programmes and curricula. These foundations and programmes have, moreover, a severely practical aim—none the less pious for that. They aim to make learning more useful and to create in consequence an elite in learning to replace the feudal aristocracy now going rapidly out of date, and already out of key with the Tudor absolutism. The story told by Richard Pace—himself a product of humanist advancement—is well known, but is worth repeating again, so typical is it of this development.

> A nobleman of this time in contempt of learning said that it was for noblemen's sons enough to wind their horn and carry their hawk fair and to leave study and learning to the children of mean men. To whom . . . Richard Pace replied, 'Then you and other noblemen must be content that your children may wind their horns and keep their hawks, while the children of mean men do manage matters of estate'.　(Camden's *Remains* (1605), p. 220)

There is an interesting variant in the last sentence here from the Latin which Camden is paraphrasing. Pace himself writes

> nam si veniret ad regem aliquis vir exterus quales sunt principum oratores, et ei dandum ei responsum, filius tuus sic ut tu vis, institutus, inflaret duntaxat cornu et rusticorum filii docti ad respondendum vocarent.　(p. 15)

> for if some foreigner, such as are the ambassadors of princes, come to the king and a reply has to be given to him, your son, educated as you desire, may blow his horn, but it is the learned sons of mean men that are called to make the reply.

One of the most obvious uses of Ciceronian Latin was in the diplomatic service, and the Humanists were much employed as ambassadors (*oratores*). The capacity to pronounce royal messages was of course only a part of the New Learning. More important was the capacity to think out the proper content for such messages. Wolsey's foundation, Cardinal's College in Oxford, and Cromwell's (and later, Henry's) support of English scholars on the continent were aimed at a flexibility of mind and width of political and social experience so that the new world of secular law and centralized administration would not have to rely on minds entirely unprepared for it.[22] By the time of the third generation of Humanists the original impulse towards a secular piety was already being distorted by court necessities into shapes that seem to bear little likeness to their originals. By the time we reach John Lyly the Humanist impulse is so strangely altered that we would not recognize it, were it not for the clear line that carries down this far.

To study the debt that John Lyly owes to this tradition it is not necessary to go outside the history of his own family. John's grandfather and the founder of the family's scholastic fortunes was William Lily,[23] who was born in Odiham, in Hampshire, in or about 1468. We know nothing of his parentage or early life, but Anthony à Wood tells us that William Grocyn, one of the foremost scholars of the time, was his godfather; it was this cause that led Grocyn to leave Lily the sum of five shillings in his will (*Oxford Collectanea* II); and we may assume that Lily did not come from totally undistinguished stock. Like Grocyn himself, Lily went to Magdalen College, Oxford, which had been recently founded by William of Waynflete and now served as one of the principal nurseries of Humanist learning. The same college was the home of Linacre, Grocyn (who was Divinity Reader there), Thomas Starkey, Cardinal Pole, and probably of John Colet, who was at Oxford at the same time as Lily. In 1486 Lily entered as a Demy of Magdalen; it has been suggested that he was one of those Demies who were to apply themselves 'so long to grammatical and poetical and other humane arts that they could not only profit themselves but be able also to instruct and educate others'—that is, that he worked as a grammar master in Magdalen School.[24]

Like the other Humanists, Lily completed his education by travelling to the Mediterranean,[25] which he did in 1488-1492. Before attending to the secular pursuit of learning, he visited the Holy places in Jerusalem. On his return from Jerusalem he stayed some time in Rhodes where he learned Greek, no doubt as the pupil of one of the many learned refugees who had fled from Byzantium to the protection of the knights of St John, there established. From Greek in Rhodes he seems to have passed to Ciceronian Latin (the other hallmark of Humanist learning) in Italy. He studied in Rome and Venice and had as instructors Giovanni Sulpicio (Sulpicius Verulanus) and Julius Pomponius Laetus [Sabinus] (also known as Pomponio Leto). This former teacher may almost be supposed to have provided

a model for Lily's own career, for he was the author of a celebrated Latin grammar and of a *Carmen Iuvenilis de Moribus*, just
as Lily was to be. In view of the close relationship that was
to grow up between the English grammar schools and the
English drama it may be worth noticing that Pomponio Leto
(also a grammarian[26]) is said to have been the first modern
European to stage the works of Plautus and Terence, which he
did at his Roman Academy from 1471 onward.

In making this Grand Tour of Learning, Lily was following
in the footsteps of Grocyn (who had returned to Oxford in
1491 to become the first teacher of Greek in the University); in
Rome he had as his companions a choice band of scholars
including Linacre, Colet, William Warham, and Christopher
Bambridge.[27] He is still in the same circle when he returns to
England. We do not know what he is doing in this period: he
is presented with a living which he subsequently resigns; he
marries a certain Agnes, and we must suppose from this that
he never went further than minor orders. In 1504 he is passing
his time with Grocyn, Linacre and Thomas More in London,
and More refers to him as his 'dearest friend'. Grocyn was at
this time Rector of St Lawrence Jewry and was lecturing in
St Paul's on the *Celestial Hierarchies* (still generally taken in this
period to be the work of that Dionysius that St Paul met,
though Grocyn (characteristically) came to have doubts).[28]
More, no doubt under Grocyn's auspices, had been lecturing
about the same time on St Augustine's *City of God*. The combination of piety and learning that is evident in these activities
was much to the taste of William Lily but we do not know if
he was engaged in any kind of teaching at this time. The
instinct which had taken Lily to Jerusalem and was to carry
More to martyrdom showed itself in the devotions which the
two of them undertook in this period among the Carthusians
in London. The taste for religious austerity as well as classical
wit which makes More's character a puzzle to many moderns
seems to have been shared with William Lily. The two men
also competed in translations from the Greek Anthology.[29]

As far as the history of English Humanism goes, the crucial
event of these years is the decision of Colet (Dean of St Paul's
since 1504) to devote his patrimony to the foundation of a new
school; this would embody in its curriculum the new Humanist

ideals of elegant Latin and ethical Greek. As early as 1508 he
began building in the southeast corner of St Paul's churchyard,
and he also set about looking for a man 'whole in body, honest
and virtuous, and learned in the good and clean Latin literature
and also in Greek, if such may be gotten; a wedded man, a
single man or a priest that hath no benefice . . .' to serve as
headmaster. He found his man in William Lily, one who was,
says Polydore Virgil, 'a man such as Horace speaks of *integer
vitae scelerisque purus.*'[30] Lily was officially appointed as the first
High Master of St Paul's School in 1510. It seems probable
that by 1509 Lily and Colet were already collaborating in a
new Latin grammar. In 1509 Colet produced his *Aeditio*
(accidence) and it must have been about the same time that he
requested Lily to write a syntax more advanced than the
Rudiments which Lily had already written (it would seem).
Lily wrote his syntax, Erasmus revised it and the *De Construc-
tione* as it was called appeared anonymously at some date
which we can hardly guess at (since the first surviving edition
is dated 1527).[31] In spite of the modesty, which prevented
either author from claiming the work of the other, Lily's name
became attached to the whole collection of these separate parts,
and 'Lily's Grammar' carried his fame down through the
eighteenth century.

The aim of 'Lily's Grammar' was an extremely humane one:
to take the pupils as quickly as possible to classical *literature* by
cutting down to a minimum the rules that had to be learned.
Set against the old method of 'Vulgars',[32] the grammar of St
Paul's was something like a 'direct method 'approach to Latin;
years later (1570) Roger Ascham was still complaining about
the 'Vulgars' of Horman and Whittington, which had allowed
the pupils to approach classical Latinity via a dog-Latin
which aped the order of English. Such an approach offended
the Humanist conscience which saw elegant Latinity as a
state of grace, not to be debased or vulgarized.[33] For this
reason the framework of grammar is always to appear secondary
and supplementary; '. . . all the varieties and diversities and
changes in Latin speech (which be innumerable) if any man
will know, and by that knowledge attain to understand
Latin books, and to speak and to write the clean Latin, let him
above all busily learn and read good Latin authors of chosen

poets and orators, and note wisely how they wrote and spake, and study alway to follow them, desiring none other rules but their examples. For in the beginning men spake not Latin because such rules were made, but contrariwise because men spake such Latin upon that followed the rules were made. That is to say, Latin speech was before the rules, not the rules before the Latin speech. Wherefore, well-beloved masters and teachers of grammar, after the parts of speech sufficiently known in your schools, read and expound plainly unto your scholars good authors, and show to them every word, and in every sentence what they shall note and observe, warning them busily to follow and to do like both in writing and in speaking, and be to them your own self also speaking with them the pure Latin very present, and leave the rules.' (Colet's epilogue to his Accidence).[34] Colet's almost clinical concern with 'cleanness' of Latinity is very evident in this extract and is embodied in the statutes which he drew up for St Paul's.

'As touching in this school what shall be taught of the masters and learned of the scholars it passeth my wit to devise and determine in particular, but in general to speak and somewhat to say my mind, I would they were taught alway in good literature both Latin and Greek, and good auctors such as have the very Roman eloquence joined with wisdom, specially Christian auctors that wrote their wisdom with clean and chaste Latin either in verse or in prose; for my intent is by this school specially to increase knowledge and worshipping of God and our Lord Christ Jesu and good Christian life and manners in the children. And for that intent I will the children learn first above all the Catechism in English and after, the accidence that I made, or some other if any be better to the purpose, to induce children more speedily to Latin speech. And then *Institutum Christiani Hominis* which that learned Erasmus made at my request and the book called *Copia* of the same Erasmus. And then other auctors Christian, as Lactantius, Prudentius, and Proba and Sedulius and Juvencus and Baptista Mantuanus and such other as shall be taught, convenient and most to purpose unto the true Latin speech. All barbary, all corruption, all Latin adulterate which ignorant blind fools brought into this world, and with the same hath distained and poisoned the old Latin speech and the very Roman tongue which in the time of Tully and Sallust and Virgil and Terence was used, which also Saint Jerome and Saint

Ambrose and Saint Austin and many holy doctors learned in their times—I say that filthiness and all such abusion which the later blind world brought in, which more rather may be called blot-erature than literature I utterly abanish and exclude out of this school and charge the masters that they teach alway that is the best and instruct the children in Greek and reading Latin, in reading unto them such auctors that hath with wisdom joined the pure chaste eloquence.' (Lupton's *Life of Colet* 279 f.)

This passionate concern with wisdom of subject matter and 'chastity' of expression, leading to the position, as C. S. Lewis somewhat unfairly remarks, that 'the boys were to be guarded from every word that did not occur in Virgil or Cicero, and equally from every idea that did' (*16th century literature*, p. 160) was a direct reflection of the educational philosophy of Erasmus; for him, 'All knowledge falls into one of two divisions: the knowledge of 'truths' and the knowledge of 'words' . . . They are not to be commended who, in their anxiety to increase their store of truths, neglect the necessary art of expressing them . . . This goes to prove that true education includes what is best in both kinds of knowledge, taught, I must add, under the best guidance. For, remembering how difficult it is to eradicate early impressions, we should aim from the first at learning what need never be unlearnt, and that only. Language thus claims the first place in the order of studies . . . But I must make my conviction clear that, whilst a knowledge of the rules of accidence and syntax is most necessary to every student, still they should be as few, as simple, and as carefully framed as possible . . . For it is not by learning rules that we acquire the power of speaking a language, but by daily intercourse with those accustomed to express themselves with exactness and refinement, and by the copious reading of the best authors . . . Some proficiency in expression being thus attained the student devotes his attention to the content of the ancient literatures . . . For I affirm that with slight qualification the whole of attainable knowledge lies enclosed within the literary monuments of ancient Greece. This great inheritance I will compare to a limpid spring of whose undefiled waters it behoves all who truly thirst to drink and be restored' (paraphrase of 'De Ratione Studii', in Woodward, *Erasmus on Education* 162-4).

Humanism and Courtship

The aim of the whole process is to produce pupils who will speak and write 'pure', 'clean' and 'chaste' Latin of their own—the moral connotations of these epithets are not accidental, for the clear and elegant arrangement of words 'The common word exact without vulgarity, The formal word precise but not pedantic, The complete consort dancing together' is seen as a symptom of an orderly mind, a mind attuned to the orders of monarch and deity:

Ye know not what hurt ye do to learning that care not for words but for matter, and so make a divorce betwixt the tongue and the heart. For mark all ages: look upon the whole course of both the Greek and Latin tongue, and ye shall surely find that when apt and good words began to be neglected and properties of those two tongues to be confounded, then also began ill deeds to spring, strange manners to oppress good orders, new and fond opinions to strive with old and true doctrine, first in Philosophy and after in Religion, right judgment of all things to be perverted, and so virtue with learning is contemned and study left off; of ill thoughts commeth perverse judgment, of ill deeds springeth lewd talk, which four misorders, as they mar man's life, so destroy they good learning withall.

But behold the goodness of God's providence for learning: all old authors and sects of Philosophy which were fondest in opinion and rudest in utterance, as Stoics and Epicures, first contemned of wise men and after forgotten of all men, be so consumed by times as they be now not only out of use but also out of memory of man; which thing, I surely think, will shortly chance to the whole doctrine and all the books of phantastical Anabaptists and Friars and of the beastly Libertines and Monks.

Again behold on the other side how God's wisdom hath wrought, that of the Academici and Peripatetici, those that were wisest in judgment of matters and purest in uttering their minds, the first and chiefest that wrote most and best in either tongue, as Plato and Aristotle in Greek, Tully in Latin, be so either wholly or sufficiently left unto us as I never knew yet scholar that gave himself to like and love and follow chiefly those three authors, but he proved both learned, wise and also an honest man, if he joined withal the true doctrine of God's holy Bible, without the which the other three be but fine-edge tools in a fool or madman's hand.'

(Ascham, *The Schoolmaster* [ed. Arber], p. 118 f.)

The Humanist schoolmasters were relying rather heavily, we may suppose, on God's providence for learning,[35] but it was this supposition indeed that gave their educational programme its drive and dynamic: the 'bloterature' of the Middle Ages, the product of minds divorced from secular reality and caught in the tenuous web of their own cunning, was at a furthest remove from the luminous certainty and order of Christ's life upon earth dwelt on so heavily in its literal meaning in Colet's epoch-making lectures on St Paul;[36] to recover the primitive harmony between wit and wisdom, word and truth, seen in the early Fathers as in Christ, was a work of piety indeed, a true *Imitatio Christi*.

It was in this spirit that Colet's school was dedicated to the boy Jesus; Erasmus describes[37] how there was 'an excellent picture of the boy Jesus, seated in the attitude of one teaching, over the headmaster's chair, to which all the boys sing a (Latin) hymn as they enter and leave the school':

> Sweet Jesus, my Lord, who as a boy in the twelfth year of thine age didst dispute in the temple at Jerusalem among the doctors so that they all marvelled and were amazed at thy most excellent wisdom, I beg thee that in this thy school, of which thou art governor and patron, in which I daily learn letters and wisdom, I may chiefly come to know thee, Jesus, who art thyself the true wisdom, and then through that knowledge come to worship and imitate thee . . .[38]

It may seem a long way from irregular verbs to our heavenly home, but to these Humanist educators the distance could be expressed simply as the distance from the bottom rung of a ladder to the top. The ladder itself bore the name of Imitation, and the stages by which the scholar mounted from grammar and rhetoric to rectitude and Grace is expressed with logal clarity by the schoolmaster, William Kempe:

> all knowledge is taught generally both by precepts of art and also by practice of the same precepts. They are practised partly by observing examples of them in other men's works, and partly by making somewhat of our own, and that first by imitation, and at length without imitation; so that the perfection of the art is not gotten at the first, but *Per numeros veniunt ista gradusque suos*. Wherefore first the scholar shall learn the precepts; secondly he shall learn to note the examples of the precepts in unfolding

other men's works; thirdly, to imitate the examples in some work of his own; fourthly and lastly, to make somewhat alone without an example. Now, all these kinds of teaching are seen in every special sort of the things taught, be it Grammar, Logic, Rhetoric, Arithmetic, Geometry, or any other art.

(The Education of Children (1588), *sig.* F2)

The pious aims of the founder of St Paul's and the pious nature of the first headmaster could not have allowed the ladder of Imitation to have stopped at this point. For them, as for Erasmus, the end of education is *sapiens et eloquens pietas*,[39] active Christian virtue rendered effective in the service of the community by the power to write and to speak. *Propositum a nobis est sapientem atque eloquentem pietatem finem esse studiorum*, is the definition that Johannes Sturm, the German pedagogue so much respected in England, gives of his aims (*De literarum ludis* (1538), p. 104). More himself uses the traditional defence of secular study when he writes his letter to the University of Oxford, putting down the 'Trojan' or anti-Greek movement there.[40] He points out how secular learning can be justified because it prepares the mind for virtue, and can be used as a road towards the awareness of things supernatural; moreover it enables the theologian to reach into and control the minds of other people, by giving into his hands the techniques of the poets and orators of antiquity. From this point of view the secular content of the authors used to teach eloquence hardly mattered, given the methods by which they were taught. As one advanced up the ladder of imitation, any grossness in Terence or Lucian could be purged away, as in the ladder of Platonic love the grosser passions are lost in the contemplation of the soul and of the deity. Colet, it is true, does not mention secular authors in his statutes quoted above, but he is specifically avoiding anything like a list of set books (which, he says, 'it passeth my wit to devise'). He writes to Erasmus in 1512 that 'a bishop . . . took our school to task, and said that I had founded . . . a house of Idolatry. I believe that he said this, because the Poets are read there.'[41] As T. W. Baldwin remarks in quoting this passage, 'the objector was certainly not referring to the "Christian Poets", which some have supposed were the only poets to be taught at Paul's' (*Small Latine*, I, 78). It was indeed inevitable that 'the very Roman [or Greek] eloquence' would have to be taught out of unChristian (though not unethical) authors, but it could be taught in such a Christian perspective that all the major authors turned out to have had *mentes naturaliter Christianae*. If, as Ascham suggests (and he was reasonably typical), outward eloquence is a sign of inward grace, then the study and the acquisition of eloquence could hardly have a bad effect. The figure of Cicero—that archetypal *novus homo*—promoting public virtue and putting down public vice by the power of his philosophical eloquence, was one that remained central to the education of the whole period.

How far it could remain central to the lives of those who, like Cicero, had actual experience of politics, is another matter. If Colet's own experience is any indication, the relation between apostolic virtue and practical politics is apt to be a little strained. While Henry VIII was preparing for war in 1513, Colet was invited to preach the Good Friday sermon at court. Like Erasmus, Colet thought that the wars of kings were insane folly and in his sermon he praised the victory of Christ as the only victory worth winning; he pointed out the difficulty of Christian conduct in time of war, and spoke much to discourage the intending soldiers.

After an interview with Henry, however, it is said that the good Dean then preached another sermon, praising a defensive war such as the king was about to undertake. If this story is true, it is not surprising that Henry should have remarked, 'Let every man have his own doctor, and everyone follow his liking; but this is the doctor for me.'[42] All the flexibility of mind that Humanist training could impart was needed by those who came close to the centres of power.

William Lily died of plague in 1523 and was succeeded in his High Mastership by John Rightwise who succeeded also to his daughter Dionysia (Lily's will suggests that this was not achieved without compulsion). She, keeping the family and school traditions well aligned, subsequently married James Jacob, the school Usher, and so procured for John Lyly a set of uncles and aunts with names like Polydore and Scholastica. But though the family continued to be what Feuillerat has called it, '*une famille d'érudits*', the heroic quality of *making* traditions disappears from the scholastic world. Rightwise, says Anthony à Wood, was the most distinguished grammarian of his day (he means in England). He revised Lily's poem on the gender of nouns, and added a vocabulary to it. He took a troop of children to present a Morality before Henry VIII, and he may have written a play (*Dido*) which was performed at Cambridge.[43] He led a useful and distinguished life, but it was the life of a follower rather than a leader. The ladder of Imitation has been planted in the schools of the country; interest passes to the question of how it is to be used by those who have to implement the ideals of Humanism in life rather than in school. The pupils of Humanism look abroad for the power that has been promised to the eloquent man, and in looking are transformed.

The career of William Lily's eldest surviving son, George, illustrates neatly and conveniently the opportunities and problems that beset the next order of Humanists. George followed his father to Magdalen in 1528 but left the University without taking a degree; and he next appears at Padua in 1534 as a member of the learned household which was assembling round Reginald Pole, the young scholarly kinsman of Henry VIII; he studied law at Padua, having as his companions men whose future was to lie in state service, such as Richard Morison, Henry Cole (who preached the funeral sermon over the dying Latimer and Ridley), Thomas Starkey and Thomas Lupset.

Pole had been sent abroad with a very generous (indeed unheard of) allowance from the king, not only because he was of the blood royal but because the Humanistic disciplines were acquiring so much importance in politics that one might expect money spent in this way to repay interest in diplomatic advantages. Pole's clients can be seen no less, though less directly, as investments by the state. Padua was not only the home of Pietro Bembo and the high-polished Ciceronian style but also of the Civil Law and of the sceptical and libertine views of Pomponazzi and Zabarella.[44] Men educated there were in a strong position to view English customs and traditions with intellectual detachment, and so to understand the purposes of a minister like Thomas Cromwell with some sympathy. Thomas Starkey tells us of himself,

> because my purpose then was to live in a politic life, I set myself now these last years past to the knowledge of the Civil Law, that I might thereby make a more stable and sure judgment of the

politic order and customs used among us here in our country . . .
ever having in mind this end and purpose at the last in this
commonalty, where I am brought forth and born, to employ
them to some use.[45]

Starkey matriculated into political service by writing for
Cromwell an exercise on 'what is policy, after the sentence
[*opinion*] of Aristotle'. Humanist education begins to appear as
if its function were to liberate the mind from the traditional
and instinctive morality of Christian societies. One can see
how this distortion of the original impulse came about. It has
been remarked that Erasmus' advice to Princes suffers from 'a
detachment and lack of concreteness which often stood in the
way of a practical application of his ideas'(Caspari, p. 76), and
this would seem to be true of the whole circle of early Humanists.
They formulated theories and principles of action in this
world, constructed Utopias of statecraft, but they sought to
avoid too close or precise a reference to the world of national
action. But the great debate on religion, sharpened in England
by the king's 'great matter' of divorce, presented the problem
in a way which they could hardly evade. Faced by the necessity,
More and Fisher chose the road to martyrdom, but noble
though their sacrifice was, it was not in itself a Humanist act; it
could provide no lessons in behaviour for the next generation—
the generation of Starkey, Pole and George Lily. It has been
suggested[46] that there was no real continuity in the principles
of Humanism, that Henry's executions and deprivations broke
the tradition; but though the tradition only survived in an
altered and perhaps a diminished form, the movement from
theory to practice was implicit in the original impulse, and
brought its tensions and potentialities to a sharper focus.
Morison, Cheke, Smith, Cole, Ponet, Ascham etc. not only
survived themselves, but passed on a living, flexible and relevant
tradition to the Elizabethans, capable of being applied to the
great days of the Queen.

The debate whether or not learning should emerge from the
cloister into the immediate political arena, which takes such a
large part of Starkey's *Dialogue between Pole and Lupset* and
of the actual life of Pole, had to be answered decisively when
the monarch required it; the nicely balanced ambiguities of
Erasmus were almost possible in a cosmopolitan and peripatetic

scholar, but were not at all open to patriotic Englishmen under the Tudors. William Lily and John Colet died in time to avoid the question, but their gravity and sweet otherworldliness could not have saved them from having to answer it. Even exile, as the career of Pole (and of his secretary, George Lily) shows, provided no shelter from the choice between the political life of schemes and shifts and the *vita contemplativa*, with its negation of Humanist involvement in *this* world. Those who persisted in the noble humanist aim 'To make all the land know *quam sit humaniter vivendum*, help to take out all barbarous customs, and bring the realm to an antique form of good living'[47] had to push their effort through the narrowing alleyways of Reformation diplomacy, and were inevitably deprived of the wide and luminous views of More and Erasmus; but it might be argued that the necessity forced them to restate their humane view in terms which were more concrete, more real and hence more poetic.

The 'refocussing' of Humanist idealism on national politics certainly meant some dislocation of the learned tradition. This was not because the Humanist dream of educating the nobility had failed but rather because it had succeeded. At Elizabeth's accession we find among the memoranda of parliament 'that an ordinance be made to bind the nobility to bring up their children in learning at some university ... the wanton bringing-up and ignorance of the nobility forces the Prince to advance new men' (H.M.C. Salisbury, I. 163). But the marriage of statecraft and learning was not one that was immediately fruitful of good. For one thing it meant a continual interference in the universities by royal favourites and interested politicians, and a loss of certainty about what learning was meant to do. This is the burden of Thomas Cooper's complaint, in the dedication of his great *Thesaurus* (1565) to Leicester (Chancellor of Oxford University):

> For that kind of life which was formerly proposed, in its dignity and greatness, as a reward for the labours of the studious, is now either (as many people hope) being debased to ignominy, or else (as the impious expect) to imminent disaster. The result is that parents, seeking the advantage of their own, prescribe other disciplines for their children; and the children themselves judge rather by popular esteem than by the inherent dignity of the

matter; and so they prefer to pursue whatever they find easy rather than endure the daily grind of studying, without any aim in sight. Hence it is that the Universities and public schools have been promptly abandoned by the best minds; and of those who were well educated as children but few are anxious to penetrate into the depth of things—except for those who go on to study law or medicine. The rest give up their studies and betake themselves to the life of a courtier, or devote themselves to the law of the land [at the Inns of Court] or withdraw to some other kind of pastime, which they think will prove more profitable. For this reason, the priests of the Christian religion and those very learned men in whose hands lies the present administration of the church complain (it seems to me with justice) that there is destitution everywhere in the churches, causing incredible detriment to the flourishing of the Gospel; and that poverty is the lot of those who take up the preaching of the Divine Covenant, who fulfil the duties of the church and who exercise the other functions of pious eloquence [*literatae pietatis*]. For though certain honour and great reward is promised to those who undertake functions in the state; the lot of rectors in churches and masters in schools is contempt rather than praise. No wonder if many are found seeking glory and dignity, but few following virtue and learning when these are joined with shame.

Cooper goes on to suppose that Leicester with Burghley (Chancellor of Cambridge) and the Queen will shortly reform this state of affairs, and his flattery was sufficiently persuasive to cause him to sprout into a bishopric in a very short time; but the supposition that anyone could understand the situation well enough to alter it fundamentally is not justified. The Humanist assumption that learning could teach a man how to live piously in the world of politics could not bring with it the creation of a learned Civil Service, and nothing less than this kind of Gladstonian Humanism could have cured the ills that Cooper complains of.

What is clear, in Cooper as elsewhere, is that the Humanist dream forced the learned into dependence on a court which did not really need them. Elizabeth's court remained, throughout its history, a largely medieval pageant of royal bounty and chivalric allegiance. The progressive and intellectual elements in the country were gradually squeezed into Puritan opposition which had as little time for eloquent classicizing as had the politicians. Yet the dream that the centre of power was the natural home of learning and eloquence was by now so ingrained that it was not to be denied; reluctance to enter the Church, together with inability to find any other niche for learning was the common lot of those Elizabethans who made the 'pilgrimage from Parnassus',[48] John Lyly among them. Lyly was at least able to indulge his dream in his writing:

> In universities virtues and vices are but shadowed in colours, white and black; in courts showed to life, good and bad. There, times past are read of in old books, times present set down by new devices, times to come conjectured at by aim, by prophecy or chance. Here are times in perfection, not by device as fables, but in execution as truths. Believe me, Pandion, in Athens you have but tombs, we in court the bodies; you the pictures of Venus and the wise Goddesses, we the persons and the virtues. What hath a scholar found out by study that a courtier hath not found out by practice?   (*Sapho and Phao*, I. ii. 12-21)

The careers of William Lily and George Lily might seem to us almost like object lessons in the futility of the Humanist dream of learning as politically effective. But we cannot expect the process of living to look like this from the inside. We can hardly doubt that the pressure of family tradition on John Lyly was such that he was driven along the same paths of expectation, regardless of the fact that the situation about 1575, when he left Oxford, was radically different from that about 1488, when William Lily went down, or from that about 1533, when George Lily left. By 1575 the scholastic innovations of the first had become a matter of routine mediocrity, though occasionally a schoolmaster (like Richard Mulcaster) could still make a mark; by 1575, no less, the pressing cry for learning to aid the state had died down. The court of Elizabeth had established a mode of life which was able to use the Humanistic training without depending upon it.

Elizabeth was in many ways a Humanist herself, as her father had been before her: she could translate from Greek and she could make a speech in Ciceronian Latin. But with her, as with him, the gloss of Humanist ideals accompanied other and probably more fundamental interests, and other more empirical modes of judgment. Anyone who approached the

Tudor court supposing that it was another Florentine Academy was liable to a series of rude shocks.

In fact, hardly anyone (except a constitutional eccentric like Gabriel Harvey) was foolish enough to apply to any Renaissance court the full Ciceronian expectation of the *novus homo*. Long before Elizabeth's reign the Humanist ideal had shrunk to that of 'the courtier'[49] who was required, within a certain elegant and disdainful playfulness of manner (what Castiglione calls *sprezzatura*), to have some knowledge of classical authors. But the courtier was to use his learning as decoration, not as part of his belief; he was the servant of his breeding and his sovereign, not of his understanding. And in the end, the Humanist's and the courtier's interests pointed in different directions. The Humanist admired peace, good government and the placid life of study; the courtier must praise war and honour. The Humanist inherited the learned tradition of misogyny, and the courtier the medieval conventions of Courtly Love. It was the Humanist's duty to remain detached and quizzical, the courtier's to lay down his life at his sovereign's feet. Thus the tradition of practical learning and ethical preoccupation which brought the Humanists to the court was met with a requirement that they use their literary gifts and forget their ideals, that they abandon their internationalist, pacific and misogynist impulses and become the encomiasts of tournaments, of hunting, and of amorous dalliance. The asceticism of the scholar was met by a demand that he praise licence and display. Petrarch could complain, 'Where do we read that Cicero or Scipio jousted?',[50] but this reaction was hardly open to the Tudor court entertainer. He could only achieve success by arranging a temporary union between the two traditions; and it was here that the 'wit' of which I have spoken was so valuable to the writers. Looking at the courtly writings of John Lyly we can see how wit is used to keep the author detached from the courtly passions of his creatures. Euphues tastes the pleasures of the metropolis, but he soon returns to his university, able to see such a life for what it is, and so to advise Livia to abjure the court. His vision of courtly love is sympathetic, but again detached by wit. He balances misogyny against adoration, 'places' his flattery by its exaggeration, and throughout remains witty

31

enough to avoid being identified with any of the views he puts forward.

The difficulties that the Humanist attitude to life and letters produced in the late Renaissance period are writ large and documented fully in the life of Lyly's contemporary and enemy, Gabriel Harvey. Harvey was born of prosperous burgher stock and went to the local grammar school; from there, as a brilliant pupil, he was sent to Cambridge, where senior, politically oriented Humanists, Sir Thomas Smith and Sir Walter Mildmay, helped to pay his expenses. At Cambridge Harvey showed the combination of brilliance and truculency which is commonly a feature of the upstart scholar, pulled up by his brains from an obscure background; this unbalance of temperament serves to magnify for our inspection the tensions which were present in the Humanist outlook in any case.

Harvey took his education, with pathological singlemindedness, to be a means of getting nearer to the life of power and becoming what he calls a 'curtisan politique' [a politically influential courtier]. Like Starkey and many another Humanist, his hopes of preferment made him transfer his career from theology to the civil law: 'being willed by my friends and set on by others' example to determine with myself to what kind of study I were best to betake me to, and having a great good liking of the Civil Law, which I know to be so highly commended of the worthiest of men, and namely of Tully . . .' (*Letter Book*, p. 162).

But Harvey's contacts with the court, when he actually made them, were (like other poor scholars') a disappointment to him. Little (or at any rate, too little) attention was paid to his gifts of intellect; he had not the power of waiting till some great person deigned to notice him; he thrust himself forward in a series of much pondered-on, but ill-timed and tactless devices, and the court soon showed that it could do without his intellect more easily than he could do without its glamour: 'He that most patronized him [*probably Leicester*], prying more searchingly into him and finding that he was more meet to make sport with than any way deeply to be employed, with fair words shook him off, and told him he was fitter for the University than for the court or his turn, and so bade God prosper his studies, and sent for another secretary to Oxford'

32

(Nashe, III. 79). This is the portrait of an enemy and we need not take the details (especially the *Zuleika Dobson*-like conclusion) too seriously; but it is certain enough that Harvey failed in the very point that his doctrines told him was crucial:

> *il pensare non importa, ma il fare.*   (*Marginalia*, p. 141)

His Humanist belief that the *vita activa* was the natural end of study deprived him even of the pleasures of contemplation which Spenser's sonnet imputes to him

> that sitting like a looker-on
> Of this world's stage, dost note with critique pen
> The sharpe dislikes of each condition
> . . .
> And the evil damning evermore to die.
> For Life and Death is in thy doomful writing;
> So thy renown lives ever by inditing.

Frustrated of the Humanist's chief end he was reduced to communicating furiously to the margins of his books those beliefs by whose light he himself stood condemned: 'Any serviceable point, either civil, courtly or militar, is very soon learned by art and practice' (*Marginalia*, p. 89). 'Visible flattery is abject and unworthy of a gentleman; invisible flattery a matter of skill and suited for men of affairs' (ibid. p. 56). But even as he did so, the would-be man of action slid from one college fellowship to another, and so out of fellowship, landing up eventually in medicine, which was of dubious social status, and certainly well off the imaginary highway which led from the University to the Privy Council.

The obsessive quality of Harvey's temperament makes the tensions in the Humanist position especially obvious, but I think that the same tensions existed for other men, and can be seen specifically in the life of John Lyly. Lyly had poise enough to make literature out of his situation between the court and the university; I shall argue below that this provides a principal interest of *Euphues*, and it appears also in *Campaspe* and *Sapho and Phao*; but the supposition that literature is a kind of courtship display of general secular capacity[51] informs and I think explains much of his life, and serves to cut him off from such mere writers as Shakespeare. At the end of his life he found that he had wasted his time (he had no post) and the beauty of his literary productions (and even their fame) was no consolation to him. The literature of the 'eighties and 'nineties is, in fact, largely a product of frustration. As we see with the students of the Parnassus Plays, literature is only a stopgap, one stage better than divinity perhaps, but not the real end of learning. As treatises on the (political) fruits of learning give way to defences of poetry, as the scope open to eloquence shrinks from statecraft through polemic to mere entertainment, so the 'University Wits' of the period have to contain their sense of divine mission within the bounds of a poor pamphlet. The eventual result of this union of learning and the need for popularity, of moral zeal and profane forms, is the greatest literature our language has known; but it was a product that theory could hardly account for, so opposed were the worlds it sprang from, the worlds of Lyly and Shakespeare. For, as C. S. Lewis has pointed out, Humanism 'would have prevented, if it could'[52] the literary masterpieces at the end of the century.

The development I have been tracing can be seen also as involving the relations between wit and wisdom. Throughout the Humanist tradition 'wit' (= cleverness) was treasured as an essential part of eloquence, always remembering what Fuller calls the 'real distinction between facetiousness and nugacity' (see *D.N.B.* s.v. Toby Mathew). *Facetudo* indeed meant elegance as well as facetiousness, and was supposed to represent that courtly virtue which stands midway between flattery and aggressiveness, an essential virtue if learning was to survive in the dangerous context of power.[53] And the earliest Humanists possessed it in plenty. Before we suppose that these men were grave divines, insensible to the frivolities of art (see Feuillerat, pp. 46ff.) we should remember that the first piece of Greek translated by an Englishman was Synesius' 'Praise of Baldness',[54] and remember likewise the well documented fondness of More and Erasmus for Lucian. Erasmus defends Lucian, it is true, as the author of works *quae faciunt ad morum institutionem* (make for instruction in morals),[55] but this didactic approach is not narrow or restrictive in its effects. In fact, More and Erasmus are so sure of the place of wit in a context of learned piety that they went much further in boldness of wit than their successors dared to. When we find one of More's letters of theological controversy headed *Doctissima simul ac elegantissima*

... *Epistola in qua non minus pie quam facete* ... [To John Bugen-hagen] the combination of learning and elegance may strike us as strange, but it is not nearly as strange as the collocation of piety and facetiousness. Yet this is a combination which is displayed at large in More's life, even to his final joke on the scaffold: 'I pray you, good Master Lieutenant, see me safe up; and for my coming down let me shift for myself'.

So long as the study of rhetoric continued to have a central place in the learned tradition, so long did wit and didacticism continue to walk hand in hand. But the reign of Elizabeth was marked by the fact that the subject-matter that seemed proper to these Cicero-inspired Humanists—the moral condition of their own time—, and the proper audience—the executive authority of the land—were more and more denied to them. Their gift for wit finds itself isolated from their belief in wisdom; at least the wisdom that is available to them is the wisdom for private life and for individual cases. But it may be thought that the pressure to make universal statements through the evocation of precise particulars is the very soul of art.

Feuillerat's view of the scholarly gravity of William Lily and his circle yields a subsequent view that John Lyly betrayed his Humanist background by writing works which would 'rather lie shut in a lady's casket than open in a scholar's study'; *wit* which is the subject of *Euphues* is supposed to have replaced the *wisdom* of the early Humanists. It has been my aim to complicate this distinction to the point of showing its in-sufficiency.[56] The earlier Humanists were wits no less than the later ones; but their wit operated in a context where it was the natural servant of wisdom aiming to be politically effective. What the court of Elizabeth allowed was a brilliant scope for wit coupled to a dislike of speechifying and a disdain for merely intellectual formulations. It was not the private degeneracy of Lyly that made a work like the *Utopia* impossible by 1575; *Euphues* did not betray the tradition that began with the *Utopia*; but it revealed what had happened to it. Its superficiality marks the drying up of a tradition beneath whose notice there was developing, in the odd and unregarded corners of the literary world, a new literary mode, which was to supersede the old and obscure it from our gaze.

II

LIFE AND *EUPHUES*

THE LIVES of William Lily and George Lily are part of the cultural history of the Renaissance. The immediate background of John Lyly is less exciting. John's father, Peter Lyly (so he seems to spell his name)[1], was one of three younger sons of the grammarian who survived the father. He is the only brother mentioned in George Lily's will (1559)[2] and is therefore likely to have been the only brother to outlive him. There is no account of his studies at school or university, though his subsequent career argues a fair standard of education, and it is unlikely that the son of his father was brought up in ignorance. But his whole early history can be deduced only from the presence of his name on legal documents. In 1544 he received the gift of lands in Odiham which had belonged to one George Lily but had been confiscated when the latter engaged in treasonable practices.[3] One may infer that these are the lands mentioned in the will of William Lily: 'also I will that mine eldest son have all my lands'[4] (William Lily came from Odiham), and understand that George Lily had committed treason by adhering to the cause of Cardinal Pole. The family was fortunate to regain its lands under these circumstances. One may also infer from this document that Peter Lyly had chosen to conform to the Anglican settlement; that this did not estrange him from his brother is indicated by the kind terms in which he is mentioned in the will of 1559. That he was in orders appears from a document of 1546 granting him the reversion of a prebend's stall in Canterbury[5]; it does not appear that he ever got nearer to the dignity than this. In 1550 he appears as a 'notary public' at the installation of John Ponet as Bishop of Rochester,[6] and thereafter his life seems settled in the

groove of minor ecclesiastical officialdom, under the Archbishop of Canterbury[7] (except for the Marian episode). He
settled in Canterbury and it is there (from 1562 onwards) that
we find the baptisms of his younger children recorded,[8] and it
was in Canterbury that he died in 1569.[9] That Peter was
married and had children before 1559 we know, for George
Lily's will refers to 'my brother Peter . . . and his poor children';
presumably John Lyly was one of these 'poor children'. We
do not know exactly when he was born, but his age is given as
seventeen in an Oxford matriculation record dated 1571 and
this would give 1554 as the date of birth. The exact interpretation of this evidence is difficult (see below p. 39) but it is
certain enough that John Lyly was born in the early 'fifties.
His mother was Jane Burgh who brought her husband lands in
Yorkshire[10]; Feuillerat plausibly conjectures that she belonged
to Burgh Hall in the East Riding,[11] and if so, the marriage
was no disgrace to the notary or registrar of Canterbury.

Whenever and wherever John Lyly was born, it is certain
that he was brought up in Canterbury, at his father's house of
'The Splayed Eagle' and in the shadow of the Cathedral where
his father was a functionary. His matriculation entry calls him
a Kentishman and the references to Kent in *Euphues* show a
self-conscious pride in this origin. In *Euphues and his England*
he takes his travellers from Dover to London via Canterbury
and stops there in order to describe 'an old city, somewhat
decayed, yet beautiful to behold, most famous for a Cathedral
church, the very majesty whereof struck them into amaze,
where they saw many monuments and heard tell of greater
[the famous jewelled shrine of Becket, despoiled by Henry VIII]
than either they ever saw or easily would believe.'[12] In *Mother
Bombie* he places his scene in Rochester and shows an easy
familiarity with the neighbourhood.

We do not know that Lyly ever went to the Cathedral
Grammar School in Canterbury, usually called the King's
School (the registers are defective), but several factors make it
probable. His father was an official of the diocese and is likely
to have exerted his influence to place a son who was certainly
not without talents. His father and John Twine, the first
headmaster, were both friends of Reginald Wolf, the King's
printer,[13] and are therefore likely to have been acquainted

with one another. Furthermore we find in the history of the school by Cape and Woodruff and in the Register of Matthew Parker that a 'Peter Lyly' and 'William Lyly' were in the school at times when Peter Lyly's younger sons bearing these names were of grammar-school age.[14] It may be worth noting in aside that 'William Lyly' appears in the same school list as 'Christopher Marley', so that we have what is, presumably, an early link here between John Lyly and his great coeval in tragedy, Christopher Marlowe.

The principal function of Tudor grammar schools, descending from the St Paul's routine established by Colet and Lily, was to inculcate good morals and clean Latinity (as we have seen above). Wherever he was educated, Lyly could not escape contact with his grandfather's Latin grammar, and his later work shows that he had learned much of it by heart. But grammar was meant by the Humanists to have more in it than the memorizing of rules. Sir Thomas Elyot (the great English vulgarizer of Humanism) calls a grammarian one 'that speaking Latin elegantly can expound good authors . . . leaving nothing, person or place named by the author, undeclared or hid from his scholars'.[15] There can be no doubt that Lyly came to know the basic principles of rhetoric and literary composition in many good authors while he was at grammar school. The intimate knowledge of Ovid which he later displays must have been partly acquired in the schoolroom, where Ovid was a favourite author.

The Humanist interest in plays as a means of educating the young bore fruit in Canterbury as elsewhere, and young John Lyly is likely to have had an opportunity to act, to declaim, or at least to witness dramatic performances. In 1562 the head-master of the King's School was voted £14, 6s. 8d., by the Dean and Chapter, for expenses incurred 'at setting out his plays at Christmas'. The amount here seems disproportionately large; had the headmaster been involved in entertaining the Queen or some other noble person? We cannot tell. In another entry we hear of a Christmas performance as consisting of 'tragedies, comedies and interludes'.[16] Of these at least the last were likely to have been in English. At any rate, living in Canterbury must have impressed on the mind of the future impresario and playwright, John Lyly, the essential connection between Humanist culture and the entertainment of the literate élite.

Wherever educated, Lyly no doubt completed his school career with a fairly fluent if occasionally inaccurate knowledge of Latin, and with a basic training in the set forms of discourse, having read, construed and explicated innumerable passages of Ovid, Cicero, Virgil, *et al.* He may even have known a little Greek (out of Erasmus' New Testament) but there is nothing in his later work to suggest that this ever grew into a real accomplishment. Like the great majority of Elizabethan authors he knew his Greek texts (such as Plutarch) out of Latin translations and was not above using an English crib, if such was available. Like the others he was, of course, fond of displaying a façade of classical knowledge, and could perhaps construe a few lines if put to this shift; but though he displays his acquaintance with Greek names, he seems quite unable to derive the nominative forms from the oblique cases.

Lyly matriculated at Magdalen College (like his uncle and grandfather). The college was still in his day, though probably less than in theirs, a prime centre of the new Humanist culture in a University which was still largely resistant to such ideals. The President in Lyly's day was Laurence Humphrey, a distinguished Calvinist theologian, whose troubles with the authorities were perhaps enough warning to avoid the obvious but thorny paths of theological writing. Perhaps we may see some connection between Humphrey's little Christian conduct-book, *The Nobles, or Of Nobility*, and Lyly's secular conduct-book, *Euphues*, but the connection is slight. The date of matriculation is given by Anthony à Wood as 1569, but the Register is dated 1571. Perhaps we may reconcile these authorities by allowing what the editor of the Register points out—that the 1571 list includes some people who were in college before that date.[17] Supposing this we are left of course with the problem whether the age of seventeen given in the Register refers to the actual date of matriculation or to the date of drawing up the list. One interpretation would give 1552 as his year of birth; the other would give 1554. He supplicated for his B.A. in 1573; this normally came at the end of four years of residence and may be thought to confirm 1569 as the actual date of entry into the University.

39

Coming to Oxford, Lyly would find himself in a home of learning which was also, as his Humanist forebears had made sure, a school of manners. Only, if the evidence is to be trusted, the manners were not always of the kind approved by Colet and Lily. In a famous passage of *Euphues* Lyly inveighs against the crimes of the University of Athens (or Oxford):

> And here I cannot but lament Athens, which having been always the nurse of Philosophers, doth now nourish only the name of Philosophy. For to speak plainly of the disorder of Athens, who doth not see it and sorrow at it? Such playing at dice, such quaffing of drink, such dalliance with women, such dancing, that in my opinion there is no quaffer in Flanders so given to tippling, no courtier in Italy so given to riot, no creature in the world so misled as a student in Athens; such a confusion of degrees that the scholar knoweth not his duty to the bachelor, nor the bachelor to the master, nor the master to the doctor; such corruption of manners, contempt of magistrates, such open sins, such privy villainy, such quarreling in the streets, such subtle practices in chambers as maketh my heart to melt with sorrow to think of it, and should cause your minds, gentlemen, to be penitent to remember it . . . . Have they not now in stead of black cloth, black velvet, in stead of coarse sackcloth, fine silk? Be they not more like courtiers than scholars, more like stage-players than students . . . Is it not become a byword amongst the common people that they had rather send their children to the cart than to the University, being induced so to say for the abuse that reigneth in the universities, who sending their sons to attain knowledge find them little better learned, but a great deal worse lived than when they went, and not only unthrifts of their money but also bankrupts of good manners.   (I. 273-75)

One must allow for rhetorical exaggeration here; but the need to apologise later in the book implies a basis of truth in the charges, which are echoed elsewhere.[18] The Humanist desire to educate the nobility had been successful in that an increasing number of the nobility went to the Universities[19]; among Lyly's contemporaries at Oxford one can name Ferdinando, Lord Strange (later Earl of Derby), Robert Sidney (later Earl of Leicester) and Lord Sheffield. But the result of this was not entirely beneficial; the most obvious effect in the University itself was not in the culture of the aristocracy but in the importation of social pretensions. The influx of gentlemen placed the scholars at an obvious disadvantage and invited competition in luxurious living. Simon Forman, the astrologer, who went to Magdalen in 1573, tells in his *Autobiography* how 'Sir Thornbury that after was Bishop of Limerick' and 'Sir Pinckney his cousin of St Mary Hall' used to 'go on hunting from morning to night . . . nor never gave themselves to their books, but to go to schools of defence [*fencing schools*], to the dancing schools, to steal deer and conies and to hunt the hare and to wooing of wenches; to go to Doctor Lawrence of Cowley, for he had two fair daughters, Bess and Martha'. If, as Feuillerat supposes, Lyly was the boon companion of these men, then we have an image of how he wasted his time in Oxford. But the context in Forman does not require us to suppose this.[20]

What he says is (continuing the above): 'Sir Thornbury he wooed Bess and Sir Pinckney he wooed Martha and in the end married her; but Thornbury he deceived Bess as the Mayor's daughter of Brackley, of which Ephues [*sic*] writes, deceived him.' Feuillerat, who discovered the passage, supposed that this turned *Euphues* into a *roman à clef*, with Lyly as Euphues, Thornborough as Philautus and the Mayor of Brackley's daughter as Lucilla. But Lucilla deceived both Philautus and Euphues, and there is nothing in the Forman passage to indicate that the Mayor of Brackley's daughter deceived both Thornborough and Lyly; the final 'him' cannot stand for both men. If the 'him' is Thornborough, then the story is one of Thornborough and Bess Lawrence, parallel to that of Thornborough and the Mayor of Brackley's daughter which *Euphues* is said to describe. If the 'him' is 'Ephues' (Lyly) then the Ephues-Brackley affair and the Thornborough-Bess affair are simply parallel. In neither case is a Euphues-Philautus relationship established between Lyly and Thornborough. We have Forman's word that Thornborough was dissolute; but we cannot go on from this to tar Lyly with the same brush.

It is true, of course, that Gabriel Harvey calls Lyly 'the fiddlestick [*plaything*] of Oxford'—presumably he means the University as well as the Earl; he also speaks of him 'horning [*committing adultery*], gaming, fooling and knaving' (II. 129), which would seem to place him squarely at the side of Sir Thornbury and Sir Pinckney. But these are the words of an enemy who is writing only in order to denigrate; we cannot regard them as objective description. Nevertheless, the image sticks, for we have nothing to set against it. Even Lyly's friend Nashe, it can be pointed out, writing to defend him, speaks of the time 'he [Lyly] spends in taking tobacco one week' (III. 138). He also says, 'He is but a little fellow, but he hath one of the best wits in England' (I. 300). Thus almost inevitably the image builds up of Lyly as a small, dapper, essentially frivolous and affected figure, his clothes to be presumed as elegant as his style was neat, forever blowing his epigrams through clouds of smoke.[21] It may be an accurate image for all we know. But the evidence hardly requires the moral bias that appears in such a description; to set him in the tradition of Humanism may be to suggest alternative explanations.

Anthony à Wood tells us that at Oxford Lyly was 'always averse to the crabbed studies of logic and philosophy' and 'did in a manner neglect academical studies', and this is often coupled to Lyly's own remarks about the unkindness of Oxford (in his 1579 addition to *Euphues*—'To my very good friends, the gentlemen scholars of Oxford') to imply that he was rusticated or sent down for misdemeanours.[22] What Lyly says is: 'Oxford . . . seemed to wean me before she brought me forth, and to give me bones to gnaw before I could get the teat to suck. Wherein she played the nice mother in sending me into the country to nurse, where I tired [*tugged*] at a dry breast three years, and was at the last enforced to wean myself' (I. 325). The passage is more remarkable for its elegance than its perspicacity. But it does not appear to be equally ambiguous at all points, and one may start at what seems to be the easiest phrase, 'give me bones to gnaw before I could get the teat to suck'. The teat must refer to the milk of learning that ought to be supplied by the *alma mater*; the bones that are substituted for this must be the dry discipline of disputation which the University did in fact offer, and which was a standard subject of complaint (see below). It follows that if this is the meaning of the second clause, it must be that of the first clause as well, for the two are presented as parallel: dry university learning was improper food for one who still sought for the liberal arts. The second sentence may be on a different tack, but it seems probable that the 'dry breast' refers once again to the logic of the schools, dry and unprofitable.

If this is the general drift, what are we to make of 'the country' where he was sent to nurse, and of the 'three years' which he spent there? The obvious explanation, that Lyly was sent away from Oxford for three years does not seem possible to justify in academic terms; 'rustication' was unknown in the period,[23] and in any case he says quite specifically that he was sent 'to nurse', that is, to be instructed. In the plague visitation of 1571 the whole university *did* go into the countryside, each college to its 'rural mansions' as Wood calls them; Magdalen was removed to Brackley (Northants) in 1571-2, when, no doubt the adventure that Forman describes took place. But Lyly's stay in Brackley in 1571-2 can hardly be described as lasting three years. I suggest that the 'sending me into the country' belongs in fact only to the 'nice mother' side of the simile, and does not refer to the geography of Lyly's education. Nice [*careful*] mothers sent their children to wet-nurses in the country where conditions were more healthy; so, says Lyly, the university sent me to a region [*of study*] which should have been health-giving but was dry and useless.

Moreover the 'three years' if intended to mean something to readers of *Euphues* who had no detailed knowledge of the personal life of John Lyly, is most likely to refer to the period of study for the M.A. (the statutory period for B.A. was four years). This makes some sense if considered in relation to what we know elsewhere of Lyly's life. To persist beyond the Bachelor's grade into that of the Master implies a fairly precise hope of academic profit, and with a poor student one must suppose that this hope is financial as well as intellectual. We know that Lyly hoped to obtain a college fellowship (see below) and was disappointed before he wrote these words. I suggest that the three unprofitable years were the years that seemed to lead to the threshold of a fellowship; Oxford is said to have a 'dry breast' because the studies followed there are dry, and also because Lyly was forced to wean himself or earn his living outside the academic circuit.

The general discontent with the academic syllabus which Wood records need not be supposed to indicate a culpable lightness in temperament. The discontent is a commonplace of the period. Rawley in his life of Bacon tells us how at the age of sixteen (that is, in 1576) his Lordship 'first fell into the dislike of the Philosophy of Aristotle . . . being a Philosophy (as his Lordship used to say) only strong for disputations and contentions'.[24] Nearer to Lyly in time, status, and University is Stephen Gosson, a fellow Canterbury (and King's School) boy, who came up to Oxford (Corpus Christi College) in 1572. Here is a man no one could accuse of lightness; yet Gosson in his *School of Abuse* speaks contemptuously of 'those lither [lazy] contemplators . . . which sit concluding of syllogisms in a corner' (sig. E2-E2v); and Gosson's tutor, the formidable Dr John Rainolds, speaks of the schools (though he was an enemy to profane letters) as a place where *contortulas tanta siccitate torquent conclusiunculas* (where they twist out in so dry a way their fantastically contorted conclusions about trifles).[25] In truth, the methods of the schools were still largely medieval, and though some of the questions disputed there show the influence of the Renaissance,[26] no alternative method of training and testing intellect was known.

Lyly may, like so many of his contemporaries, have objected to the cramping methods of academic disputation, which provided the staple of University training, but it provided the basis of his whole approach to literature. The method was not, in fact, as remote from popular literature as might seem at first sight. The practice of first listening to disputes (in the first two years) and thereafter taking part in them was one which required and encouraged the facility and copiousness which is characteristic of Nashe, Lodge, Greene, Gosson and Lyly. The disputations lasted for about two hours, in which time one 'respondent' made a speech defending his thesis, and two 'opponents' aimed to defeat his arguments; the method of argument was by the citation of authorities and the marshalling of illustrations; and this again is obviously akin to the literary methods of the 'University Wits'. The idea that the world only makes sense when it is categorized into instances of *pro* and *contra* was not in fact confined to the groves of Academe. The scholar graduated into a world still echoing with *sic* and *non*, in religion, in jurisprudence and in politics; we cannot pretend that the arts of disputation were languishing in an age which could produce (and, I suppose, read) books like *A disproof of Dr Abbott's counterproof against D. Bishop's reproof of the defence of M. Perkins' Reformed Catholic* (1614).

But it was not so much in matter as in manner that the University discipline was of immediate relevance to literary men. Literary composition of the period was largely dominated by the notion of persuasion, and so it was natural for the classical form of persuasion—the oration in its sundry varieties—to be used as a model. Professor Ringler has pointed out that the speech of Euphues at the house of Lucilla (I. 201-3) is in form a classical oration,[27] and the reply of Euphues to Eubulus earlier in the book can likewise be drawn into its formal components;[28] the dispute at Flavia's house (II. 163-83) is arranged as an academic disputation. In his exemplary account of Gosson's use of academic learning Ringler has made it clear how far a literary career could be based on the information and instruction given at the university, and has further suggested that the very style of Euphuism is derived from the Latin lectures of Dr Rainolds (see below, pp. 270 f.). At any rate it is clear when Lyly speaks of having 'tired at a dry breast three years' we must take his complaint with a grain of salt. It seems probable that it was his failure to obtain a fellowship that opened this fluent vein of academic discontent, with its *topoi* ready to hand, even if not particularly fitting.

The surviving evidence of this hope for academic preferment is the Latin letter of May 1574 which Lyly wrote to Lord Burghley, begging him to use his influence, that is, obtain mandatory letters from the Queen, requiring the college to admit him as a Fellow.[29] We need not be shocked at this; it was regularly done; the whole Humanist outlook encouraged the supposition that the court *should* control learning in the national interest; and certainly two university chancellors, Burghley at Cambridge and Leicester at Oxford often used their influence in this way.

With this letter we have the first appearance in these pages of a connection between Lyly and Lord Burghley which appears off and on throughout Burghley's life. What are we to make of this? Are we to suppose with Feuillerat that Lyly was *un protégé de Lord Burghley*, and that Burghley can be invoked to explain whatever actions Lyly takes in his early years? Or should we point out that the Hatfield Papers are the best preserved of Elizabethan archives, and that other begging letters to other Maecenases might well have perished? The evidence would seem to warrant more than this second alternative, though not perhaps as much as Feuillerat supposes. The Latin letter of 1574 calls Burghley his 'much favouring patron' [*patronus suus colendissimus*] but this may be no more than a hopeful flourish, like the qualities later prayed for— that Burghley may equal Alexander in beneficence, Trajan in humanity, Nestor in years, Camillus in magnanimity, Solomon in prudence, David in holiness, and Josiah in reforming zeal. If Oxford had taught Lyly nothing else, it had made him a connoisseur in flattery—which is not quite the same thing, however, as a successful suitor; Lyly did not obtain the fellowship.

Conventional though the flattery of this letter may be, I do not think that it was only chance that drove Lyly to aim his request at Burghley; a case has been established[30] for some degree of family relationship between the two men. If Lyly's mother was Jane Burgh of Burgh Hall, she belonged to a family connected by marriage ties to the local family of Rokeby of Morton. Dorothy, the widow of Ralph Rokeby, married Richard Browne, a second cousin of Burghley's (Edmund Browne, his uncle, having married Joan Cecil, Burghley's aunt). The likelihood that Burghley acknowledged the connection is strengthened by Lyly's later marriage to an intermediate member of the clan—the daughter of Richard Browne.

For the moment, however, the connection did Lyly no good. He persisted, none the less, in academic grooves, and proceeded to take the M.A. in 1575, and even took the further step (in 1579) of obtaining an M.A. by incorporation at Cambridge. He could thereafter (like Robert Greene[31]) sign himself *utriusque Academiae in artibus magister*, but I do not know that he ever did; so the reason for his action is not clear. Perhaps up to 1579 he was still hoping for some kind of academic preferment; *Euphues* (1578) shows his academic failure still rankling in Lyly's mind.

In any case, before this date Lyly must have left Oxford, for it was presumably in this period that he was living, as Gabriel Harvey tells us, in the Savoy (in the Strand) 'when Master Absolon lived'.[32] Feuillerat's researches have shown that Absolon was another Canterbury man;[33] and we may add that he was headmaster of the King's School from 1565 to 1566,[34] so that if Lyly was educated at the King's School he must have rejoined his old head when he went to the Savoy. Absolon was Master there from 1576 till 1586. Another remark of Harvey's narrows the date of Lyly's residence still further: he speaks of 'thy old acquaintance in the Savoy, when young Euphues hatched the eggs that his elder friends laid'. This must refer to the period before 1578 when *Euphues, the Anatomy of Wit* was published. All that we can be sure of is that the Savoy would be a convenient base of operations if Lyly was in London to pursue a double aim of literary fame and academic intrigue. That he continued to court Burghley is very probable; who would not? But that he was in the Savoy because of Burghley is not clear. At this period the hospital of the Savoy, like other pious foundations—Blackfriars and St Bartholomew's are examples that appear later in the life of Lyly—was let out piecemeal for lodgings. Perhaps Lyly had some family connection with the Savoy: his grandfather had asked for mass to be sung for him in the then newly founded institution (1517); his brother Peter was later to become a brother of the Savoy.

That Lyly's Oxford reputation (retailed by Wood) of having 'his genie . . . naturally bent to the pleasant paths of poetry' found him literary company in London is hardly to be doubted. If he came to London about 1576, what literary company could he have found between that date and the publication of *Euphues* at the end of 1578? It would be pleasant if we could link Lyly with Spenser, who was probably in London, at Leicester House, from 1576 till 1580. There is some probability that they knew one another. It appears that Gabriel Harvey was friendly with Lyly before 1580: 'in truth I loved him, in hope praised him; many ways favoured him and never any way offended him' (Grosart, II. 122). If Lyly knew Harvey then he could hardly have avoided knowing Spenser. Certainly he must have read *The Shepheard's Calendar* as soon as it came out, for he imitates it in *Euphues and his England* (1580).[35] D. H. Horne in his excellent *Life of George Peele* (Yale, 1952) has suggested that Lyly belonged to a literary group consisting of Thomas Watson and those who commended his *Hekatompathia* in 1582; *Hekatompathia* came to the reader armed with a preface by Lyly and poems by Roydon, Achelly, Peele, Buc and Downhall. On the other hand, by 1582 Lyly was in the service of the Earl of Oxford; *Hekatompathia* is dedicated to Oxford and George

Buc is said to have had 'familiar acquaintance' with the Earl. The grouping may mean no more than that here we have a number of writers associated with the patronage of a great nobleman; and this would tell us nothing about Lyly that we did not know already.

Unfortuntely, Lyly's 'letter to Watson' prefixed to *Hekatompathia*, the one document of the literary life that he must have led at this period, comes after the success of *Euphues* had made its author a famous person. I call this unfortunate because the letter takes us no nearer the author than does the romance; for it suits him better now to pose behind the *persona* of his hero than to reveal his own nature. As 'Euphues' he need do nothing but go through the motions of style and idea that are appropriate to that figure: 'The repeating of love wrought in me a remembrance of liking, but searching the very veins of my heart I could find nothing but a broad scar where I left a deep wound; and loose strings where I tied hard knots, and a table of steel where I framed a plot of wax.' The recovered lover here is Euphues, not Lyly, and there is no point in looking for biographical details.[36]

Our whole interpretation not only of Lyly's temperament but also of his conscious intentions in these early years depends on the view we take of his first published work—*Euphues, the Anatomy of wit: very pleasant for all gentlemen to read, and most necessary to remember*—which was entered in the Stationers' Register on the 2nd December 1578, and published (without date) shortly after. The book tells the story of how a young gentleman 'of more wit than wealth, yet of more wealth than wisdom, seeing himself inferior to none in pleasant conceits, thought himself superior to all in honest conditions'. We have, in short, a cautionary tale which takes a student from Athens (the University) to Naples (sophisticated metropolitan life), where he is faced with council (which he rejects), then with friendship (which he exploits), then with love (which he snatches at). Inevitably, retribution follows for these sins, since 'God who permitteth no guile to be guiltless will . . . requite this injury' (I. 233). Jilted by his mistress, Euphues comes to see that he has abused his 'little wit . . . with an obstinate will'; he repents and begins to advance in morality (retiring from the world) along the road that leads from wit to wisdom.

The moral of the story is obvious—to some minds repellantly so. As Dover Wilson pointed out long ago,[37] the narrative is a variant of the extremely popular Reformation theme of the Prodigal Son, presented in the scholastic manner adopted here by innumerable school dramas of the 'Christian Terence' tradition —from which Lyly is likely to have known at least the very popular *Acolastus*.

The relation of the *Euphues* story to the Prodigal Son theme is one which is characteristic of the Renaissance: Lyly has abstracted ideas and attitudes from the Morality and the Biblical narrative, and then re-set them in the social and courtly life of his own time. The result of this, that the work has a naturalistic surface but a non-naturalistic organization, takes us into one of the central difficulties of *Euphues*, and it is worth while pursuing the process through which Lyly has worked. Lyly found the title of his hero and probably the germ of its moral in the writing of an earlier Humanist and Protestant hero—in Roger Ascham's *The Schoolmaster* (published posthumously in 1570 and dedicated to Burghley), a work very much in the tradition of William Lily and pious pedagogy in England, and springing (so the preface tells us) out of a courtly conversation between Humanist statesmen assembled at Windsor in 1563—Burghley himself being their host. Ascham speaks of how to train the various types of mind so that the greatest benefit will accrue to the commonwealth. The first quality of mind he describes is that called 'Euphues' (because the word means, 'well-endowed'):

> Εὐφυής: is he, that is apt by goodness of wit and appliable by readiness of will to learning, having all other qualities of the mind and parts of the body, that must another day serve learning, not troubled, mangled and halfed, but sound, whole, full and able to do their office ... But commonly the fairest bodies are bestowed on the foulest purposes; I would it were not so; and with examples herein I will not meddle.   (Arber's reprint, pp. 38 f.)

The problem that Ascham was exposing here was one of the basic problems of the Humanists—how to turn the talented aristocrat into the self-disciplined administrator—and no doubt Ascham was unwilling to meddle because of an excess of highly-placed examples rather than because of a lack of them.

But what Ascham did not feel free to meddle with herein, feeling also, no doubt, the weight of his position as a royal tutor, was a natural opportunity for the Humanist as fiction-writer, for the author of *Euphues*. Lyly's Euphues has the natural endowments that Ascham praises and names; the relevance of Ascham's book to the career that Lyly describes can be seen if we travel back a few pages in *The Schoolmaster*. At this point Ascham is distinguishing between the apt or easily moulded pupil and the stubborn or hard-witted one; he questions the normal device of praising the first and punishing the second:

> Quick wits commonly be apt to take, unapt to keep, soon hot and desirous of this and that, as cold and soon weary of the same again, more quick to enter speedily than able to pierce far, even like over-sharp tools whose edges be very soon turned. Such wits delight themselves in easy and pleasant studies and never pass far forward in high and hard sciences. And therefore the quickest wits commonly may prove the best poets, but not the wisest orators: ready of tongue to speak boldly, not deep of judgment, either for good counsel or wise writing. Also, for manners and life, quick wits commonly be, in desire newfangled, in purpose unconstant, light to promise anything, ready to forget everything, both benefit and injury; and thereby neither fast to friend nor fearful to foe . . . and by quickness of wit, very quick and ready to like none so well as themselves. Moreover, commonly men very quick of wit be also very light of conditions, and thereby very ready of disposition to be carried over-quickly by any light company to any riot and unthriftiness when they be young.
>
> (Arber, pp. 32 f.)

Here we have the forecast of a prodigal career fastened on to the temperament of a Euphues, 'whose wit, being like wax, apt to receive any impression, and having the bridle in his own hands, either to use the rein or the spur, disdaining counsel' drifted naturally towards moral disaster. Here we have the system of attitudes involved in an *anatomy of wit*. What Lyly means by this phrase is, of course, that he will dissect or open up the corruptions and weaknesses of *wit*, as Lear wished to 'anatomize' Regan, as Donne supplied an 'Anatomy of the World', or as Thomas Robinson made an *Anatomy of the English Nunnery at Lisbon* (1622).

From this angle Lyly's work can be seen as a treatise on wit;

and the angle has some importance for it helps to counteract the common view of *Euphues* as a proto-novel. To see *Euphues* as a novel is, in fact, to leave most of the book outside one's sights, and to leave oneself without vocabulary for most of the effects it makes. Feuillerat says that 'ce qui sépare le peintre de Lucilla du peintre de Pamela [Richardson, not Sidney], c'est peut-être une simple question de quantité' (p. 285), but this is obvious special pleading, for the general outlook of the two books is quite different. The features they have in common can be explained by their belonging to a common tradition which is not specifically that of the novel; the rhetoric of the divided mind was established long before Lyly, most obviously in the *Heroides* of Ovid.

But what is signally ignored in the view of *Euphues* as a novel is the relevance of the series of letters with which the work concludes. I refer here to the 'cooling card' to Philautus, the letter to the grave matrons, 'Euphues and his Ephebus' and 'Euphues and Atheos'. These clearly belong together and in this order. They show a continuous development in gravity, not to say sanctity, and are linked together by a commentary which makes this clear. The end of 'Euphues and Atheos' reaches such heights of sanctimony that it is hard to imagine any development beyond it. What follows—the 'certain letters writ by Euphues to his friends'—is much more in the nature of an appendix, illustrating, but not developing the image of Euphues' regeneracy.

I speak of the 'relevance' of these letters, for I suppose they belong to and indeed complete the vision of wit and wisdom that is the subject of the book. I have suggested above that the relation of wit to wisdom was one of the central problems of the Humanist position. The Humanists hoped that a man could be made fit for responsibility in the great world of experience (that is, prudent, just, wise etc.) simply by a course of scholastic discipline. And this is just the line followed by Eubulus in his initial warning that Euphues should avoid Naples:

> As thy birth doth show the express and lively image of gentle blood, so thy bringing up seemeth to me to be a great blot to the lineage of so noble a bruit, so that I am enforced to think that either thou didest want one to give thee good instructions, or

51

that thy parents made thee a wanton with too much cockering
—either they were too foolish in using no discipline, or thou too
froward in rejecting their doctrine; either they willing to have
thee idle, or thou willful to be ill employed.   (I. 187)

Euphues, on the other hand, shows himself the Humanist
Prodigal by denying this view. He asserts that his nobility
of birth is an incorruptible asset: 'whereas you seem to love my
nature and loathe my nurture you bewray your own weakness
in thinking that nature may any ways be altered by education' (I. 191). The story exists to show how mistaken is the
view that nature is alone sufficient to deal with a corrupt
environment. 'Wit' or good endowment is only turned into
wisdom when experience breaks the mind that would not bend
to precept. It is only by passing through the Purgatory of love-
sorrow and courtly disillusionment that Euphues reaches the
Paradise or Enlightenment of his subsequent state. It is in this
state that the letters are written:

> It is commonly said—yet do I think it a common lie—that
> Experience is the Mistress of Fools; for in my opinion they be
> most fools that want it. Neither am I one of the least that have tried
> this true, neither he only that heretofore deemed it to be false.
> I was hereof a student of great wealth, of some wit, of no small
> acquaintance, yet have I learned that by experience that I
> should hardly have seen by learning . . . He that hath been
> burned knoweth the force of the fire; he that hath been stung
> remembreth the smart of the scorpion; he that hath endured
> the brunts of fancy knoweth best how to eschew the broils of
> affection. Let therefore my counsel be of such authority as it may
> command you . . .   (I. 260)

If we consider the story without the letters, and without
their rather repulsively self-satisfied admonitions on love,
education, godliness, on behaviour at court, on proper mourning for a friend, on the endurance of exile, then we consider a
work without its last scene or final movement. If we end with
Euphues' retirement from Naples, then the emphasis of the
work must rest on the brilliant temptations that have been
avoided; Euphues has escaped, but we have no idea what he
has escaped *to*. When we include the letters in our sights,
however, we have to alter our focus on the story: it is neither
an encomium on courtship nor a rejection of it, but an essential

stage in the exposition of experience as the true teacher of a ready wit. Indeed the narrative section bears much the same relation to the whole work as did the medieval exemplum to the medieval sermon: the preacher told the story to illustrate his theme, to divert his audience and to drive home his point. Though the structure of *Euphues* is less schematic than this, the analogy may serve; the letters make clear the fruits of experience as the narrative shows the nature of the experience. Of course, the image of Euphues as an *illuminatus* seems rather factitious, but this should not blind us to the structure of the work.

It is when we look at this aspect of the book that the analogy of Richardson's *Pamela* may help us. The second part of *Pamela* is a separate creation, but it is not irrelevant since it completes our image of the achieved stage of wisdom in a way parallel to the letters of Euphues. Pamela has passed through the purgatorial state of Mr B's attempted seduction, and is thereafter entitled to pronounce on all kinds of moral dilemmas. Modern readers usually dismiss the second part as a tedious appendix: when the struggling stops and the maidservant gets her man their interest flags; but clearly Richardson and his original readers did not see the relation of the two parts in quite this way, and this implies that they enjoyed Part One itself rather differently. Their interest seems to have been focussed more sharply on the moral state (allowing morals to include manners) and less narrowly on 'personality'; in consequence they did not find the prolonged demonstration of moral beatitude either boring or irrelevant. Lyly's fascination with the minutiae of elegant social intercourse is part of his Ovidian rhetoric and not, as with Richardson, part of his moral dialectic; but in both cases it is the succession of moral states that supplies the backbone of the work.

Euphues, as his name suggests, indicates a moral and social idea rather than a personality; but (as has been brilliantly demonstrated of late)[38] Lyly does show the errors within his hero's mind by means of the false logic he puts into his various arguments. He is concerned with the divided mind as the breeding-place of wrong decisions. Hence much of the narrative is made to turn on the old debate between friendship and love or, in other terms, between honour and passion. It has been plausibly suggested[39] that the basis of the plot was found in Boccaccio's story of Titus and Gisippus (*Decameron*, X. viii), which shows the same general articulation of the scenes in which the material is presented. Lyly certainly knew about Titus and Gisippus,[40] and the story was easily available in Elyot's *Book of the Governor*. But the story of the two friends divided by love, until love is outdone by generosity, is so universal[41] that it is difficult to pin anything down with precision; if *Titus and Gisippus* is not the source, however, it is a good example of the *kind* of story which stands somewhere behind *Euphues*. The story that Boccaccio tells begins as follows: an Athenian introduces to his fiancée a stranger who has become his friend. The stranger falls in love with the girl, and retires to his own lodging to debate the contrary claims of love and honour. The debate is concluded by the Athenian's entry; he offers to alleviate in any way he can the obvious misery which his friend suffers. So far the story is the same as that of *Euphues*; thereafter, however, the two diverge, and one can see good reasons why they should. Boccaccio is interested (like Shakespeare in *Two Gentlemen*) in friendship refined to an exemplary degree of purity; accordingly he makes the Athenian sacrifice his mistress to his friend. Lyly's story is not about friendship but about wit; in consequence he cannot follow Boccaccio into the sacrifice; but to highlight the falsity of wit he can show Euphues deceiving his friend Philautus by means of his wit: 'and because I resemble him in wit, I mean a little to dissemble with him in wiles' (I. 210)—on which Lyly comments 'Here you may see, gentlemen, the falsehood in fellowship, the fraud in friendship, the painted sheath with the leaden dagger, the fair words that make fools vain' (I. 215). If we imagine Lyly seeking an exemplum-story of the frailty of wit and finding some of the material he wanted in *Titus and Gisippus*, then the departure from the original and the nature of the new episodes seem perfectly understandable.

The plot-situations of *Euphues* can probably, all of them, be paralleled in the tradition of the *novelle*; but the organization of these episodes is very different. The structure of *Euphues* is, in fact, that of drama. G. B. Parks has pointed out that the greater part of the *Anatomy of Wit* can be broken down into 'scenes',[42] which are composed of soliloquies, opposed orations or (more rarely) conversations. These elements are fairly standard in the expanded versions of the *novelle* which Belleforest prepared for French taste and which Geoffrey Fenton and others transmitted to England. The rhetorically elaborated *novella*, with its endlessly drawn out soliloquies and debates and letters is, however, not a form that one naturally associates with neatness or economy of structure; if we sense these qualities in *Euphues*, we ought to look at its scenes for signs of a more pervasive structural principle. And looking at the theme of Wit and Experience one can see that there is indeed a perfectly regular development: (1) wit rejects wisdom, (2) wit meets friendship and love, (3) wit chooses love, (4) wit loses friendship, (5) betrayed by love, wit repents its wilfulness and so recovers friendship. The 'scenes' cohere to form five units of structure, whose sense I have just given. Professor Parks has roundly declared that 'Lyly shows no sign of dramatic structure',[43] but the five units I have described can be shown to correspond to the five stages of the Terentian structure, as taught in Tudor schools and analysed at large by T. W. Baldwin.[44] Moreover, the five 'acts' (as we may be allowed to call them) are separated from one another by methods which seem to be theatrical in their conception—by a 'clearing of the stage' a change of scene or a passage of time.

The first 'act' concerns Euphues' arrival in Naples and the conversation with Eubulus. It is separated from what follows by a piece of choric moralizing, 'Here ye may behold, gentlemen . . .'(I. 195), by the disappearance of Eubulus and by a two months' gap in time. In Act II we meet Philautus, and hear the pledges of friendship that the two men make; they go to the house of Ferardo where we have speeches and disputations about love, and there, subsequently, Euphues finds himself to be in love with Lucilla. Lucilla, left alone on the stage, bewails the love for Euphues which she has come to feel. This probably brings Act II to an end. The stage is cleared; we leave the house of Lucilla—'there let her lie, and return we to Euphues . . . ' (I. 207). We next hear the complaint of Euphues; then 'to him' enters Philautus with his offer of help; after a brief choric comment the two friends go to Ferardo's house; after a time Philautus is called away and the lovers are left alone to make their declarations. The act ends with the departure of Euphues (I. 226). The stage is cleared and an unspecified period of time intervenes. In Act IV Ferardo and Philautus return to Naples; Ferardo proposes that Philautus should marry Lucilla straight away; Lucilla prevaricates and finally names Euphues as already in possession of her heart; Philautus returns to his lodging, inveighs against Euphues and writes a letter of reproach; as a pendant to this comes Euphues' letter of reply. Technically this should count as a new act, since the second letter involves a change of scene, a new character and a clearing of the stage, but since nothing is made of Euphues at this point, apart from his letter, we may, I think, construe the two letters as a continuous episode. Between Acts IV and V comes another clearance, and we are told that events interrupt the action 'for a space' (237). In Act V Euphues visits Lucilla, and is told that his love is no longer acceptable; left alone he renounces wit, except when 'employed in the honest study of learning'; Ferardo returns home 'immediately' and rates his daughter with her inconstancy; in a final narrative passage we hear of the eventual reconcilement of Euphues and Philautus.

The 'five-act structure' I have been describing here would hardly be worth pursuing in such detail if it only involved moving the characters around, 'clearing the stage', etc.; for such devices could easily be copied from drama, without involving the narrative at an integral level. But I think we can see in *Euphues* the rise and fall of the Terentian structure, used in a manner which shapes the whole experience. Through the acts we can see the underlying pattern of Protasis, Epitasis and Catastrophe—or (in more modern terms) exposition, action, complication, reversal, catastrophe. Lyly's plays show that he was well aware of this structure, and the words that T. W. Baldwin uses to describe the structure of *Campaspe* serve as well for *Euphues*: 'The first act gives the argument, the second begins the action, the third presents the epitasis, the fourth the desperate state of the matter begun in the epitasis, with the occasion of the catastrophe at the exact end, and the fifth the catastrophe' (*Five-Act Structure*, p. 597); the one irregularity in *Euphues*, that the reversal (or the occasion of the catastrophe) occurs at the beginning of act V and not at the end of act IV was allowed as a variant—see Baldwin, p. 223. We may set out the structure of *Euphues* together with that of one of Lyly's plays which develops a similar theme (*The Woman in the Moon*) and note the point-by-point similarity of structure:

The Woman in the Moon

Act I. Pandora created in spite of warning.

Act II. Four Arcadians woo Pandora without success.

Act III. Pandora seems to select one lover, but soon proves unfaithful.

Act IV. The deceived lover quarrels with the other Arcadians, while Pandora elopes with the clown.

Act V. Pandora is accepted as permanently changeable.

Compare *Euphues*

Act I. Euphues comes to Naples and is warned by Eubulus.

Act II. Euphues and Philautus visit Lucilla. Euphues falls in love with Lucilla.

Act III. Euphues deceives Philautus and wins the love of Lucilla.

Act IV. Euphues and Philautus quarrel.

Act V. Lucilla deceives both. Euphues and Philautus abandon Lucilla and are reconciled.

In both plots Act I introduces the characters, Act II involves wooing, Act III a temporary success in love, Act IV a quarrel between rivals, while in Act V the changeable nature of the woman is accepted. *The Woman in The Moon* is obviously in five acts; the similarity of *Euphues* being so great it seems we should accept the five-act formula as providing its structure also.[45]

It says much for Lyly's sense of form that he has grasped here at the one type of structure sufficiently developed at this time to discipline his material. Of course he was not alone in seeing the advantages: five years before *Euphues* Lawrence Humphrey, the President of Lyly's own college of Magdalen, had treated the life of John Jewell, bishop of Salisbury, as a five-act tragedy (see the *Vita Iohanni Ieweli*). The Elizabethan translation of Appian, published in the same year as *Euphues*, calls itself (in the first part) 'four acts of that profane tragedy, whereof flowed our divine comedy', and (in the continuation) 'the last act of the woeful tragedy'. Moreover there was available as a model that variant of the epic form, in five books ('or acts') of which Sidney's 'Old' *Arcadia* is the obvious example.[46] But among the examples of five-act structure in the period Lyly is unique, I think, in applying the structure to a work of such small compass. It is as a result of this that we are so keenly aware in *Euphues* of shape, order and economy in the narrative.

I have left undiscussed till now a feature of *Euphues* which has given rise to much discussion and (I think) misunderstanding; one which is crucial for any understanding of the book as a biographical document. *Euphues* contains an account of social life of a highly sophisticated kind; Ferardo's house is free of restrictions in the social access allowed to ladies, but highly intellectual in the mode of behaviour required of its visitors. The entertainment offered to Philautus and his new friend is to pronounce on the *dubbii d'amore*, which had been favourite pastimes of refined Italianate society for some centuries before *Euphues*,[47] 'as well to renew old traditions which have been heretofore used, as to increase friendship' (II. 163). Lyly obviously enjoys the tight-rope social skill of Euphues as he balances wit against courtesy and (later) passion. But in his reformed mood Euphues denounces such courtliness, 'rather choosing to die in my study amidst my books than to court it in Italy in the company of ladies'. Are we to interpret this as *Italofobia* (as it has been called)?[48] Feuillerat bases his whole interpretation of *Euphues*, and indeed of Lyly's early career, on the assumption that the book is designed as a blow in the war of the old Humanists against a new and Italianate frivolity, and thus as a bid for Burghley's favour.

It is certainly true that Ascham's *Schoolmaster*, from which Lyly derived his approach to wit, includes a fervent attack on the Italianism which travellers bring home with them: 'for religion, papistry or worse; for learning, less commonly than they carried out with them; for policy, a factious heart, a discoursing head, a mind to meddle in all men's matters; for experience, plenty of new mischiefs never known in England before; for manners, variety of vanities and change of filthy living' (Arber, p. 78). Ascham's first point against Italy is, of course, that it is the home of Papistry; from this he sees the other evils flowing, like poisoned water from a tainted source. But Lyly shows *his* Italy as the home of love (or lust), not of sin or crime, and his treatise on godlessness ('Euphues and Atheos') never mentions Italy. If *Euphues, the Anatomy of Wit* is meant as a blow in the battle against Italianate godlessness, it must be reckoned as a particularly feeble one. It is only in the sequel, *Euphues and his England*, which Feuillerat supposes to be an acceptance of Italianism (dedicated to the 'Italianate' Earl of Oxford), that the standard attitude to Italian vice makes its appearance: 'Thou [Italy] which heretofore wast most famous for victories art become most infamous by thy vices, as much disdained now for thy beastliness in peace as once feared for thy battles in war, thy Caesar being turned to a vicar, thy consuls to cardinals, thy sacred senate of three hundred grave councillors to a shameless synod of three thousand greedy caterpillers' (II. 88 f.). We must notice that the complaint about the Roman church here appears in the context of a love-plaint (Philautus complains that Camilla will never accept him because he is an Italian) so that it can hardly be taken as a plea for an ascetic life. In any case, the speaker (Philautus) is himself an Italian.

There is no need to take the place-names in *Euphues, the Anatomy of Wit* quite literally. No one would deny that Lyly's *Athens* (where Euphues studied, and whither he returns at the end of the story) is Oxford. Since so much of the debate in the book turns on the contrast between student and courtier: 'Ah! foolish Euphues, why didest thou leave Athens the nurse of wisdom to inhabit Naples the nourisher of wantonness? Had it not been better for thee to have eaten salt with the philosophers in Greece than sugar with the courtiers of Italy?' (I. 241), it would be odd if Naples turned out to be a real geographical location, set against Athens, an allusive name. The natural supposition is that *Naples* means London, the obvious home of sophistication to an Englishman, and clearly distinguished from Oxford by its emphasis on courtship (in both senses of the term).

Moreover Lyly seems to be at some pains to copy the manner and even the matter of his fellow Oxonian, George Pettie, whose *Petite Palace of Pettie his Pleasure*—a collection of love-stories liberally sprinkled with rhetorical speeches and debates— was first published in 1576, and stayed popular enough to go through five editions in the next thirty years. By his imitation Lyly seems to invite the assumption that *The Anatomy of Wit* belongs to the same genre as Pettie's book. Pettie (or rather his introducer, 'R.B.') makes a great parade of the ('Italianate', if you will) inutility of his book, and of its suitability for ladies rather than gentlemen ('I care not to displease twenty men, to please one woman'). This anticipates the stance openly adopted in *Euphues and his England*, where it marks (according to Feuillerat) a break with the pious world of *The Anatomy of Wit* and of the early Humanists. But the introduction to Pettie is of a piece with the whole mode of his book, and Lyly must have known that, in adopting this mode in *The Anatomy of Wit*, he was making the break then (if break there was). *The Anatomy of Wit* is in any case involved in the declaration of inutility which prefaces *Euphues and his England*: 'if you be filled with the first part, put the second in your pocket for your waiting maids; *Euphues* had rather lie shut in a lady's casket than open in a scholar's study'. But even this squeak of defiance cannot be taken too literally. It is, of course, a pose, and only one among many. The rhetoric is different from anything in More or Erasmus, but there is no simple reversal of attitudes. It has been the effort of my first chapter to suggest that the split between wit and wisdom is easier imagined than discovered. *Euphues* itself (in both parts) is more a *gallimaufry* (to use Lyly's own word), more a piece of shot silk than Feuillerat was disposed to admit. Looked at one way it is sophisticated and flippant; looked at from another angle it is seriously concerned with conduct. Feuillerat thinks (pp. 259 ff.) that the narrative and the letters of *The Anatomy of Wit* may seem to elicit different and eventually incompatible reactions, and that it is proper to ask, 'where did Lyly's real interests lie?' He himself supposes that Lyly's bent shows in the elegant narrative; but that his intention appears in the moralizing framework which is meant to fix our attitude to the story. Myself, I cannot regard this distinction as proper, since I suppose that wit and wisdom, narrative and moral epistles, all belong to a single vision, even if it is one characterized by what art historians call 'Renaissance Multiplicity'.[49] The style of both sections of the *Anatomy* is the same, and the style itself is a good example of the fusion of argument with ornament which modern analysis finds difficult to handle, preferring to treat the two aspects quite separately. It is true that Lyly is fascinated by social elegance, that he eventually rejects worldly life and that there is (for us) a conflict here; but the conflict is perfectly capable of being rendered by the *non minus pius quam facetus* formula which we have already noticed in the work and life of Sir Thomas More (it turns up again in the lives of Donne and Herbert). Lyly may reconcile these opposed attitudes in a superficial way which bears little relation to the depth of charity in More; but the parallel is there and it may indicate some of the difficulty of keeping the wit and wisdom of *Euphues* rigidly separated.

One reason why the book was the most popular of its age was that it was one of the most eclectic, in an age devoted to eclecticism. It was an enchanting treasure-trove of attitudes and traditions—serious, flippant, classical, contemporary, fantastic, immediate. Pettie's praise of the ideal writer comes home to roost as a description of *Euphues*; Pettie speaks of him as writing, 'as copiously for variety, as compendiously for brevity, as choicely for words, as pithily for sentences [*thoughts*], as pleasantly for figures and every way as eloquently as any writer should do'.[50] It is typical that there is no suggestion how this list of virtues could be made to cohere in one work. The Dutch translation of *Euphues* in 1668 advertises itself as 'containing intellectual diversions, such as jests, courtly oratory, witticisms, *bon mots*, questions and answers, and letters'.[51] All that is lacking is some indication why all these elements should be in this one book; and this is not a lack that seems to have been felt strongly by Lyly or his contemporaries. The work presupposes unity, but it does not labour to prove its existence. The continuity of a dominant style suggests that all these attitudes belong together and can be reconciled at some point, but it leaves the point undetermined.

If we are to treat *Euphues* biographically, all we can say, I suspect, is that the book reads like the pipe-dream of a disappointed don. The contrast between Athens and Naples, the University and the metropolis, is an essential part of the contrast between learning and experience, wit and wisdom. In the person of Euphues, Lyly manages to have it both ways (as he had signally failed to do in real life). Plunging into experience Euphues becomes a notable figure in the great world; Lucilla (not only charming, but an heiress) falls in love with him at first sight, bewitched by his wit. But he sees through the world of courtship, and returns to his University, entitled to lecture others on all kinds of topics. He becomes 'public reader in the University, with such commendation as never any before him; in the which he continued for the space of ten years, only searching out the secrets of nature and the hidden mysteries of philosophy, and having collected into three volumes his lectures, thought for the profit of the young scholars to set them forth in print, which if he had done, I would also in this his *Anatomy* have inserted' (I. 286). We are spared the three volumes of lectures because Euphues, increasing in sanctity even beyond the status of a 'public reader' turns to divinity, and vanishes from sight in a cloud of Biblical references. The book obviously bears some relation to Lyly's hopes of an Oxford fellowship. If he had been told at the time of his application that he had not enough experience to fill the post, we might regard *Euphues* as a demonstration that he now knew quite enough about experience and its fruits. But to suppose this would be to suppose too far. Euphues and Lyly are alike, but they are not identical. It seems fair to infer that Lyly was like his hero in certain characteristics; that he fancied himself as a wit and as a scholar, that he laboured under a sense of injustice, that he felt himself entitled to stand aside and castigate both court and university. But with what immediate aim he expressed these attitudes in *Euphues* we cannot tell.

The common belief that *Euphues, the Anatomy of Wit* was intended as a moral demonstration involves, almost of necessity, a further belief about the sequel. This bears the title *Euphues and his England, containing his voyage and adventures, mixed with sundry pretty discourses of honest love, the description of the country, the court and the manners of that Isle. Delightful to be read and nothing hurtful to be regarded; wherein there is small offence by lightness given to the wise, and less occasion of looseness proffered to the wanton,* and was first published about Easter 1580. It is clear beyond dispute that this is not a work of Humanist piety. It is dedicated to the cultured and vicious Earl of Oxford, whose service Lyly seems to have entered, and (as I have noted above) makes a point of frivolity, inutility and suitability for ladies: 'handle him [*Euphues*] as you do your junkets, that when you can eat no more you tie some in your napkin for children; for if you be filled with the first part, put the second in your pocket for your waiting maids. Euphues had rather lie shut in a lady's casket than open in a scholar's study' (II. 9). Again, the narrative section, which was only a part of the *Anatomy* volume, and was the least overtly moral part, here occupies the whole book; the treatment of love becomes a much more exclusive concern. Misogyny gives way to a praise of ladies as virtuous, noble, chaste and what not; and though Euphues finishes as a hermit on Mount Silixsedra, Philautus (who becomes the central character of the narrative) ends in blissful matrimony. It follows that if the *Anatomy* is to be presented as a work of pious scholarship, then *Euphues and his England* must be seen as a recantation, and this Feuillerat argues.

There are, however, many features which show the second volume carrying on the interests of the first. The Prodigal Son motif which I take to be central in the *Anatomy*, appears again and again in the second volume. While they are travelling to England, Euphues—a regenerate prodigal—tells the story of Callimachus, a prodigal son who is eventually recalled to sense and wealth, but who endures before this a series of exemplary misfortunes:

> You must imagine (because it were too long to tell all his journey) that he was seasick (as thou beginnest to be, Philautus), that he hardly escaped death, that he endured hunger and cold, heat without drink, that he was entangled with women, entrapped, deceived, that every stool he sat on was penniless bench, that his robes were rags . . . etc. (II. 29)

Among the misfortunes to be borne by Callimachus is a visit to his hermit uncle, who is another recovered prodigal, and his story is also related at some length. When they move into England, Euphues and Philautus have their first converse with Fidus, an old bee-keeper, and he turns out to be yet another recovered prodigal; the story of his visit to court and of his unavailing pursuit of the virtuous Iffida occupies a fair proportion of the whole work. The story of Fidus and Iffida, moreover, points forward to the main story of the book—that of Philautus and Camilla; as Fidus learns wisdom through his rejection, so Philautus is taught a more humble kind of love and a less strident use of wit by *his* rejection—and behind both of these stands Euphues who, in the *Anatomy*, learned wisdom by the rejection of his wit. In his jealousy, Philautus quarrels with Euphues here, as in the previous volume Euphues had deceived Philautus. In both volumes love leads to the rejection of friendship; in England, however, the fault is not in the lady but in the Italian lover; and this would seem to be inevitable, given the change of setting. If we put on one side these inevitable changes (to be discussed below), the similarity of motifs in the two volumes is very striking. Both books end with gravity borrowed from Humanists and Classics—in this case with an epitome of Harrison's *Description of England* and a translation of Plutarch's *Conjugal Precepts*. Gravity rather than lightness is also the consequence of the later volume's praise of ladies, since this leads Lyly naturally to the sustained Humanist appraisal of Elizabeth as a Deborah, a Semiramis, an Aspasia, an Amalasuntha.

Feuillerat admits that there are similarities in the second volume; but he suggests that they gradually disappear as the work progresses. He divides *Euphues and his England* into three parts: the first (Euphues, Philautus and the Callimachus story) in the severer vein of the *Anatomy*, the second (Fidus and Iffida) involving pure narrative, without moral dissertations, and the third (Philautus and Camilla) showing courtly frivolity without criticism; he supposes that these crystallize successive states of mind in the author, the whole comprising a *'régression morale'*. It is certainly true that the book contains different attitudes to courtship, and we must endorse Feuillerat's perception that the author seems to change his mind about the nature of the audience addressed, as the work develops. He begins with choric comments of a fairly simple and severe kind: 'Now you shall understand . . .' (II. 103), 'Here, Gentlemen, you may see . . .' (II. 109) and finally arrives at teasing asides as of the ladies' confessor in love: 'Now, Gentlewomen, in this matter I would I knew your minds . . .' (II. 160).

There is also some evidence that Lyly changed his mind about the whole work as he was writing *Euphues and his England*. At the end of the *Anatomy*, Lyly prepares the reader for his second book:

> I have finished the first part of Euphues, whom now I left ready to cross the seas to England. If the wind send him a short cut,

you shall in the second part hear what news he bringeth, and I hope to have him returned within one summer. In the mean season I will stay for him in the country, and as soon as he arriveth you shall know of his coming ... where I have heard of a woman that in all qualities excelleth any man.   (I. 323)

And in the additional 'To my very good friends, the gentlemen scholars of Oxford' (first printed in the summer of 1579) he adds: 'Euphues at his arrival I am assured will view Oxford, where he will either recant his sayings or renew his complaints. He is now on the seas, and how he hath been tossed I know not; but whereas I had thought to receive him at Dover, I must meet him at Hampton' (I. 325). All this suggests a book which will survey the realm, culminating in a view of the university and the court and ending with a panegyric of Elizabeth. One might expect the misogyny of the earlier book to be complemented in this book by praise of the *English* woman. The regenerate Euphues can be brought to regret his 'cooling card for . . . all fond lovers', but after all he has said he can hardly be made into a lover again. Philautus is a less spent residue from the first volume, and his naivety is a more obvious means of recording the impact of English virtue than is the wisdom of Euphues; in consequence we might expect Philautus to be the central character of the second volume.

Whatever the nature of the sequel Lyly intended to write, he had some difficulty in writing it. By mid-1579 he is forecasting delay: I take it that the transfer of landing-point from Dover to Southampton means that Euphues will be at sea (that is, in writing) longer than expected when Lyly wrote his 'returned within one summer' in 1578. In the dedication of *Euphues and his England* he is more explicit: 'I have brought into the world two children; of the first I was delivered before my friends thought me conceived; of the second I went a whole year big, and yet when everyone thought me ready to lie down, I did then quicken' (II. 4). This would seem to imply that the delay was largely due to a difficulty in getting started, but we should not push images elaborated for the sake of parallelism too far as evidence. More integral difficulties seem to be indicated by the fact that the book actually produced in 1580 is notably different in some respects from the book promised in 1578 and 1579. Lyly can still refer to it in his dedication as 'this pamphlet containing the estate of England'; but though the book is twice as long as its predecessor, Euphues and Philautus never go to Oxford, never appear before the Queen, their comments on England are few and most of these are crushed into the concluding epitome of Harrison's *Description of England*—which reads like a hasty attempt to redeem the original promise. It looks indeed as if Lyly had got caught up in the description of manners and failed to leave himself space for the survey of the realm.

But those who look to *Euphues and his England* for objective narration, or expect the pursuit of manners for their own sake are likely to be disappointed. Lyly's interest is still stretched between wit and morality; the morality is not here separated out into a collection of letters, but letters of moral advice remain a notable feature of the work, though they are more effectively dramatized as part of the story. Even in the concluding episode of Philautus' courtship, for all its 'devotion to social frivolity', the method is purely scholastic and the aim is strictly moral—to show how the guilt of Philautus undermines his wit ('Philautus being in a maze . . .', 'Philautus astonied at this speech . . .' [II. 178 f.]) and to define the nature of true love so as to distinguish Philautus, the undeserving lover, from Surius, the deserving lover.

Feuillerat is certainly correct in seeing a variety of attitudes in the book. Philautus is conquered by love, but Euphues remains detached from its excesses (see his remarks in II. 181). Friendship, love, patriotism, piety jostle each other as its dominant value. But the attempt to stratify these attitudes into a *régression morale* seems to be unsuccessful. Once again we are faced with the 'gallimaufry' aspect of Lyly's work. We are told in the 'Epistle to the Gentlemen Readers' prefixed to *Euphues and his England*: 'If in every part it seem not alike, you know that it is not for him that fashioneth the shoe to make the grain of the leather . . . let every one follow his fancy and say that is best which he liketh best' (II. 12). The principle of variety enunciated here is one that we shall notice at greater length when we deal with the plays. We may see how important a principle it is for *Euphues and his England* by itemizing that work in terms of the *topoi* or conventional topics it contains. It seems legitimate to split up the work in this way. Lyly's works are

all, more or less, compilations from standard sources, mosaics
of references to Humanist authorities. In this he is no different
from his contemporaries—Greene, Lodge, Nashe, Dekker all
wrote in the same way. It is probable that Lyly, like many of
these, followed the Humanist discipline of keeping a commonplace book, in which the various quotations he fancied would
be entered under the *topic* he thought appropriate: Abstinence,
Adversity, Affection, Ambition, etc. It is worth noticing how
Lyly, once the topic unfolds before him, pursues it exhaustively
rather than appropriately. So the narrative tends to move,
somewhat jerkily, from one page of his commonplace book
to another. We may give an outline of the topics drawn on for
the opening section of *Euphues and his England*:

    (1) The incommodity of travel (13-14).
    (2) Carefulness versus Prodigality [Tale of Callimachus] (14-30).
    (3) Advice to travellers   ⎫
        Description of Britain   ⎬ (31-32).
    (4) The mystery of kingship (36-44).
    (5) Praise of the regiment of bees (44-46).
    (6) Expectation versus Experience (49-51).
    (7) The incommodity of love (52-53).
    (8) Wine—pro and contra (54-55).
    (9) The variousness of love (57).
  (10) Praise of beauty (59).
  (11) Wit in woman (60).

In each of these cases we see Lyly drawing on a theme of
Renaissance discourse; the attitude veers from page to page as
he picks up now one set of attitudes, now another. To make a
book as versed in the principles of debate as *Euphues* prove
anything at all, obviously we must pick up more than stray
attitudes involved in the book; we must derive our interpretation from the whole drift of the book. And the drift of *Euphues
and his England* does not show a *régression morale*.

The dedication of the second *Euphues* to the Earl of Oxford
has been much used to imply the amoral if not immoral
interests of the book. But the two dedications do not really
allow us to infer any such distinction between the volumes. If
the *Anatomy* is regarded as a bid for Burghley's favour, we
may ask why it was not dedicated to Burghley. It is in fact
dedicated to Sir William West, Lord Delaware, about whom

we know little, and whose relation to Lyly remains largely problematical. We do know that he was convicted of attempting to poison his uncle in order to hasten his inheritance—an 'Italianate' enough action, and one that ought to prevent us from seeing him as the natural patron for a moral treatise.

At the end of the *Anatomy* Lyly speaks of himself awaiting the arrival of the second volume in terms I have already quoted: 'In the mean season I will stay for him in the country, and as soon as he arriveth you shall know of his coming.' 'The country' here may refer to Wherwell Abbey, the seat of Lord Delaware, since that is conveniently situated for arrivals at Southampton. In his dedication Lyly speaks of Delaware as 'my very good lord and master', and he signs it, 'your lordship's servant to command'. These phrases are used again in *Euphues and his England*, and there we know that they reflect a status that documents unequivocally confirm as that of 'servant to the said Earl'. We may suppose that in the *Anatomy of Wit* they reflect a similar status in relation to Delaware. In 1577 there is a reference to Lord Delaware's 'players';[52] perhaps we may assume from this that he was a man of some cultural interests.

Certainly the transfer from Delaware to Oxford cannot be seen as a movement from white to black. Lyly is at great pains to make his two dedications exactly parallel: the opening and concluding formulas remain identical; the public is expected to see the relationship of author and book to patron as unchanged from one volume to the other.

Since Edward de Vere, the seventeenth Earl of Oxford, hereditary Lord Great Chamberlain, one of the few representatives of the medieval nobility to survive into Elizabethan times, was to remain the centre of Lyly's life during its most creative phase, it is worth while pausing to have a look at this gentleman—if indeed we can see through the fog blown around him by those who suppose that he wrote at other times under the pseudonym of 'Shakespeare'. Whatever the moral status of Lord Delaware, there is no doubt that in transferring to the patronage of Oxford Lyly 'improved' himself, that is, came closer to the magic circle of the court where all power and glamour lay. Oxford was a brilliant and accomplished courtier, periodically in high favour with the Queen, and was possessed of some artistic gifts. Contemporary references allow him considerable powers, but one must beware of confusing social deference with literary criticism; the poems of Oxford's which remain show that he could thump out his fourteeners as well as any other 'Drab', but do not exalt him beyond his uncle, Arthur Golding, and do not bring him within reach of Lyly, let alone Shakespeare. What mattered to Lyly as his 'servant' was, I imagine, that here was a man with a literary reputation to sustain, who was prepared to spend money on cultural display and who was capable of making the court listen to him.

That Lyly was actually in the employment of the Earl is testified by the legal documents which describe him as 'servant to the said Earl'; what his actual position was is more doubtful. Gabriel Harvey, attacking Lyly, quotes a string of rather blasphemous phrases from *Pap-Hatchet* (Lyly's pamphlet against Martin Mar-prelate) and continues, 'a whole sink of such arrant phrases savour hotly of the same Lucianical breath and discover the minion Secretary aloof'.[53] It is usually supposed, on the strength of this, that Lyly was the Earl's secretary. There is nothing inherently improbable in this; Ascham had been the Queen's Latin Secretary, Dyer was Leicester's 'confidential agent or gentleman secretary', Spenser was secretary to the Bishop of Rochester, Antony Bacon was secretary to Essex, etc., etc. It is clear that Lyly occupied a position of some trust and authority; we find him associated with Amis, the Earl's intendant, in a scheme which Burghley devised in 1584 to secure the remnants of the Earl's fortune.

That Lyly in some degree owed his place in Oxford's household to Burghley is very probable. Oxford had been Burghley's ward and was now (by a natural Tudor development) his son-in-law—an extremely troublesome one. Lyly seems to have been obliged to tread a dangerous path between two masters, sent for by Burghley to report on his lord, who then complains that any should 'think I am so weak of government as to be ruled by servants, or not able to govern myself',[54] and revenges himself on the servants involved.

The petulant, headstrong and violent Earl could never have been an easy master. But he was a generous one, and Lyly seems to have profited (temporarily at least) by his generosity. If the aim of Lyly's career was to get close to the Queen, it was by Oxford's means that he was enabled to achieve this. His debut as a dramatist and as an impresario must have been financed by Oxford; the boys for whose performances at court he was paid in 1584 were Oxford's boys, and the opportunity to rehearse and perform at the private theatre in the Blackfriars was also due to Oxford's initiative.

Of course the benefits conferred need not have been entirely one-sided. Oxford wished to out-shine his rivals in court, and some control over or responsibility for the best court plays could have been seen as one way of doing this. To what extent (if any) Lyly tailored *Euphues and his England* and his plays to fit the taste of his patron we can never know, for we cannot even be sure of Oxford's tastes. He 'commanded' his 'loving friend' Thomas Bedingfield to translate Cardan's *Comfort* into English (1573) and this argues seriousness of mind and sobriety of taste. On the other hand he was celebrated for his outlandish clothing, and for a combination of culture and violence which most historians are prepared to call 'Italianate'. At least the 'Italianate' point must have been close enough to Oxford to prick him when Lyly suggested that a satire on the Earl was to be found in Gabriel Harvey's 'Speculum Tuscanismi':[55] *in gratiam quorundam Illustrium Anglofrancitalorum hic et ubique abud nos volitantium,*

> . . .
> Delicate in speech, quaint in array; conceited in all points
> In courtly guiles a passing singular odd man,
> For gallants a brave mirror, a primrose of honour
> A diamond for nonce, a fellow peerless in England
> . . .
> This, nay more than this, doth practice of Italy in one year.
> None do I name, but some do I know, that a piece of a
> twelfthmonth
> Hath so perfitted outly, and inly, both body, both soul.

Oxford was, indeed, abroad, in Italy and elsewhere, in 1574-5, and though we cannot suppose that his faults of character derived from his foreign travel, they were not improved by it (at the fantastic cost of £3,761). But however accurate the 'Speculum Tuscanismi' (and it claims to describe several persons, rather than one) it does not follow that the moral

Lyly was forced to change his attitude by the partonage of this lord. Feuillerat paints a dramatic picture:

> Assurément, c'était une bien jolie ironie du sort qui vouait au service de cet italianisant incorrigible le moral auteur de l'*Anatomy of Wit* . . . dans la foule de flatteurs courtisanesques, de poètes besoigneux, de spadassins sans scrupules qui se pressait autour du sémillant Oxford, Lyly ne pouvait guère conserver ses airs de vieille barbe grondeuse sans encourir le ridicule.   (p. 81)

Unfortunately, when we look at Lyly's works for the proof of this change, we cannot find it. *Euphues and his England* is no flatterer of Italianism, no apologist for assassination; it is Burghley who is praised by name, not Oxford: 'Lord Burghley, high Treasurer of that Realm, no less reverenced for his wisdom, than renowmed for his office, more loved at home than feared abroad, and yet more feared for his counsel among other nations than sword or fire . . . this noble man I found so ready, being but a stranger, to do me good, that neither I ought to forget him, neither cease to pray for him . . . not unworthy to be advanced, by whose care so many have been preferred' (II. 198). The references here strongly suggest that Lyly was still, even in the household of Oxford, labouring under a sense of obligation to Burghley, which should have been enough to keep him well-balanced. And the courtly comedies which follow do no more than persist in that Humanist balance of learning and courtly grace which we have noticed as natural to Lyly and his tradition, from the beginning. That this was how contemporaries saw the author of *Euphues* would seem to be indicated by the praise which Barnaby Rich bestows on Lyly: 'and among the whole catalogue of comely scholars there shalt thou meet with a gentleman . . . who can court it with the best and scholar it with the most, in whom I know not whether I should more commend his manners or his learning, the one so exquisite, the other so general' (*Don Simonides* [1584] *sig.* I. 3).

Whatever the literary influence of Oxford, Lyly's fortunes flourished under his patronage. In 1583 he married Beatrice Browne, an heiress from Mexborough (Yorkshire), well connected with various powerful families and quite a prize in the marriage market for the Canterbury registrar's son. I suspect that the connection that counted for most in the marriage was that which led from Beatrice Browne to Joan Cecil, Lord Burghley's aunt. Everywhere we look in Lyly's career we find a Cecil connection, and I suspect that Lyly's own relationship with the Cecils was the pivot of his career, though he was never directly employed or patronized by any of them.

Besides containing this social (and pecuniary) success, the period of the early 'eighties marks the crest of Lyly's literary reputation. *Euphues* was a success without parallel in its age: by 1581 five editions of *The Anatomy of Wit* had been published and four of the sequel; by 1630 there were twenty-six editions of the separate works and three editions of a double volume. The court was completely conquered—in a literary sense at any rate. As his first editor remarked, 'All our ladies were then his scholars, and that Beauty in court which could not parley Euphuism was as little regarded as she which now [1632] there speaks not French.' The up-and-coming literary generation were equally bowled over. Thomas Nashe tells us, '*Euphues* I read when I was a little ape in Cambridge, and then I thought it was *Ipse ille*'; Nashe was at Cambridge from 1582-88. Imitations began to be published as early as 1579, and went on appearing throughout the 'eighties. At a later point (below, pp. 280 ff.) we shall trace the fortunes of Euphues; what we are concerned with here are rather the fortunes of John Lyly.

We may indeed feel surprise at the speed with which Lyly disengaged his own career from that of the *persona* he had created so successfully. We should not, however, forget the Humanist attitude to literature—that the end of rhetoric is political power. Euphues might have considerable literary life left in him; and the composite form of tale, debate and treatise went on being used and developed by other men; but the Queen could not be approached any closer by these means. The long panegyric at the end of *Euphues and his England* comes as close to the throne as the romance form allowed. Moreover, under Oxford's patronage—the patronage of 'our best for comedy', with his own players and the ear of the court—Lyly found another opening, and one which offered a more secure demonstration of intellectual fitness and a more direct means of appeal to the sovereign, an approach through court drama.

To understand why Lyly presented *Campaspe* and *Sapho and*

Phao in the court season of 1583-4 involves piecing together fragmentary evidences concerning the Earl of Oxford, the Blackfriars theatre, and the history of the boys' companies. The dissolved monastery of the Black Friars (between St Paul's and the river) became in 1576 the site of a small private theatre (46 ft. by 26 ft.), leased to Richard Farrant, Master of the children of St George's Chapel, Windsor, who aimed to collect here some profit on the plays designed for court entertainment. It seems that Farrant had William Hunnis, the Master of the children of the Chapel Royal as his partner, and that the plays were performed by a combined troupe. Farrant died in 1580; the landlord, not particularly pleased by this use of a respectable property, attempted to break the lease, and a combine of those interested in the theatre tried to outmanœuvre him. By 1583, if not before, this party included Hunnis (in control of the troupe), Henry Evans (a scrivener, able to complicate the legal issues), John Lyly (potential playwright and Oxford's agent), and the Earl of Oxford (able to give the protection of his name).

We may well ask what Oxford is doing in this company. It is improbable that he was in it simply for the sake of the drama. It has been conjectured that he was acting for the drama-loving Queen, but had this been the case, the landlord would hardly have persisted in his suit. A more probable reason for Oxford's interest emerges from his personal history.[56] In 1581 Oxford was accused of seducing Anne Vavasour, a Gentlewoman of Elizabeth's bedchamber, and he was imprisoned, partly on this account and partly on account of the confession that he had been a secret Papist since the time of his return from Italy. He was released from the Tower in June 1581, but a series of duels and brawls with members of Anne's family followed, and it was not until June 1583 that the Queen would receive the Earl again; then 'after some bitter words and speeches, in the end all sins are forgiven and he may repair to the court at his pleasure'.[57] In 1583, then, Oxford is climbing back into royal favour, and is no doubt anxious to do all he can to win back again the lost ground. To please the Queen by dramatic entertainments was an accepted method of gaining favour when she was in Progress through the provinces; there is no ground for supposing that the method would work any less well in London. This is, I suggest, the explanation of the

'Oxford boys', who appear at court in 1583-4 and then disappear again. The 'Oxford boys' for whose court performances on 1st January and Shrove Tuesday 1584 Lyly was the payee, and who appeared once again, on 27th December 1584 (Henry Evans being the payee), are usually supposed to be a combined troupe of the Chapel Royal boys and the Paul's boys, with perhaps the boys of Oxford's own chapel as a further addition. The two plays which the 'Oxford boys' performed and for which Lyly was paid are plausibly identified with his own *Campaspe* ('new year's day at night') and *Sapho and Phao* ('on shrove tuesday'), which are said on the title-pages to have been performed by 'her Majesty's children and the children of Paul's'. If the chain of evidence holds here we can develop the story of the Blackfriars a little further. With the death of Farrant, the Windsor boys would pass out of the Blackfriars combination. It looks as if Hunnis and the Chapel Royal troupe had found a new patron in Oxford and a new support in the boys of Paul's. Oxford acquired a means of raising his prestige at court; Lyly found an outlet for his literary talents, and a mode of speaking directly to the Queen.

The somewhat rickety combination of interests which produced the two plays was not likely to last long, especially when subjected to external pressure. At Easter 1584 the landlord obtained judgment in his favour; Lyly, Evans, and Hunnis were sent packing from the Blackfriars. Evans, not Lyly, is paid for the final appearance of the 'Oxford boys', in December 1584. I do not know if this means that Lyly had withdrawn from the combination. The 'ironical letter' of December 1584 (see below), speaks of Lyly making 'the boys in Paul's play . . . upon a stage'; his later plays rely upon the Paul's boys alone for their performances and the association with the Paul's boys may have been all that Lyly salvaged out of the Blackfriars venture.

We hear of Lyly disposing of his more tangible interests in the Blackfriars in 1584 and 1585. He had leased for himself (at an annual rent of £8) some 'rooms' which were probably those which had been carved out of the old 'Parlour' of the Monastery. The lease of part of this he sold to Rocco Bonetti for a fencing school: 'a hall, a chamber above the hall, a little room under the said hall, a yard, a little chamber or

vault within the said yard, a cellar adjoining the said yard . . .
an entry, a kitchen adjoining to the said hall, and a small
room within the said kitchen'. This was spacious accommodation, and there was still more, sold to Lord Hunsdon in 1585.[58]
The natural explanation is that Lyly, now a married man, had
his own house (as had Henry Evans) in the monastery; but
the accommodation seems excessive, and one is driven to wonder
what other activities were accommodated within the various
'chambers, vaults, cellars', etc. That the Lyly *ménage* occupied
at least part of the property is made probably by their sudden
appearance elsewhere when the property in Blackfriars is sold.
Though he was married in 1583, Lyly does not appear in the
London parish registers until 1586, when he is chronicled in
the parish of St Martin's, Ludgate. There he stays till 1592
when he goes to Mexborough, and from Mexborough he
returns to London about 1596 and lives at St Bartholomew's
(see below).

As a result of his experience at the Blackfriars, Lyly evidently
became something of an impresario. One may quote the
remarks of Harvey on this topic. In his attack on Lyly he says,
'He hath not played the Vicemaster of Paul's and the Foolmaster of the Theatre for naughts'.[59] Earlier critics supposed
that 'the Vicemaster of Paul's' implied a regular post as a
teacher of the St Paul's choirboys (Vicemaster = Assistant
Master). I shall discuss below (Chapter 3) the organization of
the boys, and I trust it will emerge from this that such a post
was no refuge for the author of *Euphues*. But the context in
Harvey alone should make it clear that this is not implied,
since Vicemaster is a word of the same kind as Foolmaster,
and therefore would seem to mean 'master of those who can
play the role of the medieval "Vice" as well as implying that
Lyly was vicious [and foolish]'. Even so, we are left with the
statement that Lyly had some measure of control over Paul's
boys. Harvey says again (the words may serve as a gloss on the
above), 'They [*Lyly and Nashe*] have the stage at commandment,
and can furnish out Vices and Devils at their pleasure. . . . And
all you that tender the preservation of your good names were
best to please . . . Euphues betimes, for fear lest he be moved,
or some one of his apes [*boys*] hired to make a play of you'.[60]
One might be tempted to dismiss this as the slander of an

enemy, for there is no evidence that Nashe ever had 'the stage at commandment'; but we find independent external witness in the 'Ironical Letter' of [? December] 1584, from Jack Roberts to Sir Roger Williams.⁶¹ This retails various convivial goings-on among captains and voyagers, and then adds: 'I pray you take heed and beware of my lord of Oxenford's man called Lyly, for if he see this letter he will put it in print or make the boys in Paul's play it upon a stage'. In addition to suggesting control over the Paul's boys, this seems to tell us also that Lyly had already a reputation for putting contemporary personalities into his plays.

In January 1585, Christ Church, Oxford, borrowed theatrical apparel from Lyly to furnish out the entertainment of their chancellor, the Earl of Leicester. For this, Lyly's man received twenty shillings, while Lyly himself received a pair of gloves.⁶² We do not know how they sorted out these rewards.

Whatever kind of connection Lyly kept with the boys of Paul's, there seems to have been a break in the appearance of his plays at court, between *Sapho and Phao* (3rd March 1584) and *Gallathea* (1st January 1588). *Gallathea* must have been in existence some time before this, for it was entered for publication (under the title of *Titirus and Galathea*) on the 1st April 1585. It looks as if it was written for court performance shortly after *Sapho and Phao*, since it contains a reference which would be meaningless unless the audience could remember the earlier play. Venus remarks to Cupid 'Sir boy, where have you been? always taken, first by Sapho, now by Diana' (V. iii. 85 f.). It looks as if the opportunity to perform it as originally planned disappeared when the 'Oxford boys' combine broke up, and that Lyly, in spite of his theatrical connections in the intervening period, despaired of performance and thought of publication. By 1588, however, these troubles had blown over. Thomas Giles, the Master, was paid for Paul's boys' performances on New Year's Day 1588 (*Gallathea*, I suppose) and *Gallathea* was followed rapidly by *Endimion* (2nd February). *Midas* must have been written 1588-9; obviously it follows the defeat of the Spanish Armada and it must have been performed before November 1589, when Harvey refers to it. Presumably Harvey had seen it performed at Paul's, for the most probable date for its court performance is the 6th of January 1590.

This second bout of activity as a court dramatist may be connected with a loosening of the ties which bound Lyly to Oxford. After 1588 the connection seems to have disappeared. In that year died Ann Cecil, the Countess of Oxford, who provided the link between Burghley and Oxford that may well have assured Lyly of his place. Shortly afterwards Oxford seems to have disappeared from court. In 1592 he married again and retired to Hackney. It is clear that the pension of 1586 marked the completion of his hopes; thereafter the need to shine at court may well have diminished, and with that the literary usefulness of Lyly must have come to an end. The Epilogue to *Endimion* suggests that in 1588 the Paul's company —including Lyly, I suppose—have to face some opposition at court and hope to overcome it by the Queen's favour: 'Dread sovereign, the malicious that seek to overthrow us with threats do but stiffen our thoughts and make them sturdier in storms; but if your Highness vouchsafe with your favourable beams to glance upon us we shall not only stoop but with all humility lay both our hands and hearts at your Majesty's feet.' We have no knowledge who 'the malicious' were; but we should notice that in the same year there were some signs of favour from Elizabeth.

It seems to have been in 1588 that the Queen made her ill-fated suggestion that Lyly should 'aim all [his] courses at the Revels (I dare not say with a promise, but with a hopeful item of the reversion)'.[63] It was not the Queen's way to give encouragement, even of this vague kind, to a man who could be sustained out of other men's finances, and it seems likely that the Queen's suggestion followed on the loss of some other patronage—presumably Oxford's. No doubt Lyly's appointment as 'Esquire of the Body' was another such sop. Feuillerat searched through the Exchequer books without finding any payment to Lyly, and concludes that he had the rank (largely honorific in the case of a Queen regnant) without the stipend; the Queen kept Lyly tied to the court with hope and a sense of his own dignity and avoided any loss of revenue.

This was, of course, the common lot of the Elizabethan courtier,

> To speed today, to be put back tomorrow,
> To feed on hope, to pine with fear and sorrow.

Miserable though Lyly's last years may have been, they could be paralleled over and over again. The case-history of the high-born and superlatively gifted Francis Bacon is an object-lesson in the fate of talent at the Tudor court. The particular fate reserved for Lyly was to languish in hope of being appointed Master of the Revels. The Master in possession was Edmund Tilney, who had some literary ability but who was appointed, in 1578, largely, one supposes, because he was a connection of the powerful Howard family. Lyly could not have hoped to displace Tilney, but sought, if not a promise at least a 'hopeful item' of the reversion; that is he sought a patent that he would be the next appointee when Tilney died. In fact, Tilney outlived Lyly, but even the status of Master-in-reversion was denied. Another connection of the Howards, Sir George Buc, whom we have seen associated with Lyly much earlier (1582— see above, pp. 47 f.) in the group prefacing Watson's *Hekatompathia*, pushed his claims more successfully, and was eventually appointed.

Though Lyly remained in this posture of painful supplication for the rest of his life, various small ameliorations were possible He was a member of Parliament in 1589 and on three subsequent occasions. He had powerful friends and his wife had influential connections. In the summer of 1589 he was enlisted, as a writer of known facility, to defend the bishops in their controversy with the elusive but effective 'Martin Mar-Prelate'. The sober treatises of the doctors of divinity had failed to make the necessary impact on the public, and certainly had not countered the lively vein of polemic discovered by the Martinist authors. Only one anti-Martin pamphlet can be assigned to Lyly—*Pap with a Hatchet*—and this is sufficient to show how mistaken were the ecclesiastical authorities in supposing that Lyly could be as lively in the gutter as he was in the court. It is in fact a lamentable performance, turgid and tasteless in its efforts to match Martin at his own game. When we put Lyly's effort beside the invectives which Nashe was penning in the same cause, we see how little the Euphuistic rhetoric had to offer the author in the market-place.

It may have been because of Lyly's connection with the anti-Martin campaign that he was elected, in 1589, as M.P. for the borough of Hindon in Wiltshire. Hindon seems to have been, at this time, in the pocket of the Bishop of Winchester, or else (when Winchester was weak or vacant) in the gift of the Archbishop of Canterbury.[64] Thomas Cooper, the Bishop of Winchester at this time, was the chief butt of the Mar-prelates, and he may have been Lyly's patron; or the patron may have been Whitgift himself. After all, Lyly had close family connections with the see of Canterbury.

Lyly sat in Parliament in all the subsequent Elizabethan assemblies—in 1593, 1597-8 and in 1601, though he had to keep changing the borough he represented, like the 'carpet-baggers' of the nineteenth century. Presumably he was willing to represent any borough, if he could find a patron to appoint him, and certainly he was not alone in this. Neale cites Arthur Atye, secretary to Leicester and then to Essex, who sat for Liverpool, Fowey, Shaftesbury (Wiltshire), Dunwich (Suffolk) and Berealston (Devon). All the boroughs that Lyly represented were small places controlled by a single family. He was twice the member for Aylesbury, the town that Neale calls 'the perfect Elizabethan example of a pocket borough'. Aylesbury was owned by the Packington family, and it is not clear how Lyly had ingratiated himself with them; but it is significant that his fellow member in 1593 was Sir Thomas West, pre-sumably the brother of Lord Delaware, the dedicatee of *Euphues, the Anatomy of Wit*. No doubt if we could understand the West connection we could also understand the Packington one; as it is, we understand neither.

We have no record of Lyly's activities in the printed pro-ceedings of any of these parliaments to suggest that he had found a new vocation.[65] It seems reasonable to suppose that he was no great Parliament man, but was content to vote for whatever authority required. Nevertheless we should note that membership of Parliament was an honour that few Elizabthan writers achieved. Sidney, Ralegh, Greville and Bacon were there, of course, but for quite unliterary reasons. The authors who had to rest on their pens did not get so far—Spenser did not, Harvey did not, Drayton and Daniel did not, and none of the 'University Wits' were there—Nashe, Greene, Peele, Lodge, Watson. There can be little doubt that Lyly remained, socially, a cut above these other writers. Nashe's references to him as 'Master Lyly' have always a streak of social deference

in them, which reflects this difference. But the honour of
sitting in Parliament, like so many of the other 'honours' that
Lyly collected, did little or nothing to alleviate what Ben
Jonson calls 'the poet's evil—poverty'. From the point of
view of Lyly's career, Parliament is a blind alley.

More relevant to Lyly's history is the surviving evidence
that he used his influence over the Paul's boys to present (or
try to present) anti-Martinist plays. Harvey says (as we have
already noted) that both Nashe and Lyly have the stage at
commandment, and Lyly himself remarks:

> Would those comedies might be allowed to be played that are
> penned, and then I am sure he [*Martin*] would be deciphered,
> and so perhaps discouraged.
>
> He shall not be brought in as whilom he was, and yet very well,
> with a coxcomb, an ape's face, a wolf's belly, cat's claws, etc.,
> but in a caped cloak and all the best apparel he ware the highest
> day in the year—that's neither on Christmas Day, Good Friday,
> Easter Day, Ascension nor Trinity Sunday (for that were Popish)
> —but on some rainy week-day when the brothers and sisters had
> appointed a match for particular prayers, a thing as bad at the
> least as auricular confession.
>
> . . . Would it not be a fine tragedy when Mardocheus shall play
> a bishop in a play, and Martin, Haman; and that he that seeks
> to pull down those that are set in authority above him should be
> hoisted upon a tree above all other?   (III. 408)

The anti-Martin plays may explain Harvey's curious allusion to
Lyly as not only 'the Vicemaster of Paul's' but also as 'the
Foolmaster of the Theatre'. 'The Theatre' here must be a direct
reference to the playhouse of that name, built by James
Burbage in 1576, where (so far as we know) only adults
performed. But if theatres were hired to defend the cause of
Episcopalianism then the Theatre may well have been used for
that purpose.[66] If it was so then it must have been so before
November 1589, the date of Harvey's book.

Lyly's ineptitude in polemic, coupled probably with an
over-eagerness to please authority, seems to have led to some
gaffe at this moment of licence. Like Nashe later (in *The Isle
of Dogs*) and Marston later still, Lyly seems to have offended
others beside his opponents by the satirical drama he devised
for the boys. Points of doctrine are notoriously difficult to

handle in general terms—see below (pp. 148 f.) on the Hinchin-brook episode—and the Queen's religious position was so indefinite that she could take offence anywhere. Official action brought the plays to an end; the Paul's boys were inhibited from acting for the period 1590-1600 (approx.); and when silence falls on the Paul's boys, silence is not far from the dramatic voice of John Lyly.

I have left undiscussed three plays by Lyly which must belong to the latter end of his career—*Mother Bombie, The Woman in the Moon* and *Love's Metamorphosis. Love's Metamorphosis* draws on Greene's *Alcida* (published 1588) and so must be later than it.[67] *The Woman in the Moon* contains (III. i. 50) a reference to *Love's Metamorphosis* and so must be the later of these two plays. About *Mother Bombie* nothing is so clear. When the Paul's boys were dissolved certain plays were released for publication; there is a note prefixed to *Endimion*, from the Printer to the Reader, which tells us, 'Since the plays in Paul's were dissolved, there are certain comedies come into my hands by chance, which were presented before her majesty at several times by the children of Paul's'. This accounts for the publication of *Endimion* in 1591 and of *Midas* in 1592. I think it does not account for the publication of *Mother Bombie* in 1594; but *Mother Bombie* may have come to its publishers for the same reason. Its title-page tells us that we have the play 'as it was sundry times played by the children of Paul's; the absence of any reference to the court here leads one to suppose that it was never presented before the Queen, that we have a play from the repertory of the private theatre; a study of the content also suggests that it was designed for the playhouse rather than the court. If this is so it must precede the inhibition of 1590 or so, and therefore belongs to the same period of composition as *Midas. Love's Metamorphosis* would be more suited to court performance; the title-page calls it 'A Witty and Courtly Pastoral', but it does not say that it was ever performed at court. Probably it was in the Paul's repertory when the authori-ties closed down on them, but only as a new play, for they did not sell it for publication as they did *Endimion, Midas,* and perhaps *Mother Bombie*; they retained it in their stock and it came on the boards again when the children of the Chapel Royal emerged from their long silence (about 1600). As the title-page says, it was 'first played by the children of Paul's, and now by the children of the Chapel'. As it stands at present, *Love's Metamorphosis* is the shortest of Lyly's plays, and this shortness is largely accounted for by the absence of a sub-plot of cheeky pages. It is natural to suppose that the short form represents that of the revival, and Bond has added a further conjecture that the excised sub-plot was concerned with the Mar-prelate controversy, and had to be cut for this reason. It may be so. But we should note that if Lyly was writing a play against the Mar-prelates and not merely alluding to them, he would surely put them in his main plot. There is no sub-plot in *Love's Metamorphosis*; but neither is there in *Mother Bombie* nor *The Woman in the Moon*. In this period Lyly is obviously experimenting, and the short form without sub-plot may well be one of his experiments.

The Woman in the Moon must be, as I have said, later than *Love's Metamorphosis*. It is the only play he wrote in verse and it is the only play whose title-page does not tell us who were the actors. There are other differences as well; the action is more farcical than witty, and the clown part of Gunophilus involves the kind of audience participation in the jokes that we have supposed to be more typical of the public stage than of the private one. In addition, the action demands (what Lyly nowhere else demands) an upper stage and a trap-door. The aggregation of these differences suggests a milieu completely changed from that of Lyly's other plays; and a natural assumption is that Lyly is here writing for the adult actors, forced to this by the inhibition of the boys. He obviously thinks of the play as a new venture, though one he is willing to repeat:

> Remember all is but a poet's dream;
> The first he had in Phoebus' holy bower;
> But not the last, unless the first displease.
>
> (Prologus, 17-19)

Evidently the first *did* displease, for *The Woman in the Moon* has no fellows, and I take it to be the last of Lyly's plays. It was performed before the Queen, and has many virtues as a court play; it is varied, charming and fanciful, with a certain intellectual energy and bite of wit; but Lyly has sacrificed some of the charm that belonged to the boys—the brittle wit

of their love-scenes, and the chiming formality of their disputations—yet has found no real scope for the men. In its
songs, in its short scenes, in its puppet-like treatment of the
emotions, *The Woman in the Moon* remains essentially the same
kind of coterie play as Lyly had always written; one cannot
be surprised that it was not a popular success.

All these late plays show a degree of restless experimentation
which argues an author unsettled in his *métier*. *Mother Bombie*
would seem to be for boys not for court, *The Woman in the Moon*
for court but not for boys, while *Love's Metamorphosis* is either
an experimental short play or a play whose sub-plot became
unsuitable. Obviously Lyly is battling with a changing taste,
but without much success. He is becoming the 'victim of
fashion', and it need not surprise us that the last twelve
years of his life are years of silence as far as literature is
concerned.

We can follow his life to some extent. About 1592 he left
London, and for the next couple of years had his home in
Mexborough, where his wife came from.[68] This is hardly the
action of a courtier whose affairs are flourishing. He would be in
London for the Parliament session, February to April 1593,
but he seems to have hidden in the country from other metropolitan concerns. The exile did not last very long, however;
some time after March 1595 he left Mexborough, and by about
1596 he is living in London, once again in a dissolved monastery
split up into tenements, this time St Bartholomew's.

In 1597 he was again a member of Parliament; and in the
same year he appeared in print, with a Latin epigram seconding
Henry Lok (or Lock) in his 'century of sacred sonnets' dedicated
to the Queen. Lok was up at Oxford at exactly the same time
as Lyly, and like him was a petitioner for courtly preferment,
descending as far as a request to be made her majesty's bear-
ward; Lyly might well feel himself able to patronize one whose
begging was so much less dignified than his own.

Bond supposed that Lyly filled in the literary vacancy of
these years by writing 'entertainments' offered to the Queen in
Progress, in the years 1590, 1591, 1592, 1600, 1602, 1606. He
takes this as breaking 'the improbable silence of his last
fifteen years. It shows him employed . . . and as appealed to for
aid in such matters by various noblemen wishing to entertain

the Queen' (I. 378 f.). He therefore prints eight of these entertainments in volume I of the *Works*.

It is perfectly possible that Lyly wrote some shows of this kind[69] and he was certainly capable of producing the pieces that Bond has printed. But there is no evidence that they are his, and the conception of him filling in his retirement with work as entertainment-writer in ordinary is, I am sure, misleading. He had no reputation as an author of 'devices', 'shows' or masques, and literary power is no competitor in these pieces against showmanship; so why he should be called from London to do this work I do not know. One entertainment, that which Bond called 'Speeches to Queen Elizabeth at Quarrendon', is now believed,[70] on good contemporary evidence, to have been presented at Woodstock or Ditchley and to have been written by Richard Eedes of Christ Church, Oxford. The concept of a 'man of letters' who could do such things better than the local parson or other literate body was not then so clear as it is now; and I suspect that many of these shows were written by local authors who are otherwise unknown to us. At any rate the fact that they all contain figures which may be termed Euphuistic is no evidence of Lyly's authorship; for it was Bond's error to see Euphuism as the style of a man rather than that of a generation. Moreover the figures are too often commonplaces to allow them to be used in [arguments about authorship. Thus the image of bees hiving in a helmet may appear in Peele's *Polyhymnia* and also in *Euphues*, but this is no reason for transferring the *Polyhymnia* sonnet to Lyly; for the image appeared in Alciati's *Emblems* long before either Lyly or Peele, and like Alciati's other images, had a European diffusion.

Most misleading of all is, I think, Bond's view that the silence of Lyly's last fifteen years is 'improbable'. I suspect that the Humanist author has been temporarily replaced here by a Romantic author, with a genius inside him that *must* speak out. For if we allow that Lyly's aim in writing was to demonstrate intellectual fitness for power, there is no improbability about silence when the avenues to power are blocked. And in any case Lyly was not silent in these later years. His petitions to Elizabeth are among the most celebrated of his writings, and though they are not 'literature' in the narrow sense, they carry on directly the aims that had always animated Lyly's literary life.

I do not wish to seem to say that Lyly's later years were not pitiable; they were made all the more pitiable, indeed, because he had so many powerful friends. He refers to Sir Hugh Beeston with some familiarity; he seems to count on Sir Fulke Greville as well disposed towards him; he writes without formality to Sir Robert Cotton. Toby Mathew, at this point Bishop of Durham and shortly to be Archbishop of York, writes[71] to Sir Julius Caesar, the Master of Requests, calling him 'my old acquaintance and friend' (presumably they had known each other at Oxford). But as the second petition (1601) remarks, 'twenty friends . . . though they say they will be sure, I find sure to be slow'.

Those on whom he had always relied most were dying around him. In 1598 Burghley died. Lyly was quick with condolences for Robert Cecil and Latin verses, concocted by his clergyman brother, Peter, who was now a Brother of the Savoy and Vicar of Fulham. In 1603 the Queen herself was placed beyond the reach of any further petitionary letters. Lyly was given seven yards of black cloth for the funeral; it must have seemed a poor reward for fifteen years of attendance.

The petitions[72] themselves are worth reprinting once again, for they provide a curious and pathetic final view of Humanist eloquence in its relation to royal purposes.

(1) *Tempora si numeres bene, quae numeramus egentes*
    Non venit ante suam nostra querela diem.

Most gracious and dread sovereign, I dare not pester your Highness with many words, and want wit to wrap up much matter in few. This age aimeth at Epitomies—the Pater noster thrust into the compass of a penny, the world into the model of a tennis ball, all sciences melted into sentences. I would I were so compendious as to express my hopes, my fortunes, my overthwarts in two syllables, as merchants do riches in few ciphers. But I fear to commit the error I discommend—tediousness; like him that vowing to search out what time was, spent all his time and knew it not.

I was entertained your Majesty's servant by your own gracious favour, strengthened with conditions that I should aim all my courses at the Revels, (I dare not tell with a promise, but a hopeful item of the reversion), for which these ten years I have attended with an unwearied patience. And now I know not what crab took me for an oyster, that in the midst of the sunshine of your most gracious aspect, hath thrust a stone between the shells to eat me alive, that only lived on dead hopes.

If your sacred Majesty think me unworthy, and that after ten years tempest I must at the court suffer shipwreck of my time, my hopes, my wits, vouchsafe in your never-erring judgment some plank or rafter to waft me into the country where in my sad and settled devotion, I may in every corner of a thatched cottage write prayers instead of plays—prayers for your long and prosperous life and a repentance that I have played the fool so long, and yet live.

> *Quod petimus poena est: nec enim miser esse recuso*
> *Sed precor ut possim mitius esse miser.*

(2) *Non ero qui nunc sum te miserante miser.*

Most gracious and dread sovereign: time cannot work my petitions, nor my petitions the time.

After many years service it pleased your Majesty to except against Tents and Toils. I wish that for tents I might put in tenements, so should I be eased of court toils; some lands, goods, fines or forfeitures that shall fall by the just fall of these most false traitors; that seeing nothing will come by the Revels, I may prey upon the rebels. Thirteen years your Highness' servant, and yet nothing; twenty friends that though they say they will be sure, I find them sure to be slow; a thousand hopes, but all nothing; a hundred promises, but yet nothing. Thus casting up the inventory of my friends, hopes, promises and time the *summa totalis* amounteth in all to just nothing. My last will is shorter than mine inventory—but three legacies: patience to my creditors, melancholy without measure to my friends, and beggary not without shame to my family

> *Si placet hoc meruique, qu[i]d O tua fulmina cessant*
> *Virgo, Parens, Princeps.*

In all humility I entreat that I may dedicate to your sacred hands *Lilly de Tristibus*, wherein shall be seen Patience, Labour, Misfortune;

> *Quorum si singula nostram*
> *Frangere non poterant, poterunt tamen omnia mentem.*

The last and the least: that if I be bound to have nothing I may have a protection to pay nothing; which suit is like his that having followed the court ten years, for recompense of his service committed a robbery and took it out in a pardon.

The stylistic brilliance here and the wit of the author show why these letters quickly became collector's pieces. But there is at the same time a pathetic discontinuity between the bitterness of the feelings and playfulness of the rhetoric. Lyly, obliged still to speak through the *persona* he had created for the court, is obliged to turn his real cries for help into favour and prettiness, into jests and exercises. When his feelings can inform his style then is his style of least use to him.

We can see the petitions as a despairing comment on the Humanist dream of Eloquence to move princes. And in both letters Lyly shows a strong consciousness of the superficiality and folly of mere literary entertainment—especially that of the stage. He writes to Sir Robert Cecil in 1597: 'I will cast my wits in a new mould . . . for I find it folly that one foot being in the grave, I should have the other on the stage'; Elizabethan suspicions of the stage were not confined to professed Puritans. He also mentions in the first petition his retirement to write 'prayers instead of plays—prayers for your long and prosperous life and a repentance that I have played the fool so long and yet live.' The only Humanist end which these 'toys' (as Sidney called them) might serve—that of state advancement—has failed to materialize. The first petition (probably to be dated in 1598) seems to refer to the granting of the reversion of the Mastership of the Revels to Sir George Buc. This is referred to unequivocally in the closely related 1597 letter to Cecil: 'Offices in reversion are forestalled, in possession engrossed, and that of the Revels countenanced upon Buc'. Foiled of the Revels, he turned to the Mastership of the Tents and Toils but his petition for that seems to have been cut off with a short refusal. In the second petition (to be dated in 1601) he descends further and pleads for anything, 'lands, goods, fines or forfeitures'. He is obviously aiming at the confiscated properties of the Essex conspirators of 1601. We do not know if the request achieved anything; we only know that nothing lasted. In 1602 he is still petitioning the Queen; in that year we hear of his wife presenting another letter to her Majesty.[73] It would be pleasant to think that all this effort was not in vain, and that Blount, his first editor, was right in supposing that Queen

Elizabeth 'heard, graced and rewarded' him; but there is only slender ground for the supposition. A much damaged letter to Sir Robert Cotton refers to a 'book' held by the Solicitor-General, and this may be the title-deeds of some property that had fallen to him.[74] But he was not sustained for long. The Toby Mathew letter of 1605 (I suppose the 'IX Feb. 1604' to be 'old style') tells that he is still at this date enduring 'his years fast growing on and his insupportable charge of many children all unbestowed, besides the debt wherein he standeth, which I greatly fear will lie heavy upon him to his and their utter undoing'. To the misfortunes listed by Toby Mathew perhaps we should add illness; in 1605 he did not answer a suit laid against him; as has been suggested, 'possibly he was already ill with the disease which killed him in 1606'.[75] At any rate it is on the 30th November 1606 that we find our last record—in the parish register of Bartholomew the Less in Smithfield: 'the thirtieth of November was buried John Lyly, gent.'

III

ENTERTAINING
THE COURT OF ELIZABETH

COURTLY DRAMA, like so much else in the court of
Elizabeth, was derived from ceremonies with more than a
flavour of religious ritual in their origins, and cannot be treated
as mere entertainment. Drama did not appear at court only
at irregular intervals—when the Queen felt like a play. It was
the function of a season, which took its place in a procession
of the seasons of yearly ritual—Revels, Lent, Maying, Garter-
feast, Progress, Thanksgiving, etc.—which made up the Tudor
court calendar.[1]

The Christmas 'season' was a development of revels which
were held earlier under the sway of the Lord of Misrule, who
ruled (or misruled) at court from All Hallows Eve [31st
October] till after Candlemas Day [2nd February], and he in
his turn seems to have been a courtly offshoot from the folk-lore
'Winter King', with his associations of settling into enforced
leisure in long nights. We can also see this as a secular variant
of the ecclesiastical 'Feast of Fools' with its cathartic parody of
normal social order and belief.

Under Elizabeth, 17th November ['Accession Day'] may be
said to have begun the season, with tilts and tourneys and
sermons and bell-ringing.[2] I know of no evidence that plays
were ever performed on this occasion. On the whole, they
belonged to the twelve days of Christmas, from Nativity to
Epiphany, with St Stephen's Day, St John's Day [27th
December], Holy Innocents, New Year's Day and Twelfth
Night as the normal highlights of dramatic activity—Christmas
Day itself was not a day for plays.[3]

There were subsequent outbreaks at Candlemas [2nd

February] (which marks one possible end to the period of Misrule)[4] and at Shrovetide, before the austerity of Lent, like the Italian *Carnival*, when

> The people take their fill of recreation,
> And buy repentance, ere they grow devout.

The growth of court drama, as we must understand that term to deal with Lyly's plays, was a slow and difficult process; for it is clear that much of the earlier court entertainment was concerned with mummings, disguisings, and parodies, such as those in which the Lord of Misrule 'knighted' his subjects, dispensed 'coins', organized tilts with hobby-horses, etc.[5] These were entertainments in which the courtiers and the entertainers were intermingled. In spite of the expense and the elaboration, such entertainments were domestic. Many, if not most, of the plays which were performed at the court of Elizabeth remained strongly affected by this tradition, strong in the context of the court. It is impossible to imagine an independent play like *Othello* being performed at court before the 'nineties of the sixteenth century, though no one seems to have thought it odd by 1604—so swift was the onset of the modern world round the turn of the seventeenth century.

The process of this growth can be glimpsed or reconstructed only from the administrative relics it left behind, and these tell us nothing, of course, about the quality of the things growing, or how far Lyly's plays are representative. The earliest functionaries seem to have been courtiers who were made responsible *ad hoc* for expenditure on costumes, scenery, etc. and for the general organization of revels over a short period.[6] The extent to which material objects (cloth, paint, canvas, timber) were the central interest of such an official is indicated by the appearance of the early Office of the Revels as an aspect of the Office of Tents and Toils—the office which controlled the canvas and net for the royal tents and hunting-nets. The first permanent Master of the Revels was also Master of Tents[7] and even at the end of the century the two offices seem to have been thought of as associated: when Lyly was disappointed in his hope of becoming Master of the Revels, his ambitions then moved to the Mastership of the Tents (which was likewise refused).

We must imagine drama becoming more independent as we see the Office of the Revels acquiring an identity of its own, with functions which reflect the idea of drama as an art, as well as an occasion for mimicry and dressing-up. A memorandum of 1573 tells us that 'the cunning of the office resteth in skill of device [*devising*], in understanding of histories, in judgment of comedies, tragedies and shows, in sight of perspective and architecture, some smack of geometry and other things'.[8] We know that in 1571 six plays and six masques had been performed. The plays were *Lady Barbara, Iphigenia, Ajax and Ulysses, Narcissus, Chloridon and Radiamanta* (so the account book says; perhaps we should read *Clodion and Bradamante* and refer to the 32nd canto of the *Orlando Furioso*) and finally, *Paris and Vienna*.[9] The hodge-podge of Medieval and Classical matters in this list is fairly typical. It is also typical that we do not possess any of the texts. What we do know, however, is that these plays were chosen by the Revels Office, on a competitive basis:

> which vi plays being chosen out of many and found to be the best that then were to be had, the same also being often perused and necessarily corrected and amended (by the aforesaid officers), then they being so orderly addressed (*worked up*) were likewise thoroughly apparelled and furnished with sundry kinds and suits of apparel and furniture, fitted and garnished necessarily and answerable to the matter, person and part to be played; having also apt houses made of canvas, framed, fashioned and painted accordingly, as best might serve their several purposes. Together with sundry properties incident . . .[10]

What would give us our clearest insight into the courtly milieu which shaped Lyly's plays would be some knowledge of why the six plays named were preferred to the others. On what artistic grounds did the Office of the Revels select and reject? No doubt the danger of offence to her Majesty or other powerful persons was always present, but this hardly involves an artistic principle. The image of a Master of the Revels we are given in Shakespeare's Philostrate (in *Midsummer-Night's Dream*) suggests a timidity about 'fitting and reforming their matters (otherwise not convenient to be shown before her Majesty)'[11] which is all too probable. No doubt the artistic taste of the Queen as well as her royal dignity had to be taken into account, but of that we know little. Ascham tells us that she admired metaphors and rhetorical balance;[12] her own prose shows a fondness for the fluent use of the figures of speech. It is clear that she admired spectacle and cleverness in presentation,[13] but this was a general taste of the age. In fact we cannot separate out the taste of the Queen from the general tradition of her court, and can only approach it through the plays which were 'allowed' by the Master of the Revels, and before Lyly we have no body of court drama.

In addition to choosing and censoring court plays (and later—when they appeared—public plays) the Master of the Revels was responsible for rehearsing them. The less used the players were to professional standards, no doubt the more arduous was this aspect of his duties; the later procedure by which the Master came to court 'to choose out a company of players for her Majesty'[14] must have saved a lot of effort as well as some money, and these savings may be held partly responsible for the increased tempo of the move from court ritual to court drama in the later years of Elizabeth; the non-ritualistic drama of the public and private theatres was accomplished and available, and what it lacked in ritualistic reference no doubt it made up in entertainment. The peculiar position of Lyly would seem to be that he balances so expertly the claims of court ritual and of artistic integrity; his plays belong to the tradition I wish to discuss in this chapter, but their virtue does not depend upon it. They stand at that point in the development when the domestic entertainment of the court no longer swamps the independence of the works designed for it, but before the point when the court is merely accessory to the traditions of the independent theatres. It is this, presumably, that explains why his plays were printed, while those of the other court dramatists were not.

The actors in the court drama of Elizabeth were sometimes men and sometimes boys. In the earlier Tudor period the boys seem to have been the more regular performers. The great entertainers of the court—Cornishe, Edwardes, Hunnis, etc.— were choirmasters who combined the roles of impresario, playwright, and composer with the practical direction of a troupe of choir boys, who could perform elegantly (together perhaps with some singing men)[15] in spoken drama as well as in solo and choral singing. Such entertainers were typical of the period, and that not only in England. Courtly entertainers all over Europe tended to develop their dramatic out of their musical functions, as the careers of Orlando di Lasso[16] and Alfonso Ferrabosco[17] might suggest to us. Indeed if the career of Arnoul Greban[18] was at all typical of *his* period, this association of singing and acting was yet another of the medieval traditions which survived into the court life of the Renaissance.

The use of children as choristers in divine service can be defended on purely utilitarian grounds, the range of their voices being different from that of men, and the female sex being improper for this function; but, obviously, the spectacle as well as the sound of worship must always have gained something from the idea of innocence conveyed by small choristers, in procession and in the business of service. When medieval drama moved out of the church, the children, who had been involved in the dramatic by-products of their role in ritual, moved out too. They moved from divine drama to secular drama, where their particular gifts and range of effects could still command attention and sympathy, bringing with them the experience of drama which is involved in 'the assumption of disguises, the recitation of prepared parts, in the serious pretence of being something that one is not'.[19] In 1378 the boys of St Paul's (either Grammar School or Choir School) were acting 'The History of the Old Testament'[20] and their gifts were well enough recognized by the court for Henry VII to celebrate the birth of Prince Arthur in 1487 by seeing *pueri eleemosynarii* (almonary boys, who paid for their education by singing in the choir) in a play about Christ's descent into Hell.[21]

The growth of Humanism vastly increased the scope of drama, and as the first fruits of English Humanism were educational, so the first theatrical effects of this widening scope were seen in the plays for boys. Humanism not only gave the masters model plays to imitate and ideals of perfection in that formal vein where children can shine best, but also inculcated a mode of education where play-acting and declamation were part of the curriculum. The aim of this was not to produce professional actors but to teach 'audacity to the bashful grammarian',[22] so that like Cicero (who had not scorned to learn from Roscius

93

and Aesopus, the Kemp and Burbage of Rome) they could move audiences towards virtue. As the schoolmaster John Brinsley remarks: 'The principal end of making Themes (*school declamations*) I take to be this . . . so as to work in themselves a greater love of the virtue and hatred of the vice, and to be able with soundness of reason to draw others to their opinion.'[23] And again, 'Let them take special pains to pronounce Themes or Declamations, striving who shall do best; and in all their oppositions to dispute, as if *ex animo*, in good earnest, with all contention and vehemency.'[24] The logical end of this training in the vehement handling of moral issues was the lively presentation of characters who express moral dilemmas, first in dialogues and eclogues[25] and then in proper plays: 'This acting of a piece of comedy or a colloquy sometimes will be an excellent means to prepare them to pronounce orations with a grace.'[26] Sometimes, no doubt, the taste for drama that was fostered in this way turned to an enthusiasm for modern plays which seemed less allowable. But though schoolmasters condemned playgoing, their use of drama for moral training was implanting a general interest in acting in their pupils, and they must take a fair share of blame (or credit) for the flourishing of Elizabethan drama.

The boys' companies, trained to give performances at their private theatres and before the court were not, it would seem, different in kind from the grammar-school boys who also played occasionally at court. No doubt the professionals had greater expertise, but it must have been expertise in the same tradition. This tradition was clearly very different from anything we know today. The boys' companies must have provided an extreme case of the formality of Elizabethan acting.[27] There could be no question of it being supposed that they were living rather than acting the roles they portrayed. There was a general assumption that children were only meaningful as 'apes' or mimics of the adult state, and the child companies seem to have played up this natural tension between the child himself and the adult he is imitating. Shakespeare's children—the Duke of York in *Richard III*, or Macduff's son in *Macbeth*—depict the desperate and pathetic strain of the child striving to be grown-up; clearly something of the same charm was a regular part of the appeal of the boys' companies. The swaggering in miniature, the innocence amid sophistication, the childishness at the heart of a desperate attempt to appear grown-up—these are natural and universal features of boyhood, and all the Tudor choirmasters and dramatists had to discover was a framework which would enhance rather than impede this natural charm: 'since we are turned cracks, let's study to be like cracks; practice their language and behaviours, and not with a dead imitation: act freely, carelessly and capriciously as if our veins ran with quicksilver, and not utter a phrase but what shall come forth steeped in the very brine of conceit, and sparkle like salt in fire' (Jonson, *Cynthia's Revels*, II. 1. 4 ff.).

The effects of the boys' companies, like the effects of castrato singing, are difficult to imagine today, and cannot be clearly reconstructed from works written to display these effects; it can be presumed that the continuing tradition of cathedral singing will give some ground for conjecture, but it cannot give any idea of the virtuosity the boys' companies possessed. It is a gross error to think of them as amateurs. They were hand-picked by the masters, who were given power to 'take up such apt and meet children as are most fit to be instructed and framed in the art and science of music and singing as may be . . . found out within any place of this our realm of England or Wales to be by his education and bringing-up made meet and able to serve us in that behalf when our pleasure is to call for them.'[28] This power to press-gang likely children, wherever found, was originally and properly granted only 'for that it is meet that our chapel royal should be furnished with well singing children from time to time',[29] but it is clear that the mandate was abused,[30] perhaps with the connivance of the authorities who were aware of Elizabeth's taste for drama and her unwillingness to pay for it.

Once abducted into the choirs of Windsor or St Paul's or the Chapel Royal, the boys came under the uninhibited discipline of the Tudor schoolmaster, which is described to us in the following song:[31]

The lamentation of the boys learning pricksong [written music]
He pluck'th us by the nose, he pluck'th us by the hawse [*neck*]
He pluck'th us by the ears with his most unhappy paws,
And all for this peevish pricksong, not worth two straws
That we poor silly boys abide much woe.

He saith we sing stark naught when we make a right good noise,
For I tell you he must have his knacks, yea, he must have his toys;
O the plague that we have with him, we little poor boys;
Truly poor boys abide much woe.

Such barrack-square methods could not but have produced a
virtuosity in obedience, which would fit well with the requirements of the plays that the masters wrote to show off their
own talents and to entertain a virtuosity-loving audience. No
doubt the fifty days[32] required to rehearse a masque in 1616
was more than normal, but virtuosity of a trained *corps de
ballet* order is obviously required not only for the masque
itself but for the masque-like plays devised for the Tudor court.
Such a play was that of 1582 described by Sir John Harrington:
'that comedy called the play of the cards, in which it is showed
how four parasitical knaves [*hearts, spades, diamonds, clubs, I
suppose*] rob the four principal vocations of the realm, *viz.* the
vocation of Soldiers, Scholars, Merchants and Husbandmen'.[33]
Without precision of handling such a play is nothing. Precision
is essential because the play, if it is to be topical and critical and
yet not offensive, must walk a knife-edge of wariness. The
same point could only be made about the Latin Morality
which Rightwise (Lyly's uncle), the High Master of St Paul's,
presented before Henry VIII and the French ambassadors on
10th November 1527. The play has disappeared, but it is
described by Hall in his chronicle:

when the king and queen were set, there was played before them
by children in the Latin tongue in manner of tragedy, the
effect whereof was that the Pope was in captivity and the church
brought under foot; wherefore St Peter appeared and put the
Cardinal in authority to bring the Pope to his liberty and to set
up the church again; and so the Cardinal made intercession to
the kings of England and of France that they took part together
and by their means the Pope was delivered. Then in came the
French king's children and complained to the Cardinal how the
Emperor kept them as hostages and would not come to no
reasonable point with their father; wherefore they desired the
Cardinal to help for their deliverance, which wrought so with the
king his master and the French king that he brought the Emperor
to a peace, and caused the two young princes to be delivered.

At this play wisemen smiled and thought that it sounded more glorious [*laudatory*] to the Cardinal than true to the matter indeed.

(1809 edn., p. 735)

To play the part of Henry VIII before that monarch obviously required a great deal of finesse—capacity to convey the power and dignity of the sovereign without ever encroaching upon his personality.

The same advantages and capacities were present for Lyly, when he came to write his plays for the boys. His Cynthia and Sapho are obviously intended as portraits of Queen Elizabeth; but they are portraits which avoid any personal implications.[34] The settings of his plays are remote from ordinary life and ordinary passions, but make their points as comments on existence as known at the Elizabethan court. The incapacity of the boys to represent adult passions is here no disadvantage; their capacity to act as a team and to make a single, controlled, unified effect was a positive virtue. So long as the court wished to see representations and discussions of its own rather special code of manners, so long were the boys likely to remain supreme in this somewhat perilous occupation.

But, from 1576 onwards, and possibly before, the boys were playing, not only to the Queen but also to the patrons of their 'private' playhouses in the Blackfriars and 'in Paul's'.[35] This arrangement suited Elizabeth well enough. It meant that acting companies were available without having to be maintained out of Revels expenditure. It also meant that the courtly drama of the time was seldom *sui generis*. Plays by courtiers for courtiers were always rare and became rarer; seeing what such conditions produced in Renaissance France and Italy we must be grateful that they were rare. The court play in England grew up as a compromise genre, one which increasingly diluted private content with public spectacle. By the time we reach Lyly's plays a form has been devised which can appeal equally well inside and outside the court. Lyly's personal aims may have directed his eyes back into the past, when part-time poets were full-time courtiers; but his economic status pushed him relentlessly towards a future of literary salesmanship in uncourtly places.

This does not mean, however, that Lyly's plays must have existed in two forms—a Blackfriars (or Paul's) form, and a court form.[36] The fact that some plays print both a court prologue and a Blackfriars prologue would seem to argue that the textual difference was as little as this. There are plays of the period which suddenly turn to the Queen and make unexpected genuflections, but Lyly's plays are not among them. The idea of gracious sovereignty and of courtly behaviour stands at the centre of his comic vision. I suspect that the supposition of two forms depends on a misunderstanding of what the patrons of the private theatres went to see. I do not think that there was any pressure there away from courtliness. The court continued to present throughout the period an ideal of civility towards which a private audience would naturally aspire; one of the attractions of such plays must have been the sense they gave the audience of belonging to the best circles and sharing their tastes. The Blackfriars prologue to *Sapho and Phao* speaks of venturing 'to present our exercises before your judgments'; the pretence that these private performances were only rehearsals to prepare the boys for their role at court was a convenient fiction, no less flattering to the audience than saving to the Revels.

I have suggested above that Lyly's plays represent a final stage of compromise between the closed world of the court and the larger world outside. It was a stage which, by its nature, could not last for long and which was bound to be eclipsed by the larger and more forceful emotions of the adult actors. The second half of the sixteenth century shows a steady decline in the children's status, and a corresponding increase in that of the adults.[37] One result of the establishment of a fully public and professional theatre in London (the first house, 'The Theatre', was built in 1576) was the emergence of 'stars' such as Tarleton, Kemp, Alleyn and Burbage, whose lines could hardly be imitated by the boys. These actors became notorious public figures; audiences responded to them as individuals and they in their turn answered back to the audience with a suppleness and an immediacy which must have made the boys seem hidebound and over-formal. In addition, a movement of literary taste brought more realistic and more emotional themes on to the stage, and these themes were not within the compass of boys.

A number of economic misfortunes hastened the artistic decline of the Elizabethan boys' companies; their very existence was based on a series of compromises and we can hardly be surprised when some of these broke down. In 1584, as I have said already (p. 74 above), the landlord recovered possession of the Blackfriars theatre, and the establishment was closed. In 1590 the Paul's boys were forbidden to act, so that in the last decade of Elizabeth's reign, the boys virtually disappeared. It is true that they reappeared about 1600, but this renewal need hardly concern us if we are looking at the relationship between the boys' companies and Lyly's plays. The new boys' companies appeared in and belonged to a new world of culture (as I shall suggest below). After attempting to revive some of their old plays and finding that they were regarded as 'the *umbrae* or ghosts of some three or four plays departed a dozen years since'[38]—Lyly's *Love's Metamorphosis* was probably one of these —the boys quickly adapted themselves to the cynical temper of the time. Hamlet's 'little eyasses that cry out on top of question, and are most tyrannically clapped for it' were sophisticated but not courtly, or rather courtly only in so far as that means the same as sophisticated.

Consideration of the boys' companies has usually been con-ducted in the shadow of an interest in the major Elizabethan dramatists, especially Shakespeare, and this had led to a concentration on what the boys could not do—impose the illusion of living their parts and express powerful adult emotions over a coherent range of adult life. From the point of view of Lyly, however, it is more important to return to what they were especially fitted to do—to speak clearly and move becomingly in a group, with a total effect of grace and fluency. No doubt some boys were better actors than others, but the nature of their training, the analogy of their choral exercise and the evidence of the surviving plays all suggest that their power of working as a group, in dialogue or the more complex patterns of speech, was their most impressive accomplishment. Their clear, piping voices with considerable carrying power (as their regular use in open-air civic 'entries' shows) but emotionally inexpressive, were well suited to the artifice of formal poetic declamation, where sense so often depends on a command of rhythmical nuance and a capacity to 'project' rhythm and assonance and to produce varied effects within the single dimension of sound.

It was natural that the boys' plays, often written by their

masters, should seek to include the things that they were good at and to exclude their weaknesses. For example, the boys were basically choristers, and their plays contain a large number of songs, and also use music as a means of conveying the emotions that their acting could not encompass. In an early play, like Redford's *Wit and Science* (before 1547) a song may have little or no relationship to the plot, but it is worth noticing how much more accomplished Redford is as a poet for music than as a playwright. The dullish interlude bumblings suddenly give way to sophisticated lyric:

> Exceeding measure, with pains continual
> Languishing in absence, alas! what shall I do?
> Infortunate wretch devoid of joys all,
> Sighs upon sighs redoubling my woe,
> And tears down falling fro mine eyes too.
> Beauty with truth so doth me constrain
> Ever to sue where I may not attain.
>
> Truth bindeth me ever to be true,
> How so that Fortune favour'th my chance;
> During my life none other but you
> Of my true heart shall have the governance.
> O good sweet heart have you remembrance
> Now of your own, which for no smart
> Exile shall you fro my true heart.   (M.S.R. p. 56)

In Edwardes' *Damon and Pithias* (1564-5), song is more carefully integrated into the context, but the same sense of the superior expressiveness of music is present. We find Pithias trying to express his grief in words and then turning to song[39] and the more sophisticated control of lyric poetry, as better able to convey its forces:

Ah woeful Pithias! sith now I am alone
What way shall I first begin to make my moan?
What words shall I find apt for my complaint?
Damon, my friend, my joy, my life, is in peril; of force I must now
        faint.
But, O music, as in joyful [times] thy merry notes I did borrow,
So now lend me thy yearnful tunes, to utter my sorrow.

Here Pithias *sings, and the regals play.*

> Wake ye woeful wights,
> That long have wept in woe
> Resign to me your plaints and tears
> My hapless hap to show.
> My woe no tongue can tell,
> Ne pen can well descry,
> O, what a death is this to hear,
> Damon, my friend, must die.
>
> The loss of worldly wealth
> Man's wisdom may restore,
> And physic hath provided too
> A salve for every sore;
> But my true friend once lost,
> No art can well supply.
> Then what a death is this to hear,
> Damon, my friend, must die.
> etc.   (685-707)

The songs hold up the action while they make their expressive point. In this they are typical of the art of the children's plays. On the whole we may say that the boys' plays do not present single human intrigues developing with increasing intensity towards emotional resolutions. They consist rather of a series of static tableaux; and boys were much used in the tableaux set up to welcome distinguished persons into cities. We are asked to admire the skill of setting, of static arrangement, and of the symmetry with which one scene answers another; and we can only do this if each *stasis* does not last too long.

In consequence, we find in the boys' plays little or no evidence of a concern with the tensions of human relationships. The scenes tend to be short (in Lyly's plays they average less than a hundred lines), and to be distinct from one another, often with completely different characters. Their relationship to one another is, at the most, that of different facets of a central situation. It is just in this power to relate the different aspects of a subject and to suggest a unity embracing all the scenes that Lyly reigns supreme. He engages our interest in the immediate point he is making, but the points are not too different from one another, and follow each other in a recognizable pattern.

It is clear that the courtly milieu did not encourage concentration, and this is as true in the use of the boys as in other aspects. The casts were large, and if the parts were played at the rate of one boy to one part they could almost be thought to represent another aspect of conspicuous expenditure: we know that there were at least 51 actors in the 1580 Cambridge performance of *Richardus Tertius*.[40] But the evidence suggests that the professional companies managed their lavish effects with less lavishness in reality. The formal nature of the acting, the piecemeal construction, the tableau effects, and the ever-changing sets of characters (many of whom appear only once) suggest that the traditional Tudor method of doubling roles was employed here. There is artistic justification for this: the same points were made in different scenes (though with different sets of characters) so it would be entirely appropriate for the same boys to change their roles from scene to scene, now a shepherd, now a Muse, now a god or goddess. The traditional number of the children in the Chapel Royal was ten (sometimes increased to twelve).[41] With appropriate doubling, Lyly's plays could be performed by a troupe of from twelve to seventeen persons, though the list of characters runs to twenty-eight or more in *Campaspe*.

Given these accomplishments and qualities in the boys, were the dramatists who wrote for them (and they were often the men who had some power to train them) driven to occupy any particular field of dramatic subject-matter? That there was no hard-and-fast line of demarcation between boys and men is proved by the later cross thefts of *The Spanish Tragedy* (stolen from the men by the boys) and *The Malcontent* (stolen from the boys by the men). But Hillebrand is right in saying that 'children seem rarely or never to have ventured anything serious like *Gorboduc* or *Calisto and Melibœa*'[42]; I would add, on the admittedly shaky evidence of play-titles, that the boys seem to have avoided medieval romance subjects (*The history of the solitary knight, The soldan and the duke of* . . .) and recent domestic histories (*An history of the cruelty of a stepmother, The history of murderous michael*), preferring mythological subjects—*Ajax and Ulysses* (presumably a debate-subject, from Ovid's *Metamorphoses* XIII, like Shirley's later play of the same title) and Moralities (*Truth, Faithfulness and Mercy* or *The History of Loyalty*

and Beauty). One can see good reasons for such a preference.
The Romance themes of love and war required realistic
combat and romantic emotions, which were both outside the
natural scope of the boys; the coolness and formality of their
style would be much more appropriate to a mythological
handling, even if the themes were still those of love and war.
It is of their 'feigning bawdy fables gathered from the idolatrous
heathen poets' that contemporary witness[43] accuses the boys,
and this is certainly the strain in their tradition that descended
to Lyly, and out of which he fashioned his drama.

Lyly is the most famous of the dramatists who wrote for the
sixteenth century boys' companies, and his plays can be seen
to take up all those aspects of child-acting which I have discussed above; they show a unique skill in using the talents that
were available and in avoiding the areas where the weaknesses
would show. Lyly's plays do not develop quickly by means
of 'strong' emotional entanglements. They rather proceed by
means of a series of static tableaux. They do not raise our
expectations by mystery or surprise. They rather show how
elegantly the movements we expect can be performed. They
do not involve parts that it would be difficult for boys to play,
and regularly include a number of page roles where the boys
need only to be themselves. They never concentrate the action
round a single character or give any one speaker a high proportion of the lines—such as Shakespeare gave to Richard III
or Hamlet. They concentrate instead on the consort of voices,
the quick and witty dialogue where voice chimes with voice,
idea picks up idea and image begets image.

> *Sophronia.* Ladies, here must we attend the happy return of my
> father; but in the mean season what pastime shall we use
> to pass the time? I will agree to any, so it be not to talk of
> love.
> *Suavia.* Then sleep is the best exercise.
> *Soph.* Why, Suavia, are you so light that you must chat of love;
> or so heavy that you must needs sleep? Penelope in the absence
> of her lord beguiled the days with spinning.
> *Sua.* Indeed she spun a fair thread, if it were to make a string
> to the bow wherein she drew her wooers.
> *Soph.* Why, Suavia, it was a bow which she knew to be above their
> strength, and therein she showed her wit.

Sua. *Qui latus arguerit corneus arcus erat*; it was made of horn, and therein she showed her meaning.

Soph. Why, dost thou not think she was chaste?

Sua. Yes, of all her wooers.

Soph. To talk with thee is to lose time, not well to spend it. How say you, Amerula, what shall we do?

Amer. Tell tales.

Soph. What say you, Caelia?

Cael. Sing.

Soph. What think you, Camilla?

Cam. Dance.   (*Midas*, III. iii. 1 ff.)

Moreover Lyly's plays are full of songs, whether the songs first printed in the collected edition of 1632 are by Lyly[44] or not. These are not full-throated songs in the manner of the Redford and Edwardes examples quoted above. Even at the most romantic point in his most romantic play (*Sapho and Phao*) the song style remains cool and fanciful:

> O cruel Love! on thee I lay
> My curse, which shall strike blind the day:
> Never may sleep with velvet hand
> Charm thine eyes with sacred wand;
> Thy jailors shall be hopes and fears,
> Thy prison-mates, groans, sighs and tears;
> Thy play to wear out weary times,
> Fantastic passions, vows and rhymes;
> Thy bread be frowns, thy drink be gall,
> Such as when you Phao call;
> The bed thou lyest on [be] despair,
> Thy sleep, fond dreams, thy dreams, long care;
> Hope (like thy fool) at thy bed's head
> Mock thee, till madness strike thee dead,
> As, Phao, thou dost me with thy proud eyes;
> In thee poor Sapho lives, for thee she dies.
>   (*Sapho and Phao*, III. iii. 135 ff.)

Let us admit that this is as near as Sapho ever comes to a direct expression of her passion. Lyly might seem here to be in the tradition of Edwardes' song noted above—using music to express passion where words were insufficient; but accomplished wit has now replaced the moralizing of the earlier period, and is used here as elsewhere in Lyly to distance the emotions and express a remote and refined pattern of their equivalents in wit, as suits the natures no less than the voices of the boys who were required to act it out. The most famous of the songs in Lyly's plays—'Cupid and my Campaspe played/At cards for kisses'—has the same lightness, coolness and Alexandrian charm of fancy. But mostly his songs are in a more buffo vein, with several singers involved, and a notable neatness of execution required. The songs, in short, declare in miniature the Lylian qualities which make the plays so suitable for children; the sure control of tone, so that he can remain comic without ever becoming gross, and touch sentiment without ever becoming cloying, control static relationships so that the symmetry of one situation against another adds to the total design, without developing interests improper to the genre.

As court drama was part of court ritual, and not a separate mode of entertainment, so the use of a separate 'theatre' building was unknown. The setting seems to have been the great hall of whatever palace was being used for the Christmas season—Whitehall, Richmond, Greenwich, etc. It is not clear whereabouts the stage would be erected in such a hall. What is clear (putting first things first) is that the Queen would be seated in her 'chair of estate'—her canopied and stepped-up throne—where she could be seen easily and where she herself could see and hear. A proportion of the audience was normally accommodated on scaffolding banked up against the walls. Until recently most critics supposed that the players would normally perform at one end of the hall and use the doors in the end walls (or screens) for exits and entrances. Recently, however, Mr Leslie Hotson has produced fascinating evidence which may show that the playing area was rather in the middle of the hall; and not on a platform at all, but at floor level, since on one occasion at least the play was preceded by a courtly dance, in the same space where the play was to be performed: 'as soon as her Majesty was set at her place, many ladies and knights began a grand ball. When this came to an end there was acted a mingled comedy with . . . music and dances.'[45] Dr T. W. Craik has made the point that characters in the Tudor interludes slip easily among the spectators;[46] this would not be easy if the platform was of any height, and would be easiest if there was no platform at all. On the other hand, the end of *Liberality and Prodigality* (probably performed on the 22nd February 1601) suggests a platform: 'Virtue, Equity, Liberality, Judge and all *come down* before the Queen and after reverence made, Virtue speaketh' (M.S.R. ll. 1314 f. [*my italics*]); on the other hand, this could mean simply, 'Come down the hall', that is, 'Move along the floor to the point where the Queen sat'. In the two University performances of which we have fairly full record[47]—Plautus' *Aulularia* in the chapel of King's College, Cambridge (1564), and Richard Edwardes' *Palamon and Arcite* in the hall of Christ Church, Oxford (1566)— the Queen seems to have sat on the stage itself. In the Cambridge performance, the populace (that is, the students) were on the nave side of the stage, while privileged courtiers were placed on the other side. The Queen seems most likely to have sat on one side of the stage. In the Christ Church performance it seems probable that she was placed at the 'rear' of the stage, facing down the hall, so that the mass of the audience could watch the play and see the Queen at the same time—an improvement on the methods of modern 'command' performances, which require the audience to swivel attention from royal box to stage and back again.

What is common to all the accounts is something that approximates to modern 'arena' staging, with the Queen placed in the 'best' position, and with others simultaneously fulfilling their desire to see the Queen and their desire to watch the play. When James I visited Christ Church in 1605, the authorities tried out the new art of perspective scene-painting. The king had to be placed on the same side of the stage as the rest of the audience, and complaints were made that 'the auditory could see but his cheek only'.[48]

The play was primarily an entertainment for the sovereign; she was the first spectator, and where disadvantages (of seating, perspective, etc.) had to be endured it would be the others who were sacrificed. At the same Christ Church performance for James, the perspective scenes were calculated to work ideally from the point at which the King would be seated. If others failed to get the perspective right, they had little or no ground for complaint; for they were themselves only the mute extras in a royal occasion. The actor was, indeed, in something of the same position as the court preacher whose pulpit was faced by another structure of state, a 'closet' from which the Queen watched and listened, and out of which she would give clear indications of her reaction. The clever preacher could alter his sermon, guided by these signs, into channels more pleasing; but the actor had to rely on the discretion of the Master of the Revels, exercised before the event.

Court plays were an occasion for court spectacle. The lighting seems to have been a thing which was specially impressive to contemporaries. A description of the 1566 Oxford performance of *Palamon and Arcite* speaks of 'oil lamps and torches and burning candles' making 'a brilliant light'; 'with so many lights, arranged in branches and circles, and everywhere so many torches of varying brilliance giving out their flickering light the place glowed so that it seemed to shine as with daylight, increasing the splendour of the dramatic spectacle with its own brilliance'.[49] In later times the throne of the monarch was ringed with lights,[50] and there is no reason to suppose that Elizabeth was any less spotlighted than her successor. As late as 1625 Bacon is still harping on the effect of light—'let the scenes abound with light, specially coloured and varied'—as one of the splendours of court entertainment.[51] Modern stage lighting is an aid to illusion; the lighting of this period seems only to have been an aid to splendour. This is a distinction which is important everywhere. The setting of the court play seems often to have been elaborate, but never elaborated in the direction of realism. The sets were designed to impress rather than deceive, and the basic principles of staging seem to have remained throughout near to those of the Middle Ages, either unlocalized (we know where people are because they tell us) or presented by 'simultaneous staging', where the whole acting area is divided up into *loca* or scene-indicators (forests, caverns, palaces, etc.) which remain in sight throughout the action, but are not relevant till they are in use by the actors.

From the accounts of the Revels Office we hear much of 'houses' built for the court plays of the time. These seem to have been lath and plaster pavilions, painted to represent palace façades, shops, woods, caves, grottoes, etc., often very splendid (those at Christ Church, 1566, are called *magnifica palatia*), and set (I suppose) on either side of the stage. According to Hotson the 'houses' could be put up in a few minutes between the end of an entertainment and the beginning of the play,[52] but this cannot have been the case in all court productions and may not have been the case at all. Elaborate and weighty scenes including forests, mountains and clouds, with pulleys[53] to raise and lower heavy objects, must have been set up before the evening began.[54]

The action seems to have moved from 'house' to 'house' in a perceptible visual rhythm. In early plays, which are often little more than debates between two sides, this has an obvious dramatic function. Thus in Redford's *Wit and Science*, Tediousness has one door while his enemy, Wit, has the other; each issues from his own side and retires into it again; the visible action thus paraphrases the conflict being dramatized. In Edwardes' *Damon and Pithias* the scene was presumably set to represent Syracuse on one side and the castle of Dionysius on the other; we may suppose that it is to these *loca* that the Prologue is referring when he says

> Lo here in Siracusae th' ancient town which once the Romans won,
> Here Dionisius' palace within whose court this thing most strange was done.

The staging of most of Lyly's plays does not seem to have been governed by different principles. Thus *Campaspe* requires us to see Alexander's palace on one side (represented no doubt by a classical façade), while on the opposite side stands the 'studio' of Apelles, where he can paint Campaspe. Between these, I suppose (*pace* Sir Edmund Chambers, *E.S.* III. 33), stands the tub of Diogenes, which Alexander passes on his way from the palace to the studio of Apelles (Act II, scene iv). The action flows easily and without breaks from one *locus* to another; the great advantage of this method is its flexibility. Thus Act III, scene iv begins with a conversation between Clitus and Parmenio, gentlemen in Alexander's train, who then withdraw when the conversation is taken over by Alexander and Hephaestion (his confidant); all this must be localized in front of Alexander's palace. Alexander then decides to visit Apelles, but on the way he sees Diogenes and one of his clients:

Alex: But behold Diogenes, talking with one at his tub.

Alexander and Hephaestion stand aside to observe the tub-based episode of Diogenes and Crysus; then they continue their journey to the studio where we discover Apelles painting Campaspe.

In *Sapho and Phao* there is a greater variety of scene than in *Campaspe*, but the method remains the same. Indeed, as Sir Edmund Chambers has pointed out, 'a long continuous stretch of action, not even broken by the act-intervals, begins with III. iii. and extends to the end of V. ii. and in the course of this Venus sends Cupid to Sapho and herself waits at Vulcan's forge (V. i. 50). Presently (V. ii. 45) she gets tired of waiting and without leaving the stage, advances to the chamber and says, 'how now, in Sapho's lap?'[55] Three places are required for this play: Sapho's palace, Sybilla's cave and Vulcan's forge. The other scenes, such as the ferry where Phao works, require no properties and no buildings, and may take place in open stage. Indeed we may reduce our three *loca* to two by noting that Vulcan's forge appears only once, and could easily use the same 'entrance to the underworld' as Sybilla uses on other occasions. This power to establish a type of *locus* (cave, palace, etc.), now as one person's now as another's, seems to be required by most of Lyly's plays. In both *Midas* and *Endimion* we have an opposition between palace scenes and country scenes, and I suppose that one palace-type façade did for both Midas' palace and the Temple at Delphi (established by the opening words, 'This is Delphos') while another generalized background (rural this time) served for Mount Tmolus, for the 'reedy place', and for the scene with the huntsman. In *Endimion*, I imagine, one set served for Cynthia's palace and for the Castle in the desert ('Here is the castle, fair Tellus, in which you must weave . . .'), and another for the lunary bank and for the hermitage of Geron. Act IV, scene iii seems to require us to find Endimion sleeping on the lunary bank on one side of the stage. Corsites tries to lift him and, failing, is pinched by fairies till he also falls asleep. Then Cynthia and her court enter (presumably on the other side) and after some conversation cross the stage and find Endimion and Corsites asleep. Endimion is left undisturbed; but then Cynthia emerges from the palace again, primed to attempt his recovery by a kiss. She crosses the stage again and restores Endimion, who returns to Court with her. The flow of action back and forward thus reflects the dramatic tensions in the play.

None of Lyly's plays seem to require a double level of scene (an upper and a lower stage) except *The Woman in the Moon*, where the predominant planets sit aloft in order to watch the effects of their influence on Pandora. One may guess that this peculiarity should be linked to the supposition that this play was performed by men and not by boys.[56]

The ornateness of court settings and the elaborateness of the spectacle often provided, and therefore likely to be expected, was not without its influence on Lyly's plays, especially his later ones, where transformation scenes abound. Thus in *Love's Metamorphosis* a 'thick mist' arises when the three obdurate nymphs are changed into rock, bird, and rose, and a 'shower' descends when they are changed back again. Lyly seems to have acquired a trick tree at some point in his career, which he became rather devoted to. In *Gallathea* Hebe is tied to a tree, but it does not affect her fate. In *Endimion* Bagoa is changed into a tree (off stage), and the tree is changed back into the crone at the end of the play (on stage). In *The Woman in the Moon* Gunophilus is changed into a hawthorn; in *Love's Metamorphosis* the tree is attacked with an axe and a nymph cries out inside it. All this would seem to imply a stage-tree with a hollow trunk and with a door which opens to receive or eject an actor.[57]

I have already suggested that such elaboration was quite distinct from any attempt at realism; it was far more often a part of an attempt to convey the romantically marvellous, to stun with ingenuity; it was thus the scenic equivalent to the marvels of magic and travel later to be ridiculed in the *Old Wives' Tale*, but widely popular in the prose romances (the favourite reading of a large part of the audience[58]), and memorable as the natural background to the *Faerie Queene*.

A play called *The History of the knight of the burning rock*, which the Earl of Warwick's servants played at Whitehall on Shrove Sunday (1st March) 1579, gives a good example of this. This romantic tale[59] (taken from the Spanish *Knight of the sun* cycle, later to be the butt of Ben Jonson's neoclassical wit) concerns the daughter of a magician who is wronged by a knight; her father, in revenge, imprisons him in a burning rock, only to be released by a knight bolder than he is and able to defeat him

in battle; at the same time the rescuer must be wise enough to
find the hidden entrance to the rock. Only the knight of love
has all these qualities; when applied to by the wronged but
still loving lady he defeats and releases the knight, who then
agrees to marry the lady. From the Revels Accounts[60] we can
follow the extraordinary pains that went to the serving up
of this morsel. The imprisoned knight seems to have been
accommodated in a leaden or lead-protected chair, while
flames of aqua-vitae played about it, and rosewater was
scattered 'to allay the smell thereof'. The mount itself was made
of 'long spar poles of fir' and 'pieces of elm cut compass'
[*circular wise*] and was decorated with ivy and holly and
covered with cloth made up by the botcher or patching tailor.
No doubt the ordeal of the knight combined for the audience
the pleasures of seeing what was going right and of wondering
if anything would go wrong. The pleasure in the lavishness and
the skill of the devisers of such fancies was akin to that in other
virtuoso skills[61] which we know were exhibited on the stage
and relished by the audience—juggling, feats of legerdemain,
prolonged sword-play, not to mention the clouds descending,
flowers that opened and other spectacular toys of the court
masques.

In all this we have to remember again and again that a play
was not, in this period, thought of as an exclusive 'kind', whose
'legitimate' stage-blood could not be tainted with the stuff of
mannequin parades, unarmed combat demonstrations, after-
dinner speeches, circus acts, etc. Indeed, the playwrights seem
to have sought to include as many modes of entertainment as
possible and to have regarded the narrative chiefly as a means
of stringing together as many and as diverse episodes of
traditional entertainment as possible. It is Lyly's great virtue
to give a unity to his plays while still providing a great variety
of entertainment. In reading we can easily see the first of these
virtues, but it is easy to miss the second. Thus in Act V, scene i
of *Campaspe* we have two bare stage-directions, 'Then Perim
danceth' and 'Milo tumbleth', and these do not make much
effect on the reader who notices them; but given the tradition
of tumbling and dancing at court, one may suppose that the
actions involved were fairly elaborate and applause-seeking
episodes, by highly skilled performers.

The taste for the spectacular, for conspicuous expenditure, was no doubt restricted in Elizabeth's day (as against those of James I) by the parsimony of the Queen; but it seems to have been present all the time as a pressure on poets and devisers, and on gala occasions it broke out with obvious relief. Thus the ceremonies arranged for Elizabeth when she was on progress from one great house to another always strained towards the lavishness of the Kenilworth 'Princely Pleasures' of 1575, when Leicester squandered a fortune on his mistress. Courtly entertainers do not seem to have found any virtue in the kind of restraint that often makes an unpretentious film better than a Hollywood epic.

If we compare an obvious gala performance, like that of Edwardes' *Palamon and Arcite*, as performed in the hall of Christ Church in 1566, with a later handling of the same material out of Chaucer's *Knight's Tale*, in *Two Noble Kinsmen* (1613), we can see the extent to which the court occasion produces spectacular rather than dramatic entertainment.[62] In *Palamon and Arcite* the gods descend in person, and Mars and Venus dispute on the stage their claims to power; these features recur again and again in the court plays which survive, including Lyly's. In *Two Noble Kinsmen* (which is, after all, one of the most spectacular plays of the Jacobean private theatre) the prayers are not answered by epiphanies, but by small-scale symbolic effects: 'Doves are seen to flutter', 'clanging of armour', or 'a sudden twang of instruments'. In *Palamon and Arcite* the death of Arcite is the occasion for a display of effects: the subterranean fire sent up by Saturn seems to have been presented on the stage. Virtuosity and ostentation seem to have been preferred to a use of words, which could, after all, be duplicated on any uncourtly occasion, while the expenditure could not. In *Two Noble Kinsmen* these strange events are told in a messenger speech, and are probably all the more memorable for that. Perhaps the most revealing episode in the performance of *Palamon and Arcite* was that in which Perithous cast a rich cloak into the funeral pyre for Arcite. One spectator seeing this 'would have stayed [him] by the arm with an oath', whereon the Queen remarked 'go, fool! he knoweth his part'. Could the pleasures of conspicuous waste be more plainly represented?

Another story of audience-response, and a good indication of the Queen's own tastes, turns on another celebrated effect of the 1566 play. The Queen was fond of hunting and the organizers seem to have managed a scene in which some of the excitement of the chase was brought on to the stage: 'At the cry of the hounds in the quadrant [*quadrangle*] upon the train of a fox, in the hunting of Theseus, when the boys in the windows cried, "now, now"; "o excellent!" said the Queen, "those boys are ready to leap out at windows to follow the hounds".' The authors of *Two Noble Kinsmen* have no equivalent for this, but it is possible that the Theseus in *Midsummer Night's Dream* is prompted to his long appreciation of the music of his hounds by some report of the famous occasion in Christ Church. At any rate the spectacle seems to have encouraged imitation in courtly circles; in the Revels accounts for the 1571 season we read of 'leashes and doghooks, with staves and other necessaries . . . provided for the hunters that made the cry after the fox (let loose in the court) with their hounds, horns and halooing'.[63] The play was *Narcissus*, performed by William Hunnis' children of the Chapel Royal; in a later play of the same kind only three dogs seem to have been involved.[64] When the Count Alasco of Poland was entertained at Oxford in 1583, William Gager's *Dido* was performed at Christ Church with 'a goodly sight of hunters with full cry of a kennel of hounds, Mercury and Iris descending and ascending from and to an high place, the tempest wherein it hailed small comfits, rained rosewater and snew an artificial kind of snow; all strange, marvellous and abundant'.[65]

There are certain common factors in these gala occasions, which the reactions of the narrators bring home to us—the sense of surpassing wonder at the cleverness, lavishness and newness of the devices. Indeed the 1566 *Palamon and Arcite* might serve as a paradigm of almost everything a court play could hope to contain: a tale of princely behaviour in Theseus, a glimpse of the glamour of antiquity, an intervention by the gods, a formal debate before a moderator (Saturn in this case), compliment to the sovereign, lavish spectacle, a tournament between knights, even (presumably) 'whining poetry'. It was no wonder that Elizabeth sent for Edwardes at the end of the play 'and gave him great thanks with promise of reward'.

The elements I have listed here are not to be found in every court play, but they are common enough to be worth pursuing for the sake of the various threads they show leading up to and through Lyly's courtly entertainments, for the forms that Lyly's plays preserve reached him through a long, partly forgotten and largely perished tradition.

(i) THE MASQUE

The court play often approximated to the court masque, and it is one of the distinctions of Lyly's plays that they assimilate the masque material they contain more adequately than any preceding or contemporary plays that have survived. The material of the masque seems to have developed out of folk-festivals and chivalric customs, a process which has been traced and documented by several authors.[66] In consequence it contained perhaps more primitive material than any other of the courtly forms that the Humanist had to deal with when he became a courtly entertainer, and in it the distinction between courtly customs and folk-ritual is often very hard to make. What the Humanists did was to convert the old fertility figures into classical deities or court-of-love abstractions. C. R. Baskervill speaks of Renaissance taste changing 'the May-day bower into Paradise or Castle with its presiding god or goddesses'.[67] The Humanist also sought to import some kind of plot which would make the various ritualized movements hang together in a form more like that of a regular play. As far back as the reign of Henry VI the ceremony of entering disguised, reciting praises and offering gifts, had been accompanied on some occasions by an allegorical scheme.[68] As far back as 1454 (in Lille this time) we find spectacular symbolic machinery, round which speeches, dances, tournaments and present-giving could be organized.[69] But though the masque developed affiliations with all kinds of dramatic materials—debates, tableaux, tournaments—the requirement to compliment prevented it from acquiring a plot which would lead away from the sovereign, and towards an independent dramatic experience. Thus the interlinked series of masques which was planned for the meeting of Elizabeth and Mary, Queen of Scots in 1562[70] used narrative, but did not really move away from comment on an immediate political situation to an attitude which would bear repetition in another context. This fragility was no doubt one of the charms of the masque, but it was a charm which separated it from drama, and which makes it remote from us today, except as an historical document.

Lyly preserved the complimentary aspect of the masque, and used the spectacle, the songs, and probably the dances which distinguished it; but he disciplined all these inside a plot which separated and brought together characters for reasons other than those of compliment. The resolutions of Lyly's plays are often conducted in terms of some courtly virtue; but the courtly or the queenly virtue that is celebrated (chastity, magnanimity and so on) is always one whose importance is acceptable in general terms; and the plays make sense even if we do not understand the court occasion. Thus *Endimion* may end with Elizabeth enthroned and omnipotent; but what the play attributes to its Cynthia can be explained in terms that the play itself provides.

If we compare with *Sapho and Phao* Thomas Churchyard's 'Tuesday's Device' in his *Entertainment for the Queen at Norwich* (1578), we can see the extent to which Lyly's play turns compliment into drama, for the two actions turn on the same complimentary material. In Churchyard's 'Device', while Venus is involved in argument with a philosopher, Cupid wanders away, and—

> wandering in the world, met with Dame Chastity and her maids, called Modesty, Temperance, Good Exercise, and Shamefastness; and she, with her four maids, encountering Cupid in a goodly coach, and without any honest guard waiting on him, set upon him, threw him out of his golden seat, trod on his pomp, spoiled him of his counterfeit godhead and cloak, and took away his bow and his quiver of arrows (the one headed with lead, and the other with gold), and so sent him like a fugitive away, and mounted up into the coach herself and her maids, and so came to the queen, and rehearsed what had happened (although this was done in her view); and because (said Chastity) that the queen had chosen the best life, she gave the queen Cupid's bow, to learn to shoot at whom she pleased, since none could wound her Highness' heart, etc. (Nichols, II. 189)

Churchyard has here for his framework a sound allegorical scheme, but he soon exhausts it and runs his narrative into the quicksands of moral discourse, with characters like *Wantonness* and *Riot*; the moral dialogues do not give dramatic depth to the compliment but only pad it out with loosely related material. Lyly takes the same contrast between Chastity and Venus as the basis of his compliment, but he derives this from a complete dramatic movement involving recognizably human actions and reactions: Cupid and Venus defeat Sapho (personified Chastity) by making her love Phao; but Sapho defeats Venus by refusing to admit her love and finally captures Cupid and appropriates his weapons. The same final point is made as in Churchyard, but has infinitely greater impact because it moves in a dimension free of the original occasion.

(ii) THE TOURNAMENT

One of the features of the Churchyard entertainment which strikes one as unLylian is indicated by the words, 'threw him out of his golden coach, trod on his pomp', etc. Lyly's plays are remarkable in their period for their lack of physcial violence; it is worth noting that the court tradition he inherited gave him no warrant for this. Physical contest in the form of chivalric tournament was a favourite court interest and had, long before Lyly, been incorporated into courtly drama.[71] The Oxford *Palamon and Arcite* had shown the tournament, which decides the fate of the two knights, on the stage, where *Two Noble Kinsmen* is content with '*Cornets. A great cry and noise within*' and '*Another cry, and shout within, and cornets*'. The actual contest had, even before this, become encrusted with pageantry. As Bacon remarks, 'The glories of them are chiefly in the chariots, wherein the challengers make their entry'.[72] Henry VIII's coronation (1509) was celebrated by a tournament in which the scholars of Pallas (brought in by their goddess with her crystal shield) fought the gentlemen of Diana;[73] here we can see how easily and how early the tournament was turned into a variant of the scholastic *debate*. In the show of *Love and Riches*, performed at Greenwich on 6th May 1527, we can see a further elaboration of tournament and debate. Mercury presents a contest between love and riches, and the King (as moderator or umpire) is to make the decision. Love makes a speech and then Riches replies, 'each of the choristers on either side defending their leaders by reciting a number of verses'. Then Love and Riches together decide that the 'judgment should go by battle' and a combat follows with three knights on either side. Finally an old man with a silver beard 'concluded that love and riches both be necessary for princes'.[74] An interesting variant on the romantic play with tournament, showing that this *could* be performed by children, is the play of *Paris and Vienna*, acted on Shrove Tuesday 1571. The text is lost, but we can tell that the story was taken (presumably via Caxton's translation) from the French Romance of the same name. In this Paris jousts in plain white armour for the prize of a crystal shield; the episode is referred to unequivocally in the Revels account. The entry also tells us how it was managed: it speaks of 'hobby horses that served the children of Westminster in the triumph (where Paris won the crystal shield for Vienna at the tourney and barriers)'.[75]

Storming a castle, which was one of the conventional additions to the tournament, has been noted by C. R. Baskervill as a recurrent feature of court entertainments.[76] Here again we see the tournament reaching out to the elaboration of the play, and the play seeking to include all the different elements known to appeal at court. In the tourney arranged to honour the French ambassadors in 1581[77] 'the gallery or place at the end of the tilt-yard adjoining to her Majesty's house at Whitehall, whereat her person should be placed, was called, and not without cause, "The Castle or Fortress of Perfect Beauty". The four challengers called themselves "the Foster children of desire" and issued a promise "that upon the 24th day of this month of April, they will besiege that fatal fortress, vowing not to spare (if this obstinacy continue) the sword of faithfulness and the fire of affection".' On the occasion, speeches, music, perfumes and mechanical marvels all seem to have accompanied and surrounded the actual tilting, which lasted two days and was concluded by an admission that the Fortress (or Queen) is one 'in whom nothing can obtain victory, but virtue'. Beside this elaborate tournament should be set the *Orestes* performed at court in 1568 and probably to be identified with Pickering's *Horestes*, still extant. In the court performance, in the words of G. R. Kernodle, 'the main structure is a castle gate, with battlemented gallery above . . . Clytemnestra speaks from the walls above; the city is assaulted by an army; Aegisthus is hung from the battlements by means of a ladder; the army of Orestes makes a triumphant entry through the city gates'.[78]

Lyly avoids all such demonstrations of physical vigour. Though *Paris and Vienna* shows that it was possible to engage in them with only boy-players, the full effects must have been reserved for the men. In any case we do not imagine Lyly pining for lack of opportunity to include stage fights in his plays. His Humanist interests ensured that the contests in his plays were fought out at the level of intellect rather than muscle. His ideal world of ladies and gentlemen seeks to balance the sexes in a way that fighting makes impossible; and where the gods control this world very closely, violence such as that of Erisichthon is not only out of taste, but self-defeating. Far better to debate the issue intelligently, and let the gods decide.

(iii) DEBATE

As if in compensation for his avoidance of tournament, Lyly nearly everywhere involves his dramatic interest in that of debate or disputation. Long before his time the debate was accepted as a self-sufficient mode of entertainment; when Elizabeth visited the Universities she was entertained not only with plays but also with disputes in the schools. Indeed the whole history of drama was profoundly affected by the scholastic habit of debate and its social aspects. The continuity of the process is concealed in England, partly by the upheaval of the Reformation which broke the tradition of civic drama (sponsored by the craft guilds) and partly by the loss of so much Tudor dramatic literature. But if we look at the Dutch 'Guilds of Rhetoric' we can see a road down which the English Craft Guilds could easily have advanced, and which occasional plays signpost for the observer. The 'Guilds of Rhetoric'[79] moved from religious subjects to moral subjects and to general secular topics; their annual festival came to be a contest of different plays written on one agreed theme (*spelen van sinne*); this might be a religious question: 'what was the greatest miracle God wrought for the saving of mankind?'; or secular: 'which experience of learning brings the greatest wisdom?', 'why does a rich man desire more riches?', 'what can best awaken man to the liberal arts?', 'wherein are we to be extolled above the Romans?' In these, the dramatic narrative is a means of answering the question proposed; the question provides the framework and the angle of interest, provides formal coherence round the basic drama of a conflict.

The conflict which the court enjoyed could be as straightforward as a verbal boxing-match, as in the 'flyting' or rhetorical slanging-match, of which Dunbar and Skelton have left us famous examples; here again the courtly taste is hardly distinguishable from the rustic one in which

> With growing years the pleasing license grew,
> And taunts alternate innocently flew.

More sophisticated are the conflicts in which the contestants are fictitious, or represent attitudes or principles. Of this kind are the Medieval *conflictus veris et hiemis* (9th century),[80] which points forward through the *Summer and Winter* of 1530 to Nashe's *Summer's Last Will and Testament,* and the *dialogus inter aquam et vinum,*[81] whose subject is picked up in the seventeenth century, *Wine, Beer, Ale and Tobacco contending for superiority* (STC. 11541-2). In any of these the disputants are liable to have to submit their arguments to a moderator or judge, who may (as in the Middle English *Owl and Nightingale*) be outside the poem, or who may give his decision where we can hear it, as was done at the 'Acts' of the Universities. At these academic exercises, which were, of course, the current form of examination as well as a general entertainment, one speaker (respondent) read an oration on the subject set, and then two or more opponents answered him in turn. The moderator in charge then summed up the arguments and assigned marks for the performance. Though the subjects were often topical,[82] it is clear that it was the treatment and not the subject that was of central interest; a master of the method could be expected to do equally well on either side.

Graduates who had been trained in the arts of disputation in order to obtain their degrees, and who knew that virtuosity in these techniques was a main method of courtly entertainment, were understandably loth to leave the known and practised when they came to entertain a less strictly academic audience. Hardin Craig has remarked, 'English Renaissance writers presented human relations in terms of school learning and to do so became an established mode of procedure'[83] and William Ringler has made the workings of this system abundantly clear in the particular case of Stephen Gosson—with a side-glance at the parallel instance of *Euphues*.[84]

But drama offers an even wider scope for the techniques of disputation than does romance, and it is not surprising that the earliest English comedy, Medwall's *Fulgens and Lucres*, should be a dramatized debate about true nobility, with two suitors as the contestants, and a moderator in the person of the girl whose hand they are seeking. In a continental version of the same story the debate is even more formal: the case is referred to the Roman senate, who receive the disputants before them.[85] A similar scene seems to have been staged for the 1577 court performance of *Titus and Gisippus*. Among the properties for this are 'two forms for the senators'.[86] This undoubtedly refers to that climactic episode in the story where the two friends are pleading before the senate, each claiming the honour of dying for the other (shades of *Damon and Pithias*!) and each claiming to be guilty of the crime the other is supposed to have committed: 'thus they of long time with abundance of tears contended which of them should die for the other. Whereat all the senate and people were wonderly abashed'.[87]

The earliest English comedies regularly include a strong debate element; the plays and entertainments which the Erasmus generation of Humanists produced were often close to the French *débats*. Moreover, the English Morality tradition was already close to the debate; generally these plays were concerned with the disputes between virtues and vices, and were concluded by a formal judgment (type of the Last Judgment) or in an act of choice by Humanity, or whatever other representative figure stood at the centre of the play and was disputed over.

The medieval taste for debates and the scholastic taste for disputations were reinforced in Tudor England by grammar-school dependence on Humanist *dialogues* for teaching Latin speaking. The Dialogues of Erasmus, Corderius and Ravisius Textor were elegantly worded, but they were also seriously intended, and the serious matters which were raised were often handled by a cut and thrust of opinion which is highly dramatic.

Two Tudor Interludes (*Thersites* and Ingeland's *The Disobedient Child*) are known to be based on Textor's Dialogues, while Thomas Heywood's *Pleasant Dialogues and Dramas* are largely derived from Erasmus. A full list of the Elizabethans who knew and borrowed from Erasmus's Dialogues would include most of the major names in the period; as de Vocht has shown,[88] Lyly's name would certainly be in the list.

It is out of this milieu that we find the early Tudor Humanists writing plays like Rastell's *Of Gentleness and Nobility* (1527) which shows us the obsessive Humanist question about the nature of true nobility once again on the boards, this time competed for by a knight, a merchant and a labourer, whose arguments and whose demonstrations against one another form the basis of the action. Even more significant from the point of view of debate-turning-into-play is Heywood's *Play of Love* (1534). In this we are concerned with two questions:

(1) Of loving not loved, or loved not loving
Which is the case most painful in suffering?
(2) Whether the possession of the beloved by the lover, or complete freedom from the entanglements of love is the greater felicity.

In handling these questions, the play can be seen to fall into four sections:

(a) A dispute on the first question, that is for priority in pain, between a lover-not-beloved and a beloved-not-loving.
(b) A dispute on the second question, that is for priority in pleasure, between a lover beloved and one who is neither loving nor beloved.
(c) Now the contestants of debate (a) seek out those of (b) as arbitrators; while the contestants of (b) seek arbitration from (a). There are speeches on both sides and judgment follows: both the (a) contestants are equal in pain; both the (b) contestants are equal in pleasure,
(d) An epilogue praises contentment and the love of Heaven.

What is especially interesting here is the way in which the debate not only creates the plot, but also gives the characters in the play their stances in relation to one another, and (in the context) this means their personalities. Thus the man who rejoices in his negative status (Neither-loving-nor-beloved) is naturally coarser and wilder than the others; he is the 'Vice' of the play; similarly, and just as inevitably, Both-loving-and-beloved is the Romantic lead.

The symmetrically organized structure here points forward to Lyly, whose characters are organized in the same kind of relationship to one another, round a debate theme (see Chapter IV below). The play also points forward to Lyly in its use of material debated in the Courts of Love and in the academies and polite societies of the Humanist period—the *dubbii d'amore*.

For the courtly art of the Renaissance, here as elsewhere, did not involve a break with the medieval system (in this case the system of courtly love), but rather strengthened its hold, by organizing more effectively the moral appeal and by increasing the vivacity of the social reference. The Courts of Love had long debated difficult questions by a private mode of casuistry.[89] The *questions* came to England via books like the *Filocolo* of Boccaccio, Castiglione's *Courtier*, and the *Civil Conversation* of Guazzo, and a host of others. These normally added to the debates proper a sketch of their occasion, a description of the house or garden where they took place, and some degree of characterization for the contestants. Thus we find an approach to the dramatic episode; and Lyly in both parts of *Euphues* makes full use of these social occasions to organize wit round a contest or debate.

It is notable that in his drama Lyly does not include any full representation of either the *dubbii* or other debates. While other dramatists of the time were prepared to devote whole acts to straightforward debates, Lyly abstained from what he could so easily have managed. He also avoids Morality structure, though that continued to be popular. In 1601 it seems that the court saw the play of *Liberality and Prodigality*, in which the whole of the second act is taken up by the dispute of Prodigality and Tenacity [=Niggardliness] before the throne of Fortune —a debate self-conscious enough to use the *satis disputatum* formula (l. 457). The nearest Lyly ever comes to this is the dispute in Act I of *Midas* between Wealth, War and Love. But even this, the most formal debate in Lyly's drama, is explained as a mode of presenting Midas' hesitation: Midas is uncertain what to choose when offered the gift of choice by Bacchus, and the three pieces of advice are offered by his counsellors. The debate is thus completely justified in terms of dramatic occasion. Lyly's whole effort is to evoke the society in which the questions of love would be discussed; but the debates between chastity and love (*Sapho and Phao*), love and honour (*Campaspe*), love and friendship (*Endimion*), piety and self-preservation (*Gallathea*), are rather the basis of the plot than any single part of it, and do not emerge into the open. It was common in the Italian academies, and in the English books which imitated their manners, such as Wotton's *Courtly controversy of Cupid's cautels* (1578), Whetstone's *Heptameron of civil discourses* (1582) or Tilney's *Flower of Friendship* (1568) to illustrate debate attitudes by means of stories (*Euphues* itself does the same). In his dramas Lyly shows us the stories and leaves us, on the whole, to deduce the attitudes. The courtly occasion, the brilliant company, the beauty of the setting, Lyly mentions in his prologues and epilogues; but the play itself is content to be the kind of entertainment which only a brilliant society would appreciate, and does not make open reference to that society. The powers of discrimination, the witty poise of Castiglione's court are attributed to the audience, and we, by our appreciation of the play, put them back into the world of the drama.

(iv) HEROIC LOVE

I have spoken of the traditions of courtly love, in so far as these tied in with the debate. Questions of love had long been a staple of entertainment where men and women met in sophisticated societies, and the Elizabethan court was no exception. As E. C. Wilson has remarked, 'Elizabeth and her court delighted in an atmosphere of love, full of all the ambiguities that wit could sport with'.[90] and later speaks of how 'the paradox of a life full of marriage schemes and handsome favourites on the one hand and of constant exaltation of virginity on the other, perfectly suited the divided tastes of the age'. What is described here is the debate tradition of love versus honour, which seems to be a source of unending interest to courtiers in every age.[91] The courtier is required by the cultured and sophisticated milieu in which he finds himself to accept a position of social equality with women, especially so in the court of a Virgin Queen; but at the same time he is required to assert his virility as favourite, knight or champion. The tension between the two requirements may be sublimated into a spiritual or patriotic dedication to a non-carnal ideal, where love and honour fuse, or the two may clash, as in the archetypal Dido story.

The medieval Romances had shown knights enduring trials for the sake of their ladies, or making allegorical journeys into the recesses of the loving personality (as in *The Romance of the Rose*); but it was left for the Renaissance to show honour and appetite confronting each other in the sharp opposition of drama. One convenient method of dramatizing this conflict, and one that descended to Lyly, was the plot concerned with a female captive. A beautiful girl is captured by a noble commander; he, though conscious of her charms, spares her honour and the play sometimes ends with this nobility paying off in political power. In 1579 the boys of the Chapel showed a *History of Alucius*, which must be derived from Livy, XXVI. 50; the story there gives one a clear outline of a love-and-honour plot.

> The soldiers of Scipio Africanus, after their defeat of the Celti-berians, bring before him a female captive, a mature virgin of such beauty that, wherever she goes, she attracts attention. Scipio inquires about her native city and parentage and learns, among other things, that she is the betrothed of a prince of the Celtiberians called Alucius. Scipio ensures that the maiden is kept safe and sends for her parents and her betrothed. When Alucius arrives Scipio addresses him in studied language as follows . . . 'Your betrothed has received in my camp as much respect as under the roof of her own parents. She has been kept for you that she might be presented to you in all her purity, a gift worthy of you to receive and of me to give. One reward I stipulate in return for the service I have rendered you, that you become a friend of the Roman people—and no people is more worthy of friendship.' Alucius is overcome with shame and with joy, clings to Scipio's hand and calls upon the gods to reward him. The parents wish to give Scipio the maiden's ransom money; but he insists on adding this to the dowry paid to Alucius. Filled with gratitude, Alucius returns home and sings the praises of the Roman general; he makes a levy among his people and after a few days he returns to Scipio with fourteen hundred picked horsemen.

The same situation of the fair captive appears in another courtly play of the period, and this time one which survives—*The Wars of Cyrus*, of uncertain date, but certainly written for the boys' companies.[92] Once again a famous military hero from classical history (this time Cyrus) captures in war a beautiful princess of the enemy; again his greatness in war is complemented by his clemency; the decision to spare his captive, Panthea, brings political profit as well as personal honour. Looking at this play it is easy to see the tradition to which the first part of *Tamburlaine* belongs. *The Wars of Cyrus* may well be later than *Tamburlaine*, but *Alucius* shows that love-and-honour plays existed in the court before this time, and so before Lyly. One other play, of a cognate kind, is known from its title; and from this enough can be derived to show that *Alucius* was not isolated in its early handling of the situation of the noble general and the noble female captive. This play is *Timoclea at the siege of Thebes*, referred to in the Revels accounts for 1574, and presumably derived from the story in Plutarch's *Life of Alexander*:

> Among other calamities that befell this miserable city [Thebes], it happened that some Thracian soldiers plundered and demolished the house of an illustrious matron named Timoclea; and their captain, after he had ravished her, asked her if she had any money concealed; she answered that she had, and bid him follow her into the garden, where she showed him a well, into which she told him, upon the taking of the city, she had thrown what she had of most value. The Thracian stooping down to view the place, she came behind and pushed him into the well, and then threw great stones in upon him, till she killed him. After which, when the soldiers led her away bound to Alexander, her mein and carriage showed her to be a woman of a noble rank and an elevated mind; for she did not betray the least sign of fear or astonishment. And when the King asked her who she was, 'I am,' said she, 'the sister of Theagenes who commanded in the battle of Chaeronea against your father, Philip, and fell there for the liberty of Greece.' Alexander was so surprised at both her action and speech that he gave her and her children full liberty to go whither they pleased.[93]

This play leads us directly to Lyly's *Campaspe.* Here we begin with a specific reference to *Timoclea*, since Campaspe is first found in the company of that lady, who repeats for the delectation of Lyly's audience the noble words that Plutarch had given her:

> Alexander, I am the sister of Theagenes who fought a battle with thy father, before the city of Chyeronie, where he died I say (which none can gainsay) valiantly.   (I. i. 64 ff.)

But Lyly specifically separates *his* captive from this Amazonian kind of nobility, not only in his prologue ('we calling Alexander from his grave, seek only who was his love') but in the reply of Campaspe when Alexander questions her, in her turn:

> *Alex.* . . . but what are you, fair lady; another sister to Theagines?
> *Camp.* No sister to Theagines, but an humble hand-maid to Alexander, born of a mean parentage [*of middle station*], but to extreme fortune.   (I. i. 70 ff.)

His story, though it belongs to the tradition, differs from the examples we have mentioned. It centres the conflict in the mind of Alexander. Lyly is less interested in the pose of magnanimity and more in the process of discriminating magnanimity from other forms of virtue (such as that of the creative artist). By showing the non-heroic love of Apelles and Campaspe half-laughingly and half-tenderly he gives it a quasi-pastoral simplicity and beauty, completely independent of heroic virtue but allowed to rival it in attractiveness. He thus adds a new dimension to the world of *The Wars of Cyrus*.

These changes reflect what we might expect from the author of *Euphues*, with his command over the rhetoric of the hesitant or the divided mind, and his antithetical mode of thinking and speaking. The lightness of touch which enables him to unite romance to comedy without spoiling either gives him an obvious advantage over the author of *The Wars of Cyrus*; for the Marlovian rhetoric of the latter, accomplished though it may be, commits the author to splendid generalities rather than to precise discriminations.

But the courtly tradition of romantic love does not only appear in the plays about captives. There is also, for example, the old tradition of the lady who disguises herself in order to follow her knight.[94] Bond remarks that Shakespeare derived his romantic disguise-plots from Lyly 'with whom the type was original'. A glance at the courtly literature of the time reveals the insufficiency of this. If the play of 3rd January 1585—

called 'felix and philiomena' in the Revels Accounts—was concerned, as most scholars suppose, with the story of Felix and Felismena from Montemayor's *Diana*,[95] then we have a play of Lyly's own time and milieu in which the lady disguises herself as a page in order to follow her lover—a play in fact one stage nearer Shakespeare than Lyly ever got (the Montemayor episode is the commonly accepted source of *Two Gentlemen of Verona*). Even if the play of 1585 (which comes, I suppose, before Lyly's first disguise-play, *Gallathea*) was not based on the *Diana*, the romance itself was translated about 1583 (though no English version was printed till 1598).[96] Moreover, there was the *Arcadia* of Sir Philip Sidney, in which the girl Zelmane serves her hero, Pyrocles, disguised as a page. The early version of the *Arcadia* would seem to have been in circulation from about 1580.

The same theme can be found in the *novelle*. The ninth novel of the second day in Boccaccio's *Decameron* (Bernabo di Genova) tells the story (taken up in Shakespeare's *Cymbeline*) of the wife who flies from her husband's wrath, but is able in her disguised state to restore him to wealth and herself to honour. In the thirty-sixth novel of Bandello's second book Niccuola follows her lover disguised as a page; the story is translated as the sixty-first novel of Belleforest's popular *Histoires Tragiques*, which may be a source for Barnaby Rich's *Apollonius and Sylla* (itself, in its turn, a source for Shakespeare's *Twelfth Night*). Even nearer home is the play of *Clyomon and Clamydes* (*c.* 1570) which shows a princess (Neronis) in what the author calls 'painful page's show' (l. 1261), that is, disguised as a boy in order to follow her knight in his somewhat purposeless wanderings through courts and forests.

This sketch of the background ought to prevent us from seeing Lyly's disguised girls as innovations. More important, it may enable us to guess where Lyly's real innovations lie. His disguised heroines, Gallathea and Phillida, are not designed to make the Romantic and pathetic appeal of Neronis:

But no good lady will me blame, which of my case doth know:
But rather when they hear the truth, wherefore I am disguised,
They'll say it is an honest shift, the which I have devised
Since I have given my faith and troth to such a bruit of fame
As is the knight of golden shield . . . etc.   (M.S.R. 1262-6)

Lyly's disguised nymphs are not attached to lovers in the manner of the romances. The disguise is not part of a Romantic quest for a desired object, measured in its attractive force by the power of overcoming impediments. It is rather, for Lyly, a kind of *conceit*—a *discordia concors* of male and female which can be used as part of the witty exploration of the loving mind. By bringing the two disguised nymphs into love with one another (each supposing the other to be a man), Lyly is able to separate out the first tentative and uncertain fragments of emotion for our superior and sophisticated amusement.

This is typical of Lyly's whole relation to the tradition of courtly love; he sees the charm and beauty of it, but at the same time he is rather amused by its naivety. His plays are about love, and in his treatment of love he is all the time aware of the courtly background; but he sees the background of attitudes as something that can be played with, rearranged into new patterns, rather than as a set of rules to be followed. He combines effectively, perhaps for the first time in English, the Humanist tradition of learned contempt for female weakness, and the courtly tradition of irrational adoration, finding one style for both sides of *The Book of the Courtier*—the gay misogyny of Gaspar Pallavicino as well as the mystical raptures of Pietro Bembo. *Endimion* is the play in which Lyly's detachment is least in evidence, and where the romantic heritage of knights who travel through enchanted forests for the sake of love is at its strongest. But even in this play the passionate adoration of Cynthia is distanced and given its somewhat lunatic place in a world of other kinds of love by the comments of Eumenides:

> Is Endimion mad, or do I mistake? Do you love the moon
> Endimion?   (I. i. 16 f.)

and by the whole structure of the play. This shows other couples, Eumenides and Semele, Corsites and Tellus, Geron and Dipsas, Sir Tophas and Bagoa as alternative modes of relationship.

(v) PASTORAL

Court activities such as 'Maying' and many of the more fully dramatized entertainments organized for Elizabeth when she was on Progress involved a use of rustic rituals and manners. In such cases there was an inevitable contrast between the sophisticated life of the court and the broad manners of the countryside. For example of this one may quote the 'brideale' shown among the 'Princely Pleasures' of Kenilworth (1575). 'First, all the lusty lads and bold bachelors of the parish, suitably every wight with his blue buckram bridelace upon a branch of green broom . . . some boots and no spurs, he spurs and no boots and he neither nother . . . the bridegroom . . . with this special grace by the way, that ever as he would have framed him the better countenance, with the worse face he looked, etc.' (Nichols, I. 442 f.). The attitude is that of Theseus' court to the rude mechanicals.

In other entertainments we may see a more sophisticated mingling of the rustic and the courtly. Thus in the Entertainment at Sudeley (1592), which Bond attributed to Lyly, 'an old shepherd' greets the Queen with these words:

Vouchsafe to hear a simple shepherd: shepherds and simplicity cannot part. Your Highness is come into Cotshold [*the Cotswolds*], an uneven country, but a people that carry their thoughts level with their fortunes; low spirits, but true hearts, using plain dealing, once counted a jewel, now beggary. These hills afford nothing but cottages and nothing can we present unto your Highness but shepherds; the country healthy and harmless; a fresh air where there are no damps, and where a black sheep is a perilous beast; no monsters. We carry our hearts at our tongues' ends, being as far from dissembling as our sheep from fierceness.

(Bond, I. 477)

Here the rustic way of life is seen as possessing a virtue that is desirable, though it is not one that is supposed to have a particularly close relation to the troubles of court life. And it is only when this last step is taken that Pastoral proper begins to emerge. For the world of Pastoral is dependent on the court world, indeed parasitic upon it. It only acquires force as a complementary image to the treadmill of care that a court imposes upon those privileged enough to be its victims; it is only in this context that the courtier finds virtue in the image of himself as a shepherd.

I   129

O who can lead, then, a more happy life
Than he that with clean mind and heart sincere
No greedy riches knows nor bloody strife
. . .
Free from sad cares that rich men's hearts devour.
This all his care, this all his whole endeavour,
To this his mind and senses he doth bend,
How he may flow in quiet's matchless treasure
Content with any food that God doth send, etc.[97]

This is an emotion that Elizabeth herself had sanctified when she was her sister's captive at Woodstock; 'Hearing . . . a certain milkmaid singing pleasantly [she] wished herself to be a milkmaid as she was, saying that her case was better and life more merrier than was hers in that state as she was'.[98]

But the virtue of pastoral in court entertainments had further roots and other advantages. To write about the emotions of courtiers in terms of shepherds and sheep made it possible to deal with subjects which would otherwise have been taboo. I mention elsewhere the courtly quality of *sprezzatura* (or 'disgracing' as Hoby renders it); Fulke Greville expresses the same idea by speaking of 'that hypocritical figure *Ironia*, wherein men commonly (to keep above their works) seem to make toys of the utmost they can do'.[99] The concept is an important one for the courtly culture of the period.[100] To keep the strident competitiveness of court life within some bounds it was desirable to impose a code of manners in which the courtier could make his virtue known by concealing it. Where emulation simmered all the time between individuals and factions, kept so near to and yet so far from the bait of wealth and power, it was the function of court etiquette to conceal and canalize these emotions into shows of proud humility, grace showing itself with added charm through the shadow of disgrace:

> As these black masks
> Proclaim an enshield beauty ten time louder
> Than beauty could, displayed.

This combination of a reality of competitive violence and an imposed code of humble and light-hearted appearance is responsible for much of the doubleness and indirection of court art. In particular, it was responsible for the usefulness and popularity of the pastoral tradition in court entertainments, since (as Castiglione had pointed out):

> [the courtier may have skills that it would be beneath him to display, but] a masque bringeth with it a certain liberty and license, that a man may among other things take upon him the form of that he hath better skill in, and use bent study and preciseness about the principal drift of the matter wherein he will show himself, and a certain recklessness about that is not of importance, which augmenteth the grace of the thing . . . And a man at arms in form of a wild shepherd or some other such kind of disguising, but with an excellent horse and well trimmed for the purpose; because the mind of the lookers-on runneth forthwith to imagine the thing that is offered unto the eyes at the first show, and when they behold afterward a far greater matter to come of it than they looked for under that attire, it delighteth them, and they take pleasure at it.   (Everyman edn., p. 99)

There is nothing in all this however, of love, which stands at the centre of Lyly's pastorals and of most court pastoral indeed. The imagined idleness and ease of the shepherd is largely seen as a liberty to love freely without the impediment of propriety or convention which hindered the court lover.

> O happy Age of Gold . . . happy days,
> Because that vain and idle name
> That cozening idol of unrest
> Whom the mad vulgar first did raise,
> And called it Honour, whence it came
> To tyrannize o'er ev'ry breast,
> Was not then suffered to molest
> Poor lovers' hearts with new debate;
> More happy they, by these his hard
> And cruel laws were not debarred
> Their innate freedom. . . . Hence and remove
> Thy power; and it display above,
> Disturbing great ones in their sleep;
> And let us meaner men alone
> T'enjoin again (when thou art gone),
> And laws of our forefathers keep.
>   (Tasso's *Aminta*, First Chorus, trans. Reynolds)

The world of shepherds is seen as one where the pursuit of love and its titillations is the only serious business of life, since sheep feed themselves and the weather is never inclement; where, above all, the nymphs are compliant enough to provide another antithetical image to the courtly routine of adoration and frustration, idealization and sublimation.

The world of shepherds is also seen as antithetical to that of the court in that physical impulse is there not inhibited by the powers that be, but allowed and even encouraged by the gods themselves. Commerce between men and gods is here simple and common, and the power of metamorphosis is abused quite blatantly in the interests of fruition. Dr Johnson was no friend to pastoral in general: 'A pastoral of a hundred lines may be endured, but who will hear of sheep and goats and myrtle bowers and purling rivulets through five acts?' (Life of Gay), and he found the constant metamorphoses of the tradition especially distasteful: 'A new metamorphosis is a ready and puerile expedient; nothing is easier than to tell how a flower was once a blooming virgin or a rock an obdurate tyrant' (Life of Pope). It is true that metamorphosis may sometimes be a fatally easy means of effecting *coups de théâtre*, or of avoiding the human implications of a human problem, but it should not be forgotten that Dr Johnson is here judging the obliquities of a court art from the standpoint of common sense. As a means of expressing the wish-fulfilment of desire, metamorphosis has many advantages.

Lyly's pastorals simplify the structure of life but they do not sentimentalize it. The metamorphoses enlarge the scope of human change available for expression by an artist without any means of showing psychological development in a character; they allow him to explore human capacity for regression and obsession and other aspects of the mind that psychologists have taught us to expect, and allow him to do so in a way which is at once spectacular and just.

Pastoral, like other courtly modes, enables the artist to deal with his restricted world by expressing it in a new style. The word 'style' is especially significant here. We may remember that Virgil's pastoral poems have been celebrated as the most perfect of his works, perfect, that is, in terms of euphony, sweetness in the choice and arrangement of words. Pope says in the headnote to his pastorals that 'the reason for his labouring them into so much softness was . . . that this sort of poetry derives almost its whole beauty from a natural ease of thought and smoothness of verse'. But long before Pope and Addison were expressing these Neo-classical ideals in England, poets were putting them into practice in the petty courts of Italy. In such works as Tasso's *Aminta* or Guarini's *Pastor Fido* we find the pastoral mode being used to suggest a ravishing simplicity in sophistication, a soft, even enervating, relaxation of temper that balances on the knife-edge of decadence and bodes ill for its imitators.

England was largely saved from this enervation by the closeness of the real countryside, indeed its menace in this period; for the shadow of the unconscious swine behind the *conscious swain* gave a tension to English pastorals which was absent from the Italian. As one whose triumph, in *Euphues*, had been above all a triumph of style, Lyly was a natural adept in the pastoral vein, but the vein of genuine rusticity of his shepherds in *Gallathea* (Titerus and Melebeus) in their relation to the Lincolnshire background, serves to distinguish them from the innumerable Doruses and Menalcases of the Italian drama Lyly might be supposed to have imitated.

Court pastoral is, in short, a kind of convex mirror which concentrates the landscape it records into manageable compass; it substitutes the physical impediments that low life places in the way of desire for the spiritual, intellectual and social impediments that high life knows all too well; it does so in a way that encourages its courtly auditors to see themselves in a better light. They are encouraged to think, 'I could do better than that', or, 'I could conquer that nymph, that swain, if only I were free from the duties of courtship or greatness'. Thus the allegorical potentialities of the pastoral guise accompany a direct appeal to escape from the cramping and frustrating milieu of court, into a sympathetic natural landscape, assimilated to human inclinations by a plentiful use of the pathetic fallacy:

> Go, my flock, go, get ye hence,
> Seek a better place of feeding,
> Where ye may have some defence
> From the storms in my breast breeding,
> And showers from mine eyes proceeding.
> . . .

Then, my dear flock, now adieu;
But, alas, if in your straying
Heavenly Stella meet with you
Tell her in your piteous blaying
Her poor slave's unjust decaying.
(Sidney, in *England's Helicon* [Muses Library], pp. 9 f.)

Likewise it encourages escape into a world whose gods are more accessible and more understanding of love's frailty than is the God of everyday Christian life.

The only specifically pastoral titles I can find in the Revels Accounts before Lyly are the 'Pastoral or history of a Greek maid' performed by Leicester's men on the 4th January 1579, and 'a pastoral of Phillida and Clorin' performed by the Queen's Men on the 26th December 1584. Probably we ought to add Peele's *Arraignment of Paris*, for this is usually supposed to have been performed earlier than any of Lyly's plays. All these plays come later than non-dramatic pastoral, and the only one which has survived—*The Arraignment of Paris*—declares its dependence on Spenser's celebrated pastoral very openly. The only purely pastoral episode in the play is that involving the love-lorn Colin, with Hobbinol, Thenot and Diggon—a cast and a subject-matter taken over *in toto* from *The Shepheard's Calendar*. Otherwise Peele's play uses pastoralism largely as a means of generating poetic atmosphere. It is charming to hear of Faunus, Pomona, and Pan, but as far as the structure of the play is concerned they could as well be other gods with other (non-pastoral) attributes.

Lyly's *Gallathea* may be said to mark an advance on *The Arraignment of Paris*, for it advances the *genre* in the direction it was to take for the remainder of its short career. In *The Arraignment* the loves of the nymphs are not at the centre of the play. In Lyly, as in Tasso and Guarini, they and their loves are the focus of our interest. Indeed Lyly may have learned from such Italian sources how to combine pastoral charm with the innocent loves of the nymphs; it is possible chronologically, but there is no clear evidence.[101] Much of the parallelism only shows that Lyly was a court entertainer in a European tradition. Lyly's natural bent was towards the delicate evocation of female sentiment; given his further taste for neatly manipulated plots where a magnanimous sovereign solves the complexities by cutting the knot, and the shortage of quasi-divine monarchs (like Alexander and Elizabeth) we can almost say that it was inevitable he should take to showing the gods doing this Gordian work. And the obvious scene where the gods could appear most easily to do this was the pastoral scene. I think we can see this natural development towards pastoral in Lyly's first three plays—*Campaspe, Sapho and Phao,* and *Gallathea.*

Lyly's two later plays which may be called pastorals— *Love's Metamorphosis* and *The Woman in the Moon*—are less clearly in the tradition that leads forward to *The Faithful Shepherdess.* In *The Woman in the Moon,* as Greg has pointed out, 'the shepherds are in their origin philosophical, standing for the race of mankind in general, rather than pastoral; Utopian, in fact, rather than Arcadian'.[102] In *Love's Metamorphosis* (called on its title-page 'a witty and courtly pastoral') the plot of the three foresters and the three nymphs is, again, only pastoral by convenience. It is convenient to have a setting in which the goddess, her nymphs, and ordinary mortals can meet as freely as neighbours; but nothing positive is made out of the background. The jump forward from Lyly to Fletcher's *Faithful Shepherdess* requires an elaboration of emotions and a development of sensual appeal quite foreign to Lyly's line of wit.

(vi) PARODY AND SUB-PLOT

The variety of social levels which Pastoral handles, using the lower to express the higher, can be drawn on to produce very different effects where one level is used to parody the other. Given the strict stratification of Medieval and Renaissance society and thought, parody was a natural response, and one that was built into much social custom. I have spoken already of the Winter King, of the Boy Bishop and of the Lord of Misrule—all tributes to the stability of a social hierarchy which could emerge from these temporary reversals, strengthened in its claim to divine right. The role of the last of these figures in the court festivities around Christmas[103] makes it clear that one of the functions of 'Revels' was to engage in topsy-turvy activities and by allowing every dog his day to confirm him in his status as a dog.

Such parodies of church ritual or of social order may be separately interesting as literature or art, but on the whole they are not likely to survive the beliefs or occasions to which they refer, unless as social documentation or as satiric comment. We can hardly read into the *Testamentum Porcelli* or the Birds' Masses the degree of criticism of life which they originally contained; even painstaking research can hardly bring them alive again.

The case is rather different, however, when a work of art contains within itself not only the parody but also the serious statement which is being parodied, as medieval books of hours often contained a frieze of animals to carry forward the mind of the noble owner on a lower level from that of the text.[104] In literature, one isolated medieval example makes the point with great clarity. The famous 'second shepherds' play' of the Townley Cycle of Mystery plays, shows the shepherds, who have just found the Christ child in his manger, engaged in a second search, for a lamb which has been stolen from the flock; this they find in another crib, again dressed in swaddling bands, but the 'baby' of Mak, the comic sheep-stealer, is very different from the baby of Mary and Joseph; he is the missing lamb from the flock (not the Lamb of God) dressed as a baby and placed in a crib to avoid detection.

I say this example is isolated, and it would be improper to cite it as even a remote antecedent of the court art of Elizabeth's reign, did it not seem possible to point to a common ground of shared assumptions linking the two periods. Comic scenes abound in the Mystery Cycles; the example of Noah's wife is well known to students. Her headstrong opposition to the ark and to the scheme of salvation it implies is intended to be set against the piety of Noah, though it can hardly be said to parody it. But the impulse to show up one attitude by coupling it to another and very different attitude is present here no less than in the shepherd plays. The construction of a second plot to parody the scriptural action that the Cycle *must* show is obviously a luxury that the already packed day of the Corpus Christi cycle could rarely afford; but the impulse is present throughout. I suggest, in short, that the formal parody of a serious main plot (the adoration of the shepherds) by a comic sub-plot (second shepherds' play) can be seen as an outcrop of a general late Medieval and Renaissance aesthetic, to which art-historians have given the name of 'multiplicity'.[105]

Late Medieval and Renaissance art of all kinds shows an unwillingness to subordinate one aspect of the situation being described to another, a fondness for detail and (in the earlier stages) a lack of interest in 'the general effect'. In terms of structure this often means an aggregative method by which one thing, one view, one aspect, is added to another, with no clear view of the relationship between them established at the beginning. This is evident enough in the long poems at the period (e.g. Hawes' *Pastime of Pleasure*) but it is easier to demonstrate what I mean from non-literary arts, from the Gothic cathedral and the Medieval sermon.

In the Gothic cathedral it is seldom possible to obtain a single visual impression of the whole work, such as one may obtain at the crossing of Wren's St Paul's. What we discover as we move through the building is a collection of parts—here a Romanesque column and there a Gothic one, here a side-chapel, or a grotesque carving or a rose-window or a reredos, details which we enjoy for their own sakes, without seeking the organic connection that links one with another. We may be aware that all these details do, in fact, add up to the greater glory of God, but this is only achieved because (as Hugh of St Victor tells us) 'infinite and perfect Beauty can only manifest itself properly when reflected by an infinite number of different forms'[106] and this is a unity so vast that it does nothing to narrow our range of expectations or suggest exclusive principles. Likewise, we may know that the cathedral plan is cruciform, but this affects us as an idea or (as we might say of literature) a 'theme' rather than as an expressive feature of the building; our eyes do not follow the cross; the details are not subordinated so as to direct our attention towards it.[107] The expressive vigour or 'realism' of the detail need not be played down if we accept Hugh of St Victor's outlook; each detail in its individuality is part of a universal design and can be shown to have its place in an intellectually apprehensible framework. The parallel with allegory is obvious here; the vigour and realism of Langland's seven deadly sins may seem detached from their function in the poem, but can be defended in terms of idea or *significatio*.[108]

The same general approach to structure appears in the medieval sermon,[109] whose method remained common through the Renaissance; and we should remember in this context that the sermon was the most widely practised and most generally esteemed form of discourse till long after Lyly's day. The structure of the sermon, like that of the cathedral, is in terms of idea not of recognizable unity. The separate sections of the sermon may make a direct appeal, to prayer, to amusement, to horror, to awe, but the relation of one section to another may have nothing to do with such effects, depending on the intellectual scheme which was adopted at the beginning. Thus preaching on the text, *Justus de angustia liberatus est* (Proverbs, xi. 8) a preacher is advised[110] to introduce three sections: (1) *Justus* [the just man], (2) *de angustia* [from anguish], (3) *liberatus est* [is delivered]. In each case it is the duty of the preacher to develop these separate ideas (of the just man, of torment, and of deliverance) with whatever power he can muster; it is on this and not on the continuity of effect or original meaning of the passage that the theorists concentrate.[111]

The 'multiplicity' of the handling in cathedral or sermon may be thought inseparable from the religious attitudes which clearly inform both of these. It is certainly true that the *aesthetic* of this kind of art seems to depend on religious presuppositions, but it seems clear that the *practice* went on even when the justification was forgotten.[112] The sonnet-sequences show the old method of illustrating a theme by a series of discontinuous episodes arranged radially around a theme rather than lineally, along a narrative thread.[113] Moreover, the presence of the anti-Petrarchan attitude:

> For I have sworn thee fair and thought thee bright
> Who art as black as hell, as dark as night

as a common feature of Petrarchan sequences reveals the tendency of 'multiplicity' to turn into 'parody' when the conditions make this possible. The conditions are especially favourable when serious or romantic action becomes the central interest of dramatic entertainment, and it would seem to be no accident that the earliest English comedy surviving—Medwall's *Fulgens and Lucres* (*c.* 1497)—is a prime example of parody in a sub-plot.[114]

With *Fulgens and Lucres* we are at last in sight of Lyly. Here is a Humanist play, a debate, based on the question whether nature or nurture, birth or education gives a truer basis for nobility; this theme is worked out in terms of a Roman lady choosing between two suitors. But the presentation of love is not left at this level. To the story of the two noble suitors, which he derived from his Humanist source, Medwall added the adventures of their two less high-minded servants ('A' and 'B'), who engage in an action parallel to the main plot, wooing the servant of Lucres and contending (like their masters) for her hand:

> Come forth ye flower of the frying pan
> . . .
> See that ye judge indifferently
> Which of us twain hath the mastery.   (1174-78)

The main idea of *Fulgens and Lucres* is more clearly focussed and more directly expressed than is the case in many plays before Lyly. The same qualities are apparent in the sub-plot. The Interludes normally contain a wide variety of social and intellectual attitudes, but these are seldom stratified in the simple manner of *Fulgens and Lucres*; on the other hand, one of the functions of the Vice is to parody and ridicule the serious concerns of the other characters, and to this extent parody is seldom absent from these plays. Even works as serious-minded as *Cambyses* or *Damon and Pithias*[115] have their comic servants or rustics to give a worm's eye view of the effects of tyranny. The evidence, scanty though it is, would suggest that Lyly inherited a strong tradition of 'multiple' presentation of ideas, and that this normally included some parody of serious concerns by low-life characters, often given a licence to discuss and complain about contemporary conditions. On the other hand, though these conditions sometimes produced full-scale 'parody' sub-plots, in which servants copied the actions of their masters, this is a comparatively rare development.[116]

Lyly was, I have everywhere suggested, a traditional artist who differed from his predecessors in the degree of organization he brought to his materials, not in the materials themselves. Except in *Mother Bombie* he did not choose to develop his plots in the Italian, neo-classical manner, with a single comprehensive intrigue bringing together all the elements of a simple and unified social scene—a way already indicated by contemporary translations like Gascoigne's *Supposes* and Mundy's *Fidele and Fortunio*. He wished (it would seem) to preserve the multiplicity of incident and viewpoint characteristic of the Gothic. But he wished also to make his episodes please in their relation to one another, to balance them Euphuistically (one might say). He keeps the carnal, disillusioned, comic viewpoint of the servants, but handles it more neatly and balances it more cleverly against the material of the main plot.

The techniques of Lyly's sub-plots differ from play to play, and I shall discuss them all below (p. 229 ff.); sufficient here to note that he is not an originator in this aspect of drama any more than he is in the others we have discussed.

(vii) MYTHOLOGY

I have spoken of the mythological subjects often chosen for the boy players, but the word is, though just, too vague to convey the quality of the courtly myth. Myth appealed to the poets and entertainers of the Renaissance courts for a number of reasons. It had the glamour of the antique, and so complimented the court by putting it in the line of the greatest of great traditions. To compare the sovereign to Diana or Zeus or Apollo, the ladies-in-waiting to the nymphs or the Graces or the Muses, and the poet himself to Arion or Amphion, was to draw over the realities of power and privilege a shining veil of romance, and romance which could be justified in ways not open to the medieval images of knights, ladies, enchanters and dragons. For, as Ascham had pointed out in *The Schoolmaster*, Medieval Romance was a part of medieval civilization, which it was the primary purpose of the Humanists to reject (even if it was not, as he reported 'made in monasteries by idle monks or wanton canons' [Arber, p. 80]). Such a romance might be allowed to be historical, but it was not significantly true, for it did not show the truth about living among sophisticated, ethically self-conscious and elegant purists (so by conscience if not by practice).

The idea that the Greek myths were usefully 'true' deserves

some explanation. If Greco-Roman poetry was to appear not only not sinfully heathen but even beneficial to a moralizing period, some perception that its subject-matter was more than beautiful was required. This meant, in effect, reconciling the Greek gods to the Christian one, and finding the myths proto-Christian. This is not the place for an exposition of the methods by which the myths were allegorized, first as Christian and then as ethical truths. Part of the story (as far as it concerns England) has been brilliantly told in the pages of Douglas Bush's *Mythology and the Renaissance Tradition*. What concerns us here is that the various Christian, Neo-Platonic and Rationalizing interpreters all pointed to one general attitude, that here was truth in a form at once more glamorous and more malleable than history could provide, pointing moreover with unique directness and vividness at favourite Renaissance themes— the embodiment of divine order in the human state, or, conversely, at man's capacity to rise from bestial muddle to angelic clarity by embracing reason.

The Humanists, so seriously concerned with kingship and the establishment of good rule on earth, took very literally the 'ye shall be as gods on earth' and the court entertainers often represented the courts of earthly monarchs under the guise of Olympus. This was not simply to flatter (not that they were averse to that), but to point (and even to warn) what was the ethical and religious function of a court—to be the focus of spiritual, moral and social excellence, as well as the seat of power:

> a prince's court
> Is like a common fountain, whence should flow
> Pure silver drops in general, but if't chance
> Some curs'd example poison't near the head
> Death and diseases through the whole land spread.

Thus when the court of Henri II plays at being Olympus, with Henri as Jupiter, the Constable of Montmorency as Mars, the Cardinal of Lorraine as Mercury etc., the play is self-consciously serious play, since in a poetic sense it may be supposed to be true, or indeed truer (more serious and philosophic) than history or fact.[117]

So with Elizabeth. The common representations of her as

Cynthia or Diana are not to be taken as a literal assertion of her chastity. Had she been unchaste, in fact, this would not impair the propriety of her appearance as Virgin Queen or Virgin Goddess in any way, for the myth represents what ought to be rather than what is.[118] We may take George Sandys' view here (as so often) as summing up the Renaissance attitude: 'some [myths] inflaming by noble examples, with an honest emulation and leading, as it were, by the hand to the temple of Honour and Virtue. For the poet not only renders things as they are; but what are not, as if they were or rather as they should be, agreeable to the high affections of the soul, and more conducing to magnanimity' (Introduction to the commentary on *Ovid*). It follows that Gifford's objection (to Jonson's *Cynthia's Revels*) that 'fulsome compliments paid to the "obdurate virgin" of threescore and ten, the hoary headed Cynthia of Whitehall, must have appeared infinitely ridiculous, if the frequency of the practice had not utterly taken away the sense of derision'[119] is mere mistaking of the temper of such compliments; for they refer to the queen rather than the woman, the office and not the person. The court plays at a game elaborated by its entertainers, but the game is in some ways an excavation of the real truth which lies beneath the accidents of fact.

The temper which uses the classics for such purposes may well seem to modern minds to be 'unclassical'; but then so must a high proportion of the works of ancient Greece and Rome. The 'Augustan' ideals of decorum, clarity, simplicity, impersonality never applied even to a figure as chronologically Augustan as Ovid. Ovid's enormous influence over succeeding ages down to (and including) the eighteenth century was largely due to his 'unclassical' qualities—his lack of reticence, his copiousness, his facile wit, his command of a polished and complex surface texture and of an easily imitable rhetoric. One may pretend, indeed, that it was for such barbarous and unAugustan activities as the writing of lines like

> semibovemque virum, semivirumque bovem
> (*Ars Amatoria* II, 24)

that he was exiled from Augustan Rome to Tomi (Ben Jonson virtually says this), but the sophistic influence such lines represent could not be sent to Tomi with Ovid; they remain a powerful and eventually dominant influence on Roman culture, and so in all Western literatures where education through rhetoric and the practice of Imitation prevailed.

The whole drift of classical Imitation encouraged the accumulation of 'points' as a measure of literary excellence, and what we might nowadays call 'classical' purity of form was regularly sacrificed to the virtuoso techniques of the rhetorician and even the pedant. What was true of the figures was no less true of the 'matters' or the materials for discourse. The classics, in an age which greatly admired the classical past, became a vast storehouse to be digested, indexed, moralized and combed for examples.[120] The touchstones of a modern classical taste— say the high seriousness of Sophocles and the elegiac tenderness of Virgil—seemed less important than the wit of Ovid or the sententiousness of Seneca, for the former are only applicable to modern life at its most personal level, while the latter can be broken down and reapplied to the modern court or the modern clergy in a way which combines pleasure and profit, allows us the beauties of the gods but finds behind their marble faces the grim realities of Tudor politics.

The idea that the myths of Greece conveyed important moral lessons ties up closely with their court appearance in forms derived from the Morality or the Debate. To present-day readers, the nakedness, spareness, and austerity of *Everyman* is one of its principal attractions, and a simple debate-play like *Fulgens and Lucres* has something of the same attractive directness, which disappears when the debate is turned into a gallimaufry like *Summer's Last Will and Testament*. But the Elizabethan taste for elaboration and aggregation and every other kind of piling-up of effect made the movement an inevitable one.

It is here that the tradition of the *Psychomachia*[121] came to the aid of Tudor court entertainers. The *Psychomachia* of Prudentius had combined the Christian interest in the soul of man as a battleground for virtues and vices with classical heroic combat on the Virgilian model, with *Ira* and *Luxuria* and *Sodomita Libido* rattling swords (of the spirit) against one another. The obvious extension of this, granting that Ate or Mars may stand for anger, is to show the battle proceeding between figures with some of the elaborate attributes of the Greek Pantheon. Given the tendency of poetry to seek its own splendours, the development seems almost inevitable:

> [*poesin*] expellas furca, tamen usque recurret.

'The gods', as C. S. Lewis has remarked, 'died into allegory', and the story of their death and rebirth is the story of Medieval allegory, which can best be studied in the pages of Lewis's *Allegory of Love*.

What is important to us, viewing the story of allegory from the other end, from the period of its decline, is to notice that the sixteenth century was bequeathed a whole tradition where gods and goddesses were set in postures of opposition over moral problems, postures which could be made graceful and pleasing and rich with the spoils of antiquity, yet without sacrificing the moral basis of the work in which they appeared.

The use of the phrase 'moral problems' of works like Lyly's court comedies may seem a little strange, for there is little or no overt morality in the plays. The use of court mythology is in fact an interesting area where we can see the moral, the political and the personal jostling for position. Given the supposition that the court is a fountain of morality as well as a centre of power and a meeting place for glamorous personalities, it must have seemed natural for the old fight over Man's soul to be rephrased in terms of court intrigue, with Loyalty battling against Treason and Hate against Love, Jupiter against the Titans, Ate against Venus; the moral content of this must have seemed too obvious to need saying. In the court art of Lyly and other Elizabethans we find a coalescence of the mythological and the personal which is only 'classical' by grace and favour, but was useful none the less because such classical names had become encrusted with the multiple associations that such writers sought to evoke.

Thus in Lyly's *Sapho and Phao* the 'classical' references are already completely traditional in court art and do not require any direct relation to the classics. Lyly's Venus is neither the golden Aphrodite of Homer nor the *alma Venus* of Lucretius, but the elegant court lady, intent on love and with somewhat unusual powers, that she had become through generations of court-of-love and courtly poems. From glorifying the court as an Olympus, writers turned naturally to a conception of Olympus as a modern court, with human characters as the hangers-on whose fortunes depend on the issues of the squabbles above them. This could, of course, be a satiric mode; but to Lyly and his contemporaries it seldom is. The Elizabethan court, like the Homeric Olympus, may be fickle, personal and quarrelsome, but it is none the less the source of power and meaning in the ordinary world. Moreover the powers of the gods were obviously useful to the dramatists as justifying theatrical marvels, and they also enabled them to present in physical terms what there was no language for in psychological ones. Thus the machinery of the seven gods (or planets) in *The Woman in the Moon* explains and presents an image of female fickleness which a modern author would see (and seek to present) in psychological terms.

(viii) COURT ALLEGORY

The known survival of allegorical ways of thought through the Tudor period, the passion for oblique reference which pervades Elizabethan utterance, together with the manifest reference to political matters under feigned names in some works of the period—all these have led scholars to suppose that much of the court literature of the period had a spice of this further interest for contemporaries, beyond what can be seen by uninstructed readers today. I shall have to deal with this problem more precisely as it affects the meaning and intention of Lyly's individual court comedies, but it might be thought appropriate at the moment to examine the view that Lyly was drawing on a tradition of covert reference to political matters, and was operating in an atmosphere generally favourable to such activities.

An examination of such plays as were seen by Elizabeth, and have survived, reveals that oblique reference to the Queen and to court affairs was certainly possible, in plays as elsewhere. *Gorboduc* is an obvious example, depicting the evils of an uncertain or divided succession, and giving advice on how to deal with it:

No, no; then parliament should have been holden,
And certain heirs appointed to the crown
To stay the title of established right,
And in the people plant obedience,
While yet the prince did live, whose name and power
By lawful summons and authority
Might make a parliament to be of force.

(V. ii. 264 ff.)

Though the Queen is not mentioned, it is clear that the Britain of the play is also the England of 1561-2, and that the advice of Eubulus is direct advice to the Queen. Two points should be made, however, about the nature of this advice. Firstly, it is not in any way concerned with the personal life of the Queen; it is advice to her *qua* queen, a general fable illustrating the traditional and traditionally allowed 'advice to a prince'; secondly, it does not ask for any point-by-point comparison between any passage in the queen's life and the life of any character in the play. It develops and illustrates one potentiality in the royal situation, but does not suggest that it is any feature of the Queen's character which makes this potentiality a dangerous one.

It might be argued, however, that *Gorboduc* is untypical in a number of ways. Sackville and Norton (especially Sackville, who was second cousin to the Queen) were too exalted to be considered ordinary playwrights, and should be thought of less as dramatists giving advice and more as counsellors writing a play. Also it might be said that a gala performance at the Inns of Court was rather different from a court play, for whose performance the Queen herself was ultimately responsible; also that 1561 is too early in the reign to provide a basis for generalization, the more pedagogic reign of Edward VI still being strong in Humanist expectations. All this is true, but when we turn to Richard Edwardes' *Damon and Pithias* of 1565 as on all these counts a more reliable work, we find that its references to the contemporary situation bear the same restrictions as those noted for *Gorboduc*.

Damon and Pithias is a play about friendship, tyranny and flattery. The nature of its basic interest is, in fact, fairly clearly indicated by the derivation of its subject-matter from Elyot's *Book of the Governor*—one of the most celebrated of the English

146

'advice to a prince' manuals. The play shows that friendship, even among private persons, is something that is only normally possible where the good sovereign reigns:

> *Damon.* My Pithias, where tyrants reign, such cases are not new,
> Which fearing their own state for great cruelty,
> To sit fast as they think, do execute speedily
> All such as any light suspicion have tainted.   (M.S.R. 341-4)

The natural counterpart of false friendship is flattery and courtly abuses in general, which Grim the Collier of Croydon is here given a kind of pastoral licence to criticize:

> Who invented these monsters first, did it to a ghostly end;
> To have a mail ready to put in other folks' stuff;
> We see this evident by daily proof.
> One preached of late not far hence, in no pulpit, but in wain cart,
> That spake enough of this, but for my part
> Chill say no more, your own necessity
> In the end will force you to find some remedy.   (1422-8)

or again,

> Friendship is dead in court, hypocrisy doth reign
> Who is in favour now, tomorrow is out again;
> The state is so uncertain that I by my will
> Will never be courtier, but a collier still.   (1522-5)

But the satire is reserved for details of court life like the over-dressing of the pages and the over-spending which is its corollary—themes which were already traditional in pulpit and Complaint. Kingship is treated in so generalized a way that offence taken would be an admission of guilt:

> Although your regal state Dame Fortune decketh so
> That like a king in worldly wealth abundantly ye flow,
> Yet fickle is the ground whereon all tyrants tread,
> A thousand sundry cares and fears do haunt their restless head;
> No trusty band, no faithful friends do guard thy hateful state
> And why? Whom men obey for deadly fear, sure them they deadly
>   hate.   (2082-7)

Edwardes does not, of course, press the point that Dionysius is a terrible warning. The final song to Elizabeth merely points to her as the opposite of Dionysius, as the happy sovereign surrounded by friends:

> True friends for their true prince refuseth not their death;
> The Lord grant her such friends, most noble Queen Elizabeth.
>
> (2246 f.)

In short, the atmosphere of this play is at once intensely concerned with the court and with kingship, but at the same time completely impersonal, and in this it would seem to be typical of the handling of political themes in Elizabethan courtly entertainments. One powerful reason why this impersonality should have been preserved is writ large in the treatment of those who came closer to the susceptibilities of the monarch. We may note how Elizabeth behaved to her court preachers. Of this A. F. Herr has written:

> To speak freely before her was to displease her, for one of her few consistencies was her hatred of liberty of speech, especially if the speech concerned her. To speak with great reserve was to displease her also; she put the worst possible construction on all subtleties and she perceived threats in all dark passages . . . During the sermon Elizabeth sat in a private closet, at a window facing the preacher. If she were displeased with the sermon she would close the shutters or retire to the inner recesses of the box, unless she thought stronger measures warranted. If a man preached too long, Elizabeth would simply tell him to stop, or if he wandered into forbidden ground she might call him down on the spot. Once when Dean Nowell [*Dean of St Paul's*] was preaching to her he left the main topic of his sermon and began to inveigh against images; but unfortunately it happened to be one of the days when the Queen liked images, and so she pulled him up abruptly by shouting to him to stick to his text, which the good dean thereafter did.[122]

That the Queen was capable of similar behaviour at a play is shown by the story of the student performance which pursued Elizabeth from Cambridge to Hinchinbrook in 1564. This seems to have been a satire on Roman practices in religion and to have represented Bonner, the Marian bishop of London, 'carrying a lamb in his hands as if he were eating it as he walked along, and then others with [*other*] devices, one being the figure of a dog with [*a*] host in his mouth'. The Spanish ambassador, who reports this *contretemps*, tells us that 'the Queen was so angry that she at once entered her chamber using strong language and the men who held the torches, it being night, left them [*the players*] in the dark, and so ended thoughtless and scandalous representations'.[123] One is driven to wonder if any memory of the Hinchinbrook exit informed Claudius' angry exit from Hamlet's *Mousetrap:*

Oph. The king rises . . .
Pol. Give o'er the play.
King. Give me some light. Away!
Pol. Lights, lights, lights!

At any rate it is clear that provocation considerably less than Claudius was given would cause Elizabeth to disrupt the play and dishonour the playwright.

It is also fairly clear that allegories of the Queen's relations with her favourites would provoke displeasure. Among the victims of the Essex rebellion must be included Fulke Greville's tragedy of *Antony and Cleopatra*, which he destroyed about the time of the rebellion because fact seemed to have overtaken fiction too exactly, and (the parallel having been made) 'many members in that creature [*the play*] . . . having some childish wantonness in them, apt enough to be construed or strained to a personating of vices in the present governors and government.'[124] It has been thought that in the lost play Greville drew intentional parallels with the Elizabethan situation, but the very fact that the Essex affair surprised him (and his play) argues it was history, not intention, that turned general observations into what seemed like particular references. This view is supported by the other plays that Greville left behind him and by the whole corpus of the Senecal school to which he belonged. Daniel's *Philotas* seems to have fallen under similar suspicions, and here we have the text to check that there is little more than a general parallel with the Essex situation. In 1605 Daniel thought it proper to publish an 'Apology' in which he asserts, 'I could not imagine that envy or ignorance could possibly have made it to take any particular acquaintance with us, but as it hath a general alliance to the frailty of greatness and the usual workings of ambition, the perpetual subjects of books and tragedies.'[125] And this we may allow him.

The difference between *Gorboduc* or *Damon and Pithias* on the one hand and Daniel's *Philotas* on the other would seem to be that the former deal only with the governor, and with views about government, while the latter might be supposed to touch upon the human weakness of persons in power. The former was tolerable; the latter was not.

It is true, of course, that covert references in Elizabethan literature are not always political. Private affairs are sometimes referred to, and such reference seems to have been tolerated or even encouraged by Elizabeth in the interests of that mythologizing of court business which was so important a part of her method of government.[126] There would seem to be a conflict between the Humanist's desire to advise the Queen and the Queen's desire not to be advised but only adored. It is between these contrary pressures that common sense must steer. If we try to distinguish the sphere of advice from the sphere of mythology, we find (I think) that the latter may be personal, but must treat the Queen herself as inscrutable, save as a saint or a deity whose will may be sought, whose favour may be worshipped under a variety of names (Astraea, Pandora, Dido),[127] but who may not be treated as a fallible or changeable human being, or as a spokeswoman for political interests.

The Accession-day tilts have been brilliantly adduced by Miss Frances Yates[128] to show how the mythology which emerges in the *Arcadia* and *The Faerie Queene* is part of an organized court ritual, in which the political animals of the real court take up roles as shepherds, languishing lovers, Protestant worshippers—allowed what they strove for, a relationship with the Queen, but only on terms which were of little political value to them. It was possible to change her mind, it seems, if the terms were kept to and exploited without political trespass. At least the case of Sir Edward Dyer would seem to show this.

Sir Edward Dyer,[129] a gentleman of honourable but modest gentility, seems to have come to court under Leicester's patronage and to have had some prospect of becoming a royal favourite. In 1570 the sun of royal favour shone on him with sufficient warmth to make him sprout into the stewardship of Woodstock 'for life'. By 1571, however, the sun had clouded over and the prospects of power and wealth disappeared. How could a courtier recover the position on which all else depended? A politic illness had recently worked in the case of Sir Christopher Hatton; tried by Dyer it produced some relaxation of the Queen's severity: 'Dyer lately was sick of a consumption, in great danger, and as your Lordship knoweth, he hath been in displeasure these two years. It was made the Queen believe that his sickness came because of the continuance of her displeasure towards him, so that unless she would forgive him, he was like not to recover; and hereupon her Majesty hath forgiven him.'[130] Direct appeal was also made through the form of an entertainment. When Elizabeth visited Woodstock in 1575 Sir Henry Lee organized (presumably with Dyer's connivance) an elaborate entertainment which was shot through with covert references of one kind or another, partly to convey Lee's fidelity to his mistress, but not (it would seem) entirely so. Among the pleasures arranged for the Queen was that 'in her way homeward, closely in an oak she heard the sound both of voice and instrument of the excellentest now living, whose pleasantness therein bred a great liking with a willing ear.' The song from the oak was 'The man whose thoughts against him do aspire' (ascribed to Dyer in a contemporary manuscript) and Professor Sargent has suggested that the man in the oak was Dyer himself. Here we have a fairly clear appeal to the Queen, but it is an appeal to her as a goddess to intervene *ab extra*, without conditions and without advice. On such terms an appeal might be rewarded—shortly afterwards Dyer was granted a monopoly of leather manufacturing—but the terms available are only those of servant and mistress, suppliant and goddess, lover and lady, to be used without political overtones, proffers of advice or pretexts of responsibility.

They are, moreover, terms which do not require Elizabeth's personal relations to infringe her primary role as God's representative in England. It is the supposition that this divine function is real and really important that justifies the mode of court allegory. Elizabethan moral abstractions are sometimes seen as oblique and clumsy expressions of contemporary personalities and contemporary scandals. The *Faerie Queene* alone ought to show us the inadequacy of this. If Ralegh, Leicester, Sidney, etc., appear in the poem it is only as part of the flavouring, not of the substance. Artegall may sometimes perform actions parallel to those performed by Lord Grey in real life, but this is only because Lord Grey sometimes seemed to approximate to Justice in his actions. Sometimes, that is, a human being might fill out a moral role, but his significance in that case was due to the role and not to his personality. The general attitude to the court confirms this. The court was not important because of the personalities who were in it (as, say, a modern board of directors might be) but because of its relation to the divine will. It involved, inevitably, a number of abstractions—Leadership, Virtue, Loyalty, Religion, etc. and their natural enemies, Sedition, Infidelity, Error, etc.—and contemporary men and women might appear as convenient illustrations of these qualities; but the essential matter was not personal, but abstract. Professor Lewis has said that Spenser's *Mother Hubbard's Tale* is 'probably a mass of allusions, but not a detailed and unified allegory like Dryden's *Absalom*' (*Sixteenth Century*, p. 366), and this may serve as a general distinction between the Elizabethan and the latter attitude. In *Absalom*, politics stands at the centre of human activity in a way it could not for Spenser; for Dryden, the allegory rests on a human intrigue, and the end of the unified action is a political event. For Spenser the 'action' is spiritual or intellectual and the end reached is seen in terms of what men can be rather than what they are; personal reference is therefore peripheral and inconsequential.

Lyly is obviously less sage and serious than Spenser; but when we come to examine the contemporary references in his works I do not think that we shall find that his outlook on allegory ran counter to that of Spenser (or Sidney).[131] His images of the Queen refer first to the office and only secondarily to the woman, and allegorical reference to any other English character has yet to be proved.

(ix) LYLY AND HIS PEERS

The conditions of court drama we have been describing— the kinds of actors involved, the spectacular settings, the temper of the Queen, the nature of court ritual, etc.—did not remain static throughout the Queen's reign of nearly fifty years, though enough did stay the same to allow the term 'Elizabethan court drama' a reasonably precise meaning, especially if set against Jacobean or Caroline court drama. But there *was* development, even if only in the skill and poetic power with which the conditions could be manipulated. The complex and sophisticated plays of Lyly did not spring into being without a gradual development preceding them, preparing the way, and pioneering the possibilities of a genuinely literary contribution to court ritual.

The court plays which preceded Lyly's have nearly all perished. Though the records tell us that the 'seventies and 'eighties were decades of continuous dramatic activity, Lyly's are the first plays to survive that are clearly court-plays. We are faced with a stylistic gap between *Damon and Pithias* of 1565 and *Campaspe* of 1584 as great as that between *Tottel's Miscellany* and *England's Helicon*, or (in Professor Lewis' terms) between 'Drab' and 'Golden' literature, without any indication of the path that led from one to the other.

Feuillerat has argued that if the plays of Lyly's predecessors had survived we should not now think highly of his dramatic art—an error Feuillerat avoided by rating it rather low. It is no doubt correct to react against the earlier view (found, for example, in Symonds and Dover Wilson) that the virtue of Lyly's plays lies in their originality, but this leaves the question of aesthetic merit untouched. Even if the complete drama of Westcott, Farrant and Hunnis[132] had survived, I suspect we should still find the extraordinary completeness of the imaginative world of *Campaspe* quite a new thing. For what is remarkable in Lyly is not so much the materials he uses as the sure taste with which he selects, rejects and reorganizes the materials and conventions we have been looking at in this chapter. No doubt the plays of Lyly's predecessors contained most of the elements which are fused in *Campaspe*, *Sapho* and the rest. But it is the atmosphere which fuses, not the materials fused which constitutes Lyly's claim to originality, and this cannot be taught or taken over. When C. S. Lewis says of Lyly's prose, 'Here is "Golden" literature at last' (p. 317) he is not referring to the painstaking development, but to that fusion or 'clicking' which always comes suddenly and surprisingly, though efforts may have been made to achieve the end for a long time before. The moment of success can hardly be forecast or explained; suddenly everything becomes easy; the baby begins to crawl.

Plays by Lyly's contemporaries, and especially Peele's *Arraignment of Paris* and Nashe's *Summer's Last Will and Testament* have excellencies which are closely related to those of Lyly's court comedies, and which help to relate Lyly's 'golden' manner in prose with the 'golden' versifying of other University wits. But neither Peele nor Nashe succeed as well as Lyly in forging a homogeneous world of dainty artifice and courtly reticence perfectly adapted to the boys who played or the court where they were played. Lyly's plays, no less than theirs, show the piecemeal construction which was no doubt encouraged by the conditions of performance—being shown in a world avid of novelty and fashion, where 'for music no instrument, for diet no delicate, for plays no invention but breedeth satiety before noon and contempt before night (prologue to *Midas*)'. So in all these plays we notice the short scenes, each devoted to one point, the discontinuity and variety which issued logically in plays like the 'Five plays in one' or 'Three plays in one' of 1585.[133] Gods, sovereigns, lovers, clowns appear in a bewildering procession and the wonder lies in the cunning with which 'what heretofore hath been served in several dishes for a feast, is now minced in a charger for a gallimaufry' (ibid.).

Yet for all this, Lyly's comedies never degenerate, as Nashe's and Peele's court plays do, into *shows*; they remain plays, for in them the variety is subordinated to a mode of life which contains variety, yet remains singular. The intellectual in Lyly, often distressingly obtrusive in *Euphues*, is subordinated in the plays to the elegant courtier who wears his learning lightly and keeps the scholastic possibilities of his separate scenes under a tight rein. When we set Nashe's play against Lyly's, we can see that the heady rhetoric, the enthusiasms, the violence of Nashe (the qualities which rescue his pamphlets from dullness) break up his play into a collection of entertaining possibilities, without beginning, middle or end. The play is full of pungent attitudes and comments on life, but it has neither a story to tell nor a consistent vision to expose.

The same can be said, though to a lesser degree, of Peele's *Arraignment of Paris*: the ostensible subject of the play—the judgment of Paris—does not provide a real backbone for a developing dramatic action, and Peele fills out his play with episodes, of great poetic attractiveness, which are only 'scenes from the Classical idylls', and which postpone the central action, but do not enrich it when it comes. The prologue by Ate is in fact quite misleading, since she forecasts the war of Troy, not what we get—the praise of Elizabeth. This final episode in which Diana gives the apple to the Queen does not follow inevitably from what goes before. As Miss Welsford has remarked, 'Peele keeps us among Olympians and Arcadians till the final act when we are suddenly jolted into the presence of Queen Elizabeth.'[134] Lyly never combines pastoral colouring with obvious compliments, and this in itself may be significant of the kind of tact that the others do not use. In *Endimion*, to quote Miss Welsford again, 'Instead of ending an ordinary play with a complimentary masque-like denouement, Lyly sheds his compliment over his whole plot.'[135] Lyly's advantage over his contemporaries lay in just this power to hold together in a single atmosphere the heterogeneous elements out of which his plays no less that theirs were constructed.

Two plays which are little known, and deservedly so, for they are strange and all too eventful histories, throw more light, however, on this superior power of Lyly's than do the better known works of Peele and Nashe. *The Rare Triumphs of Love and Fortune*, published in 1589 as 'played before the Queen's most excellent Majesty', was (presumably) the 'history of love and fortune' that is mentioned in the Revels Accounts as 'enacted by the Earl of Derby's servants' on 30th December 1582. It may be taken to represent the theatrical taste and expectation of the court in the period immediately preceding *Campaspe*. The second play I wish to discuss, *The Cobbler's Prophecy*, was published in 1594 as the work of Robert Wilson, who was, presumably, the actor in Leicester's Men, famous for his 'extemporal wit'. In *The Cobbler's Prophecy*, as Sir Edmund Chambers has pointed out, the stage directions '*casts comfits*' (M.S.R. l. 42) and the reference to an audience which sits, point away from a public performance towards a courtly one.[136] Presumably it was not acted before the Queen, or the title-page would mention the fact, but it seems safe to regard it as a play which aimed at the court. The date cannot be established with any precision; it must be before 1594 but later (if the comparative maturity of the style means anything) than *Love and Fortune*. I take it to represent the taste in mythological plays of a period within the span of Lyly's own play-writing.

What shows up most significantly when one places these two plays together is their similarity in tone and structure, and the contrast this makes with Lyly. Both plays are based on myth, and in both cases this involves a quarrel of the gods; in both cases it is Venus who is the culprit; she sets the other gods by the ears and requires the intervention of Jupiter. The reasons for the quarrel and the consequences of the judgment are, in both plays, stated first in terms of these divine abstractions; but we are asked to follow the abstract action in terms of particular human lives. The relation between divine decisions and human actions is handled, however, rather differently in the two plays. In *The Cobbler's Prophecy* the human story is a quasi-political one—of the good duke of Boeotia, and how he purges his court and his country of various vices. This is handled by a method somewhere between Morality and Satire, with a debate between countryman, scholar, courtier and soldier, an exhibition of the soldier's purgatory in the corrupt times of peace, a complaint by the Muses, and other demonstrations of the corrupt state. To this extent the work is a gallimaufry of Tudor conventions of 'Complaint' (as J. F. Peter has defined that word)[137] rather than an imitation of life.

In *Love and Fortune* the human story is without political overtones; it is pure romance, of a kind widely known from the prose romances so popular in the period. Fidelia, the king's daughter, loves the apparently low-born Hermione, and is obliged to go through exile and betrayal before she can marry him. The story (so strangely similar to that of *Cymbeline*) would not differ from that of the already dramatized *Paris and Vienna*, and a hundred others, were it not for the use of a debate structure to formalize into a quasi-masque what is implicit in most stories of the kind—the contest between 'Fortune' (the fathers who oppose the match) and 'Love' (the children who advance it). The use of the act structure to present a symmetrical alternation of acts ruled by Fortune and acts ruled by Venus is an obvious development of the five-act system taught in schools out of the example of Terence; his see-saw alternation of 'now fathers up, now sons' reappears here under the formal guise of a debate of the gods, dropping the bourgeois subject-matter of Terence and pouring into the Terentian mould the romantic and mythological matter of courtly entertainment. This play like the other can be seen to draw on a wide range of models to make a new and complex form.

The same general point might be made about Lyly's plays. The use of quarrelling gods to provide a framework of arbitrary decisions reappears in *Sapho and Phao*, *Gallathea*, *Midas* and *The Woman in the Moon*. But whereas in *The Cobbler's Prophecy* and *Love and Fortune* the gods merely explain, order, and circumscribe the human action, in *Sapho and Phao* and *Gallathea* they provide the natural denouement of an action which has been led forward in terms of human conduct. In order to give shape and design to the human adventures, the other dramatists have so coerced them by divine decisions that they have destroyed their independence; the play becomes the puppet of the framework. Lyly manages, however, to keep the neatness of a debate-dominated play, and yet to give a separate and sufficient charm to the human individuals who suffer under the alternatives imposed on them from above. He does this in part by avoiding the complex and emotionally weighted fables of these other plays. In *Love and Fortune* we see the 'strong' situations of love defying exile, of fatherhood lost and then suddenly recovered:

> My heart will burst if I forbear amidst this misery.
> Behold thy father thou hast found, my son Hermione;
> Thy father thou hast found, thy father I am he.
>
> (M.S.R. 952-4)

Seeing all this and being called upon for 'strong' responses in terms of real-life pathos, we are all the less willing to accept the purely formal ordering of the plot by Love and Fortune. In the Lyly plays the formality of the structure finds a natural counterpart in the formal pattern of persons; the fable moves forward by repetitions and antitheses which ask for admiration rather than involvement. Even in 'strong' situations like that of Hebe when she is bound to the stake and awaiting the monster which will devour her, we are conscious of the power of Lyly's art to rise to the situation rather than of the intrinsic power of the situation itself.

The same distinction can be expressed in terms of style. The thumping fourteeners and other metres of *Love and Fortune* express anything but that self-conscious diffidence which is the mark of the true stylist; and though the various metres of *The Cobbler's Prophecy* are an advance in this respect, they do not sufficiently control the tone of what is being said, to make the play more than a hodge-podge. Lyly's plays can be seen, when broken down into their component parts, to be no less a medley of courtly and Humanist commonplaces than the other plays; but the difference is that his variousness is not decisive against unity. The power of the stylist is just what the courtly art of the time required—the power to treat the heterogeneous strands of entertainment with tact and with grace, and while allowing each its role, to treat with elegant detachment the further claims of seriousness or enthusiasm.

IV

THE PLAYS

A REACTION that many people have to the *Brandenburg Concertos* of J. S. Bach points to a central difficulty about the comedies of John Lyly. Works like the *Brandenburg Concertos* are made up of expected elements, so far as the separate themes go; we are aware of a general difference of effect between one concerto and another, but find it difficult to analyse these differences into manageable terms. For our enjoyment in the performance arises not from the shock or emotional power of the tunes but from the formal perfection with which the expected elements are arranged, organized, combined, the skill in utilizing different parts, the unfailing resource in counterpoint—and this can be enjoyed without technical knowledge or effort. When the performance is over there is little that the uninstructed mind can lean on to re-member what makes one concerto different from another. We are left with the sensation of self-sufficient and unconfiding artifice.

To this extent the court art of 18th-century Germany is not so very different from the art of Queen Elizabeth's court. For the difficulty of remembering which of Lyly's plays is which is similar to that experienced with the *Brandenburg Concertos*, and for the same reason. The plays are exercises in a mode which is to be appreciated by the skill displayed in organizing and not by the originality of the material organized.

It is for this reason that I do not wish in this chapter to categorize the plays in the terms which are usually employed. These may be fairly represented in Dover Wilson's summary of the views of his predecessors: 'They [sc. Baker and Bond] divide the dramas into four categories: historical, of which *Campaspe* is the sole example; allegorical, which includes *Sapho and Phao, Endimion* and *Midas*; pastoral, which includes *Gallathea, The Woman in the Moon,* and *Love's Metamorphosis*; and lastly realistic, of which again there is only one example, *Mother Bombie*' (*Lyly*, p. 98). I take this to be an unsatisfactory division of the plays because it describes only the nature of the material they contain, and says nothing about the means by which the material is organized. We are made aware that Lyly is using some conventions, but it is not suggested for what purposes the conventions are being used; and this I suppose to be the important question.

I take it that Lyly's success as a dramatist lies in his power to organize his materials; certainly he differs from his predecessors and his contemporaries as court entertainers, not in the materials and conventions he uses, but (so far as we can judge from the fragmentary records that remain) in his power to hold that material within the coordinates of a single level of artifice. This is partly the literary artifice of a patterned style which is all-pervasive, and partly the mode of construction which brings together gods, kings and clowns in a dance-like progression, no one blurring the effect of the others, but each enhancing the distinctions which relate it to the others. In short, the most useful approach to Lyly's dramatic art is one, I suggest, which starts from his techniques of unification.[1]

(*a*) UNIFICATION ROUND DEBATE

(i) *Campaspe*

What is almost certainly Lyly's first play is the one known today as *Campaspe*, but more meaningfully named in the first edition *A most excellent comedy of Alexander, Campaspe and Diogenes.* It is obvious from the opening lines that this play, though his first, is, however, no piece of prentice work. Indeed it is obvious that the stylistic ease and assurance is that of a virtuoso. What may surprise us when we come to analyse its content is to find out how far this easy unity is made out of the rag-bag stock materials of Elizabethan courtly entertainment. It would seem that Lyly achieves his effect largely by arranging the various episodes, scenes, shows, as illustrations round a central debate-theme: 'Wherein lies true kingliness? Is it in the power to command others or in the power to command ourselves?' This general problem is set before us unequivocally in the opening words of the play: 'I cannot tell whether I should more commend in Alexander's victories, courage or courtesy.' and thereafter it can be found again and again, throughout the scenes.

The story of Alexander the Great's love for his captive, Campaspe, and his yielding her up to the painter Apelles appears clearly enough as an illustration of this question in the major source of the play—Pliny's *Natural History*, Bk. XXXV §10—where Alexander appears *magnus animo, maior imperio sui: nec minor hoc facto quam victoria alia*—this the play repeats when it sums up the action, 'The conquering of Thebes was not so honourable as the subduing of these thoughts.'

Again, in a book Lyly almost certainly knew, being the most famous handbook of courtliness in that age—Castiglione's *The Courtier*—, the story (taken from Pliny) is brought in to illustrate true magnanimity in a prince: 'Truly a worthy liberality of Alexander, not to give only treasure and states, but also his own affections and desire, and a token of very great love toward Apelles, not regarding (to please him withal) the displeasure of the woman that he highly loved' (Everyman edn., p. 81). The story must have appealed to a court artist like Lyly all the more in Castiglione's presentation of it, since he speaks not only of the exquisite condescension of the prince but of the special powers of the artist which made the condescension just: 'I believe Apelles conceived a far greater joy in beholding the beauty of Campaspes than did Alexander, for a man may easily believe that the love of them both proceeded of that beauty, and perhaps also for this respect Alexander determined to bestow her upon him that (in his mind) could know her more perfectly than he did' (ibid. p. 82). This is too philosophical for Lyly's play, but (all the same) would have been read gratefully by a court-artist seeking royal favour.

Another powerful means of unifying this play was found by Lyly in the setting—in ancient (though not historical) Athens. Athens was perhaps the only setting rich enough in historical and cultural memories to provide a complete cast for a variety entertainment of this kind; and certainly Lyly never found again so coherent a milieu. For the chivalric and courtly Athens of Alexander (especially the Medieval Alexander who grew up in the Western vernaculars) was easily conflated with the university Athens of the Stoa and Lyceum (again distorted by ignorant imagination in the West into a gymnasium of sages, whose lives provided Humanist alternatives to the Lives of the Saints), conflated again with the exquisite Athens of great artists—Pheidias, Zeuxis and Apelles.

Thus in one setting Lyly is able to assemble without strain a variety of elements which would appeal to the magpie taste for classical motifs, which was as much as Tudor England knew or cared to know about a Classical taste. We see (what *Doctor Faustus* suggests was popular with Renaissance princes) a vision of the greatest monarch of antiquity walking, talking and disputing with the greatest men of his civilization, and in relation to all of them showing that magnanimity (what Spenser calls 'magnificence') on which the play is centred, and which the Apelles-Campaspe story serves to illustrate. The witty sayings and quick answers of Diogenes—the Cynic philosopher who is here given some of the qualities of the 'Vice' in the morality plays, and whose popularity is attested by his appearance on the original title-page—make the same point, by showing Alexander's tolerance of criticism, and respect for intellectuals. At the same time Diogenes provides an undercurrent of gall, to sharpen our taste for the prevailing royalist adulation.

The handling of the 'intrigue' of Alexander, Apelles and Campaspe, and a welter of philosophers, pages, gentlemen, etc., gives a nice example of Lyly's use of plot as one element in his elaboration of debate. Alexander's love may be the central emotion in the plot, but Lyly only comes to it through a praise of his other virtues; and he moves away quickly to the renunciation of Campaspe as the supreme example of his virtue. We are shown first the antithesis—his prowess in war (the conquest of Thebes) and his clemency in peace, in his attitude to Timoclea, who is as proud as he is:

> *Parmenio.* Madam, you need not doubt; it is Alexander that is the conqueror.
> *Timoclea.* Alexander hath overcome, not conquered.

Parmenio. To bring all under his subjection is to conquer.
Timoclea. He cannot subdue that which is divine.
Parmenio. Thebes was not.
Timoclea. Virtue is.   (I. i. 41-7)

The tight-lipped stylization of such exchanges of self-conscious nobility gives the key to the virtue of magnanimity which is being celebrated, and we may recognize it when it reappears in the different atmosphere of Alexander's exchange with Apelles,

Alex. I had rather be setting of a battle than blotting of a board. But how have I done here?
Apel. Like a king.
Alex. I think so; but nothing more unlike a painter.
                                                        (III. iv. 109-13)

and in the more biting comedy of the exchange with Diogenes:

Alex. If Alexander have anything that may pleasure Diogenes, let me know and take it.
Diog. Then take not from me that you cannot give me, the light of the world.
Alex. What dost thou want?
Diog. Nothing that you have.
Alex. I have the world at command.
Diog. And I in contempt.
Alex. Thou shalt live no longer than I will.
Diog. But I will die whether you will or no.
Alex. How should one learn to be content?
Diog. Unlearn to covet.
Alex. Hephestion, were I not Alexander, I would wish to be Diogenes.   (II. ii. 136-49)

What is especially skilful about the management of this latter scene, and what may give us an insight into the working of Lyly's art, is its *placing*, in immediate juxtaposition to Alexander's first confession of love, with the implied inner conflict between the emotion of love and the shame that a monarch should feel this emotion, which is the subject of Hephestion's elaborate oration. The plot keeps our attention focussed on Alexander, but never concentrated on any single aspect of his life: we move round the various aspects of his courtesy—his capacity to be magnanimous to all men—gathering new information as we respectfully circle his royalty.

Lyly puts the statement of Alexander's love dilemma into Hephestion's mouth, not Alexander's; this is a good example of his tact. By so doing he avoids seeming to know anything direct about the amatory emotions of royal persons, and makes all the easier Alexander's lofty disengagement, the royal assumption that Alexander can solve all difficulties:

> *Alex.* I am a king and will command.
>
> *Hep.* You may, to yield to lust by force; but to consent to love by fear you cannot.
>
> *Alex.* Why, what is that which Alexander may not conquer as he list?
>
> *Hep.* Why, that which you say the gods cannot resist, love.
>
> *Alex.* I am a conqueror, she a captive; I as fortunate as she fair; my greatness may answer her wants and the gifts of my mind the modesty of hers. Is it not likely then that she should love? Is it not reasonable?
>
> *Hep.* You say that in love there is no reason, and therefore there can be no likelihood.
>
> *Alex.* No more, Hephestion! In this case I will use mine own counsel, and in all other, thine advice. Thou may'st be a good soldier, but never good lover. Call my page.
>
> (II. ii. 100-114)

The difficulties that modern journalists and entertainers experience when depicting the amatory emotions of royal persons may sharpen our awareness of Lyly's skill. The difficulty is one of finding a formula which will cover both the dignity of the prince and the ordinariness of the emotion; if the former is overemphasized the emotion is frozen and unreal; if the latter is played up too much we lose sight of the prince. By his carefully calculated indirection Lyly achieves both aims: Alexander is both defeated by love and a conqueror over it; the figure of the great king, always in command, is never obliterated by the image of the lover, for till the danger is over he hardly admits to the existence of the danger.

The approach to Alexander is underlined for us in a typically Lylian way, by setting against the 'plaint of love' spoken (on Alexander's behalf) by Hephestion the very different plaint of love spoken by Apelles in Act III, scene v—love again being impeded, but not by self-respect this time, but only by the fear that the lady is already the property of Alexander:

But alas! she is the paramour to a prince, Alexander, the monarch of the earth hath both her body and affection. For what is it that kings cannot obtain by prayers, threats and promises? Will not she think it better to sit under a cloth of estate like a queen than in a poor shop like a housewife? (III. v. 28-32)

Admirable humility in love is set against royal command in love and the beauty of both is enhanced by the contrast.

The plot follows romantic expectation: the humble lover wins the maid's affections, and Castiglione's unromantic Italian supposition that the lady 'was sore aggrieved to change so great a king for a painter' is given the lie. In a scene of great delicacy, well suited to the boy-actors who performed it, Lyly shows the painter and his sitter exchanging their vows, though they never come to a direct statement:

Apel. Gentlewoman, the misfortune I had with your picture will put you to some pains to sit again to be painted.
Camp. It is small pains for me to sit still, but infinite for you to draw still.
Apel. No, madam; to paint Venus was a pleasure, but to shadow the sweet face of Campaspe it is heaven . . .
. . .
But will you give me leave to ask you a question without offence?
Camp. So that you will answer me another without excuse.
Apel. Whom do you love best in the world?
Camp. He that made me last in the world.
Apel. That was a god.
Camp. I had thought it had been a man. But whom do you honour most, Apelles?
Apel. The thing that is likest you, Campaspe.
Camp. My picture?
Apel. I dare not venture upon your person. But come, let us go in; for Alexander will think it long till we return.
(IV. ii. 18-45)

But the emotions of the 'two loving worms', Apelles and Campaspe, can only be meaningful if they are recognized by the world of courtly virtue and given status by the royal assent of Alexander; the fulfilment of romantic expectations cannot end the kind of play that Lyly has written. The climax of the play is Alexander's final perception that he should not stoop to compete in love, and this completes the earlier perceptions that he should not compete in philosophy or painting: self-knowledge is the final key to royal superiority. Like Shakespeare's 'imperial votaress', who owes much in conception to Lyly, Alexander passes on, 'fancy free':

> Well, enjoy one another; I give her thee frankly, Apelles. Thou shalt see that Alexander maketh but a toy of love, and leadeth affection in fetters, using fancy as a fool to make him sport. . . .
> Go, Apelles, take with you your Campaspe; Alexander is cloyed with looking on that which thou wonderest at.
>
> (V. iv. 131-140)

The interlude of Athenian life has been but an interlude, a jest for princes, a mote in the eye of a sovereign. One of the most widely accepted signs of 'courtesy', even today, is the capacity to give up gracefully, to withdraw assertions or shrug off one's own opinions as too unimportant to matter. In this courtly art of graceful self-deprecation Lyly is everywhere a master. He describes his plays as 'dreams' or 'idle pastimes' which fade away before the real life of the court; the end of *Campaspe* renounces the action and the world and the actors of the play, leaves Alexander alone on the stage with his general, Hephestion, with a future of war before him, where magnanimity has its widest scope. There is no direct reference to Elizabeth, but the play comes to rest before her in its final definition of sovereignty. Nor does this involve any diversion of the natural movement of the plot. The final conversation sounds out in its clearest form the motto-theme which is the basis of the play: 'It were a shame Alexander should desire to command the world, if he could not command himself.' The debate-subject remains while all the action that gave it dramatic life is allowed to fall away. Royal love is a possibility, but a possibility to be mentioned in a graceful passing jest: 'And good Hephestion, when all the world is won, and every country is thine and mine, either find me out another to subdue or, of my word, I will fall in love'.

(ii) *Sapho and Phao*

Sapho and Phao is normally considered to be Lyly's second play in order of time, and some evidence suggests to us that it followed closely on the heels of the first—one being performed at court on 1st January 1584, and the other on Shrove Tuesday (3rd March) of the same year. Though it shows certain developments in the direction of the later plays, *Gallathea*, *Midas* and *Endimion*—especially in its treatment of love and its handling of court allegory—*Sapho and Phao*, however, shows nothing which may be called 'greater artistic maturity'. In some ways, indeed, it is a less successful play than *Campaspe*. The debate theme is rather hackneyed. We have here the old conflict of Venus and Diana, the principles of love and chastity, combined with a compliment to a mortal but sovereign lady who takes the place of Diana. We see her feeling but also conquering love, and being given in the end the arrows of Cupid to blunt or dispose of as she thinks fit (see above, p. 115 f. for Churchyard's handling of the same theme). The milieu lacks the definition of Athens in *Campaspe*; the mingling of mythological, allegorical and human characters is only made possible by a setting vague enough not to be noticed.

The advance from *Campaspe* is indeed less in the direction of artistry and more in the direction of the court that Lyly was seeking to entertain. Lyly's skill here is to be measured by his power to extract from a given situation the maximum compliment to the sovereign lady who was its most important auditor as well as its central image of virtue. As in *Campaspe*, he shows the love of a monarch subdued by magnanimity; Sapho's love (like Alexander's) must be felt and conquered, and can hardly be expressed as felt until it is known to be conquered. But, coming closer to the Queen, he has here made his monarch a lady, and therefore one whose power must express itself in the field of love rather than that of war; Sapho is not free to march off at the end of the play, leaving love to others. The most that Lyly can do is to show the empire of love totally subdued to its earthly goddess, its unmoved mover, and this is how the play ends: Phao in hopeless love with Sapho and disdaining Venus; Cupid disdaining Venus and adopted by Sapho; Venus helpless against Sapho, though in high rage, and finally Sapho herself—supreme in every sphere—in complete command of her own emotions, pitying Phao, controlling Cupid, despising Venus.

The plot thus constructed is indeed what Lyly calls it, 'a

labyrinth of conceits . . . now brought to an end where we first began'; the point is not that the plot leads us to any discovery, but rather that it conducts us on a tour of the landscape of love, enabling us to compare and contrast royal and less-than-royal and much-less-than-royal attitudes and so to appreciate royalty more keenly. The method of comparison and contrast (or balance and antithesis) is one that Euphuism might lead us to expect, and we have already glanced at its use in the contrast of Alexander and Apelles.

It is in pursuit of this compliment to the Queen that Lyly has altered the status and attitude of Ovid's Sapho, the main source of his picture. Ovid's heroine says of herself:

> Cupid's light darts my tender bosom move
> Still is there cause for Sapho still to love:
> So from my birth the sisters fixed my doom,
> And gave to Venus all my life to come.
>
> (Pope's translation)

Ovid's Sapho is the victim of love; but this would never do for the Queen; Lyly's Sapho can only be a conqueror, and a ruler.

It is no accident then that the play should begin with a treatment of the traditional 'dispraise of the court' topic, put into the mouth of Phao, the ferryman and rustic; and that this should be followed by a misleading 'praise of the court' from the sophisticated Venus, tired of the mechanical interests of her husband Vulcan (like many another 'motor-car widow' since): 'What doth Vulcan all day but endeavour to be as crabbed in manners as he is crooked in body? driving nails when he should give kisses and hammering hard armours when he should sing sweet amours' (I. i. 25-7). We approach the court and Sapho, the embodiment of its virtues, only gradually and circuitously, by way of the antitheses that tradition had built up round the topic. In the second scene we meet the old debate (extended by parody in the third scene) of *vita contemplativa* and *vita activa,* the one embodied in the university, the other in the court:

In universities virtues and vices are but shadowed in colours, white and black, in courts showed to life, good and bad. There times past are read of in old books, times present set down by new devices, times to come conjectured at by aim, by prophecy, or chance; here are times in perfection, not by device as fables, but in

168

execution as truths. Believe me, Pandion, in Athens you have but tombs, we in court the bodies, you the pictures of Venus and the wise goddesses, we the persons and the virtues. What hath a scholar found out by study that a courtier hath not found out by practice? (I. ii. 12-21)

The attractive centre of the play, the sovereign lady Sapho-Elizabeth, is obviously in Lyly's mind throughout this speech, but the play does not reach her yet, and the scene immediately turns away again into another 'dispraise of the court'; and it is only now that we reach the central discrimination between the 'good' court of Sapho, and the ordinary court that such as Venus might expect.

One reason for this serpentine method of exposition lies no doubt in the effort to praise the monarch and yet to suggest dissatisfaction with court-life as an occupation. Even in the good court flatterers may be at work; the goodness of the monarch does not finally answer all the criticisms that a scholar may level at the institution:

Trachinus. Cease than to lead thy life in a study, pinned with a few boards, and endeavour to be a courtier, to live in embossed ruffs.

Pandion. A labour intolerable for Pandion.

Trachi. Why?

Pandi. Because it is harder to shape a life to dissemble than to go forward with the liberty of truth.

Trachi. Why, do you think in court any use to dissemble?

Pandi. Do you know in court any that mean to live?

Trachi. You have no reason for it but an old report.

Pandi. Report hath not always a blister on her tongue.

Trachi. Ay, but this is the court of Sapho, nature's miracle, which resembleth the tree Salurus, whose root is fastened upon knotted steel, and in whose top bud leaves of pure gold.

Pandi. Yet hath Salurus blasts and water boughs, worms and caterpillers.

Trachi. The virtue of the tree is not the cause, but the Easterly wind, which is thought commonly to bring cankers and rottenness.

Pandi. Nor the excellency of Sapho the occasion, but the iniquity of flatterers who always whisper in princes' ears suspicion and sourness.

Trachi. Why then you conclude with me that Sapho for virtue hath no copartner.

Pandi. Yea, and with the judgment of the world that she is without comparison.

Trachi. We will thither straight.

Pandi. I would I might return straight.

Trachi. Why, there you may live still.

Pandi. But not still.   (I. ii. 27-56)

That love may be elegant and sophisticated without being noble, and that court ladies may be under the sway of Venus though tending the person of Sapho, is made clear by the conversations of Sapho's six court ladies, next displayed by Lyly. Here the early court comedy looks forward most obviously to the satirical comedy of Jonson and Marston, but the comparison only shows how little Lyly is concerned to attack. In the reaction of the court ladies to the beauty that Venus has bestowed on Phao he shows the cool self-interest, the lightness of concern, the self-sufficiency of court affections:

Mileta. No, no, men are good souls (poor souls!), who never enquire but with their eyes, loving to father the cradle though they but mother the child. Give me their gifts, not their virtues; a grain of their gold weigheth down a pound of their wit; a dram of 'give me' is heavier than an ounce of 'hear me'. Believe me, ladies, 'give' is a pretty thing.

Ismena. I cannot but oftentimes smile to myself to hear men call us weak vessels, when they prove themselves broken hearted; us frail, when their thoughts cannot hang together, studying with words to flatter and with bribes to allure, when we commonly wish their tongues in their purses, they speak so simply, and their offers in their bellies, they do it so peevishly.

Mileta. It is good sport to see them want matter; for then fall they to good manners, having nothing in their mouths but 'sweet mistress', wearing our hands out with courtly kissings when their wits fail in courtly discourses; now ruffling their hairs, now setting their ruffs; then gazing with their eyes, then sighing with a privy wring by the hand, thinking us like to be wooed by signs and ceremonies.   (I. iv. 22-40)

There is nothing here, however, of the ridiculous, and when we set the episode beside similar scenes in *Cynthia's Revels* we see how little of the impulse to reform there is in Lyly's art.

Lyly's concern is with feminine emotions in a courtly setting; the male side of love, here as elsewhere in Lyly, is given short shrift. Phao, made beautiful at the whim of a goddess, is important only as provoking the reactions of Sapho, Venus herself, and the court ladies. Even to the extent that he does act he stands in the shadow of his mentor, the aged Sybil (herself the victim of love), who propels him towards the court, and prophesies (for our benefit rather than his, since there are no repercussions in his history) the power of courtly infidelity.

It is only after all these aspects of the theme have been announced that Sapho herself appears (Act II, scene ii). It is typical of Lyly's lack of interest in intrigue that he gives no emphasis to the first meeting of his central characters. In a very short scene (some thirty-three lines) each, as it were, passes by the other, in a throng of courtiers. Lyly's characteristic effects are made by obliquities, and this is no exception. He has no technique for the direct statement of love, but is accustomed to aim his statements at the auditor who has a full awareness of the pattern rather than at anyone inside the play. Sapho and Phao make a series of carefully balanced statements and then pass on:

> *Phao.* What gentlewoman is this?
> *Criticus.* Sapho, a lady here in Sicily.
> *Sapho.* What fair boy is that?
> *Trachinus.* Phao, the ferryman of Syracusa.
> *Phao.* I never saw one more brave. Be all ladies of such majesty?
> *Criticus.* No, this is she that all wonder at and worship.
> *Sapho.* I have seldom seen a sweeter face. Be all ferrymen of that fairness?
> *Trachinus.* No madam, this is he that Venus determined among men to make the fairest. (II. ii. 2-12)

That Sapho and Phao should so touch and part is necessary for the plot and for the attitudes it is to convey; but the plot proceeds as an accumulation of carefully contrasted attitudes, not as the history of an emotional entanglement, so that what is given here is precisely in tune with the way the play moves. Phao suffers for love of Sapho, held back by knowledge of his unworthiness, though pressed forward by the Sybil, with a wealth of sophisticated advice plundered from the *Ars Amatoria*. Sapho suffers for love of Phao, held back by knowledge of his unworthiness and the disproportion of their estates. Her self-command (repeating Alexander's, as Phao's humility repeats Apelles') keeps the knowledge of her love even from her waiting-gentlewomen, and though they bring Phao to her, carrying medicines, the nearest the two ever come to a declaration is the delicate exchange of puns and ambiguities which follows:

> *Phao*. Indeed I know no herb to make lovers sleep but heartsease which because it groweth so high I cannot reach, for . . .
> *Sapho*. For whom?
> *Phao*. For such as love.
> *Sapho*. It groweth very low, and I can never stoop to it, that . . .
> *Phao*. That what?
> *Sapho*. That I may gather it. But why do you sigh so, Phao?
> *Phao*. It is mine use, madam.
> *Sapho*. It will do you harm, and me too; for I never hear one sigh but I must sigh't also.
> *Phao*. It were best then that your Ladyship give me leave to be gone, for I can but sigh.
> *Sapho*. Nay, stay; for now I begin to sigh I shall not leave though you be gone. But what do you think best for your sighing, to take it away?
> *Phao*. Yew, madam.
> *Sapho*. Me?
> *Phao*. No, madam, yew of the tree.
> *Sapho*. Then will I love yew the better. And indeed I think it would make me sleep too; therefore all other simples set aside, I will simply use only yew.
> *Phao*. Do, madam; for I think nothing in the world so good as yew.
> *Sapho*. Farewell for this time. (III. iv. 61-85)

It is the method of Lyly's art to accumulate parallels; having overheard the love plaints of the noble Sapho and the reticent Phao, we are now in a position to relish the effect of love on Venus, who is caught in the snare she herself constructed —Phao's beauty:

> O Venus! unhappy Venus! who in bestowing a benefit upon a man hast brought a bane unto a goddess. What perplexities dost thou feel! O fair Phao! and therefore made fair to breed in me a frenzy! O would that when I gave thee golden locks to curl thy

head I had shackled thee with iron locks on thy feet! And when
I nursed thee, Sapho, with lettuce, would it had turned to hemlock.
(IV. ii. 5-11)

This is the centre of the play, this section of contrasted images
of love, from which by a 'look here upon this picture, and
on this' technique, we may learn where true virtue lies and
what it is like. It remains only for the plot to express our
preference in a settled form by means of some displacement
of the character relationships. This Lyly effects by dispatching
Cupid as an *enfant perdu* against Sapho, so allowing Sapho to
capture and disarm him as Diana was traditionally allowed to
do. The play thus can end with Sapho alone in command of
herself, Cupid and Syracuse, with Venus departed in a whirl
of threats and with Phao bidding farewell to the queenly figure
which is left highlighted:

> This shall be my resolution, wherever I wander, to be as I were ever
> kneeling before Sapho, my loyalty unspotted though unrewarded.
> With as little malice will I go to my grave as I did lie withal in my
> cradle. My life shall be spent in sighing and wishing, the one for
> my bad fortune, the other for Sapho's good.   (V. iii. 17-22)

It is fairly clear throughout *Sapho and Phao*, and I have
assumed it without question above, that the chaste and
lovable sovereign of the play is intended to be a complimentary
image of Queen Elizabeth. The difference of the play from
Campaspe would seem to be largely dictated by this intention.
But the intention can be carried too far and the mode of
relationship made too simple. The court world of *Sapho and Phao*
is a world of love, but this hardly argues any private intention
on the part of Lyly. He assumes everywhere that 'Courtiers
[call for] comedies, their subject is love' (as he says in the Paul's
prologue to *Midas*) and there is a general agreement everywhere
that love and honour are the principal interests of courtiers.
The love-life of Sapho may stand for the court-life of Elizabeth,
but is does not follow that its image of love refers to any love
affair involving Elizabeth. Bond assumes that the play depicts
the wooing of Elizabeth by the Duke of Alençon, which
meandered on from 1578 till 1582, and Feuillerat agrees with
him. On mere grounds of date this is extremely improbable.
The Chamber Accounts tell us that Lyly was paid for two

performances in 1584 (on 1st January and Shrove Tuesday [3rd March]). It would be an odd coincidence if his first two plays, published in 1584 as 'played before the Queen's Majesty on New Year's Day at Night' and 'played . . . on Shrove Tuesday' were not the same plays. But even if this were not so, the points we have made about courtly allegory in the preceding chapter ought to rule out Alençon on *a priori* grounds. As I have already stated, there is nothing to show that Elizabeth relished interference in state business at all, and much to show that she regarded the persons of friendly princes as above criticism and even beyond discussion.

Nevertheless there are in this play references of a more particular kind than can be justified by the general concepts of courtly adoration and royal command. As I have suggested above, there is a continuing strain of reference to flattery and self-seeking which cannot be explained (as Diogenes' scorn of courtiers could be) as a sauce to make the praise more palatable; indeed it has the air of having been dragged in for a purpose outside the obvious aims of the play. I have already quoted the conversation between Trachinus and Pandion in Act I, scene ii, with its praise of Sapho, and complaint about the 'blasts and water-boughs, worms and caterpillers' which cling about her royalty. There are signs that this has been tailored to fit a particular situation. The characteristics which are applied to the 'Easterly wind' in that passage are those which properly belong to the South wind, 'commonly thought to bring cankers and rottenness'. 'The tree Salurus' in this passage looks forward to Sapho's dream in Act IV, scene iii—another passage which cannot be explained in the general terms which suffice for the main plot of the play.

> What dreams are these, Mileta? and can there be no truth in dreams? yea, dreams have their truth. Methought I saw a stock-dove or woodquist, I know not how to term it, that brought short straws to build his nest in a tall Cedar, where, whiles with his bill he was framing his building, he lost as many feathers from his wings as he laid straws in his nest; yet scambling to catch hold to harbour in the house he had made he suddenly fell from the bough where he stood. And then pitifully casting up his eyes, he cried in such terms (as I imagined) as might either condemn the nature of such a tree or the daring of such a mind. Whilst he

lay quaking upon the ground and I gazing on the Cedar, I might perceive Ants to breed in the rind, coveting only to hoard, and caterpillars to cleave to the leaves, labouring only to suck; which caused mo leaves to fall from the tree than there did feathers before from the dove. Methought, Mileta, I sighed in my sleep, pitying both the fortune of the bird and the misfortune of the tree; but in this time quills began to bud again in the bird, which made him look as though he would fly up, and then wished I that the body of the tree would bow that he might but creep up the tree . . . and so I waked. (IV. iii. 1-22)

This occurs in an episode where the waiting-gentlewomen as well as Sapho tell their dreams; but their dreams are all interpreted in the text; only Sapho's remains without explanation. Even so, certain features of the vision can be explained in terms of the play itself. The cedar, here as elsewhere in Renaissance iconography, is the noble tree whose height betokens royalty or power, and must represent Sapho herself. The stockdove is chosen presumably for its association with love (Venus), and as an image of guilelessness, in its lack of gall. Yet its feathers enable it to fly up to the height of the cedar, and even to begin to acquire a permanent position (or *nest*) with the Queen. But such feathers (? a pun on 'favours') are not lasting; while he is making a daring effort to secure his hold on a high position he falls to the base ground, his feathers (or powers of flying high) stripped from him. On the ground he complains, and he finds justification for complaint when he sees ants (the ambitious and selfish) and 'caterpillers of the commonwealth' (so Bushy and Bagot are called in *Richard II*) eating away the substance of the court, and not dislodged as he has been. Sapho sighs and wishes she could [?openly] re-establish the stockdove in royal favour.

On one level at least the stockdove must be Phao and the effort to build a nest must be Phao's desire to love the exalted Sapho; while Sapho's sighing and wishing reflects, presumably (as in III. iv. 74 ff.), her desire to condescend in love. But there is nothing at this level to touch on the question of ants and caterpillers. In the play Phao has neither lost a position of trust he formerly occupied nor has he any relation to parasites and flatterers in the court.

There is a third passage in the play which takes up the same extrinsic themes in the same mysterious way. This is the prophecy which Sybil makes in Act II, scene i:

> Thou shalt get friendship by dissembling, love by hatred; unless thou perish, thou shalt perish. In digging for a stone thou shalt reach a star. Thou shalt be hated most because thou art loved most. Thy death shall be feared and wished. So much for prophecy, which nothing can prevent; and this for counsel which thou may'st follow. Keep not company with ants that have wings, nor talk with any near the hill of a mole; where thou smellest the sweetness of serpents' breath, beware thou touch no part of the body. Be not merry among those that put bugloss in their wine and sugar in thine. If any talk of the eclipse of the sun, say thou never sawest it. Nourish no conies in thy vaults nor swallows in thine eaves. Sow next thy vine, mandrage, and ever keep thine ears open and thy mouth shut, thine eyes upward and thy fingers down; so shalt thou do better than otherwise, though never so well as I wish. (II. i. 124-38)

This seems to have little or no relevance to the career of Phao as we see it, and to be full of court innuendos. *The eclipse of the sun* must refer to the death or overthrow of the prince, and the injunction to keep *thine eyes upward and thy fingers down* must mean 'remain in a posture of supplication but do not finger the favours you hope to obtain'. This would seem to imply the expectation of some royal gift, which any ill-considered word or thought might endanger.

Have we any clue what these passages might mean? T. W. Baldwin has analysed the second passage and suggests that the stockdove is Lyly himself, and that the fall from the tree refers to the approaching loss of the Blackfriars' lease (see above, p. 72 ff.) with the consequent effect on Lyly's venture as an impresario. Lyly, he supposes, is appealing for royal favour to succour the company.[2] This interpretation has the merit of dealing only with affairs that might be supposed to lie between the dramatist and the Queen, and of detaching these affairs from the main plot (which is well enough accounted for in general terms); it may also be reinforced by the Epilogue to *Endimion* (see below); but it leaves many of the terms in the speech unexplained. The *ants and caterpillers* could refer, I suppose, to some rival theatrical enterprise, which cost the Revels Office more money (*caused mo leaves to fall from the tree*), but since this is only one of a train of references to flatterers and parasites I do not think it is sufficient. The whole situation seems to be put closer to the Queen than can be justified in the case of a theatrical enterprise. No one could pretend that the return of the Blackfriars property to the owner was due to 'flatterers who always whisper in princes' ears suspicion and sourness'. The case would seem to be nearest that of a single courtier in competition with others for a personal favour from the sovereign. The courtier could be Oxford, whose servant Lyly was, and who was still convalescing from his disgrace. But indeed it could be any courtier; for it was the perpetual habit of the court suitor

> To fret thy soul with crosses and with cares
> To eat thy heart through comfortless despairs,
> To fawn, to crouch, to wait, to ride, to run,
> To spend, to give, to want, to be undone.
> (Spenser, *Mother Hubbard's Tale*, 903-6)

I do not know the meaning of these references in *Sapho and Phao*, and I take it that I do not need to know them in order to appreciate either the aesthetic merit of the play or its general relation to the court of Queen Elizabeth. As in *The Faerie Queene*, the general reference may carry a particular reference inside it, but the particular reference can only be apposite if it particularizes the general one. Therefore, to know the 'secret history' of the play might satisfy our curiosity, but is not necessary to our understanding of the drama.

(iii) *Midas*

These discriminations are especially important when we turn to a second group of debate-plays (*Endimion* and *Midas*), where the allegorical intent is much more important as a mode of sharpening and localizing the issues at debate. The intention to refer to recent history is more obvious and more necessary in *Midas* than in *Endimion*, and I shall in consequence begin with the easier case and only move from that to the more controversial one. This is probably a reversal of the chronological order, which has also been disrupted by my postponement of *Gallathea*. I hope that the same excuse will serve for both defaults—that my primary purpose is an exposition of the various modes of the plays, not a consideration of Lyly's chronology.

The basic plot of *Midas* is taken from Lyly's favourite classical authority, Ovid, who tells two stories of Midas: first, how he desired the gift of the golden touch, how he came to repent it and was absolved; and, second, how Midas was fitted with asses ears for preferring the music of Pan to that of Apollo. Lyly, as in the plays we have so far examined, places this story inside a debate structure. He shows that Midas' judgment that gold is the best of gifts results from a dispute between War (Martius), Wealth (Mellacrites) and Love (Eristus), here presented as the counsellors of their monarch. These three appear throughout the play as the modes of temptation to which a sovereign is most subject, and serve to give a philosophic and even political tinge to activities which, in Ovid, are merely part of the arbitrary and inexplicable relationship of gods and men. In each case the end proposed to Midas is improper: war is desired to give Midas power over neighbouring states; love is to be pursued for the end of 'such a tender wantonness that nothing is thought of but love, a passion proceeding of beastly lust, and coloured with a courtly name of love' (II. i. 61-3); gold is sought because it can buy love, monarchy and even justice:

> Justice herself that sitteth wimpled about the eyes doth it not because she will take no gold, but that she would not be seen blushing when she takes it; the balance she holdeth are not to weigh the right of the cause but the weight of the bribe. She will put up her naked sword if thou offer her a golden scabbard.
>
> (I. i. 90-94)

The story of Midas' golden gift shows how gold leads to sterility. The ills attendant on the other advices are also illustrated in the course of the play, though less fully and less coherently. A point of view opposite to that of the three counsellors is also indicated, by the person of the king's daughter, Sophronia (her name is meant to be indicative of her wisdom); it is she who speaks the clearest denunciation of the different advices and their effects on Midas:

> The love he hath followed—I fear unnatural—the riches he hath got—I know unmeasurable—the wars he hath levied—I doubt

unlawful—hath drawn his body with grey hairs to the grave's mouth, and his mind with eating cares to desperate determinations ... Let Phrygia be an example of chastity, not lust; liberality, not covetousness; valour, not tyranny. I wish not your bodies banished, but your minds, that my father and your king may be our honour and the world's wonder. (II. i. 88-107)

At the end of the play when Midas comes to self-knowledge, having learned humility and discretion as a result of his double misfortune (and this final episode is, of course, added to Ovid) it is in precisely these terms that his palinode is expressed:

I will therefore yield myself to Bacchus and acknowledge my wish to be vanity; to Apollo and confess my judgment to be foolish; to Mars and say my wars are unjust; to Diana and tell my affection hath been unnatural. (V. iii. 58-61)

This framework of moral debate enables the play to make topical reference of a fairly obvious kind without disrupting the structure of the entertainment; where there is already a moral pattern worked into the play, the localization of some of the terms does not require much readjustment of focus. The assimilation of Midas to Philip II of Spain occurs in one of the spaces left open by the framework of debate—the temptation to war, for which Ovid supplies no material. The use of a contemporary reference at this point may sharpen our apprehension of ambition and ill-judgment, but the place of these qualities in the general scheme would still be clear to a reader who had not made the equation between the moral and the political aspects.

In fact, there is nothing to make the equation even plausible till we get to Act III. There, in the long complaint by Midas, which fills the greater part of scene i, we hear, among other confessions:

Have not I made the sea to groan under the number of my ships; and have they not perished that there was not two left to make a number? ... Have not I enticed the subjects of my neighbour princes to destroy their natural kings? ... A bridge of gold did I mean to make in that island where all my navy could not make a breach. Those islands did I long to touch, that I might turn them to gold, and myself to glory. But unhappy Midas . . . being now become a shame to the world, a scorn to that petty prince and to thyself a consumption. A petty prince, Midas? no, a prince protected by the gods, by nature, by his own virtue and his subjects' obedience. Have not all treasons been discovered by miracle, not counsel? that do the gods challenge. Is not the country walled with huge waves? that doth nature claim. Is he not through the whole world a wonder for wisdom and temperance? that is his own strength. Do not all his subjects (like bees) swarm to preserve the king of bees? that their loyalty maintaineth. (III. i. 31-60)

In the period of the Armada it would be hard to hear of a great fleet miraculously frustrated 'that there was not two to make a number' without thinking of Philip II, and there is nothing in the context to contradict the thought. Again, the unqualified praise of a monarch in Elizabethan court entertainment always requires us to glance towards Elizabeth, and when we hear of Midas' enemy as a paragon, whom he seeks to destroy by plots, by invasion and by lavish expenditure, it is natural to extend the meaning to cover the general opposition between Spain and England. Further, Lyly had already identified Elizabeth with Sapho, and Sapho appears in Ovid as the Queen of Lesbos. Here the ruler of Lesbos is Midas' enemy. Identification cannot be resisted when all the evidence points one way.

But the identification of Midas with Philip of Spain does not take us very far into the play or require us to interpret every scene allegorically. It does not affect the sub-plot; the scene of Sophronia and her ladies-in-waiting, engaged in a choice between story-telling, song and dancing obviously parodies the original choice between Wealth, War and Love, but it does not follow it down into its political implications. Its point would seem to be made if we accept it as a vignette of courtly grace, otherwise absent from the play.

Halpin and Bond[3] wish to extend the allegory to figures other than Midas. They would see Martius, for example, as a pseudonym for the Duke of Alva; the argument against this is simply that it seems an unnecessary restriction of the range of reference that the name and the attitude implies; but I would not deny that the persons of Alva could have occurred to

Elizabethans as well as moderns as a local representative of the ambitious bloodthirstiness which Martius represents in general.

The golden gift has an obvious and utilized congruity with the treasure which Spain extracted from the Indies—'the utmost parts of the West, where all the guts of the earth are gold' (II. i. 101)—but we need not seek for political meaning in the fact that this is the gift of Bacchus nor in the bathing in Pactolus which removes the curse. These belong to the source, and it is sufficient for court allegory if the play at some points makes clear the relevance of the modern parallel.

The second story which Ovid tells about Midas starts from his false judgment in the case of Apollo *v.* Pan, and proceeds through his sentence to wear asses ears to the final episode of the blabbing reeds—the means by which the world learns about his deformity. Lyly presents all these without notable alteration, and adds a final scene in which Midas repents of his misjudgment (and of his inordinate ambitions) and is restored to human shape. The addition of this second story does not, however, add anything to the dramatic impact of the play; can it have been intended to add to the allegorical import? Halpin wished to identify the contest between the gods with the Reformation and supposed that Midas' mistaken preference for the music of Pan stood for Philip's adherence to the Roman Catholic church. This is attractive on *a priori* grounds, since *pan* (=all) and *catholic* are cognate terms. But no one at all sensitive to literary atmosphere could read the scene of the contest and suppose that it was intended allegorically; there is nothing in the scene which is not perfectly explicable in terms of the literal meaning. Moreover Pan appears too often in Elizabethan pastoral allegory to represent approved English figures to make the identification at all provable. Pan is here, as there, the representative of rustic poetry, and the qualities ascribed to him bear only a converse relation to those ascribed in this period to Roman Catholicism: subtlety, treachery, pride, empty ostentation (Spenser's Archimago, Duessa and Orgoglio).

Indeed the figure and song of Pan (as we have it) may seem to readers less asinine than Midas to be as good (in its own way) as that of Apollo, though lacking the music we cannot be confident—and we cannot even be sure that the songs we possess mirror Lyly's intention. The 'low' rustic style has its own charm here in the vein of

> When the merry bells ring round,
> And the jocund rebecks sound
> To many a youth and many a maid
> Dancing in the chequer'd shade.

It is certainly not true that 'Pan [hath showed] himself a rude satyr, neither keeping measure nor time' in lines like

> Cross-gartered swains and dairy-girls
> With faces smug and round as pearls
> When Pan's shrill pipe begins to play
> With dancing wear out night and day.

It would be a curious malformation of intention if Lyly's supposed satire on the Roman Catholic church ended by appearing admirable for the very qualities that Protestants thought of as their own peculiars—homely honesty and down-rightness. It seems wisest to drop the whole idea of allegorical intention in this episode and view the musical contest as just another example of Midas' instability of judgment, put in to give added weight to his repentance, and providing the audience with an opportunity to call Philip of Spain an ass.

I have discussed the temptation to wealth, where Ovid supplied the material, and that to war, where contemporary history seems to be the primary source; what of the third temptation, that of Eristus or Love? Sophronia says that Midas' love is 'unnatural' (II. i. 88) and Midas repeats the word in his palinode. On the other hand, the only love mentioned in the play is that of Midas for Celia, whose conquest is anticipated in Act I ('Celia, chaste Celia shall yield'), but who remains chaste in Act II, her words being as follows:

> if gold could have allured mine eyes, thou knowest Midas that commandeth all things to be gold had conquered; if threats might have feared my heart, Midas, being a king, might have commanded my affections; if love, gold or authority might have enchanted me, Midas had obtained by love, gold and authority.
>
> (II. i. 20-25)

The rebuttal of the three temptations of gold, love and force by Celia (the name is no doubt intended to be significant) aligns her clearly with Sophronia as representing the virtue in the play, but does not in the least explain Midas' unnatural love. Bond says that Celia is the daughter of Mellacrites—on the evidence I suppose of I. ii. 1 f., where Licio says to Petulus: 'Thou servest Mellacrites, and I his daughter'; but there is nothing to suggest that the daughter is Celia. What is clear is that she is also beloved of Eristus, 'whose eyes are stitched on Celia's face, and thoughts gyved to her beauty' (II. i. 60 f.); it is also clear that she does not return any of this love, since she says of herself, 'I am free from love, and unfortunate to be beloved'. There is no evidence in the play of a mode of relationship which would make Midas' love 'unnatural', and I suspect that the pursuit of the question along these lines is misguided anyway. Eristus is nothing but the type of the lover and so Celia, I suspect, is only the object of love in general, a heaven of beauty that it is 'unnatural' to attempt by earthly love:

> Celia hath sealed her face in my heart, which I am no more ashamed to confess than thou that Mars hath made a scar in thy face, Martius. (II. ii. 81-3)

There is a case here for regarding the difficulty as likely to have arisen from too precise a conceptual framework and too slight a dramatic interest.

This play is also remarkable (and the unusualness may be related to the difficulties I have just discussed) for the lack of interest in courtly love. All Lyly's plays, except this one, turn on the emotion of love, seen as the main motive for human activities. Love shows court life at its most intense, and moves gods or sovereigns to descend into human life and reveal their powers in a context of human passion. The absence of this favourite theme in *Midas* is all the more remarkable in that the framework of debate allows for it so clearly. Martius and Mellacrites have their attitudes exposed at length, but Eristus is confined to a few undeveloped statements. Bond's suggestion that the 'unnatural' love of Midas is meant to be filled out by knowledge of contemporary scandal is completely unconvincing. It might be supposed that the topical allusions to Philip of Spain took up so much space (*Midas* is the second longest of Lyly's plays) that there was no room left for a developed image of love, natural or unnatural. On the other hand, however, one must note that the subject on which the play is centred could never have been intended for a purpose other than that of exposing foolish monarchy. Lyly's other plays of courtly intrigue centre on a divinely good monarch, but here this Alexander-Sapho-Cynthia figure has to be deduced from her opposite, Midas.

(iv) *Endimion*

No one could accuse *Endimion*, Lyly's other play supposedly devoted to court allegory, of lacking the dimension of love; for this is the element in which the whole play moves. The use of the legend of Endimion, about the hopeless love adventures of a shepherd and the moon, is a fairly obvious case of adapting the feelings of love to shadow forth the complex of fear, ambition, admiration that real courtiers felt about their real sovereign; for there can be little doubt that the Cynthia of the play is the Cynthia of Ralegh and Ben Jonson—Queen Elizabeth herself. The play uses a strain of high-flown adoration towards Cynthia, which seems to be unnaturally intense if Cynthia is only the moon. Take the oracle that Eumenides sees in the magic well:

> When she whose figure of all is the perfectest, and never to be measured—always one, yet never the same—still inconstant, yet never wavering—shall come and kiss Endimion in his sleep, he shall then rise; else never.　　　　(III. iv. 155-58)

This mood of abject admiration falls on every character when Cynthia is mentioned. Lyly nowhere gives evidence of attachment of this kind to ideal concepts, whether of Love or Truth or Heavenly Beauty or what-you-will; but this is precisely the attitude to Elizabeth that *Sapho and Phao* and *Midas* have prepared us for.

　　The outline of the plot certainly renders an image which Elizabeth could take as a graceful compliment to her virtue and attractiveness, and which it is hard not to see as a general image of court life. We have already noted the complimentary method of *Sapho and Phao*, where Sapho the queen is left constantly but hopelessly loved by the hero, who is in his turn constantly but hopelessly pursued by another lady with a strong claim on the affections. Lyly uses the same formula here, but makes it more integral to the plot. A noble gentleman hopelessly adoring, from the distance of humility, a goddess-queen who reigns over a 'court' of ladies, is betrayed by his very faithfulness and high-minded constancy to the forces of ingratitude, treachery and envy which lurk unseen around the throne. Evil spells cast him into a perpetual sleep; only the faithfulness of a friend breaks the dark night of disfavour, and reveals to Cynthia the true natures of the faithful and the unfaithful. Cynthia, ever gracious though ever distant, is willing to end the spell by her redeeming kiss. Virtue is rewarded by royal condescension and the corrupters and deceivers are known for what they are. The story reads, as I say, like a generalized transcript of court intrigue, written from the point of view of one who has an axe to grind about unfair disgrace and a hope of reaching favour again by means of judicious flattery.

Moreover, the details of the particular vision that Endimion relates when he is recovered from his sleep are strongly reminiscent of the dream of Sapho which we have already considered as possible allegory, and would seem to derive (as does the other) from an image of court-intrigue and corruption obscuring the true merit of the speaker, and carrying aloft the opportunists and the time-servers:

> There, portrayed to life, with a cold quaking in every joint I beheld many wolves barking at thee, Cynthia, who having ground their teeth to bite, did with striving bleed themselves to death. There might I see ingratitude with an hundred eyes, gazing for benefits, and with a thousand teeth gnawing on the bowels wherein she was bred. Treachery stood all clothed in white, with a smiling countenance, but both her hands bathed in blood. Envy, with a pale and meagre face (whose body was so lean that one might tell all her bones, and whose garment was so tottered that it was easy to number every thread) stood shooting at stars, whose darts fell down again on her own face. There might I behold drones or beetles I know not how to term them, creeping under the wings of a princely eagle, who, being carried into her nest, sought there to suck that vein that would have killed the Eagle. I mused that things so base should attempt a fact so barbarous or durst imagine a thing so bloody.
>
> (V. i. 119-34)

The 'drones and beetles' here, which suck the life-blood of the Eagle, closely correspond to the 'ants . . . and caterpillers'

which suck away the life of the royal cedar in *Sapho*. What is
lacking here is a figure equivalent to that of the loyal stockdove,
whose guilelessness destroyed his hope of favour; but this is
supplied by the whole history of Endimion, and more particularly by the passage immediately preceding, where he
refuses 'counsels and policies' when they are offered to him and
has to content himself in consequence with 'pictures'. I take
this to mean that Endimion could have given Cynthia political
advice or counsel which would have protected her; but he
refrained out of humility and now has to content himself with
a knowledge (?and literary portrait) of the falsehood at
court.

Perhaps we should connect with these passages part of the
Epilogue to *Endimion*, spoken at court presumably by one of
the actors:

> Dread Sovereign, the malicious that seek to overthrow us
> with threats do but stiffen our thoughts and make them sturdier
> in storms; but if your Highness vouchsafe with your favourable
> beams to glance upon us, we shall not only stoop but with
> all humility lay both our hands and hearts at your Majesty's
> feet.

The use of 'we' here suggests that the aggrieved party can be
represented by the Pauls' boys. If this is the same grievance
as is represented in the play itself (and why should we multiply
grievances without necessity?) then the relationship with
Cynthia expressed in the vision must refer to Lyly and his
theatrical enterprise. This would be a rather unexciting truth,
and would require us to dismiss the charge that 'the malicious'
'would have killed the Eagle' as rhetorical exaggeration.
Certainly, for whatever reason, the notion has found no
favour with commentators, who have preferred, now for over a
hundred years, to brave illogicality in the pursuit of more
romantic truths.

The first in this field was the Rev. N. J. Halpin, who
published in 1843 a treatise called *Oberon's Vision*; in this
(among other implausibilities) he identified Endimion with
Leicester and suggested that the sleep in the play figured the
disgrace which followed the discovery of his (third) marriage
in 1579. This view, with minor modifications, has been accepted

by G. P. Baker, in his edition of the play (1894), by Bond in the
Complete Works, by Schelling in his *Elizabethan Drama* and most
recently by F. S. Boas in his *Queen Elizabeth in Drama* (1950).
But powerfully backed though the case for Leicester may have
been, it does not seem to have had much except human
credulity to support it. There is no evidence that plays were
ever performed before Elizabeth to support Leicester or any
other faction in the court. Even if such plays existed, it seems
highly improbable that Lyly should write one in support of
Leicester. He was never a member of Leicester's faction; he
was the servant of the Earl of Oxford, who belonged to the
opposite party. Again, it is clear that Halpin was ignorant of
dates, and that Bond (and Feuillerat for the sake of his own
theory) distort the external evidence. The title-page tells us
that the play was performed at Candlemas before Elizabeth
when she was at Greenwich; there is only one Candlemas in our
period which the records say was spent at Greenwich—2nd
February 1588—and we must give this as the date of the play.
This is too late, however, to give any relation to Leicester's
disgrace, or to the affairs of James VI that Feuillerat thinks
relevant.

If we must find, in the plot of *Endimion*, any reference to
the court affairs of the time, it seems better to retire altogether
from the state affairs and to look at the more private intrigues
of the court. From this point of view the theory of Professor
Josephine Waters Bennett has much to recommend it.[4] Mrs
Bennett accepts the 1588 dating and remains inside the
framework of Lyly's known allegiance to Oxford. As I have
noted above, Oxford quarrelled in 1580 with associates whom
he accused of secret Papism. As a result he was entered into
temporary custody and disfavour. In the following year he was
accused of adultery with Anne Vavasour, one of the Queen's
ladies, and this time the disfavour was more lasting. It was not
until 1583 that the Queen consented to receive him again.
Anne Vavasour had also been imprisoned, and in the Tower
she may have been in the custody of Sir Henry Lee, who had
apartments there. Certainly she later became Lee's mistress.
In the Woodstock or Ditchley Entertainment in 1592 Lee
refers to a long sleep with which the Fairy Queen had punished
him for not guarding the pictures left in his care, pictures first

seen at the Woodstock Entertainment of 1575. Lee failed in his duty, because

> lo, unhappy I was overtaken,
> By fortune forced, a stranger lady's thrall,
> Whom when I saw, all former care forsaken,
> To find her out I lost myself and all,
> Through which neglect of duty 'gan my fall.[5]

The 'stranger lady' would seem to be Anne Vavasour, and Mrs Bennett supposes that the sleep refers to a disgrace which she conjectures to have been suffered by Lee after the seduction of his fair captive. If *Endimion* is taken to refer to this affair, viewing it from the side of Oxford, then Tellus who casts Endimion into an enchanted sleep must be Anne Vavasour, who accused Oxford of being the father of her child and so cast him into the dark night of royal disfavour; and Corsites the 'captain' who guards Tellus in her imprisonment must be Sir Henry Lee. Mrs Bennett supposes that the 'kiss' which restores Endimion is the pension of one thousand pounds per annum which the Queen granted to Oxford in 1586.

As I have stated, Mrs Bennett's interpretation of the play has many advantages; but it also contains some improbabilities. If the play was performed in 1588, the matters it refers to were finished and done with. Mrs Bennett thinks that it *commemorates* the granting of the pension, and gives Oxford's side of the earlier difficulties. On the face of it this seems unlikely. We do not know that the pension and the disgrace were in any way connected, and it would seem impolitic to rake up the disgrace in order to commemorate the pension. But even if we were to grant the possibility of such a play, we should still have to prove that the play as we have it lives up to the intention, and this is not clear at all points. Oxford's apologia would, presumably, move along the following lines: Oxford was innocent of the accusations that Anne Vavasour levelled against him; she on the other hand was not innocent, witness her seduction by Sir Henry Lee. If this was Lyly's brief, the play mismanages it grossly. Mrs Bennett supposes the 'picture of Endimion' which Tellus weaves in her imprisonment, and which she is allowed to keep at the end of the play (V. iii. 251-5) is the child born to Anne Vavasour. But Oxford denied paternity, and it would have been indiscreet of Lyly to suggest that the child was his. Again, the play makes nothing of Anne Vavasour's promiscuity; Tellus loves only Endimion; she answers Corsites' love with deceit, and accepts him at the end only because Cynthia commands it. The play does not, in fact, come anywhere near a competent defence of Oxford, and this must make us doubtful that the play was ever intended for this purpose.

But quite apart from the plausibility or implausibility of these different identifications, is there not an assumption shared by them all which runs counter to the nature of courtly art as we have described it? The argument that it is so has been put persuasively by J. A. Bryant Jnr. in a paper read before the Southeastern States Renaissance Conference in 1956.[6] Professor Bryant starts from the point of Lyly's alteration in the classical myth. The myth told of the moon's love for a shepherd; Lyly alters this to one more flattering to the English Cynthia—the moon herself must be loved but cannot be treated as the victim of love. But the alteration involves Lyly in difficulties: in order to show the virtue of the goddess he has to depict an alternative love (to play the Venus to her Sapho, so to speak) and this produces the central design of Endimion between the moon and the earth, Cynthia and Tellus, his higher and lower destinies. Further, if he is to show Tellus as worthy of love, though unequal to Cynthia, he has to counter Endimion's rejection by another man's zealous pursuit, and this introduces Corsites. The whole play can be built up in this way as a functional development of a desire to flatter the Queen. Given Lyly's taste for symmetry and fondness for the conventions of courtly love (the conventions of his art) nothing else need be imported to explain the general structure of the play, with its final pairing-off of couples— Corsites and Tellus, Geron and Dipsas, Sir Tophas and Bagoa.

The perception that Lyly's play grows naturally out of the conjunction of the myth and the desire to flatter Elizabeth does not, of course, explain away any of the particular elaborations, which appear most obviously in the vision of Endimion, twice presented, and which strongly suggest particular reference to a contemporary situation, which may (as we have seen above) be Lyly's own situation. But does remove the necessity to suppose that Lyly began with a contemporary event, and then set about dramatizing it, finding equivalents in myth and story which would clothe his meanings. I have argued already that the search for point-by-point correspondences in courtly allegory is a vain one and I rejoice to find Mr Bryant writing in a similar vein: 'such academic attempts at explanation usually proceed upon the assumption that the subject at hand is a dead fact, to be dissected, described, tabulated and provided with an index . . . But . . . the assumption is wrong'. This objection applies to those who have supposed *Endimion* to clothe a philosophic scheme,[7] no less than to those who have seen it as a description of history. In either case the form of the play, as we have it, is judged incompetent and unsuccessful, except as a means—and even as a means it is rather inefficient (Bond has to suppose that Lyly did not know enough to get his facts right)—a means to convey a hidden truth, which will then pay back some of its own coherence and importance to the action that Bond and others suppose to be (in itself) 'incoherent and purposeless'.

Yet *Endimion* has often been reprinted, and students are invited to read it on what are, I suppose, literary grounds; moreover the play has been performed on the modern stage with some degree of success.[8] This would seem to argue that Lyly gave his play some measure of literary coherence, and that the 'meaning' that emerges need be no more than an audience can deduce from any myth-like or archetypal situation. The historical critics seem to begin with the perfectly legitimate observation that this situation is *like* court life, and that Cynthia must reflect Queen Elizabeth. Their next assumption is, however, that the coherence of the play must then be pursued at the historical not at the literary level. Halpin and Bond ask, 'if Cynthia is the Queen, who is Endimion her suitor?' and come to the conclusion, very proper in its terms, that Leicester is the obvious suitor. Feuillerat and Bond ask, 'if Cynthia is the Queen, who is Tellus her rival?' and reach the conclusion, very proper in its terms, that Mary, Queen of Scots is the obvious rival. None of these critics has asked, 'is the relationship between Cynthia, Endimion and Tellus one that has any dramatic or artistic justification?' Concentration on this question would at least avoid methods of argument such as are provided (*inter alia*) by Bond's mode of identifying Eumenides with Sir Philip Sidney:

There is one name that rises instinctively to the lips when acts
that are lovely and noble and of good report are mentioned
—one that still falls upon the ear like refreshing music in this
hard heart-wearying age of brass, even as its bearer softens and
shames with his mild lustre the coarser fames and gaudier
heroics of that iron time—the name of

> that pensive Hesper light
> O'er Chivalry's departed sun,

Sir Philip Sidney. Can the relations of Eumenides in the play be
made to square with him? (III. 95)

The method being used here is one which relies on stiffening
the play with romantic responses to history and so by-passing
the appeal of the play as a play. If Eumenides fulfils the role
of a friend, we look for an historical 'friend' to make the play
more real to us instead of looking for an artistic pattern that
justifies the role.

If we look in the play for artistic pattern we find quite enough
to stimulate discussion and response: we can find in it the major
elements which appear everywhere in Lyly's plays—debate,
mythology, romantic love, symmetrical arrangement—but
ordered in a new and individual sequence. The play certainly
contains a debate-theme—the old favourite of love *versus*
friendship—which is announced unequivocally. Eumenides
the faithful friend and lover is entitled to any one wish he may
ask for; he is then faced with the problem of having to prefer
either friendship or love:

> Why do I trifle the time in words? The least minute being spent
> in the getting of Semele is more worth than the whole world:
> therefore let me ask . . . What now, Eumenides? Whither art thou
> drawn? Hast thou forgotten both friendship and duty? Care of
> Endimion and the commandment of Cynthia? Shall he die in a
> leaden sleep because thou sleepest in a golden dream? Ay, let
> him sleep ever, so I slumber but one minute with Semele. Love
> knoweth neither friendship nor kindred.
>
> Shall I not hazard the loss of a friend for the obtaining of her
> for whom I would often lose myself? Fond Eumenides, shall the
> enticing beauty of a most disdainful lady be of more force than
> the rare fidelity of a tried friend? The love of men to women is a
> thing common and of course; the friendship of man to man
> infinite and immortal. Tush! Semele doth possess my love.

Ay, but Endimion hath deserved it. I will help Endimion. I found Endimion unspotted in his truth. Ay, but I shall find Semele constant in her love. I will have Semele. What shall I do?

(III. iv. 103-19)

We can see the relevance of this conflict to that between the higher love that Endimion feels for Cynthia and the lower love he is offered by Tellus, but there is no explicit conflict in Endimion's situation, and the debate frames the action much less than it does in *Campaspe* or *Sapho and Phao*. In both these plays the different emotional states of the central characters are arranged in a static pattern which allows them to be debated; Alexander debates magnanimity against love, and the play contrasts magnanimity in Alexander against love in Apelles; so Sapho debates love against chastity, and the play contrasts chastity in Sapho against love in Venus. But Cynthia is *semper eadem*, and the play studiously refuses to debate the issue between her and Tellus. The contrasted emotional states in this play are treated as developing out of one another in a narrative sequence, rather than as existing in a static design.

It follows that as the debate is less important so the narrative is more elaborate. Of all Lyly's plays, *Endimion* is the one which is nearest to medieval romance. The succumbing of the hero to an enchanted sleep, specially devised for him by a malignant witch, and the adventures of his friend while pursuing a remedy, the encounter with the lover-hermit Geron, the enchanted fountain, only useful to the pure in heart—all this reads like a survey of romance motifs.

Given the story, it is not surprising that *Endimion* is the longest of Lyly's plays, and that in which the symmetries of treatment are most developed towards the Shakespearian mode of parallel human instances—it is also the play which seems to have influenced Shakespeare most directly.[9] The adoration of Cynthia by Endimion is paralleled by the courtship of Semele by Eumenides, by Corsites' pursuit of Tellus, and (in the subplot) by Sir Tophas' pursuit of Dipsas. The cruelty of Tellus to Endimion is paralleled by the cruelty of Dipsas to Geron; the sublime chastity of Cynthia is parodied by the merely coquettish chastity of Semele. The denouement, in consequence, works out a broad survey of reconciliations:

Well, Endimion, . . . thou hast my favour, Tellus her friend,

Eumenides in paradise with his Semele, Geron contented with
Dipsas.   (V. iii 271-3)

The function of this denouement is no doubt the same as that
of *Sapho and Phao*—to highlight the wisdom and sympathy of the
Queen—but the effect is very different. In *Sapho* the focus is on
the mind of the Queen; Phao is a poor shadow. In *Endimion*
the hopeless love of the hero has its own vein of madly poetic
appeal:

> Tell me, Eumenides, what is he that having a mistress of ripe
> years, and infinite virtues, great honours and unspeakable
> beauty, but would wish that she might grow tender again?
> getting youth by years and never-decaying beauty by time;
> whose fair face neither the summer's blaze can scorch nor winter's
> blast chap, nor the numb'ring of years breed altering of colours.
> Such is my sweet Cynthia whom time cannot touch because
> she is divine nor will offend because she is delicate. O Cynthia,
> if thou shouldest always continue at thy fulness, both gods and
> men would conspire to ravish thee. But thou to abate the pride
> of our affections dost detract from thy perfections, thinking it
> sufficient if once in a month we enjoy a glimpse of thy majesty,
> and then, to increase our griefs, thou dost decrease thy gleams,
> coming out of thy royal robes wherewith thou dazzlest our eyes
> down into thy swath clouts beguiling our eyes.   (I. i. 50-65)

As the love of the subject has come into focus, so the mind of the
sovereign has retreated to an altitude out of descriptive range.
Cynthia is different in kind from the other characters in the
play, and though the action takes place under her benign
influence she is not part of it. The contrasts made by the
different modes of love reconciled at the end of the play do
not affect our conception of Cynthia, even by a process of
contrast, for she cannot be conceived to have been tempted to
any of these attitudes. In *Endimion*, in fact, we can see the
goddess-sovereign figure, who has dominated Lyly's drama
up to this point, retreating into a state of aloofness where she
ceases to have much effect on the conduct of the play.

(b) HARMONIOUS VARIETY

We have seen the debate-theme 'What is true royalty?'
controlling the form of *Campaspe* and *Sapho and Phao*, and we

have seen the same formal method applied in a more negative way in *Midas*: 'What interests ought a true monarch to avoid?' We have also seen *Endimion* developing the world of *Sapho and Phao* in a rather different direction. The desire to compliment the Queen does not here involve a contrast of her royalty with other emotional states, but rather requires a demonstration of her influence on the world of courtiers beneath her. As a result, most of *Endimion* is concerned with the interlocking intrigues of a spectrum of characters, all held together in a single situation.

In this respect *Endimion* reaches out to the mode of play construction we are to discuss in this section, where the interest is no longer centred on a single royal figure, Alexander-Sapho-Cynthia-Midas, but is diffused among many parallel instances, these being so organized that they complete a recognizable range of cases. Take away Cynthia, or replace her by a force about which the play has no particular feeling, and the construction of *Endimion* begins to resemble very clearly that which Lyly had first essayed in *Gallathea*.

(v) *Gallathea*

The only approach to pastoral we have met so far in Lyly's plays is the rather thin wash of rusticity to be found in *Sapho and Phao*, serving there to start off the praise of courtliness when such a one as Sapho is queen; to this we may add the isolated scene of the shepherds in *Midas* (Act IV, scene ii) in which we meet 'we poor commons (who tasting war, are made to relish nothing but taxes)'; but this is proletarian rather than truly pastoral in function. It is clear enough, however, from the opening words of *Gallathea* that this is to be a deliberate exercise in the pastoral mode:

> The sun doth beat upon the plain fields; wherefore let us sit down, Gallathea, under this fair oak, by whose broad leaves being defended from the warm beams we may enjoy the fresh air which softly breathes from Humber floods.

It might be objected that the desire to escape from the warm sun into the shade is not one that characteristically affects the shepherds or other swains on the banks of Humber. As Warton pointed out, 'complaints of immoderate heat, and wishes to be conveyed to a cooling cavern, when uttered by the inhabitants of Greece have a propriety which they totally lose in the character of a British shepherd'. But the objection is irrelevant to the banks of Lyly's Humber. The lines translate and are, I presume, meant to recall words that have universally been allowed to stand for the pastoral world in general—

> Tityre tu patulae recubans sub tegmine fagi

—the opening line of Virgil's eclogues. And as Virgil is recalled in the opening lines of the play, so the title itself and the main motif of the plot is probably intended to recall the other prime pastoral authority, Theocritus, whose sixth idyll tells of the unwelcome attentions that the nymph Galatea has to endure from the monster Polyphemus, and whose eleventh idyll gives the song with which the monster wooed the shrinking nymph. The monster that is due to prey upon Lyly's Gallathea is not a cyclops, however; for, like Hesione and Andromeda and Ariosto's Angelica she is likely to form the virgin-tribute paid to a sea-monster. The name of this monster—the Agar—Lyly seems to have taken from the *eagre* or tidal-wave of the Humber estuary, but for the attendant circumstances he seems to have gone back to the story of Neptune and Hesione, derived it would seem through Natalis Comes, the famous Renaissance mythographer.[10]

The pastoral setting, which the opening of the play establishes, is one that is preserved throughout. No courtiers or royal persons appear. The gain in homogeneousness (as against *Sapho and Phao*) is very great. And the appearance and inter-vention of the gods does not really affect this. For the pastoral world here presented is one where man and nature interact continuously. The gods act like the forces of nature pressing on man: Cupid pressing him into love, Diana into chastity, Neptune into fear and obedience. And this is indeed what the play is about—the interrelation of gods and men, obedience and deceit. The motto of the play might be taken from what Gallathea says to her father in the first scene: 'Destiny may be deferred, not prevented' which finds a more particular application to the facts of the play in Tyterus' 'dissemble you may with men, deceive the gods you cannot', and this Neptune in his turn takes up and repeats, as if summarizing his whole intention in the play—which is to pay out those who seek to circumvent the destiny he imposes: 'their slights may blear men, deceive me they cannot'. The narrative with which the play opens mirrors in little this theme which pervades the action:

> In times past, where thou seest a heap of small pebble, stood a stately temple of white marble, which was dedicated to the god of the sea—and in right, being so near the sea; hither came all such as either ventured by long travel to see countries, or by great traffic to use merchandise, offering sacrifice by fire to get safety by water; yielding thanks for perils past and making prayers for good success to come. But Fortune, constant in nothing but inconstancy, did change her copy, as the people their custom; for the land being oppressed by Danes, who instead of sacrifice, committed sacrilege, instead of religion, rebellion; and made a prey of that in which they should have made their prayers, tearing down the temple even with the earth, being almost equal with the skies; enraged so the god who binds the winds in the hollows of the earth that he caused the seas to break their bounds, sith men had broke their vows, and to swell as far above their reach as men had swerved beyond their reason. Then might you see ships sail where sheep fed, anchors cast where ploughs go, fishermen throw their nets where husbandmen sow their corn, and fishes throw their scales where fowls do breed their quills. Then might you gather froth where now is dew, rotten weeds for sweet roses, and take view of monstrous mermaids instead of passing fair maids.

(I. i. 13-34)

This story might serve as a natural introduction to a play in which men once again seek to evade the wrath of the gods, though this time there is no element of terror involved.

It will be seen even from the little that has been said so far that the unity and construction of *Gallathea* is very different from that of the plays which have been discussed. A greater homogeneousness is achieved by removing direct reference to the world of courtly manners, but is achieved only at the cost of losing direct comment on formulated ideals of living. To illustrate this point we may compare the debate structure here with that in *Sapho and Phao*: both plays deal with the conflict between Venus and Diana or Love and Chastity. When we compare them in this way it is immediately apparent that the debate matters much less in *Gallathea* than in *Sapho and Phao*.

The pressure on the earlier play was to convey the nature of the excellence which cancels any natural opposition between love and chastity, by taking the best things out of both positions

> [so] that your Dian
> Was both herself and Love.

In the earlier play the opposition between the two sides in the debate had to be sharpened in order that the nature of this excellence should emerge, showing Sapho to possess both the humanity to feel love and the magnanimity to conquer it. In *Gallathea* no one is really shown to suffer by the opposition between Cupid and Diana. It is true that the Nymphs of Diana, wounded by Cupid, utter plaints of love not unlike those we have met in the earlier plays:

> Can Cupid's brands quench Vesta's flames, and his feeble shafts headed with feathers pierce deeper than Diana's arrows headed with steel? Break thy bow, Telusa, that seekest to break thy vow and let those hands that aimed to hit the wild hart scratch out those eyes that have wounded thy tame heart. O vain and only naked name of chastity, that is made eternal and perisheth by time, holy and is infected by fancy, divine and is made mortal by folly! (III. i. 10-17)

But the focus of the play does not rest on the pathos of such a plaint. Sapho's sufferings in love have a central interest, for Sapho (like Alexander) is the obvious centre of the plot; and the whole force of its intellectual discriminations press down on her situation. In so far as the plot has weight, the weight lies here. But in *Gallathea* the love-plaints of the various nymphs are so laid together that we do not rest our interest on any single one of them. The tension between the mortals who hope to deceive both men and gods, and the gods who are lurking in the very same woods, determined not to be outdone in deception—this tension is conveyed by means of a whole series of interrelated episodes which illustrate and make general their points by their very variousness and not by their capacity to be brought to bear on a single situation. We have said that *Campaspe* and *Sapho and Phao* ask and seek to answer in their various ways the question, 'Where lies true royalty?' But no question of this kind will serve to focus the meaning of *Gallathea*. Instead, a whole series of cross-intrigues is used to present a vision of pretensions and limitations, self-will and destiny which is reminiscent of both Greek Romance and Shakespeare's last comedies.

In handling this new technique in *Gallathea*, Lyly produces one of the most beautifully articulated plays in the period. Almost all the plot material is made out of one motif—the attempt to deceive destiny by means of disguise. From this starting-point one can see the play being built up by methods almost exactly analogous to those of fugue in music. The first statement of the *subject* shows Tyterus disguising Gallathea in order to deceive Neptune. The second entry shows Cupid disguising himself to deceive Diana. In the third entry Melebeus disguises Phillida, again in order to deceive Neptune. Finally, in a fourth entry Neptune declares that he will disguise himself as a shepherd, to deceive all the other deceivers. The *exposition*, mathematically exact, is complete. Next, the play moves on to development of this material; by a dramatic equivalent to the contrapuntal texture of a fugue we sound together the themes of Phillida's disguise and Gallathea's disguise, and so arrive at the developing love-plot of these two nymphs, each knowing herself to be a woman and hoping that the other is a man. Add to this the voices of the second entry and one finds the nymphs of Diana, also inflamed, some for Gallathea and some for Phillida—again supposing that they are as male in fact as they are in attire. The re-entry of the fourth voice is delayed to its most dramatic moment. Neptune reiterates the 'subject' in a thunderous bass:

> And do men begin to be equal with gods, seeking by craft to overreach them that by power oversee them? Do they dote so much on their daughters that they stick not to dally with our deities? Well shall the inhabitants see that destiny cannot be prevented by craft nor my anger be appeased by submission. I will make havoc of Diana's nymphs, my temples shall be dyed with maidens' blood, and there shall be nothing more vile than to be a virgin. To be young and fair shall be accounted shame and punishment, in so much as it shall be thought as dishonourable to be honest as fortunate to be deformed. (V. iii. 10-19)

By now, however, the tangle of mistaken loves, of nymphs in love with one another, and of supernatural powers promoting one side or another, is sufficiently complex to take the bite out of

Neptune's threat. Diana and Venus enter in what in music would be called 'close imitation' after him. In a *stretto* of all the gods on the stage at one time, the discordant self-deceptions that have resulted from the attempt to deceive others are resolved into concord.

It is tempting to carry the fugal analogies to the structure of *Gallathea* still further, and talk of entries inverted or *cancrizans* (as when the gods invert the human point of view) but probably to take them further would be to reduce their usefulness, which is, of course, only that of analogy. But the analogy is worth using, if only to counteract complaints like that of Feuillerat, '*Gallathea*, de toutes les productions lyliennes . . . c'est . . . une de celles dont la composition est le plus hétérogène' (p. 337) and to show that the 'lack of development' is not due to lack of formal control. By using a critical vocabulary which does not import assumptions that the end of drama is to develop characters, organize intrigue and show personality at work, we take ourselves a little nearer the true excellencies of Lyly's plays.

For the 'dispersed' interest of *Gallathea* does not, for the sympathetic reader, lower the dramatic temperature or cause his attention to wander before the next appearance of these same characters. Where all the characters are arranged to imitate one another, and where the focus of interest is on the repetition and modification and rearrangement of a basic pattern of persons, we do not ask how the persons will develop individually, but how the situation can be further manipulated. Having seen Tyterus disguise Gallathea and hide her in the woods, then Melebeus disguise Phillida and dispose of her in the same way, we are then anxious to hear the two disguises chiming together. Having heard that, we then wonder how the pursuit of the other nymphs by Cupid will affect the first situation; for his threat to 'use some tyranny in these woods' and 'confound their loves in their own sex' is expressed in terms that bring Gallathea and Phillida within its compass. The process is one of agglomeration, by which similar experiences are continually being added together to produce new and piquant situations. As the wheel turns and the same episode comes round again, it is never quite the same, for new confusions and accompaniments are always being added or taken away.

This formal unity is not, however, so oppressive that no space is left for that delicate observation of manners and witty evocation of refined attitudes that gives Lyly's comedy its characteristic charm. The comedy of errors between the two nymphs is handled without ever invoking the slapstick of Plautus or Shakespeare—people punished or abused for things they never did—but produces instead the 'soft smiling, not loud laughing' over human capacity for self-deception. Each maiden retreats into herself in order to imitate the signs of maleness she finds in the other:

> *Gallathea.* . . . But whist! here cometh a lad; I will learn of him how to behave myself.
> *Enter* Phillida *in man's attire.*
> *Phil.* I neither like my gait nor my garments; the one untoward, the other unfit, both unseemly. O Phillida! But yonder stayeth one, and therefore say nothing. But O Phillida!
> *Galla.* I perceive that boys are in as great disliking of themselves as maids; therefore though I wear the apparel, I am glad I am not the person.
> *Phil.* It is a pretty boy and a fair; he might well have been a woman; but because he is not I am glad I am, for now under the colour of my coat I shall decipher the follies of their kind.
> *Galla.* I would salute him, but I fear I should make a curtsey instead of a leg.
> *Phil.* If I durst trust my face as well as I do my habit, I would spend some time to make pastime; for say what they will of a man's wit, it is no second thing to be a woman.
> *Galla.* All the blood in my body would be in my face if he should ask me (as the question among men is common), 'are you a maid?' (II. i. 10-30)

It is characteristic of Lyly to organize a situation where we in the audience can watch his characters failing to understand one another. We alone are given the total understanding that is required. Lyly offers us the pleasure of a smiling superiority to and enjoyment of the accidents and misunderstandings that affect others in their lives and (more especially) loves. He repeats the method a little later in the same play. We watch the plaints of love following one another in a regular order, and then witness what follows when each nymph attempts to disguise her feelings from the others

Eurota. . . . why blushest thou, Telusa?

Tel. To hear thee in reckoning my pains to recite thine own.
I saw, Eurota, how amorously you glanced your eye on the
fair boy in the white coat, and how cunningly (now that you
would have some talk of love) you hit me in the teeth with
love.

Eur. I confess that I am in love, and yet swear that I know not what
it is. I feel my thoughts unknit, mine eyes unstayed, my heart
I know not how affected or infected, my sleeps broken and
full of dreams, my wakeness sad and full of sighs, myself in all
things unlike myself. If this be love, I would it had never been
devised.

Tel. Thou hast told what I am in uttering what thy self is. These
are my passions, Eurota, my unbridled passions, my intolerable
passions, which I were as good acknowledge and crave counsel
as to deny and endure peril.

. . .

But soft, here cometh Ramia; but let her not hear us talk.
We will withdraw ourselves and hear her talk.

        Enter Ramia.

Ramia. I am sent to seek others, that have lost myself.

. . .

Eur. . . . Ah, would I were no woman!

Ramia. Would Tyterus were no boy!

Tel. Would Telusa were nobody! (III. i. 39-111)

The play is, of course, basically a play about love, and of the
three gods who appear on the stage (I take Venus to be a mere
extension of Cupid) only Cupid seems willing to do more than
preserve the *status quo*. He is the only agent of change, for love
is the only emotion in the play which involves the interaction
of people and allows their natures to move forward. This
remains true even though love here is only the courtly and witty
game which is all that Lyly ever touches on, and probably
all that his instruments were capable of expressing. I have
spoken of the play as lacking direct reference to the court;
this is true, in that it is totally unconcerned with magnanimity
or honour, but in another sense the play is courtly enough, the
loves of the nymphs reflecting the love ideals of refined ladies—
ideals which can be indulged here with complete impunity,
since there are no male suitors within sight. Here is the supreme
example in Lyly of the delicate precision of his style, used to

discover in wit-combat the delicacy of virginal sensations about love.

Phillida. It is a pity that Nature framed you not a woman, having a face so fair, so lovely a countenance, so modest a behaviour.

Gallathea. There is a tree in Tylos whose nuts have shells like fire, and being cracked, the kernel is but water.

Phil. What a toy is it to tell me of that tree, being nothing to the purpose. I say it is pity you are not a woman.

Galla. I would not wish to be a woman unless it were because thou art a man.

Phil. Nay, do not wish to be a woman, for then I should not love thee, for I have sworn never to love a woman.

Galla. A strange humour in so pretty a youth, and according to mine, for myself will never love a woman.

Phil. It were a shame if a maiden should be a suitor (a thing hated in that sex) that thou shouldest deny to be her servant.

Galla. If it be a shame in me, it can be no commendation in you, for yourself is of that mind.

Phil. Suppose I were a virgin (I blush in supposing myself one) and that under the habit of a boy were the person of a maid; if I should utter my affection with sighs, manifest my sweet love by my salt tears, and prove my loyalty unspotted, and my griefs intolerable, would not then that fair face pity this true heart?

Galla. Admit that I were as you would have me suppose that you are, and that I should with entreaties, prayers, oaths, bribes and whatever can be invented in love desire your favour, would you not yield?

Phil. Tush, you come in with 'admit'.

Galla. And you with 'suppose'.

Phil. What doubtful speeches be these? I fear me he is as I am, a maiden.

Galla. What dread riseth in my mind! I fear the boy to be as I am, a maiden.

Phil. Tush, it cannot be, his voice shows the contrary.

Galla. Yet I do not think it, for he would then have blushed.

Phil. Have you ever a sister?

Galla. If I had but one, my brother must needs have two; but I pray have you ever a one?

Phil. My father had but one daughter, and therefore I could have no sister

Galla. Ay me, he is as I am, for his speeches be as mine are.

Phil. What shall I do? Either he is subtle or my sex simple.
. . .
Phil. Come let us into the grove, and make much one of another,
    that cannot tell what to think one of another.

(III. ii. 1-59)

In the discovery of this vein of delicate innuendo, Lyly does
more than anticipate Shakespeare; he advances his own art.
It is well worth pausing to notice the skill with which he
orchestrates (so to speak) the advance and retreat of the two
maidens, the desire to speak out and the fear of being under-
stood. The passage is made up entirely of repetitions, but the
formality does not in the least impede the movement round a
circuit of maidenly daring; so that we end the scene knowing
better what sensitivity and delicacy are like. Small wonder that
Shakespeare should have remembered the scene, and tried to
transplant its easy control of verbal ballet, advance and retreat,
into his own richer idiom.

The play thus uses the somewhat savage story of Neptune's
anger, and the annual sacrifice of virgins exacted to appease
him, to frame a world of exquisite refinement in the emotions.
The evocation of the tenderness of virginal feelings acts as a
foil to the dangerous and bitter state of virginity most feelingly
evoked in Hebe's speech of farewell when she is due to be
devoured by the Agar:

Farewell the sweet delights of life and welcome now the bitter
pangs of death. Farewell you chaste virgins, whose thoughts are
divine, whose faces fair, whose fortunes are agreeable to your
affections, enjoy and long enjoy the pleasure of your curled locks,
the amiableness of your wished looks, the sweetness of your tuned
voices, the content of your inward thoughts, the pomp of your
outward shows; only Haebe biddeth farewell to all the joys that
she conceived and you hope for, that she possessed and you shall;
farewell the pomp of princes' courts, whose roofs are embossed
with gold and whose pavements are decked with fair ladies,
where the days are spent in sweet delights, the nights in pleasant
dreams, where chastity honoureth affections and commandeth,
yieldeth to desire and conquereth.
. . .
Come, Agar, thou unsatiable monster of maiden's blood and
devourer of beauty's bowels, glut thyself till thou surfeit and let
my life end thine. Tear these tender joints with thy greedy jaws,

these yellow locks with thy black feet, this fair face with thy foul teeth. Why abatest thou thy wonted swiftness? I am fair, I am a virgin, I am ready. Come Agar, thou horrible monster, and farewell world thou viler monster. (V. ii. 25-55)

What would have been rather cloying without the spice of danger, what would have been rather heartless without these hints of flowery tenderness, becomes by the combination of the two a more affecting and effective image.

The loves of the all-female cast are brought to a happy conclusion in the only way possible—by sex-change or metamorphosis. It is often supposed, with Dr Johnson, that 'a new metamorphosis is a ready and puerile expedient'; and the onset of this trick for ending the play may be seen as marking a decline in Lyly's dramatic art. Actually, Lyly's adoption of this mode of denouement coincides with his adoption of the whole mode of play construction which I have called 'harmonious variety', and can be seen as an integral part of its method. The plays I have dealt with as debates showed a controlling royal figure, who could end the play by rejecting the errors and re-establishing the right. But in *Gallathea* and the other plays of my second group the cast is not controlled from the centre in this way; the cast is grouped in such a way that there is a state of permanent unbalance, keeping the action in movement; balance can be restored at the end only by some *fiat* from outside. It may be that this is a poor thing beside a logical development based on character, but the latter is not possible within the terms of Lyly's art; the interest is focussed on the groups, and the individuals inside the groups are arranged to complement one another, not to establish separate individualities.

(vi) *Love's Metamorphosis*

All the qualities which I have discussed above as separating *Gallathea* from the plays in my first group—the lack of topical reference, the weakness of the debate structure, the dispersion of interest over groups of characters, the lack of intrigue, the 'musical' methods of organizing the plot—all these appear in *Love's Metamorphosis* at a yet further remove from the other plays. The range of *Love's Metamorphosis* is still narrower than that of *Gallathea*. *Gallathea's* local allusions to Lincolnshire and the Humber have no counterpart in the later play, whose setting is uniformly that never-never pastoral country where nymphs and shepherds work out endlessly the permutations of love, under the benign sovereignty of Pan and Cupid. In a country without history (as without geography) the action moves through a timeless continuum, sometimes resembling a chess problem more than an image of life.

From one angle we can see that the play represents a dramatic shaping of the Petrarchan situations, as these appeared in the English sonnet-sequences which were getting under way in the 'eighties. Three foresters are in love with three nymphs, attendant on the goddess Ceres. But the three ladies are really only three aspects of one person—the Petrarchan unkind mistress—alternately cruel (as Nisa), coy (as Celia), and inconstant (as Niobe); from their own point of view, of course, these qualities are to be read as 'virtuous', 'fair' and witty'. The three foresters who languish under these several displeasures may also be taken to represent aspects of the Petrarchan poet-lover, his desire for absolute possession, his acceptance of merely physical pleasure, his jealousy, his humility, but these discriminations are not developed as clearly or as consistently in the case of the three nymphs. In any case it is clear enough that the relationship between lovers and beloveds is presented by methods which are entirely formal and unindividualizing. For the first time in Lyly (apart from the anomalous *Midas*) there are no love plaints or other extended expressions of emotion. The play is an 'anatomy' of love, which almost manages without the story normally used to illustrate and bring alive the texture of the discriminations involved, and which certainly manages without any picture of their effects on personality. The foresters enter, discriminate between their kinds of love and the kinds of opposition it has to deal with; they then hang up the mottoes relevant to these different oppositions on the sacred tree (actually Fidelia, a trans-shaped virgin). Next the nymphs enter and, again by means of symbolic properties, reveal their separate but interrelated attitudes to love; they discover the foresters' mottoes and reply to them in other mottoes. It is only after this highly stylized preparation, and after sermons on love (proper and improper) from Ceres and Cupid that we are allowed to see the nymphs and foresters together; and then only in a triptych of tableaux, in each of which the lover is defeated by the kind of opposition which characterizes his nymph. And this is the end of conversation between lovers and beloveds till we get to the denouement, for in the next act Cupid agrees to metamorphose the ladies into objects which clearly emblematize their fixed characteristics—which is all they have of character; the cruel one is turned into a stone, 'that being to lovers pitiless, she may to all the world be senseless', the coy one into a rose, 'that she may know beauty is as fading as grass, which being fresh in the morning is withered before night', and the inconstant one into a bird of paradise, 'that liveth only by air and dieth if she toucheth the ground', so that 'she may know her heart fed on nothing but fickleness'. Even when equilibrium is restored at the end and the ladies de-metamorphosed into their stony, flower-like and airy selves, the final consent is managed without any attempt at emotional expression, in a stanzaic form which presents each individual instance as a variant form of the type:

> *Ceres.* Well, my good nymphs, yield; let Ceres entreat you yield.
> *Nisa.* I am content, so as Ramis, when he finds me cold in love, or hard in belief, he attribute it to his own folly, in that I retain some nature of the rock he changed me into.
> *Ramis.* O my sweet Nisa! Be what thou wilt, and let all thy imperfections be excused by me so thou but say thou lovest me.
> *Nisa.* I do.
> *Ramis.* Happy Ramis!
> *Celia.* I consent, so as Montanus, when in the midst of his sweet delight shall find some bitter overthwarts, impute it to his folly, in that he suffered me to be a rose, that hath prickles with her pleasantness, as he is like to have with my love, shrewdness.
> *Mon.* Let me bleed every minute with the prickles of the rose so I may enjoy but one hour the savour; love, fair Celia, and at thy pleasure comfort and confound.
> *Celia.* I do.
> *Mon.* Fortunate Montanus! (V. iv. 131-48)

What I have been saying may seem to charge this play with poverty of effect; but in fact it is one of the best of Lyly's plays. The lack of characterization in the nymphs and foresters involves no real loss; Lyly's characters were never notable for

depth or richness of humanity. On the other hand, the clarity
with which he has fixed the position of each character allows
him to develop his anatomy of love with a constructive precision
and economy we do not find elsewhere. This is the shortest
of Lyly's plays, and not only because it lacks a sub-plot of boy
pages; there is a crispness in the dialogue and an absence of
incidental decoration:

> *Ramis.* Stay cruel Nisa . . . let me touch this tender arm and say
> my love is endless.
> *Nisa.* And to no end.
> *Ramis.* It is without spot.
> *Nisa.* And shall be without hope.
> *Ramis.* Dost thou disdain Love and his laws?
> *Nisa.* I do not disdain that which I think is not, yet laugh at
> those that honour it if it be.
> *Ramis.* Time shall bring to pass that Nisa shall confess there is
> love.
> *Nisa.* Then also will love make me confess that Nisa is a fool.
> *Ramis.* Is it folly to love, which the gods account honourable, and
> men esteem holy?
> *Nisa.* The gods make any thing lawful, because they be gods, and
> men honour shadows for substance, because they are men.
> *Ramis.* Both gods and men agree that love is a consuming of the
> heart and restoring, a bitter death in a sweet life.
> *Nisa.* Gods do know, and men should, that love is a consuming
> of wit and restoring of folly, a staring blindness and a blind
> gazing.
> *Ramis.* Wouldst thou allot me death?
> *Nisa.* No, but discretion.
> *Ramis.* Yield some hope.
> *Nisa.* Hope to despair.
> *Ramis.* Not so long as Nisa is a woman.
> *Nisa.* Therein, Ramis, you show yourself a man.
> *Ramis.* Why?
> *Nisa.* In flattering yourself that all women will yield.
>
> (III. i. 1-33)

There is less charm here than in *Gallathea*, but there is an edge
to the wit which is a kind of strength.

As in *Gallathea*, the world of witty love-exchange is joined
to a violent fable from Ovid, this time the story of the atheist,
Erisichthon, who offends Ceres by cutting down her sacred oak

tree, and who is punished by Famine; he postpones death by selling his daughter (unnamed) to various masters, from whom she then escapes by means of a disappearing trick, taught her by Neptune. Lyly takes over this story more or less as it stands, except that (as in *Midas*) he gives it a happy ending. But this does not mean that it remains extraneous. Greg says that 'this plot is even more crudely distinct from the principal action of the play than is usual with Lyly'.[11] But the story of the blasphemer and despiser of virginity ('there is none that Erisichthon careth for, but Erisichthon') is clearly related to the other thematic interests of the play. Erisichthon is saved by the piety of his daughter—here called Protea because of her protean capacity to change her shape—and her love serves to balance the frigidity of Ceres' nymphs in the main plot, as his arrogance balances the humility and piety of the foresters. Thus at the end of the play when (as in *Gallathea*) the gods come together to bargain their punishments one against another, Cupid can say to Ceres with perfect propriety, 'thou seekest to starve Erisichthon with thy minister, famine, whom his daughter shall preserve by my virtue, love', and the bargaining proceeds as follows:

> *Ceres.* How may my nymphs be restored?
> *Cupid.* If thou restore Erisichthon, they embrace their loves, and all offer sacrifice to me.
> *Ceres.* Erisichthon did in contempt hew down my sacred tree.
> *Cupid.* Thy nymphs did in disdain scorn my constant love.
>
> (V. i. 29-33)

The function of Erisichthon is thus to balance with his pride the pride of the unkind nymphs, and to offend Ceres in the same way that they offend Cupid.

I suppose that it is the same interest in balance that dictates the curious addition of a 'siren' (here only a classical name for the Teutonic mermaid) to the story of Protea. As Protea seeks her true lover Petulius, 'Ay me, behold, a siren haunts this shore. The gods forbid she should entangle my Petulius!' The scene which follows—the exhibition of a well-known classical episode—is of a kind that is popular with Lyly and probably with his contemporaries: one can think of the competition of Pan and Apollo, staged in *Midas*, and of the interviews of Alexander and Diogenes in *Campaspe*. Petulius enters, the mermaid sings (twice, once 'with a glass in her hand and a comb'), and Petulius is about to follow her when Protea enters, now disguised as the ghost of Ulysses, and dissuades him:

> *Pet.* Is this a siren, and thou Ulysses? Curst be that hellish carcase, and blessed be thy heavenly spirit!
>
> *Siren.* I shrink my head for shame, O Ulysses! is it not enough for thee to escape, but also to teach others? Sing and die; nay die, and never sing more!
>
> *Protea.* Follow me at this door, and out at the other.

At this point they pass through one of the 'mansions' I suppose, and Protea finds means to discard her cloak and false beard, re-emerging as herself:

> *Pet.* How am I delivered! The old man is vanished and here for him stands Protea. (IV. ii. 91-8)

The clanking mechanics of this episode tempt one to dismiss it as mere theatricality, a patently devised opportunity for more metamorphoses; but when the lovers next appear one finds that there is some structural justification for the episode of the syren. Protea's labour to save her father engages Cupid on her side; but she is only able to help because Neptune, having ravished her long ago, is now in her debt and willing to help. If she is not to be left unaccounted for at the end of the play, she too must have a lover, and if her career is to match the others', her love must proceed via quarrel and compromise to some reconciliation. This the siren episode allows: she has to forgive Petulius his moment of weakness, and he has to forgive her yielding to the assault of Neptune. The scene of the siren ends with following preparation for what follows:

> *Pro.* Here standeth Protea that hath saved thy life; thou must also prolong hers. But let us into the woods and there I will tell thee how I came to Ulysses and the sum of all my fortunes which happily will breed in thee both love and wonder.
>
> (IV. ii. 99-102)

When Protea and Petulius emerge from the woods, in the next scene but one, they discourse as follows:

> *Pet.* A strange discourse, Protea, by which I find the gods amorous and virgins immortal, goddesses full of cruelty and men of unhappiness.

o   209

Pro. I have told both my father's misfortunes, grown by stoutness, and mine by weakness; his thwarting of Ceres, my yielding to Neptune.

Pet. I know, Protea, that hard iron, falling into fire waxeth soft; and then the tender heart of a virgin being in love must needs melt; for what should a fair young and witty lady answer to the sweet enticements of love but

> *Molle meum levibus cor est violabile telis?*

Pro. I have heard too that hearts of men stiffer than steel have by love been made softer than wool; and then they cry,

> *Omnia vincit amor, et nos cedamus amori.*

Pet. Men have often feigned sighs.

Pro. And women forged tears.

Pet. Suppose I love not.

Pro. Suppose I care not.

Pet. If men swear and lie how will you try their loves?

Pro. If women swear they love, how will you try their dissembling?

Pet. The gods put wit into women.

Pro. And nature deceit into men.

Pet. I did this but to try your patience.

Pro. Nor I but to prove your faith. But see, Petulius, what miraculous punishments here are for deserts in love: this rock was a nymph to Ceres, so was this rose, so that bird. (V. ii. 1-25)

And so the various themes come together before the end of the play. The argument does not, of course, affect the actual virtue of the siren episode in itself, but it does suggest Lyly's care for the symmetry of his argument, and imply that it was seen by the author in terms other than those of theatrical effect.

In respect of debate-structure, the points that were made about *Gallathea* apply also to *Love's Metamorphosis*. This play deals with an opposition between love and chastity no less than does *Gallathea*, but even less than in *Gallathea* is the debate between these forces a structural support for the play. The debate between Cupid and Ceres has not the same function as that between Cupid and Diana in the earlier play, for Ceres is never the proponent of chastity as a self-sufficient way of life; her nymphs exemplify frigidity rather than chastity, are pathological exceptions rather than genuine votaries of a possible order. The catechism of love that Cupid provides in his temple is nowhere provided with contradiction:

Ceres. . . . But that my nymphs may know both thy power and thy laws, and neither err in ignorance nor pride, let me ask some questions to instruct them that they offend not thee whom resist they cannot. In virgins what dost thou chiefest desire?

Cupid. In those that are not in love, reverent thoughts of love; in those that be, faithful vows.

Ceres. What dost thou most hate in virgins?

Cupid. Pride in the beautiful, bitter taunts in the witty, incredulity in all.

Ceres. What may protect my virgins that they may never love?

Cupid. That they be never idle.

Ceres. Why didst thou so cruelly torment all Diana's nymphs with love?

Cupid. Because they thought it impossible to love.

Ceres. What is the substance of love?

Cupid. Constancy and secrecy.

Ceres. What the signs?

Cupid. Sighs and tears.

Ceres. What the causes?

Cupid. Wit and idleness.

Ceres. What the means?

Cupid. Opportunity and importunity.

Ceres. What the end?

Cupid. Happiness without end.   (II. i. 90-113)

The evident wisdom of Ceres in the play, the reverence with which she is treated throughout (though Cupid does say, 'thou Ceres dost but govern the guts of men') and the balance of her position, neither denying the force of love nor wishing to infringe the beauty of her own virginity—all this has led to the position indicated by Bond's statement: 'that the Queen is represented in the person of Ceres has been generally allowed'. Nevertheless, it is difficult to find evidence in the play itself of any intention to depict the Queen. There is none of that strained adulation of the goddess, in excess of what the action requires, which we meet in the descriptions of Sapho and Cynthia, and no reference to courtly or royal virtues such as appears in the Alexander of *Campaspe*. The activities of Ceres and her nymphs are restricted to what the fairly rigid limits of the drama allow. She punishes Erisichthon (exactly as in Ovid), pays her respects to Cupid and forces her nymphs into marriage. The image of Ceres is never detached from or raised above these activities, and the activities themselves cannot be plausibly translated into happenings in the court of Elizabeth.

(vii) *The Woman in the Moon*

Lyly's only play in verse, and possibly the last play he wrote (though published nine years before his death) is usually considered among his pastorals; probably it should be put beside *Gallathea* and *Love's Metamorphosis* in terms of construction also. Like them, it does not concentrate on an intrigue round a central dilemma, but disperses its interest through a series of symmetrically arranged episodes, which show in their interrelation the different phases of the world depicted. It is true that one central character, Pandora, who gives the play its name, appears throughout *The Woman in the Moon*; but against the continuity of the person of Pandora must be set the deliberate variation from scene to scene in the characteristics she displays, as now one planet, now another exercises 'influence' over her. I have spoken of the three nymphs in *Love's Metamorphosis* as three phases or aspects of the Petrarchan unkind mistress. In the same way one may speak of the different aspects of Pandora as adding up to what she becomes by the end of the play:

> idle, mutable,
> Forgetful, foolish, fickle, frantic, mad;
> . . .
> For know that change is my felicity,
> And fickleness Pandora's proper form.
> (V. i. 307 f., 301 f.)

The fact that the nymphs are three persons and Pandora only one is not particularly relevant to this argument; the nymphs are never really separable except in terms of idea, and in terms of idea Pandora is just as divisable as they are; as she moves through saturnine, martial, venereal, and lunatic phases she becomes in effect a different person, though the plot turns on the attempts of her shepherd lovers to believe that she is still the same, and in the end some kind of psychological unity is implied by the decision that 'fickleness [is] Pandora's proper form'. Moreover, as metamorphosis is the means by which, in *Love's Metamorphosis*, the puppet-like emotions of the nymphs and shepherds are manipulated into a final pattern of agreement (and something of the same kind is true of *Gallathea* as well), so in this play another outside force, this time astrological influence, is the main motive of the plot movement. As in all these later plays by Lyly, there are no inner debates, and no personal responsibility is implied for the emotions felt or the actions undertaken. Like chess pieces the characters have only one or two moves open to them; the mastery of the playwright and the virtue of the play lies in the skill with which these moves are combined, and the surprising and piquant new patterns of movement produced.

At the opening of the play certain dramatic moves are obviously implicit in the situation. Four shepherds beg Nature to create a woman,

> To have as every other creature hath
> A sure and certain means among ourselves
> To propagate the issue of our kind;
> As it were comfort to our sole estate,
> So were it ease unto thy working hand.
>
> (I. i. 40-44)

Since Pandora is one and they are four it is obvious that difficulties or unorthodoxies will arise in one way or another. When the seven planets join in a league against Pandora, 'Nature's glory and delight, / Compact of every heavenly excellence', a further twist is given to the intrigue opening up between Pandora and the shepherds. Notice that this contest between Nature and the Planets offers an opportunity to handle the play as a debate; but Lyly does not now seem to be interested in developing this aspect of the situation. By giving each planet a period of 'influence' so that Pandora's moods alternate unpredictably, he keeps the shepherds busy endeavouring to cope with the lady; thus he can postpone any issue of their numerical difficulties till near the end of the play. In fact, the action can be seen to be developed in two ways: the earlier scenes are a series of 'shows' in which Pandora displays the Saturnine or Jovial temperament, with no more connection between the episodes than there is between the planets. Later, a more continuous intrigue begins to emerge and to override the alternation of planets.

In the first episode Saturn makes Pandora melancholy; she receives the supplications of the shepherds that she should choose one of them with 'winks and frowns', with swooning, and in the end runs away from them. They sing to revive her, but all the response they get is

> What songs, what pipes and fiddling have we here?
> Will you not suffer me to take my rest?   (I. i. 225-6)

The second bout of influence subjects her to Jupiter, who 'fills her with ambition and disdain'; but Lyly shows less interest in his plot here than in a classical 'show' of Jupiter wooing Pandora for himself, while Juno exhibits her well-known jealousy. Nevertheless, we do not lose the thread of the plot; the difficulty of obtaining Pandora for a wife remains clear enough.

The third fit, when she is subjected to Mars and 'becomes a vixen Martialist' carries this interest to a climactic point, for Pandora here encourages battle between her suitors, and herself wounds one of them (Stesias). The first three episodes have thus led Pandora through a scale of increasing violence and disdain, in which she rejects, spurns and finally injures her suitors. It is now the turn of Sol (who turns out to be the classical Apollo, god of poetry, phrophecy and medicine) to dominate her temperament, and this seems to be leading the original impetus of the plot to a full close. Regretting her violence, Pandora agrees to marry Stesias, the shepherd she injured in her martial mood:

>   unhappy me
> That so unkindly hurt so kind a friend!
> But, Stesias, if thou pardon what is past,
> I shall reward thy sufferance with love.
> These eyes that were like two malignant stars,
> Shall yield thee comfort with their sweet aspect,
> And these my lips that did blaspheme thy love
> Shall speak thee fair and bless thee with a kiss,
> And this my hand that hurt thy tender side
> Shall first with herbs recure the wound it made,
> Then plight my faith to thee in recompence.
>   (III. i. 12-22)

The plot has reached a point which more or less exhausts the original tension; it is not surprising, in consequence, that the next alteration in temperament begins the second line in plot development which I mentioned above. Venus comes into the ascendant, and Pandora in consequence begins an action to set the shepherds against one another, inspired for the moment by a venereal passion for them all; this jolts the plot out of its statuesque movement as a series of tableaux, and turns it into a web of intrigues and counter-intrigues, in which the audience is constantly invited to share (by means of asides) the pleasures of manipulating men against one another:

> *Pan.* Now have I played with wanton Iphicles,
>   Yea, and kept touch with Melos, both are pleased;
>   Now, were Learchus here! But stay, methinks
>   Here is Gunophilus; I'll go with him,
> *Gun.* Mistress, my master is in this cave, thinking to meet you
>   and Learchus here.
> *Pan.* What, is he jealous? come, Gunophilus
>   In spite of him I'll kiss thee twenty times.
> *Gun.* O look how my lips quiver for fear!
> *Pan.* [*louder, for* Stesias *to hear*] Where is my husband? Speak,
>   Gunophilus.
> *Gun.* [*ditto.*] He is in the woods, and will be here anon.
> *Pan.* [*aside*] Ay, but he shall not.
>   [*for* Stesias' *benefit*] His fellow swains will meet me in this
>   bower,
>   Who for his sake I mean to entertain;
>   If he knew of it he would meet them here.
>   Ah! wheresoere he be, safe may he be!
>   Thus hold I up my hands to heaven for him,
>   Thus weep I for my dear love Stesias.
>
>   (III. ii. 219-36)

The dramatic method here is something new in Lyly and nearer Ben Jonson that Lyly usually comes; the complications mount dizzily and we are drawn to wonder how far Pandora's skill in intrigue will stretch in her elaborate play of husband against lovers, and servant against all.

The ascent of Mercury in Venus' place, to make Pandora 'thievish, lying, subtle, eloquent' does not really affect this intrigue. The command that Pandora should not longer be in love hardly matters, once the intrigues started by love are under way; she has to pretend love in order to keep the intrigue from collapsing on her own head, and Mercury's augmentation of her power to deceive only pushes the complications into a further stage of complexity. The busyness of the scene, with characters dashing on and off in pursuit of one another, the punch-and-judy beatings when the rivals meet, is at the furthest remove from statuesque court comedy which we have come to associate with Lyly, as is the consequent loss of obvious patterning and balancing. The parallelism between the three lovers, Melos, Iphicles and Learchus, is a basic factor in the play, and sometimes Lyly presents them in the patterned manner we have come to expect of him:

> *Enter* Melos, Learchus, Iphicles.
>
> *Iphi.* Unkind Pandora to delude me thus.
> *Lear.* Too kind Learchus that hath loved her thus.
> *Melos.* Too foolish Melos that yet dotes on her.
>
> *Lear.* Black be the ivory of her ticing face
> *Melos.* Dimmed be the sunshine of her ravishing eyes.
> *Iphi.* Fair may her face be, beautiful her eyes!
>
> *Lear.* O Iphicles, abjure her, she is false!
> *Iphi.* To thee, Learchus, and to Melos false.
> *Melos.* Nay, to us all too false and full of guile.
>
> (IV. i. 12-20)

But, in the main, such parallelisms are absorbed into the cut and thrust of dialogue which relies for its effect on the mounting tension of the intrigue:

> *Melos.* What makes Learchus here?
> *Iphi.* Wherefore should Melos banquet with my love?
> *Lear.* My heart riseth against this Iphicles,
> *Pan.* Melos, my love! Sit down, sweet Iphicles.
> [Pandora *and* Iphicles *confer apart.*
> *Melos.* She daunts Learchus with a strange aspect.
> *Lear.* I like not that she whispers unto him.
> *Iphi.* [*aside to* Pandora] I warrant you.
> *Pan.* Here's to the health of Stesias my love;
>   Would he were here to welcome you all three.
> *Melos.* I will go seek him in the bosky groves.
> *Gun.* You lose your labour then; he is at his flock.
> *Pan.* Ay, he weighs more his flock than me.
> [*She weeps.*

Iphi. Weep not, Pandora, for he loves thee well.
Pan. And I love him.
Iphi. But why is Melos sad?
Melos. For thee I am sad; thou hast injured me.
Pan. Knows not Melos I love him?
Iphi. Thou injurest me and I will be revenged.
Pan. Hath Iphicles forgot my words?
Gun. [*aside*] If I should hollow, they were all undone.
Lear. [*aside*] They both are jealous, yet mistrust me not.

(III. ii. 278-97)

The final bout of 'influence' on Pandora is given to *Luna*, the moon, and this brings the intrigue to a sudden end by making the principal intriguer, Pandora, *lunatic*. There is quite a bit of slapstick comedy in the spectacle of the intrigue of the jealous lovers running downhill on its own momentum and then bumping into the central character's irremovable unconcern:

Ste. Ah whither runs my love Pandora? stay,
    Gentle Pandora stay; run not so fast.
Pan. Shall I not stamp upon the ground? I will!
    Who saith Pandora shall not rend her hair?
    Where is the grove that asked me how I did?
    Give me an angle, for the fish will bite.
Melos. Look how Pandora raves; now she is stark mad.
Ste. For you she raves that meant to ravish her.
    Help to recover her or else ye die.
Lear. May she with raving die! do what thou dar'st.
Iphi. She overreached us with deceitful guile;
    And Pan, to whom we prayed, hath wrought revenge.

(V. i. 179-90)

But in the main it may be said that in Act V the play returns to its statuesque mode of tableau presentation, and what is left of the intrigue is transferred to Gunophilus, Pandora's comic servant, who is the Vice or tormentor of the play, and who in his irreverent or anti-romantic interventions in the action takes up the role of Lyly's pages (a role still to be discussed) and carries it forward towards Shakespeare's Speed and Launce. The return to a more statuesque mode of presentation restores stanzaic order and patterning to the speeches of the shepherd lovers, and here Lyly draws more fully than elsewhere in the

217

play on the poetic material of pastoralism. The palinode of the shepherds, with which their part in the forward action is concluded, brings the intrigue to rest on a note of pastoral charm which Lyly has not cared to use much elsewhere in the play:

> *Melos.* O that a creature so divine as she,
> Whose beauty might enforce the heavens to blush,
> And make fair Nature angry at the heart
> That she had made her to obscure herself,
> Should be so fickle and so full of slights,
> And feigning love to all, love none at all.
> *Iphi.* Had she been constant unto Iphicles
> I would have clad her in sweet Flora's robes;
> Have set Diana's garland on her head,
> Made her sole mistress of my wanton flock,
> And sing in honour of her deity,
> Where now with tears I curse Pandora's name.
> *Lear.* The springs that smiled to see Pandora's face,
> And leaped above the banks to touch her lips;
> The proud plains dancing with Pandora's weight;
> The jocund trees that vailed when she came near,
> And in the murmur of their whispering leaves
> Did seem to say, 'Pandora is our queen',
> Witness how fair and beautiful she was,
> But now alone how false and treacherous.
>
> (V. i. 149-68)

It only remains after this for Stesias, the nominal husband, to make the same discovery and to react to it in the opposite way:

> *Ste.* Go life, fly soul; go, wretched Stesias!
> Curst be Utopia for Pandora's sake!
> Let wild boars with their tusks plough up my lawns,
> Devouring wolves come shake my tender lambs,
> Drive up my goats unto some steepy rock,
> And let them fall down headlong in the sea.
>
> (V. i. 243-8)

With typical Lylian balance the action returns to the point from which it started—with Nature and the seven planets disputing on the stage, numbering down the line in formal order; and the play ends, as many another mythological show has done, with a justification of the myth in terms of natural phenomena: Pandora becomes the woman in the moon, Stesias the man in the moon, while Gunophilus is metamorphosed into the bush that the man in the moon carries.

It has been suggested (by E. C. Wilson) that *The Woman in the Moon* is an 'unreserved satire of woman';[12] Greg speaks of 'the satirical conception and representation of womankind which gives the tone to *The Woman in the Moon*'.[13] How far are these critics justified in regarding the play as satirical in intention or effect? Pandora ends as 'forgetful, foolish, fickle, frantic, mad', and it is true that this glances from the first woman to all women. But the play does not require us to consider any of its details as pointing out of the action towards woman in general; the moods of Pandora are explained entirely by the planetary influence to which she is subjected, and in her true nature she is said to be 'innocent, / And fully fraught with virtuous qualities'. The satire on woman was a well established medieval and Humanist genre and had its standard topics or commonplaces —the love of finery, the concealment of ugliness, vanity, pretentiousness, sensuality and false modesty. It will be seen how few of these *topoi* Lyly actually draws on, and yet how easy it would have been to draw on them. Certainly on the question of *tone* I must emphatically dissent from Greg. The tone of satire may be savagely angry (as in Juvenal) or urbanely supercilious (as in Horace), but it can hardly be pastorally poetic and pageant-like in showing the actions of the gods, and yet remain satiric. Satire invites us to make a judgment, and this is no part of the appeal of *The Woman in the Moon*.

The further extension of this idea that the satire on woman is pointed at Queen Elizabeth should be too absurd to require refutation. Elizabeth was sometimes known as Pandora (because the name means '[endowed with] all the gifts') but the mere coincidence of names proves nothing, especially if we remember the source in Fenton's Belleforest, pointed out by Bond (III. 235), where Pandora is 'a young lady of Milan' who 'long abused the virtue of her youth and honour of marriage with an unlawful haunt of diverse young gentlemen'. No court dramatist could show in a play 'as it was presented before her Highness' a picture of the royal Pandora as 'sullen . . . proud . . . bloody-minded . . . idle, mutable, forgetful, foolish, fickle, frantic, mad' and then suppose that this would entertain as a personal portrait the lady whose motto was *semper eadem*. The possibility implies a general migration of *lunacy* out of the play and into the author, the Master of the Revels, the licenser for the press, the actors and the worshipful company of stationers. But in fact the Master of the Revels did not disappear, and the author remained at liberty; indeed he was soon writing begging letters to the peremptory Pandora implying some obligation on her part. We cannot, to be brief, allow the allusion.

(c) SUB-PLOT INTRIGUE

(viii) *Mother Bombie*

Mother Bombie differs from all other comedies by Lyly not only in its subject-matter but even in its *genre*. It belongs to that line of comedies which domesticate the Roman comic muse among English manners—a line which always occupies a disproportionate space in histories of English drama; disproportionate, that is, to the worth of the plays involved, but understandable, given the ease with which it can be used to tie up influences and developments. Hitherto Lyly's interest in Classical literature had been confined to imitation of its motifs—collecting its apophthegms, anecdotes, *exempla* etc., but now he makes a formal imitation of the order, regularity, neatness, and clarity of the Terentian mode in comedy, and abandons the 'gallimaufry' technique of his other plays, their rich and surprising variousness.

Even so, the play is clearly marked with the mind of Lyly. The cross-talk, on which any such comedy depends, is neater and defter than anywhere else in the tradition. Take the following exchange from *Ralph Roister Doister*:

> *Dobinet Doughty.* Whether is it better that I speak to him first
> Or he first to me, it is good to cast the worst.
> If I begin first, he will smell all my purpose,
> Otherwise I shall not need anything to disclose.
> *Truepenny.* What boy have we yonder? I will see what he is.
> *D. Dough.* He cometh to me. It is hereabout ywis.
> *Truepenny.* Wouldest thou ought, friend, that thou lookest so about?
> *D. Dough.* Yea. But whether ye can help me or no, I doubt.
> I seek to one Mistress Custance house here dwelling.
> *Truepenny.* It is my mistress ye seek to, by your telling.
> (II. iii)

Compare with this a similar meeting in *Mother Bombie*:

> *Dromio.* Now, if I could meet with Risio it were a world of waggery.
>
> *Risio.* O that it were my chance, *obviam dare Dromio*, to stumble upon Dromio, on whom I do nothing but dream.
>
> *Dro.* His knavery and my wit should make our masters that are wise, fools; their children that are fools, beggars; and us two that are bond, free.
>
> *Ris.* He to cozen and I to conjure, would make such alterations that our masters should serve themselves; the idiots, their children, serve us; and we to wake our wits between them all.
>
> *Dro. Hem quam opportune*; look if he drop not full in my dish.
>
> *Ris. Lupus in fabula*: Dromio, embrace me, hug me, kiss my hand; I must make thee fortunate.
>
> *Dro.* Risio, honour me; kneel down to me, kiss my feet; I must make thee blessed.
>
> *Ris.* My master, old Stellio, hath a fool to his daughter.
>
> *Dro.* Nay, my master, old Memphio, hath a fool to his son.
>
> *Ris.* I must convey a contract.
>
> *Dro.* And I must convey a contract.
>
> *Ris.* Between her and Memphio's son, without speaking one to another.
>
> *Dro.* Between him and Stellio's daughter, without one speaking to the other.
>
> *Ris.* Dost thou mock me, Dromio?
>
> *Dro.* Thou dost me else. (II. i. 1-25)

What we notice at once here is the greater integration between the speech and the speaker. Lyly's basic method, as usual, is repetition and balance:

> Grove nods at grove, each alley has a brother
> And half the platform just reflects the other.

But this so functionally reflects the plot, and so precisely catches the exuberance of the boy players, that the usual objections can hardly apply. Lyly has found a style exactly fitted to his intriguers, who are revealed as pert and comically self-satisfied, but completely disengaged from any world where moral judgments might apply. The pursuit of wit is presented as disinterested, and with no justification but the value of wit itself. Udall's dialogue is painstakingly caught up in moving the plot forward; Lyly's plot seems to move effortlessly, drawn by the featherweight wit of the pages. He puts the boys at the centre of the play and makes all the other characters their victims; the wit thus becomes the motive of the plot, and the plot-values become centred on the pleasures of wit. The most beautiful example of wit carrying plot comes right at the begining:

Memphio. Boy, there are three things that make my life miserable: a threadbare purse, a curst wife and a fool to my heir.

Dromio. Why then, sir, there are three medicines for these three maladies: a pike-staff to take a purse on the highway, a holly wand to brush choler from my mistress' tongue, and a young wench for my young master; so that as your worship, being wise, begot a fool, so he, being a fool, may tread out a wise man.

Memp. Ay, but, Dromio, these medicines bite hot on great mischiefs: for so might I have a rope about my neck, horns upon my head, and in my house a litter of fools.

Dro. Then, sir, you had best let some wise man sit on your son to hatch him a good wit. They say, if ravens sit on hens' eggs, the chickens will be black, and so forth.

. . .

Memp. I'll have thy advice, and if it fadge, thou shalt eat till thou sweat, play till thou sleep, and sleep till thy bones ache.

Dro. Ay marry, now you tickle me; I am both hungry, gamesome, and sleepy and all at once. I'll break this head against the wall but I'll make it bleed good matter.

Memp. Then this it is: thou knowest I have but one son, and he is a fool.

Dro. A monstrous fool.

Memp. A wife, and she an arrant scold.

Dro. Ah, master, I can smell your device; it will be excellent.

Memp. Thou canst not know it till I tell it.

Dro. I see it through your brains; your hair is so thin and your skull so transparent I may sooner see it than hear it.

Memp. Then, boy, hast thou a quick wit and I a slow tongue. But what is't?

Dro. Marry, either you would have your wife's tongue in your son's head that he might be a prating fool; or his brains in her brain-pan that she might be a foolish scold.

Memp. Thou dream'st, Dromio, there is no such matter. Thou knowest I have kept him close, so that my neighbours think him to be wise, and her to be temperate, because they never heard them speak. etc. (I. i. 1-61)

Basically this is a series of cross-talk jokes, handled with Lyly's usual virtuosity in accumulating parallels. But through the jokes Lyly is managing to conduct an exposition; the purse and the wife are irrelevant, but we do not know that at this stage in the play, and they serve to draw on the plan for palming off the third tribulation, the idiot son, on his rich neighbour's daughter. The basic facts about Memphio and Dromio, their simple characteristics, their relationship and their aims in the play are outlined for us without effort (it would seem) and without intrusion. Similarly throughout the play the cross-talk of the servants is never used solely for the purpose of displaying wit. The bouts of wit by their effervescence carry the plot forward.

What is lacking here is, of course, a comedy of situation such as one meets in Plautus and some of his English imitators— the comedy of seeing the errors of individuals catching up with them, embarrassing them, probing their delusions and the lies they tell themselves and us. Nobody in *Mother Bombie* is tested in this way, for everyone (except the idiots) is too wittily in control of himself to be liable to such attack. It is perhaps this aspect of the play that best explains the use of Mother Bombie herself, a figure whose exact function is difficult to assess in terms of ordinary plot construction. For Mother Bombie seems to foreknow everything in the play:

> *Pris.* Why, have you all been with Mother Bombie?
> *Lucio.* All; and as far as I can see, foretold all.

But this foreknowledge is not used to much dramatic purpose. No one's course of action is altered by Mother Bombie, except (at the end of the play) Vicinia's—when she reveals the true relationship of Maestius, Serena, Accius and Silena. This trips the switch for the catastrophe, but Vicinia's confession could have been motivated by less clumsy methods, if Lyly had not fancied the figure of Mother Bombie in his play for other reasons. One reason I may suggest is that Lyly, feeling the shallowness of a plot where wit is so much in the ascendant, and characters so much in control of themselves, sought to give the dimension of mystery and misunderstanding to his play (it was not a dimension he was accustomed to doing without) by means of a prophetess, in whose mind the whole action may be supposed to take place. Mother Bombie's function is certainly different from that of the Sybil in *Sapho and Phao*. The Sybil forecasts the career of Phao and advises him throughout its progress, but she has no connection with the other characters; she is not depicted as looking in upon the whole action; she does not give her name to the play.

Another reason for the introduction of Mother Bombie may be indicated by the analogy of works like Spenser's *Mother Hubbard's Tale* (published 1591, but probably written about a decade earlier) and Peele's *Old Wives' Tale* (published 1595). *Mother Hubbard's Tale* is so called because the character of the old woman indicates the level at which the style is to be placed:

> I'll write in terms, as she the same did say,
> So well as I her words remember may.
> No Muse's aid me needs hereto to call;
> Base is the style, and matter mean withall.

Similarly, Mother Bombie may serve as an excuse or explanation of the uncourtly *genre* of the play which bears her name. Unlike Mother Hubbard, or Peele's Madge, she does not *tell* the story, but she *knows* it all. Moreover, she belongs to that very precise social background which Lyly elsewhere fills in by his many references to Rochester, Ashford and Canterbury. These are quite different from the references to Lincolnshire we noticed in *Gallathea*. For the sense of place is only a convenience in *Gallathea*: but the action of *Mother Bombie* needs the real world of houses and taverns and distances to the next town, in order that we should understand the relationship between the different people.

As a comedy of cross-intrigue, with symmetrically organized groups of characters trying to deceive one another by identical devices, *Gallathea* is an obvious play to compare with *Mother Bombie*. Both plays begin in the same way: with two parents, one after the other, planning to use their children in deception. In the first scene of *Gallathea* Tyterus disguises Gallathea as a boy; in the third scene Melebeus disguises Phillida in the same way and for the same reason—to prevent her being sacrificed to Neptune. The later development of the play shows the two daughters meeting, nonplussing their fathers and overthrowing their schemes of deception. Similarly in *Mother Bombie*: the first scene shows us Memphio planning to foist his idiot son on the heiress of Stellio; the next scene shows us Stellio planning to foist his idiot daughter on the heir of Memphio. The development of the play reveals the idiocy of both children and overthrows the plans of both parents.

This similarity in plot outline is, however, only a framework which contains interests and effects very different in kind. The intrigue in *Gallathea* moves very slowly; very few lines are taken up with planning the moves; even the scenes of disguising the daughters are conducted without any elaborateness of plotting, for the main spotlight there is fixed on the moral problems involved in such deception, not on the practical ones—especially on the question if deceit is justified when it is fate or the gods that have to be deceived. But in *Mother Bombie* it is men who must be deceived, and a complication of intrigue is directly functional to that end. Moreover, when the characters are once disguised in *Gallathea* they are pushed off stage into 'the woods'; behind the whole of the presented action in this pastoral play is a vaguely conceived bosky retreat where actions grow to maturity, and we never need enquire how they do this; loose ends do not matter, indeed are not noticed, in this god-infested twilight of causality. *Mother Bombie* is, however, without *chiaroscuro*. It is a completely urban and daylight and entirely human play with every stage of the intrigue shown; each human endeavour is keyed into others; each person's intrigue leads directly to another person, who is usually found to be engaged in another endeavour and a counter-intrigue. It is only the unremitting effort and resourceful ingenuity of the pages that keeps the action moving forward; by making themselves the agents for the various sectional interests that press upon the plot, they manage to channel its multifarious activities into a single line of development.

It is in this effort to keep the intrigue at once extremely complicated and yet bound within a recognizable shape that the Roman Comedy method of carrying on the intrigues through the agency of servants is of obvious use to Lyly. It enables him to keep up what I may call a *density* of intrigue which compensates for the loss of shadow and the supernatural. The servants in *Mother Bombie*, like the slaves in Roman Comedy, are poised between the aims of the fathers who possess the power and the counter-aims of the children who possess more attractive qualities; thus, like the slaves, they are obliged to intrigue in a veering manner, tacking back and forth in a complex course of plotting, so that they may seem to satisfy the fathers while in fact they aim to satisfy the children. Lyly alters the Roman Comedy situation, however, by emphasizing the purely formal symmetry of the plot. Instead of the one servant (or at most two) of Roman Comedy, Lyly gives us four servants serving four masters, the masters all desiring different and incompatible ends, the servants determined to act in consort and reach a witty solution, which may amuse sufficiently even those who are disappointed and cause a general reconciliation to close the play. By forming a coherent group the servants are able to fit together their individual fragments of knowledge, and so are able to manipulate by a superiority of wit the whole course of the plot.

In Lyly's other comedies the audience alone knows the whole situation. We in the audience watch with compassion and superior amusement the self-revealing efforts of individual characters to grasp whatever fragment of the situation is revealed to them. When we watch the efforts of the disguised Gallathea and Phillida to understand their situation, we watch from above: no one in the play (not even the gods) controls the action as it moves along. The wit arises from the situation and the maidens amuse us because they are its puppets. On the other hand, when Dromio meets Risio (I have quoted the exchange already—see above p. 221) the wit, though it arises from the plot, is (like the plot) far more in the control of the speakers. We in the audience identify ourselves with *their* enjoyment of the symmetrically arranged situation; we do not stand above them and judge the adequacy of their responses; their wit is our means of entrance into the plotting, and admiring their agility we plot along with them, seeing the plot from the point of view of this central group of manipulators.

By creating this central group, Lyly also creates a central area of value for his play, which may be defined as 'wit'. 'Wit' is of course the cleverness which enables the servants to play off one master against another, and even to dispose of stray enemies like the Hackneyman *en passant*; but it is also the love of fun and conviviality for its own sake, a good which no one in the play is prepared to question, and which in the end carries the work to a denouement of feasting and marriage and good fellowship. Wit has always been an important element in Lyly's comedies. But the wit of *Sapho and Phao* or *Love's Metamorphosis* is chiefly a means of evoking the spirit of courtly gallantry: it is the index of a mind so poised above the ordinary struggle of living that it can afford to play with all its elements, having them all within easy control. In *Mother Bombie* wit is no longer a means of displaying this effortless superiority to life; it is rather a means of avoiding the oppressions of life and working towards a goal of ordinary sensual happiness. In Lyly's other plays wit is the servant of a structure concerned chiefly with moral exposition and demonstration—of (for example) the nature of magnanimity, or lovable virginity or honourable love. In such plays the debates or the antitheses carry the meaning; the wit is used to reveal the detachment of the truly lofty soul from the immediate ends of action. *Mother Bombie*, however, is without debate-structure and without the moral discriminations involved in images of Love and Honour. Wit is here a real value on its own, and not merely a means of conveying to the audience the nature of other and loftier values.

Another way of looking at this difference between *Mother Bombie* and Lyly's other plays is to consider their attitudes to love. In most of Lyly's plays love is depicted as an emotional test, measured as good or bad by the degree of poise or self-control which remains with the individual, even in the middle of his loving. In *Mother Bombie*, however, love is not treated as an emotion at all; it is an animal impulse, thinly disguised as a social duty, and worried over only because of its social implications. We have here none of the plaints of love with which Apelles or Phao or Gallathea were wont to unload their hearts and reveal their minds. In avoiding these features Lyly is of course entirely within the tradition of Roman Comedy; but we should notice that Lyly does not simply follow the tradition in this one play; he even goes beyond it in the un-romantic attitude he takes up. Of the three sets of lovers (or rather, persons destined for marriage) one pair is without sense (and so no love-talk can be expected from them), one pair is (or seems to be) incestuous, and they must be content with the avoidance of love-talk, with the mere exposure of their dilemma:

> *Maestius.* Sweet sister, I know not how it cometh to pass, but I find in myself passions more than brotherly.
> *Serena.* And I, dear brother, find my thoughts entangled with

affections beyond nature, which so flame into my distempered
head, that I can neither without danger smother the fire nor
without modesty disclose my fury.

Maest. Our parents are poor, our love unnatural; what can then
happen to make us happy?

Ser. Only to be content with our father's mean estate, to combat
against our own intemperate desires, and yield to the success
of fortune, who though she hath framed us miserable cannot
make us monstrous.   (III. i. 1-12)

Even Candius and Livia, who have neither incest nor folly to
impede them, are shown as more concerned in their exchanges
with their fathers' opposition than with their own feelings; and
the few phrases directly concerned with love that we have from
them are wittily oblique, where they are not pedantically
frigid. Clearly, Lyly is more interested in the conduct of the
intrigue than with the emotions of those involved in it.

Mother Bombie comes comparatively late in Lyly's work as
a dramatist, and the question naturally arises whether its
difference from the other plays represents an advance in Lyly's
dramatic power. Bond refers to the 'far greater skill in weaving
a plot' which it shows, and to its advance on the 'conventional
allegorical fashion of *Midas* and the three preceding plays'
(III. 168). The skill of the plotting in *Mother Bombie* cannot be
denied, but there is some danger in comparing what is clearly
the central interest of this play with what is only of peripheral
importance in the earlier work. The concentration of interest
on the intrigue of *Mother Bombie* involves loss as well as gain.
There is a loss of that delicacy of observation which characterizes
Lyly's art in plays like *Sapho and Phao* or *Gallathea*; there is loss
of that just poise between love and honour, between self-
forgetfulness and self-consciousness, which belongs to the court
plays proper; in the clear hard world of Roman Comedy there
is no space for reticence in expression or the tentativeness of
approach which measures delicacy of thought. This is Lyly's
only play in which the values of the female mind are completely
ignored. Comparison between *Mother Bombie* and Lyly's other
plays can only, in fact, reveal the difficulty of using these simple
concepts of advance or retreat in Lyly's dramatic art where
difference of *genre* is involved. *Mother Bombie* differs from the
other plays, in part at least because it was designed (it seems)

not for the Queen and the court, but for the well-educated society audience at the Paul's boys' private theatre. It is without opportunities for spectacle; it is without the beauties of mythology; there is no hint of allegory; pastoral grace is absent. All these were popular at court; they are not present in *Mother Bombie,* one might suppose, because the tastes of the court were not those that the play was designed to satisfy.

(ix) Sub-plot

One way of describing the difference between *Mother Bombie* and Lyly's other plays I have postponed till now: for it involves a reconsideration of the whole corpus of plays in terms not so far used. We may say that Lyly puts at the centre of his action in *Mother Bombie* the group of pert pages who are elsewhere confined to a sub-plot, indeed hardly ever allowed contact with the major characters. In my discussion of the individual plays I have not mentioned these page roles at all; for they are separable, and the plays can be described more coherently and more intelligibly if we confine our attention to the main plots. But it would be mere falsification to leave the plays thus, without attempting to re-attach the page plots to the main plots we have described.

From one point of view the sub-plots may be seen as supplying yet another strand to a fabric already devoted to variousness. They supply a worm's eye view of the heroic and courtly world of the main plot; the two taken together may incline us to accept the world of royal artifice, where artifice could hardly deceive us. Against the Love and Honour, Chastity, Chivalry and Magnanimity of the main plot is set a world of people who everywhere claim freedom from such enchantments. Thus the servants in *Campaspe* complain continually of the asceticism and dedication of their philosopher masters; what is virtue to Diogenes or Apelles is vice in the eyes of those who aim principally to fill their own bellies:

> *Manes.* I serve in stead of a master, a mouse, whose house is a tub, whose dinner is a crust, and whose bed is a board.
> *Psyllus.* Then art thou in a state of life which philosophers commend. A crumb for thy supper, an hand for thy cup, and thy clothes for thy sheets. For *Natura paucis contenta.*

Manes. . . . Plato is the best fellow of all philosphers. Give me
him that reads in the morning in the school and at noon in the
kitchen.
Psyllus. And me.
Granichus. Ah sirs, my master is a king in his parlour for the body
and a god in his study for the soul. Among all his men he
commendeth one that is an excellent musician; then stand I by,
and clap another on the shoulder and say, this is a passing
good cook.
Manes. It is well done, Granichus; for give me pleasure that goes
in at the mouth, not the ear; I had rather fill my guts than my
brains.   (I. ii 1-5, 43-54)

It is this narrow range of interest that gives the wit of the pages
its bite; for they know exactly what they want and see how
little is romance or philosophy able to supply the basic needs of
the body. They have the forms of learning at their fingertips,
but the forms are filled by interests remote from scholarship,
and turn naturally into parody:

Manes. I did not run away, but retire.
Psyllus. To a prison, because thou wouldest have leisure to
contemplate.
Manes. I will prove that my body was immortal because it was
in prison.
Granichus. As how?
Manes. Did your masters never teach you that the soul is immortal?
Gran. Yes.
Manes. And the body is the prison of the soul.
Gran. True.
Manes. Why then, thus to make my body immortal, I put it to
prison.   (I. ii. 27-39)

Wit is not for the pages a gloss upon the world reduced to order
by the magnanimous spirit, but a means of survival in a world
of harsh compulsions. Their gaiety is the gaiety of the *gamin*,
without background and perhaps without future, but keeping
an end up with what valour wit can muster. It is significant in
this respect that Lyly's plays end by reconciling or defining
in some noble pose the principal characters in the action; but
they leave the pages just where they started, in a limbo made
out of physical dependence and independence of spirit; they
have not even (except rather tenuously in *Mother Bombie*) the
aim of manumission which animates the slaves in Roman

Comedy and gives them their assurance of success at the end
of the play. And here again we should remember the suitability
of these roles for the boys by whom they were first played. As
the noble characters in Lyly's plays draw on such qualities as
the beautiful gravity and innocence of youth, so the page-roles
draw on the aimless love of mischief, the spontaneity and
unquenchable high spirits of the same age.

The attitude of the pages being, on the whole, one which
parodies the dominant attitudes of the main plot, we find that
the interests of the pages vary from play to play. In *Campaspe*,
where the masters are high-thinking philosophers, the servants
concentrate on the terrors of plain living. In *Sapho and Phao*,
where the main plot is more courtly, the pages Criticus and
Molus carry on at a lower level the debate between courtship
and scholarship begun by their masters, Trachinus and Pandion.
But whereas the debate is handled by the masters in terms of
Sapho's godlike magnanimity, and takes up the problem of the
dangers to virtue found at court, the servants treat the contest
as one between rival spheres of irresponsibility:

> *Criticus.* Then is it time lost to be a scholar. We pages are polit-
> [ic]ians; for look what we hear our masters talk of, we determine
> of; where we suspect, we undermine; and where we mislike for
> some particular grudge, there we pick quarrels for a general
> grief. Nothing among us but, instead of 'good morrow',
> 'what news?' We fall from cogging at dice to cog with states;
> and so forward are mean men in those matters, that they
> would be cocks to tread down others before they be chickens to
> rise themselves. Youths are very forward to stroke their chins,
> though they have no beards, and to lie as loud as he that hath
> lived longest. (I. iii. 24-33)

Or else the contest between Court and University is seen by the
pages as one between starvation (associated with scholarship
here as in *Campaspe*) and the courtly dueller's 'honour'. For
a worm's eye view of 'honour' the following witty variation on
the proverb *plures occidit crapula quam gladius* (cf. *Campaspe*
I. ii. 77) may stand as a not unworthy introduction to Falstaff's
famous diatribe:

> *Molus.* Now thou talkest of frays, I pray thee, what is that whereof
> they talk so commonly in court, 'valour', 'the stab', 'the pistol',
> for the which every man that dareth is so much honoured?

Criticus. O Molus, beware of valour! He that can look big and wear his dagger pommel lower than the point, that lieth at a good ward and can hit a button with a thrust, and will into the field, man to man, for a bout or two, he, Molus, is a shrewd fellow, and shall be well followed.

Molus. What is the end?

Criti. Danger or death.

Molus. If it be but death that bringeth all this commendation, I account him as valiant that is killed with a surfeit as with a sword.

Criti. How so?

Molus. If I venture upon a full stomach to eat a rasher on the coals, a carbonado, drink a carouse, swallow all things that may procure sickness or death, am I not as valiant to die so in a house as the other in a field? Methinks that epicures are as desperate as soldiers; and cooks provide as good weapons as cutlers.

Criti. O valiant knight!

Molus. I will die for it; what greater valour?

Criti. Scholars' fight, who rather seek to choke their stomachs than see their blood.

Molus. I will stand upon this point: if it be valour to dare die, he is valiant howsoever he dieth.   (II. iii. 6-31)

It is easy enough to devise parody of scholarship and courtship, whose under-sides are as real as their glamour (more real, some would say). But the case of pastoral is not so easy; since the world of pastoral is only a convention anyway, it lacks perforce an obvious and solid world of under-stairs. Moreover, it is a convention made up of elements blended from high life as well as low life so that capacity to contrast these two in main plot and sub-plot is blunted. Sidney had, of course, contrasted the base household of the true shepherd Damoetas and the noble household of the shepherd king, Basilius; but that contrast is based on the chivalric element in the *Arcadia*, rather than on anything specifically pastoral. If deeds of war and bravery were not a recurrent feature of the *Arcadia*, the distinction between Dorus, the prince disguised as a shepherd, and Damoetas, the shepherd jacked-up as a royal counsellor, would not be so striking.

Shakespeare also, in *As You Like It*, manages a contrast or parody relation between Audrey, the true rustic, Phebe, the

Dresden-china shepherdess, and, between these, the comprehensive sanity of Rosalind, both elegant and feeling; but it is easy to see that this, with its roots in a deep understanding of human variousness, and its flowering in a unique power of individual expressiveness, is beyond the art of Lyly.

What Lyly does for his pastoral *Gallathea* is to devise a sub-plot which is completely coherent in itself, but bears no relation to the main plot—the boys are no longer the servants of main plot characters. The same Humber shore, of course, sees the shipwreck of the boys' attempt to go to sea as well as the sacrifice to Neptune; the same woods hide the Alchemist and the Astronomer of the sub-plot as well as Cupid, Diana and Neptune of the main plot; at the end of the play the boys appear as minstrels to play at the wedding of Phillida and Gallathea.

But these features must be counted as absence of contradiction rather than reality of connection. What Lyly has done is to devise a story whose provenance is distinct from the pastoral of the main plot, but which in no way compromises its atmosphere. The boys of *Gallathea* are not the disillusioned observers of sophisticated high life that we meet in *Sapho and Phao*; their circumstances are humbler, and their wit less assertive. They are, in short, closer to the soil and to the folk life in which pastoral superstitions about the gods grow up. The story is basically of fairy-tale provenance: the three sons of a miller go in search of their several fortunes, and agree to meet again after a year and a day to discover how fortune has treated them. Lyly handles this as a series of episodes which draw on the tradition of 'estates-satire'—that progression through the different 'estates' or classes of the country, observing their various foibles—which elsewhere joins up with the picaresque and feeds into better known Elizabethan works like Nashe's *Unfortunate Traveller*, Chettle's *Piers Penniless* and *The Pilgrimage from Parnassus*. It is typical of Lyly, however, that his observation of the lives of Mariner, Alchemist, and Astronomer is without the dimension of social injustice which appears in the other works mentioned. Seamanship, alchemy and astrology are presented as crabbed mysteries, only fit to be made the target of the deflating wit of the boys. This largely takes the form of ridiculing the specialized jargon of these 'mysteries', and it might be argued that we ought to see this as an attempt to do what Jonson managed later in the period—measure moral depravity by a depravity of speech. The terms of such an argument, however, bear little relation to the conduct of Lyly's sub-plot; for the seaman is treated in much the same way as the alchemist, and there is no suggestion that he is a quack. The point is rather that all three are imprisoned within the jargon of their own trades; they are proper subjects for ridicule, for they lack the all-round gracious dilettantism of the gentleman. As Sir William Cornwallis remarks: 'a gentleman should talk like a gentleman, which is, like a wise man. His knowledge ought to be general; it becomes him not to talk of one thing too much or to be weighed down with any particular profession' ('Of Discourse', *Essays*).[14]

The sub-plot of *Midas* must be considered next if we are to trace a clear line of development up to the apex of Lyly's art in sub-plotting, in *Endimion*. The evidence suggests (as I have said already) that *Midas* in fact followed *Endimion*; but there is no good reason why an author's development should proceed along a straight line, and for purposes of critical exposition it is sometimes convenient to reverse chronology.

The story of Motto, the king's barber, and his sudden enrichment when he cuts off the beard which Midas has touched and turned to gold, and of the feud between him and the three pages for the possession of the beard—this has the coherence of the sub-plot in *Gallathea*, and has, in addition, a closer connection with the main plot, since the wealth which brings about the conflict derives from Midas' golden gift. Against this, however, we should set the fact that this plot only begins in Act III, up to which point Motto the barber and Dello his assistant are never mentioned. Instead of the earlier part of the beard story, which is told us indirectly, we have conversations about gold between the pages and Pipenetta, a female page, with the same qualities of wit as the boys (compare Rixula in *Mother Bombie*), drawing largely on the topics of female vanity:

> Pipenetta. . . . But this is the matter: my master is gone abroad and wants his page to wait on him; my mistress would rise and lacks your worship to fetch her hair.
> Petulus. Why, is it not on her head?

Pip. Methinks it should; but I mean the hair that she must wear today.

Licio. Why, doth she wear any but her own?

Pip. In faith, sir, no; I am sure it is her own when she pays for it. But do you hear the strange news at the court?

Pet. No, except this be it, to have one's hair lie all night out of the house from ones head.

Pip. Tush! everything that Midas toucheth is gold.

Pet. The devil it is!

Pip. Indeed, gold is the devil.

Licio. Thou art deceived, wench; angels are gold. But is it true?

Pip. True? Why the meat that he toucheth turneth to gold, so doth the drink, so doth his raiment.

Pet. I would he would give me a good box on the ear, that I might have a golden cheek.

Licio. How happy shall we be if he would but stroke our heads, that we might have golden hairs.   (I. ii. 113-33)

The somewhat truncated nature of the debate-structure in this play (see above) makes it difficult to be sure, but there is at least a suggestion that the triple indictment of Midas' court (as covetous, tyrannical, and lubricious) was meant to be reinforced by an under-stairs view of its deficiencies. The intrigue for possession of the beard only accounts for a small number of the lines in the sub-plot (proportionately the largest in the canon) which is mainly composed of a series of traditional paradoxes and joke situations. The estates joke reappears in the person of the huntsman, with his outlandish vocabulary:

Licio. Is not hunting a tedious occupation?

Petulus. Ay, and troublesome; for if you call a dog a dog, you are undone.

. . .

Licio. Dost thou not understand their language?

Minutius. Not I!

Pet. 'Tis the best calamance in the world, as easily deciphered as the characters in a nutmeg.

Min. I pray thee, speak some.

Pet. I will.

Huntsman. But speak in order or I'll pay you.

Licio. To it, Petulus!

Pet. There was a boy leashed on the single, because when he was embossed he took soil.

Licio. What's that?

Pet. Why, a boy was beaten on the tail with a leathern thong, because when he foamed at the mouth with running, he went into the water.

Hunts. This is worse than fustian! Mum! you were best! Hunting is an honourable pastime, and for my part I had as lief hunt a deer in a park as court a lady in a chamber.

Min. Give me a pasty for a park, and let me shake off a whole kennel of teeth for hounds; then shalt thou see a notable champing; after that will I carouse a bowl of wine, and so in the stomach let the venison take soil.

(IV. iii. 1-3, 18-38)

There is a suggestion of the same kind of joke when we first meet Motto the barber:

... I instructed thee in the phrases of our eloquent occupation, as 'how, sir, will you be trimmed? Will you have your beard like a spade or a bodkin? a penthouse on your upper lip or an alley on your chin? a low curl on your head like a bull or dangling lock like a spaniel? your moustaches sharp at the ends like shoemakers' awls, or hanging down to your mouth like goat's flakes? your love-locks wreathed with a silken twist or shaggy to fall on your shoulders?'

Dello. I confess you have taught me *Tully de oratore*, the very art of trimming. (III. ii. 37-46)

But the main role of Motto is rather different, and we soon lose sight of barbering as a source of jargon. Much of the last scene of the sub-plot turns on the barber's traditional inability to keep a secret, where we watch the pages' exploitation of this weakness to secure their own advantage:

Petulus. But tell us, Motto, why art thou sad?

Motto. Because all the court is sad.

Licio. Why are they sad in court?

Motto. Because the king hath a pain in his ears.

Pet. Belike it is the wens.

Motto. It may be, for his ears are swollen very big.

Pet. [*to* Licio] Ten to one Motto knows of the ass's ears.

Licio. If he know it, we shall; for it is as hard for a barber to keep a secret in his mouth as a burning coal in his hand. Thou shalt see me wring it out by wit. Motto, 'twas told me that the king will discharge you of your office because you cut his ear when you last trimmed him.

Motto. 'Tis a lie; and yet if I had, he might well spare an inch or two.

Pet. [*to* Licio] It will out; I feel him coming.

Dello. [*to* Motto] Master, take heed! You will blab all anon. These wags are crafty.

Motto. Let me alone.

Licio. Why, Motto, what difference between the king's ears and thine?

Motto. As much as between an ass's ears and mine.

Pet. O, Motto is modest. To mitigate the matter he calls his own ears, ass's ears.

Motto. Nay, I mean the king's are ass's ears.

Licio. Treason, treason!   (V. ii. 123-47)

The baiting of the older man by the darting wit of the pages is here strongly reminiscent of the sub-plot episode of the pages and Grim the Collier of Croydon in Edwardes' *Damon and Pithias*.

I have said that in sub-plot construction *Endimion* represents the furthest reach of Lyly's art. Here, for the only time in his works, we meet a coherent sub-plot which moves throughout in parody of the main plot. Lyly does this without altering his usual materials. In nearly all the plays there has appeared in the sub-plots one or two older persons (presumably singing bass in the concerted numbers—see *Damon and Pithias*, 1659 f.) whose dramatic role has been to blunder slowly on while the nimble boys tack round them and plant darts where they will. Calypho, in *Sapho and Phao*, is the earliest of these and the nearest to the prototype in Edwardes' Grim the collier (the Cyclops being conceived of as a kind of mythological collier). Of the same family are the Mariner, Alchemist, Astronomer of *Gallathea*, the Hunstman in *Midas*, and the Hackneyman in *Mother Bombie*. All these, however, with the exception of Motto the barber, have appeared only in separate episodes, and have not affected the development of the sub-plot.

Endimion not only puts a character of this kind at the centre of the sub-plot, but also (and this represents the development from *Midas*) makes his career imitate, at the level of parody, the career of the hero. Sir Tophas was played, I think, by a boy rather than a man—he is said to be growing his first beard (V. ii. 17 ff.) and the inane schoolboy humour of his part, and

237

the tradition of Ralph Roister Doister to which it belongs, both point to a juvenile rather than an adult actor. The version of *miles gloriosus* habits found here is without the menace that accompanies its adult presentation, in Pyrgopolynices (*Miles Gloriosus*) or Thraso (*Eunuchus*) or even Captain Spavento (of the *Commedia dell'Arte*). The pursuit of love and honour in Sir Tophas (love for the witch-crone, Dipsas, and the honour of killing sheep and blackbirds) is never so realistic as to throw the mad infatuation of Endimion into contrast; unless indeed by a more inane code of behaviour he cancels out the madness and highlights the nobility of Endimion's behaviour.

Endimion, with a model courtier's constant passion for the impossible, sighs for the moon:

> *Eumenides.* Is Endimion mad, or do I mistake? Do you love the moon, Endimion?
>
> *Endimion.* Eumenides, the moon.
>
> *Eum.* There was never any so peevish to imagine the moon either capable of affection, or shape of a mistress; for as impossible it is to make love fit to her humour which no man knoweth as a coat to her form, which continueth not in one bigness whilst she is measuring. Cease off, Endimion, to feed so much upon fancies.
>
> . . .
>
> *End.* O fair Cynthia, why do others term thee unconstant whom I have ever found unmoveable? Injurious time, corrupt manners, unkind men, who finding a constancy not to be matched in my sweet mistress, have christened her with the name of wavering, waxing and waning. Is she inconstant that keepeth a settled course which since her first creation altereth not one minute in her moving? (I. i. 16-36)

So Sir Tophas abandons his mad pursuit of war to follow an equally mad pursuit of love:

> *Tophas.* . . . to tell thee the truth, I am a noun adjective.
>
> *Epiton.* Why?
>
> *Tophas.* Because I cannot stand without another.
>
> *Epi.* Who is that?
>
> *Tophas.* Dipsas.
>
> *Epi.* Are you in love?
>
> *Tophas.* No; but love hath as it were milked my thoughts, and drained from my heart the very substance of my accustomed courage; it worketh in my head like new wine, so as I must

hoop my sconce with iron lest my head break, and so I bewray my brains; but I pray thee first discover me in all parts that I may be like a lover, and then will I sigh and die. Take my gun and give me a gown: *cedant arma togae.*

Epi. Here.

Tophas. Take my sword and shield and give me beard-brush and scissors: *bella gerant alii, tu Pari semper ama.*

Epi. Will you be trimmed, sir?

Tophas. Not yet; for I feel a contention within me, whether I shall frame the bodkin beard or the bush. But take my pike and give me pen: *dicere quae puduit, scribere iussit amor.*

Epi. I will furnish you, sir.

Tophas. Now for my bow and bolts give me ink and paper; for my smiter, a pen-knife: for *scalpellum, calami, atramentum charta, libelli, sint semper studiis arma parata meis.*

Epi. Sir, will you give over wars, and play with that bauble called love?

Tophas. Give over wars? No, Epi: *militat omnis amans, et habet sua castra Cupido.*

Epi. Love hath made you very eloquent; but your face is nothing fair.

Tophas. Non formosus erat, sed erat facundus Ulisses.

Epi. Nay, I must seek a new master if you can speak nothing but verses.

Tophas. Quicquid conabar dicere versus erat. Epi, I feel all *Ovid de arte amandi* lie as heavy at my heart as a load of logs. O what a fine thin hair hath Dipsas! What a pretty low forehead! What a tall and stately nose! What little hollow eyes! What great and goodly lips! How harmless she is being toothless! her fingers fat and short, adorned with long nails like a biter. In how sweet a proportion her cheeks hang down to her breasts like dugs, and her paps to her waist like bags! What a low stature she is, and yet what a great foot she carrieth! How thrifty must she be in whom there is no waste! How virtuous is she like to be over whom no man can be jealous!

(III. iii. 17-60)

Endimion falls into an enchanted sleep; similarly, in the case of Sir Tophas, love leads directly to sleep:

Epi. . . . But what? begin you to nod?

Tophas. Good Epi, let me take a nap; for as some man may better steal a horse than another look over the hedge, so divers shall be sleepy when they would fainest take rest.

. . .

Samias. What, Epi! Where's thy master?
Epi. Yonder, sleeping in love.   (III. iii. 64-7, 79 f.)

The parallel is pointed very obviously in this latter case by the
lines immediately preceding:

Samias. Thy master [sc. Endimion] hath slept his share.
Dares. I think he doth . . .   (III. iii. 71 f.)

Endimion in his sleep has visions of courtly and perhaps
political import; Sir Tophas has his love-dreams too:

There appeared in my sleep a goodly owl, who sitting upon my
shoulder, cried twit, twit, and before mine eyes presented herself
the express image of Dipsas. I marvelled what the owl said till
at the last I perceived twit, twit 'to it', 'to it',; only by contraction
admonished by this vision to make account of my sweet Venus.
(III. iii. 130-35)

Finally, as Endimion is recovered from his sleep by the kiss of
Cynthia, and learns that the reward of constant adoration
is royal favour, so Tophas is recovered from his infatuation
by the discovery that Dipsas has a husband, and learns that
another woman will do as well. The difference between the
Tophas-plot and the other sub-plots in Lyly is indicated by the
short coda which prolongs the play by a few lines, and brings
Tophas into the general reconciliation of husband to wife,
lover to mistress and servant to sovereign:

Cynthia. Well, Endimion, nothing resteth now but that we
depart. Thou hast my favour, Tellus her friend, Eumenides
in paradise with his Semele, Geron contented with Dipsas.
Tophas. Nay, soft; I cannot handsomely go to bed without Bagoa.
Cynth. Well, Sir Tophas, it may be there are more virtues in me
than myself knoweth of; for Endimion I awaked, and at my
words he waxed young; I will try whether I can turn this tree
again to thy true love.
Top. Turn her to a true love or false, so she be a wench I care not.
(V. iii. 271-80)

The sub-plot of *Endimion* is thus interwoven into the movement
of the main plot from beginning to end; and the wit of the pages
is concentrated on an object which reflects the interests of the
main action. This is a technical achievement of some order;
and we must honour Lyly for being the first we know of to

achieve a unified dramatic structure by this means, and Shakespeare's direct model in this particular. But we should not overlook the fact that, as far as Lyly himself is concerned, the structural advantage involves some loss in the quality of the wit: the Tophas-plot is in many ways the silliest of Lyly's sub-plots. It is without the sharpness or bite of the pages' comments on courtliness or scholarship, as found in the preceding plays. Though the sub-plot is closer to the main plot structurally, it is more remote intellectually. The decline of the debate-interest in the plays has removed much of the intellectual function of the pages—to represent an alternative and unfashionable view of the subject being discussed. By concentrating their wit on an unworthy object, however important structurally, Lyly has here debased their function, and the loss weakens the whole play.

Lyly's last three plays—*Love's Metamorphosis, Mother Bombie,* and *The Woman in the Moon*—show a casting loose from the formulae he had employed fairly consistently up to this time, including that of a sub-plot of cheeky pages. *Love's Metamorphosis* is short enough to have had a sub-plot at some earlier stage of its existence, but there is no evidence one way or the other. In *Mother Bombie* the sub-plot has taken over the whole play: the pages are able not only to be witty about the loves of their masters but even to arrange the outcome of their loves. *The Woman in the Moon* is different again: here there is no sub-plot in the ordinary sense of the word, but the function of the pages, who comment on the action from a point of view beneath that which is accepted, is caught up by one character—Gunophilus, Pandora's servant. He keeps up a series of sardonic asides to the audience as the shepherds one by one get dusty or deceiving answers from the planet-ridden Pandora. Like the pages he plumes himself on his cleverness: having told Stesias of Pandora's infidelity, he then persuades him to enter into a 'cave' (probably the stage 'trap'):

> Were't not a pretty jest to bury him quick? I warrant it would be a good while ere she would scratch him out of his grave with her nails, and yet she might too, for she hath digged such vaults in my face that ye may go from my chin to my eyebrows betwixt the skin and the flesh! Wonder not at it good people! I can prove there hath been two or three merchants with me to hire rooms to

lay in wine: but that they do not stand so conveniently as they would wish (for indeed they are every one too near my mouth, and I am a great drinker) I had had a quarter's rent beforehand. Well, be it known unto all men that I have done this to cornute my master, for yet I could never have opportunity. You would little think my neck is grown awry with looking back as I have been a-kissing, for fear he should come; and yet it is a fair example —beware of kissing, brethren! [*the trap begins to open*] What! doth the cave open? ere she and he [*sc. Pandora and Iphicles*] have done, he'll pick the lock with his horn.   (III. ii. 203-18)

The tone of this, with its 'we're-all-good-fellows-here' invitation to complicity, is very different from the earlier sets of wit, which invite the audience to admire but not to take sides; one is tempted to equate the difference with that between the court and the public theatres, between the formal patronage of entertainers and the more robust traditions of audience participation, and to see it as another sign of *The Woman in the Moon*'s having been written for an adult company.

When Gunophilus is enrolled in the list of Pandora's lovers (when Venus is in the ascendant), his comic lechery serves to set off the more romantic attachment of the shepherds, as in the earlier plays the realism of the sub-plot helps to define the stately romanticism of the main plot. One difference (and it is one of many that align this play with *Mother Bombie*) is that the disillusioned view of Pandora is one that the play as a whole endorses. Thus when he elopes with his mistress at the end of the action:

> *Gunophilus.* Well I am revenged at last of my master. I pray God I may be thus even with all mine enemies, only to run away with their wives.
> *Pandora.* Gunophilus, for thee I have done this.
> *Gun.* Ay, and for yourself too; I am sure you will not beg by the way.
> *Pan.* For thee I'll beg and die, Gunophilus.
> *Gun.* Ay, so I think; the world is so hard that if ye beg ye may be sure to be starved.
> *Pan.* I prithee be not so churlish.
> *Gun.* O this is but mirth; do you not know
>
> > *Comes facetus est tanquam vehiculus in via.*
>
> A merry companion is as good as a wagon; for you shall be sure to ride though ye go a-foot.

Pan. Gunophilus, setting this mirth aside, Dost thou not love me
    more than all the world?
Gun. Be you as steadfast to me as I'll be to you, and we two will
    go to the world's end; and yet we cannot, for the world is
    round, and seeing 'tis round, lets dance in the circle: come,
    turn about. [*they dance*]
Pan. When I forsake thee, then heaven itself shall fall.
Gun. No, God forbid! then perhaps we should have larks.

                                      (IV. i. 271-91)

As a means of comic relief Gunophilus has many obvious
advantages over the groups of pages, but this should not blind
us to the fact that he belongs to a different kind of play. Lyly's
clowns come into closest relation to Shakespeare's here,
because Lyly has begun to write Shakespeare's kind of play.
Moreover, the formal advantage does not everywhere com-
pensate for the sparkle of the wit that has been lost. The failure
of the earlier page sub-plots to be concerned about anything
but wit ensures them a brilliance of manner that is lost with
greater integration. Compared with *Campaspe* and *Sapho and
Phao*, *The Woman in the Moon* is a clownish work. The integration,
here as in *Mother Bombie*, blurs into something more generally
acceptable the separate harsh brilliances of these earlier plays.
Though Shakespeare has made an integrated humanity seem
to modern readers to be the key virtue of Elizabethan drama,
we should see that as far as Lyly is concerned the movement
towards Shakespeare is not all gain.

(*d*) STYLE

The success of Lyly's plays is commonly said to represent a
triumph of style, and in general this must be allowed. The
materials of the play could hardly keep them fresh, were it not
for the effervescent liveliness, resourcefulness, virtuosity and
even beauty of the manner. But this manner is often damned
under the blanket name of Euphuism; charts are drawn (as if
this were a stylistic fever) to show the extent of infection or
health in each of the plays—and this can hardly be assented
to as a sufficient view of the matter.

    The principal objection to be made is that this view treats
the artist as the passive victim of his own stylistic habits, as

if the highly patterned prose which appears especially in the
early comedies, were a mere excrescence, added arbitrarily to a
perfectly sound artistic structure—like Baroque stucco on top
of Romanesque stone. But it is not there simply because Lyly
was suffering from a bad dose of agnomination or isocolon. It
is there because it is a means to keep the plays together; no
manner less strongly marked would give unity to materials so
various; this is what we must mean I suppose, when we talk of
'a triumph of style'.

I shall discuss below the general topic of 'Euphuism' and
its relation to contemporary styles, but it is necessary to
anticipate here and point out that Lyly's style, when set beside
the styles of his contemporaries, seems more notable for the
faults it avoids than for those it commits. Lyly wrote in prose,
not verse and we may suggest that he was the first prose-
writer in English who could manage the range of effects that
well-bred mixed conversation requires.[15] But the real comparison must be with verse, not prose, since this was the vehicle
that seemed to contemporaries to be natural in drama, and we
must suppose Lyly to have rejected it, deliberately. One can
see why. In the period in which Lyly was writing, verse was
clearly impossible for his purposes. It was perhaps *easier* to
write in verse, but in this very ease lay much of the disadvantage.
The rhythms of verse supplied a unit of repetition to which
syntax could be accommodated, and this gave some kind of
structure to the long sprawling sentences. But this very dependence of syntax on rhythm takes away the power of verse,
playing syntactic rhythm against the basic stress-pattern, to
mirror the subtlety of speech; the long lines suitable for dramatic
verse are, through most of Elizabeth's reign, only capable of a
bouncing and inflexible rhythm, as remote as possible from the
requirements of witty conversation:

> Come cruel griefs, spare not to stretch our strengths,
> While baleful breasts invite our thumping fists;
> Let every sign that mournful passions work
> Express what piteous plights our minds amaze.
> (*Misfortunes of Arthur*, IV. iii. 1-4)

Once the powerful rhythmical impetus of such verse is set going
(the case with 'fourteeners' or 'poulter's measure' is even more

obvious) it is very difficult for an unsophisticated ear to break
the flow, without demolishing the verse; and the Tudor poets
showed no desire to attempt such sophistication. We speak of
'Marlowe's mighty line' as if the lines before him had been
distinguished by timidity or reticence; but this is not what
we find. Where Marlowe's achievement lies, I suspect, is in
the discovery of a tone of voice able to carry off the inflexible
rhythms, a content 'high-astounding' enough to fill out the
'proud full sail of his great verse'. However this be, Lyly's
achievement lies in the opposite direction—in his power to
avoid raising those expectations of vehemence which inform
the verse of Churchyard no less than that of Marlowe. This
may seem negative praise. It may seem less so if we remember
that Churchyard was an obvious rival for the ear of the Earl
of Oxford (himself addicted to fourteeners), and a rival
encomiast of the Queen, whose enemies (of 1588) he rebukes
in the following terms:

> Mine eyes they weep, my heart it bleeds in breast;
> My soul doth sob, my body quakes for fear;
> My wits they roll, my mind can take no rest,
> My senses blush, as sp'rits amazed were.
> My knowledge shrugs at rumours in mine ear,
> My head doth muse, my reason sore doth rue
> These quarrels old that rise on brabblings new,
> These bold attempts that rebels set abroach
> To God's dislike and country's great reproach.
>
> (Nichols, II. 603)

The effects of this kind of versification on drama may be
seen if we turn back again to *Love and Fortune* and *The Cobbler's
Prophecy* as representative courtly plays of Lyly's own time.
The kinds of verse we find in these two plays are too various
and too laboured ('painful' is the Elizabethan word for it) to
be the result of carelessness. We must treat the various styles
we find as serious attempts to uncover rhythmical equivalents
to the different shades of emotional atmosphere that are
involved. There seems to be a principle involved here, which
was natural enough in Elizabethan England, but which has
not (so far as I know) been discussed by modern critics. It was
known that the Greek and Roman dramatists had written their
plays in a variety of metres (and even of dialects); the metrical

varieties in Terence were certainly a matter of common text-book instruction. Vernacular literature in this case did not provide any counterpoise against classical example. The Mystery Plays and many of the interludes, were written in a variety of metres, ranging from dignified rhyme-royal down to unscannable doggerel.[16] All agreed that

> it is certain that one and the same sort of style is not called for in the case of a rich man as of a poor one; in plain, straightforward narrative as in thrasonical boasting; in soothing consolation as in complaint; in a voice from heaven as in the wailings that arise from hell. Consequently, the work ought to be done so in accordance with the nature, the change, and the manner of the action, that at one time the verse may creep along in an unpretentious measure, shunning, as it were, the adornments and forms of oratory, whereas at other times it may speed along in a fuller and more precipitous course. Often, however, with marshalled words in battle array, it makes an onset like the snowstorms of winter, and its eloquence bursts forth unchecked, and gains the fields in which it can revel.
>
> (Nicholas Grimald, *Christus Redivivus* (1542), Preface)

Given this background, the modern assumption that there ought to be a single metrical unit for the whole play would not necessarily recommend itself; and in the court plays of the period I do not find it. In *Love and Fortune*, for example, there is a bewildering variety of metres employed, to match the variety of episodes, social levels, and moods that the play contains. Sometimes the expressive intention behind the choice of metre is fairly obvious: when Bomelio, falling into madness, simultaneously drops into prose, we understand; again, when a comic dialogue is expressed in anapaests the point can be accepted. But not all the changes can be explained so easily, and even in those where it is easy, the explanation is *ex post facto*; as we hear the play we are aware only of a dreadful uncertainty where the next accent will fall; the gears crash alarmingly as we move from fourteeners to heroic couplets, to poulter's measure, to hexameters.

In *The Cobbler's Prophecy* the metres are better metres (owing, I must suppose, to the example of Marlowe), but the capacity to sustain a stylistic norm against which the various metres of the play are seen to be variations, is still beyond the author.

He is interested in the effects of his individual scenes, and tries to use metres which will be expressive of their individual tones; but he is less interested in the continuity from scene to scene, so that the 'gallimaufry' effect (which I have discussed above) is one that applies to the metres no less than to the structure.

Even *The Arraignment of Paris*, a far better play than either of these, succeeds by giving in to this outlook rather than by seeking to advance beyond it. Like these others, the play is an exercise in several modes, the Senecan violence of Ate's prologue, the pastoral charm of the Oenone story, the forensic dignity of the final Olympian judgment, etc. The metres show a similar, though not an expressive variation:—fourteener couplets for conversations, decasyllabic couplets (sometimes breaking into fourteeners) for speeches in dialogue and blank verse for formal orations (not to mention songs in English, Latin and Italian). The effect again, emphasizes the local effect at the expense of continuity, turning what might have been a play into a 'show'.

Having written *Euphues* and established his fame as a stylist of unrivalled virtuosity, Lyly was an obvious person to rescue drama from this defect. The finesse he brought to the task is obvious as soon as we open the first page of his first play:

> *Clitus.* Parmenio, I cannot tell whether I should more commend in Alexander's victories, courage or courtesy; in the one being a resolution without fear, in the other a liberality above custom. Thebes is razed, the people not racked; towers thrown down, bodies not thrust aside; a conquest without conflict and a cruel war in a mild peace.
>
> *Parmenio.* Clitus, it becometh the son of Philip to be none other than Alexander is; therefore seeing in the father a full perfection, who could have doubted in the son an excellency? For as the moon can borrow nothing else of the sun but light, so of a sire, in whom nothing but virtue was, what could the child receive but singular? It is for turquoise to stain each other, not for diamonds; in the one to be made a difference in goodness, in the other no comparison. (*Campaspe*, I. i. 1-13)

This is not a style suitable for every occasion, but it is flexible enough to cover a fair range of courtly emotions; even more important, it is a style of sufficiently marked individuality to impose its 'key-signature' on the whole drama, from kings and lovers down to clowns.

Take the following love exchange from *Love and Fortune*:

Hermione. Why then my dear what is the greatest price in love?
Fidelia. Absence of other's griefs the greatest that loving hearts can prove.
Herm. Yet absence cannot minish love or make it less in ought.
Fid. But nevertheless it leaves a doubt within the other's thought.
Herm. And what is that?
Fid. Lest change of air should change the absent mind.
Herm. That fault is proper but to them whom jealousy makes blind. (M.S.R. ll. 285-91)

Compare this with the amorous catechism in *Campaspe*:

Campaspe. What counterfeit is this, Apelles?
Apelles. This is Venus, the goddess of love.
Camp. What, be there also loving goddesses?
Apel. This is she that hath power to command the very affections of the heart.
Camp. How is she hired, by prayer, by sacrifice or bribes?
Apel. By prayer, sacrifice and bribes.
Camp. What prayer?
Apel. Vows irrevocable.
Camp. What sacrifice?
Apel. Hearts ever sighing, never dissembling.
Camp. What bribes?
Apel. Roses and kisses; but were you never in love?
Camp. No, nor love in me.
Apel. Then have you injured many.
Camp. How so?
Apel. Because you have been loved of many.
Camp. Flattered perchance of some.
Apel. It is not possible that a face so fair and a wit so sharp, both without comparison, should not be apt to love.
Camp. If you begin to tip your tongue with cunning, I pray dip your pencil in colours, and fall to that you must do, not that you would do. (*Campaspe*, III. iii. 29-51)

The ideas here (repeated elsewhere in Lyly—e.g. *Love's Metamorphosis* II. i. 104-117) may be derived from Ovid, but this can hardly be taken to infringe the originality of Lyly's manner; for the whole of Golding's *Metamorphoses* comes from Ovid; and that is hardly a monument of crisp wit. The sharp-

ness of the expression here, and the awareness of social tone
that it shows, the undercurrents of irony that it expresses—
all these show the advantages of Lyly's prose. It may not
individualize those who are speaking, but it does convey the
pleasure of speaking such lines; the mind dances on the tautness
of the dialogue. In the other, half way along the blundering
lines the interest begins to flag; the impulse of the idea is
exhausted before the rhythm has concluded its bouncing
progression; and in the dreary monotony of superfluous
rhythm the dramatic impetus is lost.

I argue, in short, that Euphuism was as important to Lyly's
success as a comic dramatist as blank verse was to Marlowe's.
It made the transition from low comedy, farce and slapstick
to courtly comedy of ladies and gentlemen a possibility, by
providing a norm of prose rhythm against which the personal
and social variations of the characters could be brought alive.
Take the following examples:

(1) I serve Apelles who feedeth me as Diogenes doth Manes; for
at dinner the one preacheth abstinence, the other commendeth counterfeiting; when I would eat meat, he paints
a spit; and when I thirst, 'O' saith he, 'Is not this a fair pot?'
and points to a table [*picture*] which contains the banquet
of the gods, where are many dishes to feed the eye, but not
to fill the gut. (*Campaspe*, I. ii. 55-60)

(2) Treacherous and most perjured Endimion, is Cynthia the
sweetness of thy life, and the bitterness of my death? What
revenge may be devised so full of shame as my thoughts are
replenished with malice? Tell me, Floscula, if falseness in
love can possibly be punished with extremity of hate. As
long as sword, fire or poison may be hired, no traitor to my
love shall live unrevenged. Were thy oaths without number,
thy kisses without measure, thy sighs without end, forged to
deceive a poor credulous virgin, whose simplicity had been
worth thy favour and better fortune? If the gods sit unequal
[*partial*] beholders of injuries or laughers at lovers' deceits,
then let mischief be as well forgiven in women as perjury
winked at in men. (*Endimion*, I. ii. 1-12)

(3) *Sapho.* Sir boy, will ye undertake to carry us over the water?
Are you dumb, can you not speak?
Phao. Madam, I crave pardon; I am spurblind; I could
scarce see.

249

Sapho. It is pity in so good a face there should be an evil eye.
Phao. I would in my face there were never an eye.
Sapho. Thou canst never be rich in a trade of life of all the basest.
Phao. Yet content, madam, which is a kind of life of all the best.
Sapho. Wilt thou forsake the ferry and follow the court as a page?
Phao. As it pleaseth fortune, madam, to whom I am a prentice. (*Sapho and Phao*, II. ii. 18-30)

The antithetical dance of words here is fully dramatic, for the antitheses are not only of words but of characters and emotions in the plays, and serve to convey these relationships. The farcical balance of the hungry page against the ascetic painter helps to define both figures in a sharp and memorable way. The tirade of Tellus in (2) sets out equally sharply the paradoxical hate-love complex in her mind, and again by means of the balanced clauses that are the staple of Euphuism. The third example may serve to indicate the power of Euphuism to lighten dialogue and at the same time show the opportunity that dialogue gave Lyly to free Euphuism from too narrow a range of repetitions. For the necessity to keep up a strict pattern of antithesis as a framework for his essentially disjunctive wit, is hardly pressing where dialogue provides its own antiphony. The *tic-tac* being obvious enough as we move from speaker to speaker, Lyly can concentrate on the antitheses of *idea*, and though he does not succeed in turning the speakers into witty persons, he at least goes beyond the 'quick answers' on which the scene is based, to some evocation of the complexity of real responses. The indirections and uncertainties of Phao's replies suggest a tongue more glib than the heart that informs it. There is a kind of casuistry in his distinctions which points beyond the chop-logic of the pages towards a mode of speaking which expresses the natural indirection of the loving heart.

(e) HIGH COMEDY

One pitfall I have sought to avoid in this survey of Lyly's plays is that of dwelling too long on a supposed central 'Lylian' quality; I have sought to present each play as a separate

experience, and to keep such generalization as a subordinate
issue; for it is important to notice the variety of Lyly's achievement, and the several integrities of several plays. But there is
also danger on this other side. If we leave the plays as separate
achievements we distort the question of influence, which is
obviously important in any assessment of Lyly. If we are to
speak of Lyly as having influence on his contemporaries and as
handing forward 'ideals' of writing we must be prepared to
hazard definitions of these ideals.

If we ask what qualities separated Lyly's comedies from those
of his contemporaries we are involved, of necessity, in the
attempt to define what is nowadays usually called 'High
Comedy'—in contradistinction to the 'low' comedy, farce or
slapstick which was already in Lyly's day (with *Roister Doister*
and *Gammer Gurton* to its credit) a powerful part of the English
tradition.

That there was some self-consciousness in Lyly's departure
from this tradition would seem to be indicated by the Blackfriars Prologue to *Sapho and Phao*:

> Our intent was at this time to move inward delight, not outward
> lightness: and to breed (if it might be) soft smiling, not loud
> laughing; knowing it to the wise to be as great pleasure to hear
> counsel mixed with wit, as to the foolish to have sport mingled
> with rudeness. They were banished the theatre at Athens, and
> from Rome hissed, that brought parasites on the stage with
> apish actions, or fools with uncivil habits, or courtesans with
> immodest words. We have endeavoured to be as far from un-
> seemly speeches to make your ears glow as we hope you will be
> from unkind reports to make our cheeks blush.

The terms used here, and the general outlook, have often been
seen as a response to Sidney's plea in his *Defence of Poesy* for a
comedy of delight:

> So falleth it out that, having indeed no right comedy, in that
> comical part of our tragedy we have nothing but scurrility,
> unworthy of any chaste ears, or some extreme show of doltishness,
> indeed fit to lift up a loud laughter and nothing else; where the
> whole tract of a comedy should be full of delight, as the tragedy
> should be still maintained in a well-raised admiration. But our
> comedians think there is no delight without laughter; which is
> very wrong, for though laughter may come with delight, yet

cometh it not of delight, as though delight should be the cause of laughter; but well may one thing breed both together. Nay rather in themselves they have, as it were, a kind of contrariety; for delight we scarcely do but in things that have a conveniency to ourselves or to the general nature; laughter almost ever cometh of things most disproportioned to ourselves and nature; delight hath a joy in it, either permanent or present; laughter hath only a scornful tickling. For example, we are ravished with delight to see a fair woman, and yet are far from being moved to laughter; we laugh at deformed creatures wherein certainly we cannot delight. We delight in good chances; we laugh at mischances. We delight to hear the happiness of our friends, and country, at which he were worthy to be laughed at that would laugh; we shall, contrarily, laugh sometimes to find a matter quite mistaken and go down the hill against the bias, in the mouth of some such men as, for the respect of them, one shall be heartily sorry he cannot choose but laugh, and so is rather pained than delighted with laughter. Yet I deny not but that they may go well together; for as in Alexander's picture, well set out, we delight without laughter, and in twenty mad antics we laugh without delight, so in Hercules, painted with his great beard and furious countenance, in a woman's attire spinning at Omphale's commandment, it breeds both delight and laughter. For the representing of so strange a power in love procures delight; and the scornfulness of the action stirreth laughter. But I speak to this purpose that all the end of the comical part be not upon such scornful matters as stir laughter only but mix with it that delightful teaching which is the end of poesy.

(Feuillerat's *Sidney*, III. 40 f.)

What we would seem to have here is the distinction, common enough among Shakespearian critics, between laughter *at* a character (Dogberry, Armado, the Falstaff of *Merry Wives*) and laughter *with* a character (Berowne, Rosalind, the Falstaff of *Henry IV*). And in terms of this distinction, Lyly is certainly Shakespeare's most important predecessor. His comedy of love involves our amused sympathy rather than our scorn—for, as Sidney says, 'the representing of so strange a power in love procureth delight'. Lyly makes it possible to view love's power as 'strange' in this sense by placing his lovers in a cultured and self-conscious context, which neutralizes our scorn for love's absurdity by showing either (in his major characters) the preference for self-control (in Alexander, Sapho, Cynthia) or (in his minor characters) an approach so delicate and tentative that we see the impulse to action rather than the action itself, and so for this reason react with 'soft smiling, not loud laughing'.

This attitude to love involves a further aspect of 'High Comedy' which neither Sidney nor Lyly talk about, but which is clearly illustrated in Lyly's plays. I refer to the prominent part played by educated women in such comedy. This has been most elaborately described by Meredith in his famous essay 'On the Idea of Comedy' (1877). Meredith tells us that 'the higher the comedy, the more prominent the part they [the ladies] enjoy in it.' When he says 'higher' here he is not, of course, thinking of 'high' as descriptive of a kind of comedy, but only of its degree of closeness to an ideal; but since his ideal is what we now call 'High Comedy', it is not unfair to apply it here. Meredith does not mention Lyly, but his praise of Congreve is one that could apply (with certain historical allowances) to Lyly's plays: '*The Way of the World* may be read out currently at a first glance, so sure are the accents of the emphatic meaning to strike the eye, perforce of the crispness and cunning polish of the sentences.' The world of High Comedy is a world of *style*, in which literary polish is used to evoke the polished minds of its characters. We watch them move, with a sense of our own muddling grossness, and fascinated by the sparkle, flippancy and independence of their wit. We peer into what Meredith calls, 'that lively quicksilver world of the animalcule passions' with something of the wonder we bring to the sight of an exquisitely made watch—the flickering jewelled movement dazzles the eye as it teases the mind, while the sense of it being a toy lightens as it complements the sense of coherence and purposiveness providing a criticism of our own lives.

Artistic power here is above all the power to prevent the 'toy-like' nature of the world created from degenerating into the 'insignificant'. Swift's Lilliputians and Pope's sylphs are exquisite enough, but it is the satirist's intention to use this to point their insignificance, their less than human status. The writer of High Comedy must ensure the opposite reaction. Shakespeare clearly does so in his various pictures of exquisite refinement, Rosalind, Viola or the Princess of France; but Shakespeare's capacity to use the world of 'play' so as to lead us into a new perception of reality is (of course) a thing in itself. But even if we leave Shakespeare on one side, the line of High Comedy in English—which may be represented by the names of Lyly, Congreve and Wilde—can be seen to involve a narrow passage between loss-of-exquisiteness on one side and loss-of-significance on the other.

Lyly, Congreve and Wilde are all concerned to paint an image of 'high life' which is at once impossibly elegant and yet a reflection of what inelegantly human beings actually desire—or at least admire. Theirs is a world in which idleness never bores, flirtation never palls (and never burgeons, disturbingly, into passion), in which wealth does not oppress and where power exists without responsibility; it is, in short, a world of permanently poised potentiality, indeed of wish-fulfilment; but the wish-fulfilment is everywhere curbed by self-awareness, by knowledge of the destructive capacities of appetite, and sharpened everywhere by respect for the rational intelligence.

This 'respect for the rational intelligence' is the point at which the female wits of High Comedy most clearly affect the nature of its world. The poise of life in High Comedy is presented chiefly through an imagined balance between male and female forces, in a state of equality which is only possible where intelligence rather than passion or social valuation governs the terms of contact. Their emotions are restricted by rules with their own intellectual beauty, to be savoured for this by actors and audience alike, and we measure their natures by their power to use the rules to their own advantage. Within this formal setting the female wit has a natural advantage over the male, as well as a natural opposition to it. For the male intelligence has certain qualities which hamper it in dealing with such formalities of living: we may notice especially a tendency to take all or nothing, to be rash in action, and to be self-deceived about motives. Female passivity, on the other hand, tends to keep the ladies detached and 'sensible' about games, wise before as well as after the event. Hence it is the natural role of the man in High Comedy to be infatuated and forget that it is all a game; while the natural role of the woman is to remain unimplicated in any belief that the rules are absolutes, to be more sure of feelings than of any system for expressing them, and so to act as a moderating influence, usually by mocking male pretensions. As Meredith says: 'Comedy is the fountain of good sense, not the less perfectly sound on account of the sparkle; and Comedy lifts women to a station offering them free play for their wit, as they usually show it, when they have it, on the side of sound sense'.

The role of Millamant as a witty curb on breaches of good sense is obvious, as is the verbal elegance of the world over which it is her right to reign. The same may be said of the Honourable Gwendolen Fairfax in Wilde's *The Importance of Being Ernest*, though Wilde's epicoene fops take over some of the female roles from the earlier comedy. Rosalind, Beatrice, Viola and the ladies of *Love's Labour's Lost* are obviously the crown of this tradition. But has Lyly any right to stand at the beginning of it? Certainly he has no heroines to enter into the competition; but his world is recognizably the world which the later heroine will make her own—a world of stylish balance between good sense and genuine sensibility, in which the loving male can be kept at a distance:

Mileta. No, no, men are good souls (poor souls!), who never enquire but with their eyes, loving to father the cradle though they but mother the child. Give me their gifts, not their virtues; a grain of their gold weigheth down a pound of their wit; a dram of 'give me' is heavier than an ounce of 'hear me'. Believe me, ladies, 'give' is a pretty thing.

Ismena. I cannot but oftentimes smile to myself to hear men call us weak vessels, when they prove themselves broken hearted; us frail, when their thoughts cannot hang together, studying with words to flatter and with bribes to allure; when we commonly wish their tongues in their purses, they speak so simply, and their offers in their bellies, they do it so peevishly.

Mileta. It is good sport to see them want matter; for then fall they to good manners, having nothing in their mouths but 'sweet mistress', wearing our hands out with courtly kissings when their wits fail in courtly discourses; now ruffling their hairs, now setting their ruffs; then gazing with their eyes, then sighing with a privy wring by the hand, thinking us like to be wooed by signs and ceremonies.

Eugenua. Yet we, when we swear with our mouths we are not in love, then we sigh from the heart and pine in love.

Canope. We are mad wenches, if men mark our words; for when I say, 'I would none cared for love more than I' what mean I

but, 'I would none loved but I'. Where we cry, 'away' do we
not presently say, 'go to'; and when men strive for kisses we
exclaim, 'let us alone' as though we would fall to that ourselves.

(Sapho and Phao, I. iv. 22-47)

The harsh Ovidian brilliance of the stratagems in love that the
ladies describe here, lacks the extra dimension of female tenderness; for though the ladies tell us they are in love, this information does not fuse with their earlier trickery to give us a sense
of a complex human response. None of Lyly's characters, in
fact, prepare us for the complexity of temperament that Shakespeare handles; but the complexity of Lyly's situations is not far
away. Of the Elizabethans, only Lyly succeeds in making wit
the basis of comedy, detaching speech from its immediate
(persuasive) function and characters from their practical
purposes, to re-establish both in a pattern of courtly (and to
that extent serious) *play*. If High Comedy can be made to exist
by creating a world of witty elegance, without depending on
characters of witty elegance, then Lyly is undoubtedly the first
English dramatist in this genre.

THE VICTIM OF FASHION

WE HAVE looked at Lyly's *Euphues* and his plays as literary experiences worthy of comment in their own right. They may be seen, however, from another angle—as part of a tide of fashion which swept them up, sustained them for a moment, and then, as relentlessly, swept them away. This indeed is how they must have looked to contemporaries, and to Lyly himself at the end of his life. The obscure Henry Upchear who praises Greene's *Menaphon* in 1589 tells us,

> Of all the flowers a *Lily* once I loved
> Whose labouring beauty branched itself abroad
> But now old age his glory hath removed,
> And Greener objects are mine eyes' abode.[1]

In many ways the isolation of Lyly from his background may seem just enough; *Euphues* was the most popular work of the period and therefore must be supposed to have been most influential, and most representative; the style may have been popularized by Pettie and worked to death by Greene, but we still call it 'Euphuism'. Yet if we look more closely at the period, the uniqueness and indeed the separateness of *Euphues* begins to disappear; instead of seeing a distinct blob, we only notice the convergence of a number of different lines, and our interest moves from the point of convergence to the lines themselves.

In 1567 the *novelle* of Bandello, or rather the French elaborations of Bandello by Belleforest, were Englished by Geoffrey Fenton. Fenton added still further to the elaborations and rhetorical digressions of his original. In the same year was published the wide-ranging but essentially similar collection by William Painter—his *Palace of Pleasure*. In 1573 George Gascoigne published a single story of love-adventure ('The Adventures of Master F. J.'). In 1576 George Pettie sought to rival Painter with a *Petite Palace of Pettie his Pleasure*, which contains stories from non-Italian (usually classical) sources and further augments the rhetorical digressions and the style (reaching a kind of proto-Euphuism). Also in 1576 comes Whetstone's *Rock of Regard* miscellany, with a love-adventure story ('Rinaldo and Giletta') clearly descending from that of his friend Gascoigne. Dated 1577 is Grange's *Golden Aphroditis*, a single, long, rhetorically digressive love story. In 1578 there is *Euphues*; in 1579, Gosson's *Ephermerides of Phialo*, similar to *Euphues*, but not deriving exclusively from it. In 1580 comes Mundy's *Zelauto*, Austen Saker's *Narbonus*, and *Euphues and his England*, all indebted to *Euphues*, but also showing lines of descent which by-pass that work. In 1581 there is Barnaby Rich's *Don Simonides*. In 1583-4 we have Melbanke's *Philotimus*, Barnaby Rich's *Don Simonides* again ('the second tome'), with Greene's first effort, *Mamillia*. Up to this point the fashion for love-stories moralized in the manner of Lyly would seem to be in full flood; thereafter, in the long series of Greene's romances we can see a recession from it. Indeed even in the list I have given there are elements which belong to alternative traditions, and the 'decline of the fashion' can be seen largely in terms of separating out these descriptive and narrative elements from the specifically 'Lylian' debating and speechifying ones and developing them independently; the drift from Lyly is part of a larger drift of Elizabethan taste.

Indeed it is hard to describe the drift of Lyly's reputation except as part of a general movement; for what a writer may have taken from Lyly he may also have taken from other sources. The tradition is a network of imitations: Lyly imitates Pettie, Pettie imitates Painter, Painter imitates and translates Belleforest, Belleforest translates Bandello; and Bandello himself is seldom an original.[2] Lyly was the most successful of these authors; few of the others saw their novels pass beyond a single edition. But Lyly's success was not (as the earlier critics supposed) due to his originality; rather it would seem to be due to a unique skill in combining, balancing and interrelating the various strands he inherited from others. *Euphues* takes us into the society of polite ladies to listen to their conversation, but so did Hoby's *Courtier* (1561), Edmund Tilney's *Discourse of Duties in Marriage* (1568), and Wotton's *Courtly Cautels* (1578); Euphues draws on the themes of the *dubbii d'amore*, but so do Gascoigne's *F. J.*, Grange's *Golden Aphroditis* and Tilney's book. It addresses itself to the ladies, but so does Pettie. It contains long moralizing digressions, but so did the whole tradition of sentimental romance. It notes the deceitfulness of wit, but so did Ascham and the Prodigal Son plays. It makes some point of its contemporary relevance, but so did Pettie; and so on. It is difficult to find a single point in which *Euphues* introduces a motif which is later incorporated into the tradition. I have spoken indeed of Lyly's interest in debate and his lack of interest in description; in the proportions of his mixture he may well be unique, and the relevance of his style to this feature of his content is important; but both debating and descriptive techniques were part of the tradition long before *Euphues* was written.

Every aspiring author in the period must have read *Euphues*, but few can have read only *Euphues*; and much of the apparent reference turns out to be a completely superficial cashing-in on the manner or the name. Greene's *Euphues his censure to Philautus* (1587) is a collection of tales to illustrate a debate between Hector and Achilles concerning 'the exquisite portraiture of a perfect martialist'. The Epistle to the reader makes it quite clear that the use of Euphues' name is only catchpenny:

> Gentlemen, by chance some of Euphues' loose papers came to my hand, wherein he writ to his friend Philautus from Silexedra certain principles necessary to be observed by every soldier . . . hoping . . . that you will for Euphues' sake vouchsafe of the matter. (Grosart's *Greene*, VI. 154)

The title of Greene's later *Menaphon: Camilla's alarum to slumbering Euphues in his melancholy cell at Silexedra* (1589) may perhaps be justified in so far as the book aims to mock Euphuism as a style, but this is at best a slender excuse. There is no more to be said in favour of Lodge's use of the name in his *Euphues' Shadow* (1592) or his *Rosalind: Euphues' Golden Legacy found after his death in his cell at Silexedra. Bequeathed to Philautus' sons* (1590). Arthur Dickenson's *Arisbas: Euphues amid his slumbers* (1594) is, in fact (like *Menaphon*), an imitation of Sidney's *Arcadia*. As we shall see below when discussing the style, the exact quality of Lyly's mind was not caught by any of his imitators, whose pastiche productions can be seen usually as reversions to traditional modes of writing and constructing which he had been careful to avoid or to rearrange.

It is not, of course, for its content that *Euphues* was chiefly remembered; and if we wish to trace the history of its reputation, it is most convenient to do this in terms of style rather than subject. It is the style that has given the word 'Euphuism' a permanent place in the English language and characterized John Lyly as a man whose significance is fixed if we attach to his name the pejorative label of 'the Euphuist'. I call the label pejorative for 'Euphuism' has come to mean in general, a perversely elaborate style, and historically, a faddish aberration which affected English prose for a period of ten years or so 1578 to *c.*1590. Smith's Latin Dictionary nicely sums up this attitude in its definition: *'putida quaedam dictionis affectatio quem euphuismum appellant'*. This being so, it becomes a work of mere piety to remove the distorting incubus from the name of John Lyly. For 'distorting' it certainly is, most obviously in the historical aspect. Lyly did not invent Euphuism; he merely brought to focus tendencies and tricks in style which were everywhere around him, and which had been a fairly regular feature of rhetorical prose since the days of Gorgias of Leontini (5th century B.C.). Even if Lyly had never existed, Euphuism (no doubt under another name) would still be a strand of Elizabethan style that the historian would have to deal with.

Moreover the common idea that Euphuism *distorted* the course of English prose is not, I think, one that can survive an acquaintance with the writers immediately before Lyly; and I shall argue below that its power was one of clarifying the style of the time. The earlier estimates of its place seem to have been based on plain ignorance. Thus we have Gifford (in 1816) telling us that

> These notable productions [the two volumes of *Euphues*] were full of pedantic and affected phraseology (as Whalley truly says) and of high-strained antitheses of thought and expression. Unfortunately they were well received at court, where they did incalculable mischief, by vitiating the taste, corrupting the

language and introducing a spurious and unnatural mode of conversation and action.

(note on Jonson, *Every Man Out*, V. vii)

This view was given its most naïve and therefore most revealing expression in 1862. The author (George P. Marsh) speaks of

that brief period of philological and literary affectation which for a time threatened the language, the poetry, and even the prose of England with a degradation as complete as that of the speech and the literature of the last age of imperial Rome. This quality of style appears in its most offensive form in the nauseous rhymes of Skelton, in the most elegant in Lyly, in its most quaint and ludicrous in Stanihurst. Spenser and Shakespeare were the *Dei ex machina* who checked the ravages of this epidemic.

(quoted in Arber's *Euphues*, p. 25)

These ideas appear often enough elsewhere, expressed in more sophisticated ways; the obviously affected forms of Elizabethan prose are often seen as a distortion (more or less wilful) of plain, downright English, represented by the authors we now think best in the period. R. W. Chambers has seen a continuity in plain prose,[3] against which the extravagances of Euphuism or Arcadianism must seem wilfully aberrant. But some acquaintance with the mass of literary prose between Malory and Lyly shows that the plain prose of which Chambers writes may be continuous but is not representative. C. S. Lewis, the most recent student of the subject has this to say about Sir Thomas More who stands at the centre of Chambers' picture: 'The man who sits down and reads fairly through fifty pages of More will find many phrases to admire; but he will also find an invertebrate length of sentence, a fumbling multiplication of epithets, and an almost complete lack of rhythmical vitality' (*Sixteenth Century*, p. 180); and More is in these respects completely the man of his age. Lewis again has an admirable warning at the beginning of his chapter on prose before Lyly: 'Not all plain prose is good. Such efforts as ink-horn terms or euphuism may have been misdirected, even barbarous, but those who made them were not wrong in their belief that our prose needed to be heightened and coloured and "strongly trussed up". We forget too easily the faults of the plain Drab' (p. 272). To

261

exemplify this we may notice two passages from the *Hundred Merry Tales* (1525), as enjoyed by Queen Elizabeth, if not by Shakespeare's Beatrice.[4]

> In a certain town there was a rich man that lay on his death-bed at point of death, which charged his executors to deal for his soul a certain sum of money in pence, and on this condition charged them as they would answer afore God that every poor man that came to them and told a true tale should have a penny, and they that said a false thing should have none.
>
> (Collier's reprint, p. 110)

> A certain fellow there was which proferred a dagger to sell to a fellow, the which answered him and said that he had right nought to give therefore; wherefore the other said that he should have his dagger upon condition that he should give and deliver unto him therefore, within three days after, right nought or else forty shillings in money; whereon the other was content.
>
> (*ibid.* p. 71)

The invertebrate sentences here are pleasing enough, given the quaint simplicity of the subject-matter; but they are obviously incapable of expressing any complexity of relationship. The author is not in control of the random consonances and repetitions which occur (fellow/fellow; therefore/wherefore), and our attention wanders round the statements instead of being carried along by them.

When the author becomes conscious of the dignity or complexity of the occasion in which his prose is involved, his normal resource, in this early Tudor period, is to augment his statements by means of synonyms. Lord Berners can render Froissart's slow-moving narrative into simple English; but the Preface shows him incapable of using one word where three will do:

> What condign graces and thanks ought men to give to the writers of histories, who with their great labours have done so much profit to the human life? They show, open, manifest and declare to the reader, by example of old antiquity, what we should enquire, desire, and follow, and also, what we should eschew, avoid, and utterly fly: for when we (being unexpert of chances) see, behold, and read the ancient acts, gests and deeds, how and with what labours, dangers, and perils they were gested and done,

they right greatly admonish, ensigne and teach us how we may lead forth our lives.

One can see from the Berners' passage how the desire to 'exornate' would lead to the practice of 'inkhornism'—the coining of strange words, or the dumping of them from foreign sources [*condign, ensigne*]. Here the pursuit of a rich fluency has defeated its own aims (at least from our point of view); the total impression is rendered less impressive rather than more so. But the flourishing of synonyms is not all to be explained as a barbaric display of verbal splendours. The strange word is the emphatic word, the reduplicated idea stands out of the sentence, and given the kind of basic sentences I have quoted from the *Hundred Merry Tales*, one can see why the more self-conscious authors were driven to linguistic folly in their effort to communicate emphatically. C. S. Lewis, quoting a particularly egregious example, remarks on the 'effect as of a man speaking with his mouth half full of gravel' (p. 273); the problems of verbal emphasis in such a condition hardly need to be explained.

The style of Cicero was not, in these circumstances, a fortunate model; for Cicero's long and interwoven periods were sufficiently like the long loose sentences of the vernacular tradition to encourage the pursuit of the one by the other, but too embedded in the linguistic pattern of Latin to make imitation possible. The periodic style requires, if it is to make its effect, a tight control over the different co-ordinate or antithetical ideas which appear in it; this Cicero manages by organizing his word-order in a way not open to an analytical language like English, and by organizing the rhythm, jingling and balancing his clauses one against the other.

Take the following very average piece of Ciceronian prose:

Sed sunt non nullae disciplinae, quae propositis bonorum et malorum finibus officium omne pervertant. Nam qui summum bonum sic instituit, ut nihil habeat cum virtute coniunctum, idque suis commodis, non honestate metitur, hic, si sibi ipse consentiat et non interdum naturae bonitate vincatur neque amicitiam colere possit nec iustitiam nec liberalitatem; fortis vero dolorem summum malum iudicans aut temperans voluptatem summum bonum statuens esse certe nullo modo potest.

(*De Officiis* I. § 5)

The emphasis here is distributed by subordination (quae propositis . . . finibus . . . pervertant), by separating co-ordinate ideas (neque amicitiam colere possit nec iustitiam nec liberalitatem) and by balancing clauses (as in the chiastic 'dolorem summum malum iudicans aut temperans voluptatem summum bonum'). Whittington, trying to translate this in 1534, follows the Latin so closely that he produces a no-language: 'But there be many disciplines which the end of miseries and felicities purposed do pervert all office and good manner', etc. Grimald's later translation (1553) is much better, and deserved to go on being reprinted throughout the sixteenth century:

> But there be sundry doctrines, which in setting forth the ends of good and bad do misturn all duty. For who in such wise appointeth the sovereign good that it hath nothing adjoined with virtue, and measureth the same by his commodities and not by honesty, it cometh to pass that this man, if in himself he agree, and be not sometime overcome with the goodness of nature, can use neither friendship, neither justice, nor liberality, and in no wise doubtless can he be a manly man, who judgeth pain the utterest evil, nor he a temperate man who counteth pleasure the greatest good. (1566 edn., sig. A3)

The long sentence is managed here with considerable dexterity; but the strain shows in the rather over-emphatic phrases used to join the clauses ('it cometh to pass that', 'and in no wise doubtless'), which wreck the fine balance of the original—the ironic tone of 'et non interdum naturae bonitate vincatur' is completely lost.

The relation of Euphuism to these inherited and adopted styles is not simple; we may briefly suggest that Lyly gave definitive form to a taste for patently balanced shorter clauses, which had existed long before his time; but before his time this taste had appeared as only one among several, competing for the attention of the reader, as an occasional effect in Ascham, for example, inside a general dependence on long aggregative sentences. Lyly isolates this taste to a state of almost chemical purity, and substitutes for the uneasy aggregate of clauses which was the staple of Tudor prose a style based on a very small number of easily recognized patterns, rhythmic and syntactic, repeated over and over again.

Euphuism can thus be defined in terms of a restricted number of figures, and I may be permitted to give a rapid survey of its characteristic elements:

(1) *Parison* (the use of what is observably the same structure in different clauses); see the example under (3).

(2) *Isocolon* (the balancing of clauses which are related by having the same length); see the example under (3).

(3) *Paromoion* (the balancing of clauses which have the same sound-patterns): 'not the carved visard of a lewd woman, but the incarnate visage of a lascivious wanton' (I. 189).

(4) *Quasi-rhymes* (*similiter cadens, similiter desinens, anaphora, epistrophe*, etc.—jingling or rhyming the beginnings or endings of clauses): 'Ay, but Euphues hath greater perfection. Ay, but Philautus hath deeper affection' (I. 205); 'Artistippus a philosopher, yet who more court[e]ly? Diogenes a philosopher, yet who more carterly?' (I. 190).

(5) *Alliteration*, and especially transverse alliteration: 'the blossom before the fruit, the bud before the flower' (I. 195); 'a sweet panther with a devouring paunch, a sour poison in a silver pot' (I. 202).

(6) *Extended similes derived from 'unnatural natural history'*: 'though the camomile the more it is trodden and pressed down the more it spreadeth, yet the violet the oftener it is handled and touched the sooner it withereth and decayeth' (I. 196).

(7) *Proverbs and Exemplums* (especially when arranged in lists): 'Tush! the case is light where reason taketh place; to love and to live well is not granted to Jupiter. Whoso is blinded with the caul of beauty discerneth no colour of honesty. Did not Giges cut Candaules a coat by his own measure? Did not Paris though he were a welcome guest to Menelaus serve his host a slippery prank?' (I. 210).

(8) *Rhetorical questions* (especially in lists): 'And canst thou, Lucilla, be so light of love in forsaking Philautus, to fly to Euphues? Canst thou prefer a stranger before thy countryman? a starter before thy companion?' (I. 205); 'Didest not thou accuse women of inconstancy? didest not thou account them easy to be won? didest not thou condemn them of weakness? What sounder argument can he have against thee than thine own answer? what better proof than thine own speech? what greater trial than thine own talk?' (I. 206).

What Lyly is doing in relation to the whole development of Tudor prose-style may be seen in little by the relation of these figures to those of the most obvious proto-Euphuist—George

Pettie. Dr Swart, who has written learnedly on this relationship, points out how Lyly tightens up the whole system of balance as that existed in Pettie: 'in Pettie's prose we are struck by the alliteration rather than by the balance of phrases. By restricting the alliteration, shortening the isocolon—thereby making it more obvious—and combining parison and patterned alliteration to a higher degree than had been done by Pettie, Lyly created a systematic style, which has a certain elegance'.[5] The elegance and the reasons for the elegance are somewhat similar to those more familiar to us from the heroic couplet. By establishing an obvious basic pattern of expectation the author can distribute his emphases with greater finesse.[6]

This may be seen if we compare Lyly's translation of Plutarch (in 'Euphues and his Ephoebus') with the earlier translations of Sir Thomas Elyot (1535) and Edward Grant (1571)[7]; in the following extracts '(a)' represents Elyot, '(b)' Grant, '(c)' Lyly.

(a) For sloth destroyeth the power of nature, and she herself by doctrine is destroyed. And light things fleeth from men that be negligent; and nothing is so difficile but by cure it is obtained. Also you shall lightly perceive in many things (if ye take good heed) what speediness and efficacy is in labour and diligence. For the small drops of water (with often falling) pierce the stones. Iron and brass is worn out with much occupation (Sig. B1).

(b) For as luskishness and sluggishness doth corrupt, mar and adulterate the goodness of nature, so doth learning and discipline correct and amend the fall and vitiosity thereof. Likewise very easy things do escape and fly those that pamper themselves in negligence, and implunge themselves in the filthy puddles of idleness. And the hardest things with diligence, labour and sedulity be obtained and won. If thou turn thy eyes to learn the things which in common use are accomplished, thou shalt soon most evidently perceive, that diligence and labour are most convincible to the finishing and quick perfecting and absolution of things. For the small drops of water do pierce and penetrate the dure rocks and flint stones, and hard iron and brass with the often handling of the craftsman's hands are mollified and softened (Sigs. B1-B1v).

(c) Sloth turneth the edge of wit, study sharpeneth the mind; a thing be it never so easy, is hard to the idle; a thing, be it never so hard, is easy to the wit well employed. And most plainly we may see in many things the efficacy of industry and labour. The little drops of rain pierceth hard marble, iron with often handling is worn to nothing (I. 263).

One can see from this how Lyly abbreviates and sharpens into opposition. Elyot is anxious to preserve the continuity of thought and introduces every sentence with a connective ('For ... And ... and ... Also ... For ...'). By this means he only succeeds in blurring the real relationship of the ideas; the attempt at chiasmus in the first sentence is a dismal failure. The one metaphor he uses ('fleeth from') has no structural function; the change from the third person to the second and back again to the third does not make the effect which we find in Lyly—the effect of summing-up in personal experience the factual antitheses described elsewhere. Grant's translation avoids the paratactic monotony of Elyot's 'for, and, also, and', but his syntax is so lost or overborne by the torrent of his synonyms that we do not really see the benefit. The wealth of his metaphors is no less embarrassing. Compared with both his predecessors, Lyly's compression is clarification: the *tic-tac* of his rhythm expresses his syntax and conveys his sense. The nouns are wonderfully precise; one feels that the author has thought out the difference and similarity of 'wit' and 'mind', 'industry' and 'labour'; the relation between the Latin and Germanic elements is pleasantly adjusted.

We may take a more obviously Euphuistic passage in Lyly and find the same contrast between the three translations:

(*a*) A little water maketh herbs to grow, and with too much they be soon glutted. In like wise the mind with moderate labour is quickened, and with inordinate labours is oppressed and drowned (Sig. D4).

(*b*) Even as young plants are nourished with the sprinkling of moderate water, but suffocated and choked with dismeasured liquors poured upon them; likewise a child's tender young wit with moderate labours is augmented, but with superfluous pains and immoderate toils extinguished, overwhelmed and drowned (Sig. F3).

(*c*) Plants are nourished with little rain, yet drowned with much; even so the mind with indifferent labour waxeth more perfect, with much study it is made fruitless (I. 277).

It can be seen how the transverse alliteration in the second of Lyly's sentences here (on *m* and *f*) aids the sense as well as contenting the ear, underlining the words that the sense requires to be emphatic. Set against that of his predecessors, Lyly's verbal organization seems functional and efficient. Instead of debauching the language, he seems to be clarifying it. His vocabulary is remarkable for its purity, avoiding all those 'hard words' which a reliance on synonyms requires us to digest. By restricting the stylistic interest of his prose to those few and easily recognized patterns, Lyly carved a world of order and relationship out of the general imprecision of his predecessors. We may think that precision, order and relationship are bought at too high a rate in Euphuism, but it is hardly open to us to deny that these qualities on which Lyly concentrates are important for prose style, or that the effort to isolate them from the undifferentiated mass of Tudor prose must have exacted from the author, of necessity, a narrow concern with his own two inches of ivory.

The rediscovery of Euphuism occurred in the nineteenth century at a period of time when the sophistic prose that Lyly uses could not but be judged remote and eccentric; it was also a time when serious critical study and source study were virtually interchangeable terms. To explain the extraordinary phenomenon of the style, its earliest students therefore looked around for sources from which Lyly could have learned it.[8] The first source proposed was found in the writing of Antonio de Guevara, a Spanish bishop whose popular moral fantasies about classical life were available in English from 1532 onwards. The English translations, however, are found to lack the tricks of style which connect Guevara and Lyly;[9] and the idea that Lyly knew Spanish, which finds no support elsewhere, is only to be entertained as a desperate conjecture if no other explanations of the style can be found.

A second line of explanation was in fact opened up by the publication in 1892 of Eduard Norden's massive *Die Antike Kunstprosa*, which catalogued the fortunes of sophistic prose styles from the time of Gorgias to that of Lyly. Professor Norden pointed to Isocrates as the great Renaissance model of a patently balanced style, and explained the coincidence of style between Guevara and Lyly as due to a common imitation of the Classical model.

It might be argued, however, that though Lyly had many of

the same figures as Isocrates, the total effect produced was very different, and could not have resulted from imitation unless the imitator had already clearly in his mind the kind of figures he was looking for. This has been clearly demonstrated by M. W. Croll:

> Although they [*the sound effects in Lyly's sentences*] are present in both Isocrates and Cicero, they appear there in a minor relation to other features of their style, and with a wholly different effect upon the total result. In Cicero the cumulative and comprehensive period is the normal unit of expression, and the members of the period have a noble and varied rhythm; whereas in Lyly there is no periodicity, and the members are usually short and sharp. And in Isocrates the particular figures used by Lyly appear with comparative infrequency and are always used with a careful study of variety in form and rhythm which is in sharp contrast with Lyly's study of uniformity and exactness. (pp. xxv f.)

In consequence of this, Croll goes on to reject the theory of classical imitation and finds a closer parallel to the style of *Euphues* in the jingling Latin prose of certain Fathers of the Church and their medieval descendents—'a stream of Latin prose-style which runs on with almost unabated volume into the sixteenth century itself' (lvii). It is in consequence of this undercurrent of sophistic Latin prose that we find sporadic English examples of 'Euphuism' in authors as far apart as Aelfric and Lyly.[10]

Croll's point of view has held the field from his time till our own (with minor modifications), and one can see with what justice his explanation has replaced the earlier ones; his examples are nearer to Lyly in general effect and also closer to him in time. The argument from unlikeness of total effect, which Croll uses against his predecessors, is, however, quite damaging when turned back on himself; for the view he takes of Euphuism is at best a partial one. He selects the elements which I have numbered (1) to (5) above (p. 265) as sufficiently representative of the style: 'The essential feature of the style . . . is a vocal, or oral, pattern, and all its other characteristics, such as the use of antithesis, and the constant use of simile, are only means by which the Euphuist effects his various devices of sound-design' (xvi). But, as has been pointed out in a brilliant recent article, isocolon, parison, etc. are essentially involved in syntax and so are figures of thought as well as of sound: 'to describe it [*parison*] as ornamental [*i.e. sound only*] is to suggest that thought itself is ornamental'.[11]

If we are to describe Euphuism as it appears not only in Lyly but (before him) in Pettie's *Petite Palace* or as copied in the work of his imitators Greene, Lodge, Mundy, etc., we have to find a means of grasping not only the sound of the clauses, but the effect of the whole complex of sounds, illustrations, images and attitudes conveyed. This general effect has been brilliantly evoked by G. Wilson Knight,[12] lucidly described by Jonas Barish,[13] and learnedly analysed by W. G. Crane;[14] but an attempt to fit their perceptions into a general history of Tudor prose has not been made. Yet a pointer in the direction such work might take can be found in the work of William Ringler.[15] He has found some very precise parallels to the various aspects of the Euphuistic style in lectures which William Rainolds was giving at Oxford while Pettie, Lyly, Grange and Gosson were there— thus documenting after thirty years Dover Wilson's penetrating guess about 'that Oxford atmosphere which, I maintain, sur- rounded the birth of full blown Euphuism' (p. 39). Ringler agrees with Croll that a sophistic style was generally available in Latin, but suggests that the peculiar combination of rhetor- ical features which make up Euphuism is only to be found in Rainolds, and that Rainolds must therefore be held to be 'the immediate source of Euphuism'.

One must agree. But, as with much source study, this only puts the question one stage further back, into the form, 'Where did Rainolds get the idea of Euphuism?' Henry Jackson, who collected Rainolds' orations in 1613, defends him by the example of St Augustine and St Bernard, and this fits in with Croll's view of the Church Fathers as principal transmitters of the sophistic style through the Middle Ages.[16] But a more useful filiation has been pointed out by Ringler. He shows how 'Rainolds, imitating Cicero, takes a Ciceronian passage and repeats each of its ideas three times, jingling the repetitions with one another to produce a Euphuistic pattern—so following the ideas of Erasmus' *De Copia* for augmentation. . . . Thus it was possible for a student to begin with Cicero but by the process of Erasmian imitation or accumulation to produce a style which was essentially anti-Ciceronian' (*Oratio*, pp. 12-15). Here at last is an outlook which may be used to reconcile Norden's view of Euphuism as resulting from Classical imitation and Croll's perception of the medieval and patristic background, and so to fit Lyly into the development of Tudor prose as I have described it. For Lyly does not seem to have been eccentric either in his choice of models or in his method of imitation, though he was perhaps more systematic than others. He too is a Ciceronian, but his Ciceronianism operates on the wavelength of debate and definition rather than that of narrative, description or harangue; it is significant that Rainolds' Euphuism is confined to his Latin lectures; it does not appear in his English sermons or treatises. So perhaps we should see Lyly's Euphuism as the function of a mind which is basically analytic in its methods, concerned to define by distinctions and antitheses, and changing Cicero by the light of these interests.

For the much-admired Ciceronian *concinnitas* depends on a delicately adjusted balance between the forward momentum of the period and the pauses which define the different members, *cola* or *commata*. Though Cicero (like Lyly) uses jingles and balance to link the members, 'the period must move forward from the beginning to the conclusion, sweep on so comprehensively that when it reaches the end, the halt seems natural' (*Orator*, § 199). As soon as the different members rhyme or jingle with one another in too obvious a way, the balance is lost, and the separateness becomes more obvious than the continuity. This is why, I suppose, Cicero and others object to repetitions of too regular a kind (e.g. *Orator*, § 40). Cicero's own speeches show a cunning use of the separate eddies of repetition to ornament without impeding the whole flow of the period round its central idea. Cicero had written:

> Atque sic a summis hominibus eruditissimisque accepimus, ceterarum rerum studia et doctrina et praeceptis et arte constare, poetam natura ipsa valere et mentis viribus excitari et quasi divino quodam spiritu inflari. Quare suo iure noster ille Ennius sanctos appellat poetas, quod quasi deorum aliquo dono atque munere commendati nobis esse videantur.
>
> (*Pro Archia Poeta*, 18)

The Victim of Fashion

With this as a basis, Rainolds constructed the following:

> Namque poetarum facultas, non ut ceterarum rerum studia, literarum doctrina constat, sed divino instillatur afflatu, non ex praeceptorum artificio coalescit, sed mentis viribus excitatur; non usus assiduitate conficitur, sed naturae praestantia comprehenditur: quae non humanis artibus aquiritur, percipitur, ediscitur; sed instinctu coelesti inseritur, imprimitur, infunditur: ad quam non docemur, sed nascimur; non instituimur, sed imbuimur; non informamur, sed effingimur: cuius vis non acerrima contentione, non infinita diligentia, sed excellentioris quodam impetu naturae arripitur, hauritur exprimitur.
>
> *(Oratio in laudem artis poeticae,* ed. Ringler & Allen, p. 34)

The fullness of Cicero's repetition 'et doctrina et praeceptis et arte' is never for a minute in danger of halting the onward movement of the sentence; the jingle of 'excitari . . . inflari' is likewise used in the service of the single forward-moving central idea, which finally comes to rest on the idea of *divinus* or *sanctus*, taken up in the next paragraph. But Rainolds is not concerned to use this central distinction between poetry and the other arts as part of a developing argument; he is concerned to make it straight away and then to play clever variations upon the theme, to turn it round and round showing the different opportunities for development that it reveals. And this is the method of Lyly.

The *tic-tac metronomique* of Lyly breaks the fundamental rules of Ciceronian eloquence but it does not do so as a result of mere clumsiness or inattention. For Lyly by his methods reaches a different kind of elegance—one that is essentially static, expository and definitive. He hardly shows any attempt to subordinate; his clauses are linked loosely by present participles, by *and . . . and* or *as . . . so* conjunctions, and its movement is only towards a superior definition, a sharper focus on the qualities he is concerned with. The style is thus entirely functional to a mode of analytical thinking which is natural only to a specialized kind of mind. The authors who took over the tricks of Euphuism in an attempt to become as popular as Lyly failed to use the style effectively because their minds and their rhetoric were operating on different frequencies.

The obvious example of this is Robert Greene, the style of whose early Romances derives from the grossest imitation of

Lyly. But however Greene may borrow the appearance of Lyly, he is always closer in the fundamentals of his writing to the older narrative and persuasive rhetoric of Romance than he is to the Lylian kind of dramatized argument. Even in Greene's first Romance, *Mamillia*, the innumerable letters, speeches, etc., which fill out the action are felt as impediments, for the narrative is sufficiently complex to require an attention to which these digressions are irrelevant.[17] Greene remained a digressive writer, but he developed by concentrating more attention on the narrative interest and turning his digressions from analysis towards persuasion. Similarly, Greene's natural idiom is the long invertebrate sentence, and though he may fall into short-breathed paromoions as tricks of style these do not reflect his natural way of looking at experience, and he constantly relapses into his native idiom.

Let us consider in this respect the parallel speeches in which Greene's Ferragus greets his friend Pharicles, finding him in a depressed state of mind (due to love sorrow), and that in which Lyly's Philautus greets Euphues, found in the same condition.

(1) I am sorry, friend Pharicles, to find you in this dump, so am I the more grieved because I cannot conjecture the cause: and although it be the duty of a friend to be copartner of his friend's sorrow, yet I dare not wish myself a partaker of your sadness, because I suppose you are offering incense at the altar of such a saint, at whose shrine you will not so much as once vouchsafe that I should but sing *placebo*. If this be the care that cumbers your mind, good Pharicles, find some other time for your amorous passions; but if it be any sinister mishap which hath driven you into this dump, either want of wealth, loss of friends or other frown of Fortune, only reveal, Pharicles, wherein I may pleasure thee and I will supply thy want with my weal, and cure thy care with such comfortable counsel as my simple wit can afford. The fairest sands, Pharicles, are oftimes most fickle. When the leaf of the Seahulver looketh most green, then is the root most withered; where the sea breaketh with greatest billows, there is the water shallowest; so oftimes in the fairest speech lies hid the falsest heart, in flourishing words, dissembling deeds, and in the greatest show of good will, the smallest effect of friendship. I cannot, Pharicles, paint out my affection towards thee with coloured speeches, nor decipher my

amity with the pencil of flattery, but if thou wilt account me for thy friend, and so use me when thou hast occasion, thou shalt (to be short) find me far more prodigal in performance than prattling in promises; and so I end.

(Grosart, II. 208-10)

(2) Friend and fellow, as I am not ignorant of thy present weakness, so I am not privy of the cause; and although I suspect many things, yet can I assure myself of no one thing. Therefore, my good Euphues, for these doubts and dumps of mine, either remove the cause or reveal it. Thou hast hitherto found me a cheerful companion in thy mirth, and now shalt thou find me as careful with thee in thy moan. If altogether thou may'st not be cured, yet may'st thou be comforted. If there be anything that either by my friends may be procured, or by my life attained, that may either heal thee in part or help thee in all, I protest to thee by the name of a friend that it shall rather be gotten with the loss of my body than lost by getting a kingdom. Thou hast tried me, therefore trust me; thou hast trusted me in many things, therefore try me in this one thing. I never yet failed and now I will not faint. Be bold to speak and blush not; thy sore is not so angry but I can salve it, thy wound not so deep but I can search it, thy grief not so great but I can ease it. If it be ripe it shall be lanced, if it be broken it shall be tented, be it never so desperate it shall be cured. Rise therefore, Euphues, and take heart at grass; younger thou shalt never be; pluck up thy stomach; if love itself have stung thee it shall not stifle thee. Though thou be enamoured of some lady thou shalt not be enchanted. They that begin to pine of a consumption, without delay preserve themselves with cullisses; he that feeleth his stomach inflamed with heat cooleth it eftsoons with conserves; delays breed dangers, nothing so perilous as procrastination. (I. 211 f.)

The opening sentences of the two passages reveal at once the different manners of the two authors. Greene proceeds through a series of antitheses, but one can see behind this mannerism the outline of a sentence which develops without depending on them: 'I am sorry, friend Pharicles, to find you in this dump, and although it be the duty of a friend to be copartner of his friend's sorrow, yet I dare not wish myself a partaker of your sadness, because I suppose you are offering incense at the altar of such a saint, at whose shrine you will not so much as once vouchsafe that I should but sing *placebo*'. The mind wanders in this sentence from topic to topic and one's impression is of new things turnings up at the end of each clause in a further extension of complex relationships. In Lyly's opening clauses, on the other hand, there is no suggestion of the mind wandering through different topics. The necessity of the antitheses to the structure of the thought makes excision impossible; the logicality of the procedure is insisted upon by the precise distribution of the emphasis inside the clauses: '. . . not ignorant . . . not privy; . . . suspect many things . . . assure myself of no one thing. Therefore . . . remove . . . or reveal . . . companion in thy mirth . . . careful with thee in thy moan . . . cured . . . comforted,' etc. Interest is focused on the verbs and their objects (by the jingling methods characteristic of Euphuism), not on the relatives which serve, in Greene, to take us from one topic to another. Lyly avoids any suggestion that Philautus *knows* the reason for his friend's melancholy; this keeps his speech, as it were, pointing always in one direction. Its statements move forward by enlarging the scope of the antithesis proposed at the beginning, accumulating elements in either side of the opposition in the series of short parallel sentences, and so leading up to the more complex and directly emotional statement in the long sentence, 'If there be anything . . . getting a kingdom'. Another series of short parallel sentences (or clauses) follows this, now setting the two friends (not the situation) on the two sides of the antithesis. Finally we have a series of advices to act quickly, not connected formally with what goes before (by relative pronouns, subordination, etc.) except by a logical 'therefore'. The final position is reached, without considering side issues and other wanderings of the mind, by a process of argumentative deduction from the first antithesis.

Greene, on the other hand is unwilling to postpone the discovery till the end of the argument; he wishes to suggest straight away the full piquancy of a multi-dimensional situation: we are shown not only the relationship of Ferragus to his friend, but his relationship to the lady. And yet in spite of the supposition about the lady Greene wishes to make parallels about 'want of wealth, loss of friends or other frown of Fortune' in the manner of Lyly; these have a different effect from the parallel clauses in Lyly, for they belong to a side issue, an elaborate hypothesis which the situation does not require. Ferragus' protests that, though appearance and reality are not always the same, he will be true, is a romantic excursion from the situation in hand. Greene does not use his piled-up figures to augment our understanding of the argument, but in augmentation of the emotional penumbra within which the argument is placed.

What Lyly has done here, and what he does regularly throughout his work, is to trace a line of scholastic logic which is at the same time a line of rhetoric and a means of personal discrimination. The neatness with which he dovetails these different interests is a neatness beyond the power and probably outside the interest of Greene. I have not found it either in any of the other imitators of Lyly.

The functional description of Euphuism which I have attempted to give has not yet been applied to what is the most obvious feature of the style—the strings of similes drawn from remote or marvellous nature; it was this that contemporaries referred to when they noticed Euphuism as a special style; for they seem to have been much more impressed by Lyly's similes than they were by the features that Croll points to as representative—isocolon, paromoion, etc. If we are to describe the *whole* style as functional we must try to justify these similes in relation to the analytical vision which we have seen behind the other features.

Take one extract, which is (I hope) representative:

Though all men be made of one metal, yet they be not cast all in one mould; there is framed of the self same clay as well the tile to keep out water as the pot to contain liquor; the sun doth harden the dirt and melt the wax; fire maketh the gold to shine and the straw to smother; perfumes doth refresh the dove and kill the beetle; and the nature of the man disposeth that consent of the manners. Now whereas you seem to love my nature and loathe my nurture, you bewray your own weakness in thinking that nature may any ways be altered by education, and as you have ensamples to confirm your pretence, so I have most evident and infallible arguments to serve for my purpose: it is natural for the vine to spread; the more you seek by art to alter it, the more in the end you shall augment it. It is proper for the palm tree to mount; the heavier you load it the higher it sprouteth;

though iron be made soft with fire it returneth to his hardness; though the falcon be reclaimed to the fist she retireth to her haggardness; the whelp of a mastiff will never be taught to retrieve the partridge; education can have no show where the excellency of nature doth bear sway.   (I. 190 f.)

We are likely, in strict logic, to find these similes something less than 'evident and infallible instances', but we should notice how they relate to Euphues' distinctions cited at the beginning of the quotation. The distinctions do not only apply to abstract entities, or to human and social behaviour: they extend into the world of animal and vegetable life. Nature no less than man is susceptible of pattern and organization; and when we look through the list of Lyly's similes we find that natural history is most often being drawn on to provide analogues for human behaviour.[18] The strangeness of the similes may be justified by the extent to which they create a world entirely dominated by the patterns of man's social life. Nature is not here a norm against which man can be measured, but rather an arras of richly worked instances reflecting back the centrality of the human mind in its power to perceive and create relationships and correspondences. And the interest of *Euphues* is, of course, just in this matter of social relationships, attitudes and correspondences, not in the impact of individual passions; the style is an extension of the subject-matter. This use of the similes to turn Nature into a pattern is especially obvious in those that Lyly seems to have invented for himself. The 'hedgehog who evermore lodgeth in the thorns because he himself is full of prickles' (II. 139), or 'Lavia' 'who seeing her beauty in a true glass to be but deformed, washed her face and broke the glass' (II. 190), have their attributes given to them only by Lyly's random extension of appearance (the prickles of the hedgehog suggest the prickles of the thorn) or etymology (*Lavia* from lavo, lavare= to wash). The patent unreality of the facts is no disadvantage, for it adds everywhere a certain daintiness of artifice which is perfectly in keeping. The modern reader may also feel a lack of solidity, of concreteness, in the instances, a lack of sensory impact; here are no 'coming musk-rose[s] full of dewy wine', not even any 'sea-shouldering whales'; but again this is quite appropriate to an interest focused on relationships rather than particulars.

It is in terms entirely appropriate to Lyly, and which help to explain his use of the book, that Erasmus defends his *Similia*, the compilation from which Lyly got most of his material. Some may object, Erasmus says, that a noble subject-matter will throw up its own instances; that may be so, he says, but it will not throw up similes of the kind I have collected here—exquisite jewels from the hidden treasury of the Muses, from the inmost secrets of Nature, and from the central shrines of the arts.[19] The theoriests of the *Emblem* were to develop the same point; Henry Estienne tells us

> there is nothing so proper, so gentile, so powerful, nor so spiritual as those similitudes and relations which we discover walking in the spacious fields of the wonderful secrets of nature and qualities of things, as also of the proper effects of our intentions, to find therein the correspondency of qualities natural and usage of things artificial with your own thoughts.
>
> (*The Art of Making Devices*, trans. by Thomas Blount
> (1646), pp. 41 f.)

Of the factual untruth of many of these 'secrets of nature' Estienne has this defence:

> Here we must also observe that it is lawful to use the propriety of a natural subject, be it animal, plant, fruit or other thing, according to the general approbation or received opinion of ancient authors, though the moderns have lately discovered it to be false, because the comparison which is grounded upon a quality reputed true by the generality, though indeed it be false, shall be more universally received and better understood than if it were grounded upon a true property which nevertheless were held false. (ibid. p. 46)

It is odd to see how Aristotle's preference for a probable impossibility over an improbable possibility has here come to the defence of similitudes which seem to us so exquisitely improbable. But more important than a detection of sources is a perception of the whole world-picture on which these defences draw. It is a world-picture which is entirely Medieval, and the Humanists were, of course, still Medieval in their attitude to the subject-matter of science. The likeness of Lyly's natural history to that of the medieval Bestiaries has long been noticed,[20] and the whole of Lyly's background in this respect has been nicely summed up by S. L. Wolff:

Lyly employed these supposed facts of natural history in a way that is humanistic in a very authentic sense, a way coincident with the Renaissance turn from *litterae sacrae* to *litterae humaniores*, from theology to 'the humanities'. The bestiaries, lapidaries and volucraries of the Middle Ages systematically assuming a necessary parallelism between the phenomena of nature and the scheme of salvation, used birds and beasts and stones as symbols of things divine . . . But Lyly assumes a necessary parallelism between the nature of things and the nature of *man*; so that, with him, natural phenomena, supposed or invented, became arguments not of matters divine but of matters human, of human nature.

(*Sewanee Review* (1923), p. 25)

I have said several times that Lyly's gift was never that of an innovator, but always that of a man born to blend, refine and unify received methods and opinions. Nothing shows this better than his handling of the predigested materials of moral discourse, those Wolff mentions here and innumerable others, found in Erasmus, Mexia, Cornelius Agrippa and innumerable other forgotten polymaths. The heaping up of materials, the recital of authorities, the listing of instances, the endless antitheses of *sic* et *non*, show Lyly completely in the tradition of Medieval moral discourse. It may be that he draws on Humanist compilations rather than those of the Middle Ages, but the Humanists are only doing more efficiently what the Middle Ages had believed was worth doing. Erasmus's *Adagia* can be seen as a secular version of Peter Lombard's ever-popular *Book of Sentences*, and in reducing classical literature to a heap of topics Erasmus was only fulfilling desiderata laid down by Bernard of Chartres in the twelfth century.[21] Behind the *Similia* (or *Parabolae*) of Erasmus lie the *Parabolae* of Alain de Lille (Alanus ab Insulis)—again of the twelfth century—and the dictionaries of Christian symbols.[22] We tend not to think of Lyly as a writer of this kind, but this is only a tribute to his skill in organizing and unifying.

To see *Euphues* in the stream of medieval moral discourse, though applying its methods to a courtly and Romantic subject is to see how little Lyly could offer in fact to the history of the novel. Imitation of *Euphues* never went more than skin-deep, and as soon as the court-craze faded, romance writing slipped back to its natural channel. The style of Euphuism likewise summed up a whole age of English prose; though it contributed to the clarification of vernacular style (as I have suggested above) it had no real heirs; and prose style developed not by imitating it but by reacting against it.

It is difficult to tell at what point Euphuism came to seem patently old-fashioned and to that extent ridiculous. In 1585, in the preface of 'N.W.' to Samuel Daniel's *The worthy tract of Paulus Jovius* we heard that 'your argument is such as can both move and delight, tickle the ear and satisfy the mind. And our time also hath learned to loathe that odd rhyming vein, and to persecute the letter is clean out of fashion, which begun by a bad portraiture of wit, and is ended by a ripe direction of judgment'. This is not specifically aimed at Euphuism, but Lyly is within its scope, and a further reference to 'the silly interlude of Diogenes' (*Campaspe*, I suppose) makes it probable that he is at least one of the objects of 'N.W.'s scorn. Four years later we hear the same complaint from William Warner, speaking of the danger 'that to run on the letter we often run from the matter; and being over-prodigal in similes we become less profitable in sentences and more prolixious to sense' (*Albion's England*, 1589).

On the other hand, Webbe's *Discourse of English Poetry* (1586) shows admiration for Lyly still in full flood:

> whose works, surely in respect of his singular eloquence and brave composition of apt words and sentences, let the learned examine and make trial thereof thorough all the parts of rhetoric, in fit phrases, in pithy sentences, in gallant tropes, in flowing speech, in plain sense, and surely, in my judgment I think he will yield him that verdict which Quintilian giveth of both the best orators, Demosthenes and Tully, that from the one nothing may be taken away, to the other nothing may be added.

The decline in Lyly's reputation from this point on, may be traced conveniently in the context of Robert Greene. In 1588 J. Eliot placed a French poem comparing Lyly and Greene before the latter's *Perimedes the blacksmith*

> Euphues qui a bien connu fils-aisné d'Eloquence,
> Son propre frere puisné te pourroit reconnoistre
> Par tes beaux escrits, GREENE, tu fais apparoistre
> Que de la docte Soeur tu as pris ta naissance.

Marot et de-Mornay pour le langage François:
Pour l'Espaignol Guevare, Bocace pour le Toscan
Et le gentil Sleidan refait l'Allemand:
GREENE et Lylli tous deux raffineurs de l'Anglois.
GREENE a son Mareschal monstrant son arte divine
Moulé d'une belle Idée: sa plume essorée
Vole viste et haute en parolle empenée;

It is clear that Lyly is still, at this point, in the circle of Greene's admirers, a dominant figure on the literary horizon; to compare Greene to Lyly is still a generous mode of praise. Additional evidence of this is provided, in the same year, in a Latin poem before Greene's *Alcida*:

Floruit Ascamus, Chekus, Gascoynus, et alter
Tullius Anglorum nunc vivens Lillius, illum
Consequitur Grenus, praeclarus uterque poeta.

Lyly here is linked (no doubt through the memory of his grandfather) with an earlier generation of Humanists, and Greene is his pupil.

It is in the following year, with the appearance of Greene's *Menaphon*, that we notice a slump in the respect paid to Lyly. I have already quoted Henry Upchear's poem, with its clear statement that Greene has now replaced Lyly (see above p. 257). Prefixed to *Menaphon*, beside Upchear's poem, we find another, by Thomas Brabine, which tells the same story:

One writes of love and wanders in the air;
Another stands on terms of trees and stones
. . .
Sweet verse, sweet prose, how have you pleased my vein!
Be thou still *Greene* while others' glory wane.

If, as seems probable, it is Euphuism that is pointed at in the second line, one can see how Lyly can be linked with the Petrarchists as the exponent of a worn-out style. Greene himself reinforces the sense that *Menaphon* is meant to mark a decisive break with Lylian imitation. Having brought together his hero-in-disguise and his heroine-in-disguise, he proceeds:

Melicertus, esteeming her to be some farmer's daughter at the most, could not tell how to court her; yet at length calling to remembrance her rare wit discovered in her last discourses, finding opportunity to give her both ball and racket, seeing the coast was clear and that none but Samela and he were in the field, he left his flock in the valley and stepped unto her and saluted her thus.

'Mistress of all eyes that glance but at the excellence of your perfection, sovereign of all such as Venus hath allowed for lovers, Oenone's overmatch, Arcady's comet, beauty's second comfort, all hail! seeing you sit like Juno when she first watched her white heifer on the Lincen downs, as bright as silver Phoebe mounted on the high top of the ruddy element, I was by a strange attractive force drawn, as the adamant draweth the iron, or the jet the straw, to visit your sweet self in the shade and afford you such company as a poor swain may yield without offence; which if you shall vouch to deign of I shall be as glad of such accepted service as Paris first was of his best beloved paramour.' Samela looking on the shepherd's face, and seeing his utterance full of broken sighs, thought to be pleasant with her shepherd thus: 'Arcady's Apollo, whose brightness draws every eye to turn as the Heliotropion doth after her lode, fairest of the shepherds, the nymphs' sweetest object, women's wrong, in wronging many with one's due, welcome, and so welcome as we vouchsafe of your service, admit of your company as of him that is the grace of all companies, and if we durst upon any light pardon, would venture to request you show us a cast of your cunning.' Samela made this reply because she heard him so superfine, as if Ephoebus had learned him to refine his mother tongue, wherefore thought he had done it of an inkhorn desire to be eloquent. And Melicertus thinking that Samela had learned with Lucilla in Athens to anatomize wit and speak none but similes, imagined she smoothed her talk to be thought like Sapho, Phao's paramour.

(ed. Harrison, pp. 58 f.)

Having thus dimissed what he wishes to represent as Lylyan rhetoric—in fact the parody draws on a far wider range of stylistic excesses than Lyly ever used—Greene then proceeds to give an example of his own skill, and has Melicertus sing the roundelay,

> Tune on my pipe the praises of my love
> And midst thy oaten harmony recount
> How fair she is that makes thy music mount
> And every string of thy heart's harp to move.

When Melicertus has thus displayed Greene's prowess, Samela

perceived by his description that either some better poet than himself had made it, or else that his former phrase was dissembled.

(p. 60)

In short, Euphuism is now a style whose use marks the user as démodé and uncourtly in his tastes. Finally, there is a reference in Nashe's preface to *Menaphon* which, given the generally anti-Lylyan bias of the book, may be taken also as weighted against Euphuism: 'Let other men (as they please) praise the mountain that in seven years brings forth a mouse, or the Italianate pen that, of a packet of pilfries, affordeth the press a pamphlet or two in an age, and then in disguised array vaunts Ovid's and Plutarch's plumes as their own; but give me the man whose extemporal vein . . .' (p. 5). The distinction here would seem to be between Greene's 'extemporal vein' and the laborious work of some other [?Romance] writer. The reference to 'Ovid's and Plutarch's plumes' strongly suggests that the other writer was Lyly, for these are the authors that *Euphues* leans on most heavily.

This accumulation of sneers is hardly countered by the favourable notice given to Lyly the dramatist in Meres' *Palladis Tamia* of 1598: 'The best for comedy amongst us be Edward Earl of Oxford, Doctor Gager of Oxford, Master Rowley, once a rare scholar of learned Pembroke Hall in Cambridge, Master Edwardes, one of her Majesty's Chapel, eloquent and witty John Lyly, Lodge, Gascoigne, Greene, Shakespeare, Thomas Nashe, Thomas Heywood, Antony Munday, our best plotter, Chapman, Porter, Wilson, Hathway and Henry Chettle.' It is of some interest to note where Meres places Lyly, between the gentlemen, and the professionals— the players—who toil in the dusty rear of his procession; in this he shows a nice sense of social discrimination. But we need not look to Meres for any sense of literary discrimination; his generalizations are too sweeping and too facile to count, except where we have no other evidence at all. And in Lyly's case there is plenty of other evidence of the reaction against him.

As might be expected, Jonson and Marston quickly pinpoint Lyly as a purveyor of faded elegancies. Little attention need be paid to Bond's idea that Jonson portrayed Lyly in the figure of Fastidious Brisk (in *Every man out of his humour* (1599)); there is nothing but gallant commonplace to link the two. We are on safer ground in noting that Jonson (in the same play) puts approval of *Euphues* into the mouth of Fallace, the admirer of false courtliness. In Marston's *Antonio and Mellida* (1599) the same scorn for courtly affectation, which turns Castiglione into a foolish gallant,[23] fixes on Euphuism as a courtly style suitable for vapid minds: 'you know the stone called *lapis*; the nearer it comes to the fire the hotter it is . . . etc.' The same point is made in the academic *Return from Parnassus* (about 1600), where Lyly's unnatural natural history is again the object of ridicule: 'there is a beast in India called a polecat that the further she is from you the less she stinks, and the further she is from you the less you smell her' (ed. Leishman ['First Part'] ll. 1475 ff.). And finally there is the famous parody of Euphuism with which Falstaff amuses Hal and posterity in *I Henry IV*—earlier in date than the other dramatic examples I have quoted, though without the critical acerbity which characterizes them.

All this proves that before the turn of the century Lyly was no longer avant-garde and no longer being imitated by the smartest wits—even that it was now smart to decry the style. But against this one must set the plain fact that *Euphues* went on being reprinted, all through the 'nineties, and through the first three decades of the seventeenth century. Who was buying and reading Lyly's book when it had ceased to be 'smart' in literary circles? We cannot tell, but the point that Jonson makes *Euphues* the bible of Fallace, the citizen's wife with pretensions to courtly culture, is suggestive. Marston's *Dutch Courtesan* (1605) tells the same story: Crispinella, who is a bourgeois version of Shakespeare's Beatrice, is blamed for tartness 'because you have read *Euphues and his England*, Palmerin de Oliva and the Legend of Lies'.[24] One can tell the status of *Euphues* by the company it keeps. Anthony Mundy's translations from the Spanish Palmerin Romances were favourite bourgeois reading and favourite butts of the new intellectual élite. *Euphues* has sunk to the level of the kind of reading enjoyed by the citizen and his wife in *The Knight of the Burning Pestle*. And there was much in *Euphues and his England*, as has been pointed out by Louis B. Wright, to appeal to the patriotic instinct of the Londoners; he notes how the 'good morality and copious advice in the manner of the conduct books . . . could not fail to attract the attention of burgher readers' (*Middle Class*

Culture, p. 383). It is for these qualities that *Euphues* may have become a school-book. In a seventeenth-century list of 'Schoolbooks and philosophy given to Kingsnorton library', *Euphues* appears among the Latin classics in company with a few other books sufficiently similar to suggest its status in this context— Peacham's *Complete Gentleman*, More's *Utopia*, Ascham's *Schoolmaster*, Barclay's *Argenis* and *Euphormio*.[25]

Lyly's very success in crystallizing and synthesizing Elizabethan social attitudes into literary form was the source of his undoing. He expressed his own period so perfectly and was so easy to identify with its ideals that his literary merits could hardly be disentangled from its notions of elegance. He himself must have heard the speech with which Sir Christopher Yelverton, the Speaker, closed Parliament in 1597.[26] Sir Roger Wilbraham expressed neatly the new attitude to the old eloquence when he noted in his Diary: 'the speaker (Yelverton serjeant) made a most fine and well filed speech: very short and many well-couched sentences somewhat imitating but bettering Euphues . . . this speech was full of elegancies, sweetly delivered; but thought too full of flattery, too curious [i.e. carefully composed] and tedious.' Quoting this, Sir John Neale remarks that the speech was 'perhaps too obsequious to the younger ear' (*Elizabethan House of Commons*, p. 421). This is precisely the point. The style belonged to a more flattering, more flowery, more relaxed period and could hardly survive the chill winds of Jacobean satiric realism. The brief afterlife that remained to Lyly was to accompany the gradual descent of the Elizabethan ideal of elegance; when this ceased to be courtly, it became the plaything of lower social classes, now scorned and now patronized:

> words alter as the times
> And soonest their fantastic rhetorics
> Who turn their poesies with school-boy tricks.
> That which this age affects as grave and wise
> The following generation may despise.
> Greene's phrase and Lyly's language were then in fashion
> And had among the wits much commendation;
> But now another garb of speech with us
> prized, and theirs is thought ridiculous.
>
> (Wither, *Britain's Remembrancer* (1628))

There was, of course, a factitious revival of 'Elizabethan' tastes in Stuart times. It is this that would seem to be responsible for the 1632 printing of the *Six Court Comedies*. It is to such nostalgia as had produced the *Memorial of Queen Elizabeth* in 1630 that Blount, the publisher, appeals in his prefaces: 'It can be no dishonour to listen to this poet's music, whose tunes alighted in the ears of a great and ever-famous Queen; his invention was so curiously strung that Eliza's court held his notes in admiration . . . Reader, I have (for the love I bear to posterity) digged up the grave of a rare and excellent poet, whom Queen Elizabeth then heard, graced and rewarded.' The author is now 'old John Lyly' a 'witty companion' who will be 'merry with thee in thy chamber', a genial figure speaking the quaint dialect of an age without gall, belonging to a never-never land where virtue was always rewarded.

We may say in general that only two Elizabethan authors remained strong in reputation through the Jacobean onslaught —Sidney and Spenser. It was Lyly's misfortune to come into early conflict with one of these; and it is in the conflict with Sidney that Lyly's weaknesses show themselves most clearly. The first literary reaction against Lyly centres on Greene's *Menaphon*, and it would seem to be no coincidence that *Menaphon* is the first work of Greene's which borrows extensively from the *Arcadia*. Was it the discovery of a new hand to feed him that encouraged Greene to bite the old one, now that 'old age his glory hath removed'?

At any rate it appears to later connoisseurs of style that it was Sidney, not Lyly who was the 'raffineur de l'Anglais'. It was Sidney who

> did first reduce
> Our tongue from Lyly's writing then in use;
> Talking of stones, stars, plants, of fishes, flies,
> Playing with words and idle similes
>
> . . .
>
> So imitating his ridiculous tricks
> They spake and writ, all like mere lunatics.
> (Drayton, Epistle to Henry Reynolds)

In a conflict with Sidney, Lyly has no cards in his hand. His wit was based on pedantry aspiring to courtliness; Sidney's was courtly in essence, a natural development of the elaborated styles of courtly Romance. Lyly's style was basically argumentative; Sidney's was basically descriptive. The most obvious figure of Arcadianism is periphrasis, not balance; which allows Sidney greater scope in varying the appearance of his figures, and so he is able to avoid the stiffness and repetitiveness of Euphuism.[27] In Sidney, no less than in Lyly, the natural world is evoked only in order to describe man, but the pathetic fallacy as Sidney uses it is suppler and less obtrusive than the simile from natural history, which is Lyly's equivalent. Sidney himself first made this point:

> Now for similitudes in certain printed discourses, I think all herbalists, all stories of beasts, fowls and fishes are rifled up that they may come in multitudes to wait upon any of our conceits; which certainly is as absurd a surfeit to the ears as is possible; for the force of a similitude not being to prove anything to a contrary disputer, but only to explain to a willing hearer, when that is done the rest is a most tedious prattling, rather overswaying the memory from the purpose whereto they were applied than any whit informing the judgment, already either satisfied or by similitudes not to be satisfied.
>
> (Feuillerat, *Sidney*, III. 42 f.)[28]

What Sidney would seem to be objecting to here is not the simile from unnatural natural history in itself but the rows of such similes that Lyly delighted in. The power of a simile, he says, is to illustrate and explain; but this is done as well by one simile as by many; therefore all similes after the first are superfluous. Repetition may be of great force in vehement orations (he has just alluded to Cicero's . . . *consul videt: hic tamen vivit. Vivit? immo vero etiam in senatum venit* (*In Catalinam I*, I. § 2)) but this does not apply to the simile. We may suppose that Sidney is unfair to Lyly here in not allowing the use of repeated similes to create the world of *préciosité* through which Euphues moves; but in terms of his own aesthetic virtues he is correct. The style of *Euphues* lacks the richness, depth and romantic glow of Arcadianism; its logic and its symmetry confine it to a predictable range of effects, and it cannot encompass the sphere of magnanimity where Sidney is supreme.

But though Sidney was bound to defeat Lyly in any appeal to seventeenth-century courtly taste, Lyly went on being reprinted. Editions of both authors in fact went on appearing fairly regularly until the eighteenth century. The last (the 'fourteenth') reprinting of Sidney's *Works* came in 1724, in a period which marks the end of the taste for heroic romance by substituting another 'Pamela' as the model of female excellence. Only eight years before (in 1716) appeared what was also to be the final reprinting of *Euphues*—this time in a modernized version, or (as the Epistle calls it) a 'New Translation', with a new and more piquant title for the whole work: *Euphues and Lucilla, or The False Friend and Inconstant Mistress.*

It is worth the time of anyone interested in Lyly's style to look at this modernized version, for the remodelling brings out, with a minimum of change, how truly Congrevian are the virtues of the style. If Sidney survived into the tradition of the French heroic romance, we can see that Lyly is a natural ancestor to the sharp elegance of Restoration wit, and so of the witty couplet in the next century. Confined to a more narrowly argumentative range than Sidney, he remains closer, for this very reason, to the cadences of speech. It needs only a little loosening of the vocal pattern[29] to bring it into line with the ideals of cultivated female conversation in the Augustan period:

> O my Euphues! Little do you suspect what sorrows I sustain for your dear sake; whose wit has charmed me, whose good qualities have shocked my former resolutions, whose courteous behaviour without affectedness, comely features without blemish, eloquent speech without fraud have wrapped me in this misfortune—and can you, Lucilla, be so light as to forsake Philautus, and fly to Euphues?—prefer a stranger before your own countryman?— Why, Euphues perhaps desires my love; but Philautus has merited it. Euphues (it's true) is worthy of me; but Philautus deserves better than I am.—Ay, but the later love is more fervent; yet the first may be more faithful.—Euphues has greater perfections; but Philautus has deeper affection.   (p. 23)

Compare this with the original and notice how little has been changed:

> O my Euphues, little dost thou know the sudden sorrow that I sustain for thy sweet sake; whose wit hath bewitched me, whose rare qualities have deprived me of mine old quality, whose courteous behaviour without curiosity, whose comely feature without fault, whose filed speech without fraud hath wrapped me in this misfortune. And canst thou, Lucilla, be so light of love

288

in forsaking Philautus to fly to Euphues? canst thou prefer a stranger before thy countryman? a starter before thy companion? Why, Euphues doth perhaps desire my love; but Philautus hath deserved it. Why, Euphues' feature is worthy as good as I; but Philautus his faith is worthy a better. Ay, but the later love is the most fervent. Ay, but the first ought to be most faithful. Ay, but Euphues hath greater perfection. Ay, but Philautus hath deeper affection. (I. 205)

It is a curious paradox that the noble Sidney should become the patron of bourgeois idealism, while the *arriviste* Lyly (the word is Feuillerat's [p. 39]) forecasts the laconic elegance of a later vision of aristocracy.

A survey of the reputation of Lyly's plays reveals the same curve as that we have already described for *Euphues*, but the terms of the decline are rather different; the plays were more closely linked to the court than was the romance, and could hardly support the bourgeois after-life which was the fate of the other. Plays, which depend on performance before they are fully alive, are much more likely to be the victims of external events. History acts on them in a sharper way, and one can see the author much more clearly as the victim of the historical events which act upon the theatre.

The inhibition imposed on the Pauls' Boys in 1590 (presumably for some part in the anti-Martinist revels) marked the end of Lyly's career as court dramatist in ordinary the only continuous literary work that lay ahead of him was the writing of eloquent begging letters. Mercifully, no doubt this was concealed from him, but we can see from the playwriting of his last period that he was already conscious of some difficulty or disadvantage in the kind of plays he had made his own. *Mother Bombie, The Woman in the Moon,* and *Love's Metamorphosis* all show a restlessness about the form they use, perhaps an attempt to find a *métier* outside court-comedy for boy actors. *Mother Bombie* would seem to be for boys but not for court; *Woman in the Moon* for court but not for boys; while *Love's Metamorphosis* is either a new kind of short play, or a play which was truncated when it came back on the boards with the new Chapel Royal company—about 1600. But the new age can hardly be thought to have welcomed Lyly on his reappearance as a dramatist;

T

Love's Metamorphosis is presumably one of those revived Elizabethan plays that Marston calls the 'musty fopperies of antiquity'. Another of the new men—Ben Jonson—tells us in the
Induction to *Cynthia's Revels* that 'the *umbrae* or ghosts of some
three or four plays departed a dozen years since have been seen
walking on your stage here . . . take heed, boy, if your house
be haunted with such hobgoblins 'twill fright away all your
spectators quickly'.

One can see why Lyly's later plays failed to re-establish his
fame as a dramatist, or even to keep up with the change in
public taste. Different from one another though they may be,
none of these later plays really succeed in breaking away from
the courtly formulae of the Tudor revels. *Woman in the Moon* is
in blank verse, but though the verse is accomplished it never
suggests anything that could have been as popular as Marlowe's
bombast. The verse of *The Woman in the Moon* gives no drive
to the action; indeed it is less successful than Lyly's prose in
establishing a world of light-hearted intrigue. The play itself
is still organized on the piecemeal lines of the older drama,
setting complete episodes one against the other, within a framework of divine intentions, and it is arbitrarily concluded by the
inexplicable will of the gods. This play was very probably
written to be played by men rather than boys,[30] but Lyly does
not make any capital out of this. The roles still show the same
pert, shallow variations on the theme of love—Arcadian shepherds with set figures to dance through, but no passions to
expose. Lyly could not become another person, an artist deeply
involved in his characters, or a daring individual innovator.

Again, *Mother Bombie* may be less courtly and elegant than
Lyly's other plays, but it is no less firmly inside the conventions
of Tudor dramaturgy; it belongs to a different convention we
may say, but this is Tudor none the less. Its 'realism' is that of
Ralph Roister Doister, The Birth of Hercules, and of Erasmus'
Colloquia, not that of Jonson or even Dekker.

Lyly did not succeed anywhere in reaching the new taste,
which was replacing that of his youth—the taste that Greene
was pursuing when he moved from Lylian romance through
Sidneian showers of eloquence towards the familiar button-
holing style of the coney-catching pamphlets. Jonson, Chapman and Marston are the models of the new Jacobean taste as

it affects the theatre, and when we compare their plays with Lyly's we see that much of the change revolves round the word 'satire'. Professor Harbage has suggested that, 'If, as seems probable, *Endimion* actually adumbrates a recent imbroglio of treachery, adultery and bloodshed among the socially eminent . . . the progression from Lyly to Marston, from the amatory and satirical to the erotic and cynical, was more predictable than at first appears' (*Rival Traditions*, p. 70). I suspect that this is to lay too much weight on the idea of satire. Whatever recent imbroglios are adumbrated in *Endimion*, it remains a play of completely different atmosphere and outlook from *The Malcontent*; however predictable the progression is, it remains a progression from one pole to another. For if we say that *Endimion* contains 'satire', where shall we look for it? Sir Tophas is a fool and his infatuation with Dipsas is there to be laughed at; but he is too fantastic to be *satirized*. His praise of old women is absurd or mad, but is no more satire than is the tumbling of a clown. Moreover the serious points that *Endimion* makes are made positively, by evoking the magnanimity and beauty of the Queen, not negatively or satirically by dramatizing their absence.

The obvious play to make the contrast here is Jonson's *Cynthia's Revels* of 1600-1601. Written for the Chapel boys and for the court of Elizabeth, with gods and men and a presiding Queen-goddess, it reproduces very closely the conditions of Lyly's court drama. More than this, the story of *Cynthia's Revels* is close to that of *Endimion*: a good man (Crites/Eumenides) finally reveals to Cynthia the Queen the defacing of virtue in her court; she accepts his version of the truth and at the conclusion reforms what is amiss.

The similarity of the framework only serves, however, to show up the difference of the material inside it. Jonson's Cynthia is an image of withdrawn godhead, powerful in the awe she evokes, but hardly revealed, and always acting through others. We learn about the values of the court only by witness-ing the absurd travesty of courtliness in the affectations oɪ self-love. It may be urged, of course, that Crites is a positive figure; he is so, but only as a scholar; his courtliness is entirely theoretical. The action of the play shows us only the parody; the virtues of the court are presented only in terms of idea. But in *Endimion* (see Act III, scene i) we are shown how virtue can be effective in courtly action. In Jonson, the fop is set against the scholar, and courtly virtue is reduced to the power to prefer the scholar; in Lyly the scholars (Trachinus and Pandion) spend their time in trying to be courtiers. Lacking any image of the positive virtues of courtly action, Jonson's scholar (Crites) has to be sustained in his bitterness and self-regard by the theory that the highest powers really approve of him, but there is no clear image of how their approval will affect the court— except (as I say) in the negative way of repressing vices. In Jonson's refusal to visualize the exact nature of the courtly end of study we may, indeed, see a final despairing comment on the Humanist position.

Jonson's play is realistic in a way that Lyly's could never be —with the realism of man's corruption. But Lyly's play is nearer to the reality of court life as it must have looked to those who were involved in it, showing the pursuit of elegance as a virtue, and the strange mingling of the personal, the mythological, the economic and the moral. Both plays involve what we may call allegories; but the dealings of court-slander (in the intrigue of Tellus with Dipsas) are presented in so remote a way in *Endimion* that we are given no sense of indignation about the action. What the allegory *does* make us aware of is the simplified and exaggerated states of love, jealousy, disdain and aspiration which explain the relations between the various characters:

> *Dipsas.* Who is he whom you love, and what is she that he honoureth?
> *Tellus.* Endimion, sweet Endimion is he that hath my heart; and Cynthia, too too fair Cynthia, the miracle of nature, of time, of fortune, is the lady that he delights in and dotes on every day, and dies for ten thousand times a day.
> *Dipsas.* Would you have his love either by absence or sickness aslaked? Would you that Cynthia should mistrust him or be jealous of him without colour?
> *Tellus.* It is the only thing I crave, that seeing my love to Endimion, unspotted, cannot be accepted, his truth to Cynthia (though it be unspeakable) may be suspected.
> *Dipsas.* I will undertake it and overtake him, that all his love shall be doubted of and therefore become desperate; but this will wear out with time that treadeth all things but truth.

(I. iv. 33-47)

Inside the framework established by such emotional relationships it is the attractive power of Cynthia that makes her the
centre of the play; she is known as a goddess by her over-
whelming virtue and beauty—necessary to adore and worthy
to be adored; no one in the play is unaffected by this power
and virtue, though Tellus and Semele wish to escape from its
pressure. Jonson's Cynthia, on the other hand, is not appre-
hended by the poetic force of adoration directed towards her,
but by the general awe of her moral integrity. His allegory is
of virtue displaced and then replaced; the court is a natural
focus for the conflict, but is not a boundary for its significance,
for affectation and pretension are everywhere around us.
Jonson's is a play of judgment where Lyly's is a play of love:
the characters are all the time judging one another rather than
loving, hating, despising, etc. Here indignation is the cutting
edge of judgment, and it is the combination of these two that
makes the play a satire; conversely the absence of these qualities
keep the word from having any applicability to *Endimion*. It is
the strong sense of judgment in Jonson that 'places' for us the
court we see:

> The strangest pageant fashioned like a court
> (At least I dreamt I saw it), so diffused,
> So painted, pied, and full of rainbow strains
> As never yet, either by time or place,
> Was made the food to my distasted sense;
> . . .
> Here stalks me by a proud and spangled sir etc.
>
> (III. iv. 4-12)

In Lyly's court, though unvirtuous things happen, the relation
between immoral and moral (not being coterminous with that
between real and ideal) is never so simple as to enforce judgment. We see static passions set in relation to one another—
adoration for Cynthia, regret at having resorted to magic,
faithfulness and lightness in love (in married and unmarried
states) etc.—and we have no doubt which is good and which
is evil; but these are not so arranged that the whole play folds
down a line between the good and the bad. In the denouement
all are reconciled in much the same way, from the wicked
Dipsas and Tellus, through the light-minded Semele, the disobedient Corsites, the inane Tophas, to the virtuous Geron,

Eumenides and Endimion. In Jonson the middle ground of minor weakness is left vacant; virtue, vice and folly are all shown in their most exaggerated and mutually opposed forms. The denouement is not a series of small reconciliations, but by lining up the virtues and vices against one another it shows the complete reversal that is needed if evil is to be turned into good; the supposed masque of virtues is shown up as, in truth, a dance of their opposites—the vices, and in the following Palinode the courtiers are made to deny all the qualities which have given them their dramatic being.

Jonson's play belongs to a tradition of royal entertainment in showing the conflict between Cynthia and Cupid (see Chapter 3); but where for Lyly and other Tudor entertainers the gods are outside the human scene, and reflect the kind of pressure that was a condition of Elizabethan court life and gave it its shape, Jonson sees the myth as possessing a general psychological truth. This is obvious enough in the Echo scene at the beginning of *Cynthia's Revels*. Like the contest between Pan and Apollo in *Midas*, this presents a well-known classical episode in a pleasing and fluent way; but Jonson is not content to leave it at this: he treats the myth as containing the seed of all the subsequent action. Narcissus is 'that trophy of self-love' whose relation to flattery and such courtly vices is made explicit:

> But self-love never yet could look on truth
> But with blear'd beams; slick flattery and she
> Are twin-born sisters.   (I. ii. 36-38)

Similarly, Echo is seen as the type of the clear-eyed and eloquent scholar-satirist, condemned to be only a voice, and for most of the time a voice disregarded by those who hear her. For Jonson, the myth is one mode of presenting the explicit moral intention of the play; and it is round this intention that the whole structure of his play revolves.

The opening episodes of *Cynthia's Revels* are as diversified as those of *Endimion* or *Gallathea*, but the diversity is organized by Jonson both to point forward to later events and to suggest the pervasive nature of the theme the narrative will enforce. In Act I of *Cynthia's Revels* we have

(1) the humanized, lightly mythological quarrel of Mercury and Cupid (prose).

(2) The episode of Mercury and Echo; the explicit statement about self-love and the cursing of the fountain (stately verse and song).

(3) The fools come to drink of the fountain; while Crites observes and comments (prose).

(4) Epilogue by Crites (moral verse).

If we compare this with the first act of *Gallathea*, taking this as the most perfect example of Lyly's method, the change of handling becomes obvious. The *Gallathea* episodes run as follows:

(1) We hear about the oracle and intended sacrifice; Tyterus disguises Gallathea.

(2) Cupid decides to torment the nymphs of Diana.

(3) Melebeus disguises Phillida (close imitation of (1)).

(4) four boys recover from shipwreck and decide to seek their fortunes.

Jonson is careful to link his episodes: Mercury stays on stage to become the interlocutor of Echo, and the observer of the fools, and as the god of wit is the presiding deity of the act. Echo is the cause of Amorphus' entrance: 'Dear spark of beauty, make not so fast away', while Crites naturally remains after his observation of the fools to confide his judgment to the spectators.

Lyly on the other hand shows no interest in the *liaison de scenes*; his interest is to set the episodes against one another, and to evoke the pleasure of hearing the same theme handled in different ways. Jonson is interested in 'theme', but theme for him is not found in the situation (attempts to deceive) but rather in the weakness (self-love) that drives men into action. The light-mindedness of Cupid and the sense of injustice in Echo point forward to the folly of Asotus and the self-justification of Crites. So the whole play is linked, and centred on the moral judgment of the varieties of folly.

The variety of expressive means that Jonson commands is used to reinforce this aim, so different from Lyly's. The elegance of Lyly's prose evokes a world of wit and cultivation where rudenesses can be excluded and the chances of life controlled; even his pages share something of this power to control life through wit. But the elegance of Jonson's opening page-talk

between Cupid and Mercury draws on a world of low-life
social observation that Lyly only treats marginally:

> why, my light feather-heeled coz, what are you any more than
> my uncle Jove's pander? a lackey that runs on errands for him,
> and can whisper a light message to a loose wench with some
> round volubility? wait mannerly at a table with a trencher,
> warble upon a crowd a little, fill out nectar when Ganymede's
> away? one that sweeps the gods' drinking-room every morning,
> and sets the cushions in order again, which they threw one at
> another's head over night. etc.   (I. i. 21-30)

The Lucianic particularity of this satire seems stronger than
the witty detachment of the pages in handling it. Again, Jonson
follows Lyly in his interest in the vocabulary of different
occupations. But Lyly's alchemist, etc., in *Gallathea* are only
there to add their interesting oddity to the total mixture; in
Jonson, linguistic oddity is a sign of moral obliquity, or inability
to form a central and humane viewpoint. Jonson's style asks us
all the time to apply a moral response to the splendid objects
he describes, setting their ideal contexts against their real ones.
Lyly's style asks us to wonder rather than judge—to wonder
at the ubiquity of pattern, which can hold diverse objects in
meaningful relationships.

These differences between *Endimion* and *Cynthia's Revels* or
even between Lyly and Jonson are not, I think, to be seen as
merely particular. The prevalence of *satire* (the invitation to
make adverse judgment of the world depicted) in Jonson, and
its absence from Lyly is symptomatic of a whole shift of temper,
which was to make Lyly obsolete and isolated before his natural
term was over. We may, if we wish, call *Midas* a 'satire' on
Philip II, but it is still distinct from the Jacobean mode, for
no standard of judgment is either invited or sustained; it is a
free fantasy on contemporary themes, and this seems to be
distinct from satire. The same may be said of *The Woman in the
Moon* which has sometimes been considered to be a satire on
woman. The structure and tone of the play invites us to enjoy
its elegant fantasy rather than its telling blows. Whatever name
we give to the genre of such a play we cannot disguise its
difference from the Jacobean plays for the boys' companies in
the private theatres, or in the court. It is easy to see why
Lyly's plays should have failed to win a place in the repertory

of the seventeenth century, even at court. For though satire does not play any clear part in the Jacobean Court Masque, the same shift from evocation to judgment has its effects there. In Jonson's masques the monarch is the focus of moral influence on human life; the gods walk the earth again through the modern representatives (or would-be representatives) of their virtues in the court. In Lyly it is rather in the grace and dignity of the court that Olympus comes alive again. To the Jacobeans it must have seemed that Lyly's myths were superficially handled, neither used systematically nor interpreted thoroughly; for in them the Queen is hardly shown to have a precise moral function, independent of her glamour. And in the dark mood of the Jacobeans, glamour was liable to be written off as a deception.

The rapid eclipse of the attitudes that Lyly took for granted is partly to be explained by his Humanist background which, I have suggested, governed his outlook, and out of which he could not escape. But we should also notice the curious gap in the literary life of the time which can hardly be explained in these terms. 'The University Wits' expired quickly as a generation, leaving no obvious progeny. By the time the 'Parnassus Plays' were presented (*c.* 1601), the literary life they depict was finished; Greene died in 1592, Peele in 1596, Nashe in 1601, and about the same time Lodge turned his interests to medicine. A new generation had taken over, which was in revolt against the facility, decorativeness, and remoteness from direct experience of most Elizabethan literature. Only one considerable dramatist moved into the new age still carrying with him the techniques and the attitudes of the 'University Wits', and developed not by rejecting the past but by combining, assimilating and elaborating the new and the old. In this single mind of unique flexibility the vision of John Lyly was given new life, and a renewed claim on our attention, for the mind was that of William Shakespeare.

If Lyly lives on and exercises a continuing influence on drama it is through the attitudes he bequeathes to Shakespeare; to analyse this heritage is the purpose of my concluding chapter.

VI

LYLY AND SHAKESPEARE

SHAKESPEARE MAKES a clear reference to Lyly only
once in his plays, and that, if anything, is a gesture of rejection;
I refer to the famous parody of Euphuism in *Henry IV*. But the
influence of the ideals implied by Lyly's style are evident
throughout Shakespeare's comedy. Shakespeare never wrote a
romance, but one might argue that it was he rather than
Greene who carried on, developed and fulfilled what was
unique in Lyly's vision of high life.

Lyly's romance shows wit competing with love as an indicator
of what is noble and generous in youthful minds. The mood
of *Euphues* and of the plays lies between sentimentality and
acerbity, sentiment being sharpened by wit, and wit being
humanized by sentiment. The ideal of life presented is one
which will perfectly balance these two sides of human nature
and social intercourse. And this remains, on the whole, the
ideal of Shakespearian Comedy.

This was not an inevitable heritage; it was not a major
tradition of Comedy; it was not even the commonest way of
writing about the nobility of love. Sidney's *Arcadia* represents
a far more powerful tradition, in which love is ennobled by an
all-or-nothing pursuit through trials of every kind. The tendency to regard love as farcical, debilitating and irrational,
which Lawrence Babb has recently documented,[1] was countered in this medieval and Petrarchan strain of writing by
crossing it with honour (in honourable minds) and allowing it
to be measured by the martial virtues of the nobleman who
pursued his lady through fantastic obstacles. It is true that
there is a measure of self-mockery in the romantic love of the

Arcadia, but wit is not used to provide a continuous level of self-awareness, balancing the absurdity of loving against the sense of honour. Indeed, before Lyly, it is difficult to think of an English author, now extant, who writes of love in this latter way. Early plays about love like *Clyomon and Clamydes* or *Love and Fortune* take the obvious line of medieval romance and derive their standards of love from the prowess of the man involved. But for Comedy, the Lylian handling of love has many advantages. Most obviously it allows an *integration* of noble sentiment with Comedy—that is, Lyly's kind of Comedy, whose intent is 'to move inward delight, not outward lightness, and to breed (if it might be) soft smiling, not loud laughing'. Otherwise we are all too liable to find a mere alternation of brutish farce (in the sub-plot) with stilted heroics (in the main plot).

The line Lyly took was not, I suppose, very obvious to his age, for in such a Comedy the comic vision must, almost of necessity, focus on female rather than male sentiments and virtues. For the man who detaches himself from his passions, and (though he feels them strongly) does not pursue them with valour but rather observes them with wit, will almost certainly be judged unvigorous and so unheroic. On the other hand, a woman showing the same kind of diffident self-awareness will be supposed (by a male audience, at any rate) to have added sense to her sensibility, head to her heart, and so to be more admirable rather than less.

The most reputable authorities take it that Shakespeare began his career by writing the *Henry VI* plays. If so, he began without any particular interest in love as a dramatic subject. Even if we restrict ourselves to the comedies and take *The Comedy of Errors*—presumably the first play in this genre—we find that he begins with interests and antecedents that are not Lylian in themselves and which seem unlikely to develop towards Lyly. It is worth noting, however, that the early comedies, though they were written for men acting on a public stage, could equally well have been played by boys, and could have graced a more courtly occasion. We may explain this as mere incapacity on Shakespeare's part: he could not yet write 'big' roles for the men or express powerful personal emotions. But this argues, even if it is admitted, a specialized kind of incapacity, unlike that of Greene for example, and still puts Shakespeare by the side of Lyly. Moreover, the intrigue of *The Comedy of Errors*, of *Two Gentlemen of Verona*, or of *The Taming of the Shrew* shows an interest in patterning human behaviour, setting one level against another, which was an art in which Lyly was the obvious master.

Whatever area of common ground Shakespeare shared with Lyly's mode in comedy, there can be little doubt that the earliest Shakespearian plays show interests which are quite divergent from Lyly's, and that later comedies (such as *A Midsummer Night's Dream* or *Love's Labour's Lost*) show definite traces of a study and imitation of Lyly. But the interest of the relationship is not, I take it, to be measured by a list of parallel passages, which is, in any case, much smaller than is usually supposed; a book like Rushton's *Shakespeare's Euphuism* measures only the extent to which Lyly is a repository of Elizabethan commonplaces. I suppose that the point of comparing Lyly and the early Shakespeare is not to find out what Shakespeare took from Lyly; that question can only be answered by a few hard but possibly irrelevant facts, set in a vast penumbra of conjecture. What may be a more fruitful as well as a safer process is to seek a standpoint from which we can see the young Shakespeare *differing* from his models. We normally judge Shakespeare's early plays as preparations for his later achievements; it may be worthwhile to see them (for a change) as deliberate departures from norms and excellencies already established; and this the comparison with Lyly allows us to do.

The order of composition in Shakespeare's early plays is a vexed question, and to argue the meaning of the details which constitute evidence in this field would take space quite disproportionate to the value. I have sought in what follows to talk about the plays as showing different relations to Lyly's works, without basing interpretation on supposed positions on an imaginary curve of development. It has not been possible, of course, to exclude altogether idea of development, and where this begs the question of chronology I have assumed E. K. Chambers' order (*William Shakespeare*, I. 243-274) to be the correct one.

The Comedy of Errors would seem to show Shakespeare's natural tastes in comedy at a point where he had not absorbed

(or else absorbed and then rejected) the influence of Lyly.
The play is, of course, largely dependent on its sources, the
Menaechmi and *Amphitryon* of Plautus, and if we are to compare
Lyly's work with Shakespeare's it would have to be in the
additions and alterations to the originals. These changes *do*
reflect a viewpoint materially different from Plautus' and in
some ways close to Lyly, who can be represented in this case by
Mother Bombie—not because *Mother Bombie* was necessarily
known to Shakespeare when he wrote *The Comedy of Errors*, but
because it represents 'Lylian Comedy' at work on materials
basically similar to those of the *Errors*, and therefore most
convenient for comparison. Though no original for Lyly's play
is known, 'in *Mother Bombie*' Professor M. W. Wallace tells us,
'we have a comedy . . . in which the typical situations of Latin
comedy have been brought together in such a manner that it
would not be difficult to imagine the play as a transcript of
some lost comedy of Plautus'. (*Birthe of Hercules*, p. 75.)

Shakespeare's major alterations of his original are: the
addition of the romantic frame-plot of old Aegeon, an expan-
sion of the part given to the wife, Adriana, the creation of her
sister Luciana (to be pursued by the love of the unmarried
twin), and the creation of another slave, twin to the first, so
that the two servant parts balance and repeat the errors of
their twin masters. These changes may be characterized as
breaking up the classical purity, simplicity and heartlessness of
the original, widening the range of emotions involved—especially by the exhibition of the more tender feelings—and creating
a more circuitous, florid, and less logical narrative line. *Mother
Bombie*, in spite of Professor Wallace's somewhat exaggerated
statement, is unPlautine in much the same way. It is much less
simple, sensual and direct; its range of characters—pages, half-
wits, fiddlers, farmers, a hackneyman, a wise woman, etc.—is
much wider than in any Plautine comedy; it is more concerned
with the emotion of love than Plautus ever is.

To this extent, Lyly's treatment of classical comedy and
Shakespeare's coincide; and they can be lumped together in
contrast to Ben Jonson's satirical exploitation of Plautus'
Captivi and *Aulularia* for his *The Case is Altered*. But to suppose
that Shakespeare treated Plautus thus because he imitated
Lyly is to put too much weight on the coincidence of common

Elizabethan tastes. Shakespeare's approach to Plautus is of a piece, both with itself and with the subsequent trend of his writing. Either Lyly's influence has been so absorbed at the beginning of Shakespeare's career that it does not show, or else it exercises little or no power. I take it that the latter is the more probable inference, for Shakespeare's play is in many respects quite unLylian.

To say this is, of course, to deny the usual claim that the essential difference between *The Comedy of Errors* and the *Menaechmi* is seen in the love-emotion between Antipholus of Syracuse and Luciana, his alleged sister-in-law, which has been described in the following terms: 'Luciana brings into the play a range of sentiment utterly incompatible with the atmosphere of *The Comedy of Errors* . . . Between Plautus and Luciana are the centuries in which chivalry and its achievement in life and letters had evolved the love which, like God, makes man and earth new.' (Charlton, *Shakespearean Comedy*, p. 70.) This leads naturally to the further assumption that we have here 'a kind of love and wooing not found in Plautus, but already popular in England through the works of John Lyly' (Bullough, *Sources*, I. 8 f.).

I cannot find, however, that the scene where Antipholus 'woos' Luciana marks a basic or pervasive break with tradition, or that Lyly is to be held responsible for its manner. It shows us the fairly obvious comedy of the innocent abroad, and of the man who protests too much—though in language of a new eloquence, I admit. What is new in the poetry is not its Lylian elegance, however, but rather the strong pathos of man's loneliness, and this is something that runs counter to Lyly's flippant and detached view of the man in love:

> Teach me, dear creature, how to think and speak;
> Lay open to my earthy-gross conceit,
> Smoth'red in errors, feeble, shallow, weak,
> The folded meaning of your words' deceit.
> Against my soul's pure truth why labour you
> To make it wander in an unknown field?
> Are you a god? Would you create me new?
>
> (III. ii. 33-39)

Shakespeare was later to adopt Lyly's kind of courtship, in which the lady holds the gentleman at bay by means of her

wit, and in which all the moves of love-play are organized as
a game; but there is no hint of this half-fun, whole-earnest
approach in *The Comedy of Errors*. It seems correct to treat the
play as indicating a pre-Lylian phase in Shakespeare's comedy.

I have already indicated what I take to be essentially
Shakespearian in this play, and therefore distinct from both
Plautus and Lyly; it is the pathos with which Shakespeare
indicates man to be the *victim* of error. In *Mother Bombie* the
different groups—pages, fathers, children—exploit one another
and are exploited, fall into *errors* or *supposes* (as Gascoigne calls
them in the source play so seminal for this whole period oɪ
Shakespeare's development) as part of an enjoyable and consciously devised web of intrigue. The errors by which Lyly's
avaricious fathers, Memphio and Stellio, are prevented from
fulfilling their unpleasant schemes result exclusively from the
clever trickery of the pages. The central value of the play is
wit, which allows the pages to manipulate others and to lead
essentially self-frustrating plans into paths of fulfilment and
benefit. In all this there is no question of 'earthy-gross conceit,
Smoth'red in errors'—no question, that is, of the pathos of
human capacity to get lost in the labyrinth of error. But this is
the question that Shakespeare raises again and again in *The
Comedy of Errors*, even to the point where he seems to be ques-
tioning the nature of human identity. It is the threat of lost
identity that draws forth the most powerful poetry in the play:

> O time's extremity,
> Hast thou so crack'd and splitted my poor tongue
> In seven short years that here my only son
> Knows not my feeble key of untun'd cares?
> Though now this grained face of mine be hid
> In sap-consuming winter's drizzled snow,
> And all the conduits of my blood froze up,
> Yet hath my night of life some memory,
> My wasting lamps some fading glimmer left,
> My dull deaf ears a little use to hear;
> All these old witnesses—I cannot err—
> Tell me thou art my son Antipholus.
>
> (V. i. 306-17)

We may notice that the same betrayal of the father-son relationship draws forth the most powerful poetry in the *Henry VI* plays also (*2 Henry VI*, V. ii. 39 ff.).

Mother Bombie shows us characters who *could* be treated as victims. Maestius and Serena are involved in incestuous love which they abhor, but there is nothing in their scene (III. i) which invites us to become involved in their emotions; their situation is too obviously parallel to that of the other lovers in the play, too obviously a facet of a plot which moves forward by laying such facets together, to invite us to pause and imagine the mental states involved. And apart from Maestius and Serena there are no *victims* in the play; Lyly's attention is concentrated on the positive intrigues being set to work.

Shakespeare, on the other hand, chose as his model the one Roman play in which no agents, jokers or intriguers are shown on the stage, in which the errors result from fate. It is not the purpose of Plautus, of course, to dwell on the power of Fate, let alone the mental attitudes of those who endure its power. In the *Menaechmi* the short scenes are fully taken up with efforts to outwit other people: Menaechmus is trying to steal his wife's dowry; Peniculus is trying to secure a decent dinner or (alternatively) a satisfactory revenge; the wife is trying to gain her father's support and so defeat her husband; the other Menaechmus is trying to get away with the goods he had been given (by mistake). All this is dropped by Shakespeare; the characters become much more the passive victims of the mistakes, and the interest comes to rest on what they feel rather than what they do. This new focus appears as early as Antipholus' first soliloquy. 'Sir, I commend you to your own content', says the First Merchant; Antipholus' comment on this is as unnecessary to an intrigue as it is essential to an understanding of Shakespeare's outlook:

> He that commends me to mine own content
> Commends me to the thing I cannot get.
> I to the world am like a drop of water
> That in the ocean seeks another drop,
> Who, falling there to find his fellow forth,
> Unseen, inquisitive, confounds himself.
> So I, to find a mother and a brother,
> In quest of them, unhappy, lose myself.

(I. ii. 33-40)

Following, as this does, the scene of 'Hapless Aegeon, whom the fates have mark'd, To bear the extremity of dire mishap', Antipholus' soliloquy suggests a view of error which raises the uncomic question, 'Who am I?' or even (more particularly), 'How, outside family relationship, is identity sustained?' The importance of some such question to the author of the play is suggested by the recurrence of the same image as Antipholus uses, in a later scene, where Adriana reproaches her supposed husband:

> How comes it now, my husband, O how comes it,
> That thou art then estranged from thyself?
> Thyself I call it, being strange to me,
> That undividable, incorporate,
> Am better than thy dear self's better part.
> Ah, do not tear away thyself from me;
> For know, my love, as easy mayst thou fall
> A drop of water in the breaking gulf,
> And take unmingled thence that drop again
> Without addition or diminishing,
> As take from me thyself, and not me too.
>
> (II. ii. 118-28)

The view I have suggested here is not to be taken to mean that the play is 'The Tragedy of Errors' misnamed. The business remains comic, but the comic action is accompanied by a more searching regard for the human condition than is usually allowed by critics. A nice example of the combination of pathos and farce that the play seems to be aiming at occurs at the end of Antipholus' first soliloquy, quoted above. We may suppose he feels a little ashamed of his emotional outburst, and spying his servant returning—the return of routine and normality as he thinks—he remarks cheerfully, 'Here comes the almanac of my true date'. The pathos lies in the irony, for the servant is the wrong twin, who fails to recognize him, and neither Antipholus nor Dromio is to know the 'true date' till the end of the play. But the fact that this is pathos to Antipholus cannot conceal the complementary fact that it is farce in respect of the action. These darker interests only tint, never colour the surface of the play. But they persist throughout, none the less. 'I think you all have drunk of Circe's cup' says the Duke at the beginning of the denouement (V. i. 270); and the image is not fortuitous, for there is much reference throughout to the witchery which transforms men into appearances where their reality cannot be known. The conception of *error* here would seem to be linked to that of fate through the *Metamorphoses* of Ovid—Shakespeare's (and many another Elizabethan's) favourite reading, and liable to be taken very seriously, as a repertory of the deformations to which human nature was liable.[2] Lyly, much less concerned with the integrity of his characters, subjects many of them to metamorphosis; Shakespeare is content most of the time to keep it as a threat, to use it only to hint at the uncertainty around our assurance of personal identity. And so he uses it here.

It is this underlying seriousness about error which smoothes the transition from the frame-plot of Aegeon to the intrigue of the twins and stops the former from being what Charlton supposed: 'romantic matter [which] frames a realistic picture, but exercises no control over it' (p. 113). From our point of view, the frame-plot can be seen to catch up what is a minor strain in the intrigue and invert it to major status.

What I have called the problem of identity in *The Comedy of Errors* can be seen to be related to a well-known and persistent interest of Shakespeare's—concern with appearance and reality. The *Menaechmi* intrigue is given a different focus by asking seriously, 'What does it feel like to be mistaken for another person?' This is obviously a first form of the question about disguise which Shakespeare asks again and again—'Is disguise concealment or discovery?' For the first form of the question there is no obvious precedent in Lyly to 'explain' *The Comedy of Errors*; but there is an interesting parallel which shows up neatly what I take to be a basic factor in the relationship of the two dramatists. Lyly was evidently interested in the idea that his plays were 'unreal' and he recurs to it in several of his court prologues. Thus in the prologue to *Sapho and Phao* he says: 'Whatsoever we present, whether it be tedious (which we fear) or toyish (which we doubt), sweet or sour, absolute or imperfect, or whatsoever, in all humbleness we all, and I on knee for all, entreat that your Highness imagine yourself to be in a deep dream, that staying the conclusion, in your rising your Majesty vouchsafe but to say, *And so you awaked.*' The image here is repeated in the prologue to *The Woman in the Moon*:

> Our poet, slumb'ring in the Muses' laps,
> Hath seen a woman seated in the moon,
> A point beyond the ancient theoric;
> And as it was so he presents his dream
> Here in the bounds of fair Utopia
> Where lovely Nature, being only queen,
> Bestows such workmanship on earthly mould
> That heavens themselves envy her glorious work.
> . . .
> This, but the shadow of our author's dream,
> Argues the substance to be near at hand;
> At whose appearance I most humbly crave
> That in your forehead she may read content.
> If many faults escape in her discourse,
> Remember all is but a poet's dream.

In the prologue to *Endimion* we find yet another expression of the same idea: 'Most high and happy Princess, we must tell a tale of the man in the moon; which, if it seem ridiculous for the method or superfluous for the matter, or for the means incredible, for three faults we can make but one excuse: it is a tale of the man in the moon.'

The relation of these statements to Shakespeare is most obvious in *A Midsummer Night's Dream*, where it has been remarked; but in fact Shakespeare's interest in the relation between play and reality, appearance and truth, is one that goes back to the beginning of his art. But he never uses the distinction in the same way as Lyly. What Lyly says, in effect, is that the court audience is the reality (he never uses this image in his prologues for the private theatres) and the fount of truth; the play can only approach truth by mirroring the court's virtues, and can be at best but a shadow of that true perfection. This is to present the whole action as a homage to the audience; the relation is that of servant to master, complimenting, humbly insinuating, and suggesting that this cannot be taken too seriously since it is known and realized already in the lives of the audience. This parasitic relationship is shown in the nature of Lyly's denouements: his characters can hardly be said to achieve their own reconciliation; their lives are reversed and rearranged for them by the gratuitous benevolence of the sovereign-goddess, and this again points out of the play towards the audience, attributing to that the power which makes reconcilement possible.

Shakespeare's plays show a completely different relation to the audience. He does not assume that it represents a single ideal of conduct which he must attempt to imitate in his action. The life inside his plays is a life which is complete in itself, and cross references from the life of the play to that of the audience are handled on a basis of equality, most often in terms of a kind of rough cameraderie (for example, the Epilogue to *As You Like It*). If Shakespeare is going to talk about the 'unreality' of his play he must oppose it to a 'reality' which is also presented in the play, as part of *its* world. The reconciliations at the end of his comedies must set the different artificialities we have seen in action in an order or hierarchy of importance which the life of the play itself guarantees. It follows that the theme of Appearance and Reality involves for Shakespeare, as it need not do for Lyly, the problem of interconnecting his levels of reality, of making his action complete in itself and convincing though fictional. The difference is there, I suggest, in *The Comedy of Errors*, in the handling of fate's victims in both the frame-plot and the *Menaechmi* plot, but it becomes much more plain when we look away from the more abstract idea of 'disguise' in *The Comedy of Errors*, at the more normal use of disguise for intrigue in *The Taming of the Shrew* or at the romantic disguisings of *Two Gentlemen of Verona*. This is a movement of attention towards Lyly, and at the end of it a comparison between the two dramatists becomes natural; but even where they are most alike we can see that Shakespeare approaches disguise from a direction which is different from that of Lyly, a direction which *The Comedy of Errors* helps to explain.

Bond has suggested that Lyly was Shakespeare's model for his scenes of romantic disguise [II. 297]; however, as we have suggested above, Shakespeare is here much closer to the tradition of narrative prose romance than he is to Lyly. We should also notice that what is unique in Shakespeare's handling of the motif can often be explained in terms of the interest in Appearance and Reality discussed above. A comparison of

Gallathea with *The Taming of the Shrew* and *Two Gentlemen of Verona* may show the different direction of pull in the two authors.

The narrative function of disguise in *The Taming of the Shrew* is fairly obvious: Lucentio disguises himself as a schoolmaster in order to gain access to his love, while his servant Tranio pretends to be Lucentio; these are the 'supposes' (Gascoigne defines them in the source play of *Supposes,* as 'nothing else but a mistaking or imagination of one thing for another') which propel the plot forward. I should like, however, to look at these 'supposes' from a rather different angle from that of plot—to see how Shakespeare conducts his audience towards these disguisings; and this is a route that is not charted in the source play.

We move forward into *The Taming of the Shrew* as if into a series of Chinese boxes, as group after group 'stands aside' to allow the next group to perform. We begin with Christopher Sly, swine-drunk and penniless; he is obliged to 'play' as the lord takes over and turns Sly into his 'show'; then the troupe of players enters, and the lord and Sly 'stand aside' to watch them. In the play that the troupe performs we begin with Lucentio and Tranio, whose flowery blank verse is at the opposite pole from Sly's vernacular, suggesting a further level of artifice; the same effect is made by their glamorous Italian background, set against Sly's Warwickshire particularity: 'ask Marian Hacket the fat ale-wife of Wincot if she know me not'. But the Chinese boxes do not end even here. Having defined their persons and places, and then discoursed on the conflict of love (or experience) and learning, which Shakespeare uses as a minor theme in the play, Lucentio and Tranio in their turn stand aside:

> *Luc.* But stay a while: what company is this?
> *Tra.* Master, some show to welcome us to town.
> *Enter Baptista with his two daughters, Katherina and Bianca, Gremio a pantaloon, Hortensio, suitor to Bianca. Lucentio and Tranio stand by.*
> (I. i. 46 ff.)

The 'show' that follows is almost a complete 'play within the play'. Baptista imposes the condition that Kate must be married before he will consider the suitors to Bianca; Gremio and

Hortensio counter by promising to find some man who will woo Kate. In its Italianate, *Commedia dell'arte* conventionality this episode would seem to represent the limit of static artifice. It is just at this point, however, that Shakespeare begins to cross the plots and complicate his levels of reality. We return to Lucentio and Tranio. Lucentio, having fallen in love with Bianca, decides to add yet another couple of actors to the 'show' ('now 'tis plotted'). He will appear in the part of Cambio, a schoolmaster, while Tranio will 'keep house and port and servants' in the role of Lucentio.

We thus approach the disguising of Lucentio and Tranio in a way that clearly differentiates that from the disguising in *Gallathea*. We approach by a series of alternations between playing and watching: who was but now the player is now the auditor to another player. We watch the lord watching Sly watching Lucentio watching Bianca. When we next see Baptista taken in by the 'suppose' that Cambio is indeed a schoolmaster we cannot confine this error to the action of Baptista versus Lucentio. The motif of 'playing a part' has been repeated too often for the disguise to be seen only at this level of intrigue. Baptista's error joins the others throughout the play as a type of the human liability to suppose that the appearance is the reality, the actor the real man. Shakespeare has disrupted the standard audience assumption that 'we' are all real while 'they' (the actors) are all unreal, in a way that was hardly open to Lyly, faced by *his* audience; and so the play conveys the suggestion that the errors of the plot represent a condition to which all men are liable. Shakespeare has arranged his action in a series of planes of reality, in a way that reminds us of perspective planes in scenery. But there is no proscenium arch to separate the scenery from his audience; 'we' are only a further stage in a progression which demonstrates that all reality is relative—handy-dandy, which is the real man, which is the player?

The Taming of the Shrew is like *The Comedy of Errors*, I suggest, in raising problems of identity which can hardly be dismissed as merely functional to a disguise plot. The conditions of Lyly's art (and no doubt temperamental adaptation as well) make *his* handling of disguise very different. Lyly's patterning depends on a clear separation of one part of his play from another. Thus in *Gallathea* we have the deceivers on one side and those they wish to deceive on the other; to raise the question of their comparative 'reality' would be to destroy the delicate balance of the two sides, and so to destroy the effect of denouement, when they come together. It is inside a structure composed of parallel facets building up this central antithesis that we see the disguising of Gallathea and Phillida. The disguising of one is carefully paralleled in the disguising of the other, and in a landscape of such parallels, the action is taken as a masked figure to be danced through for the sake of the total effect rather than as an exploration of the feelings involved in situations of Appearance and Reality; the effect of the disguising is measured by its contribution to the whole plot, its power to supply a new facet to the static plot-situation of 'Destiny cannot be prevented by craft'.

This is not to say that Lyly fails to use disguise as a means of exploring the emotions of the nymphs who are disguised. He does do so, and of the dramatists before Shakespeare he shows the highest degree of accomplishment in such matters. But it is the *situation* that his control over the oblique statements of disguised persons leads him to explore. Phillida and Gallathea neither choose disguise nor try to use disguise; the disguise exists as a datum and the maidenliness of their approach is shown by the delicacy with which they move through its maze of problems. We savour this delicacy as connoisseurs, but do not feel that we share the problems as *our* problems. Shakespeare, on the other hand (even the Shakespeare of *The Comedy of Errors*), presents the problems of 'seeming' rather than 'being' as personal and so appeals to *our* feelings directly. When we come to a situation as apparently Lylian as that in *Two Gentlemen* where Julia (disguised as Sebastian) woos Silvia on behalf of her own love, Proteus, we can see how far the pressure of Shakespeare's own interests has changed the motifs. The 'suppose' that Julia is really Sebastian is one that Julia herself has chosen, because it enables her to be implicated in the love of Proteus even when she herself is not its object. The disguise is part of a 'history' of Julia's love, which we follow with sympathetic attachment and a sense of 'getting somewhere'. The condition of being in love is certainly something that Lyly is concerned with; *Euphues* was probably the first work in

English to convey the half amused, half fascinated quality of male reaction to female coquetry, which Shakespeare develops for example in that scene of *Two Gentlemen* where Julia tears her lover's letter before she will condescend to read it. But Lyly does not aim to carry us forward steadily from a witty view of the state of loving to the fruition of love in marriage; he is perfectly capable of Julia's witty equivocation but he is not capable, I suggest, of showing a developing view of her love, through the pathos of disguise, and into the eventual reconcilement. The extreme balance of *Gallathea* may seem to make the contrast with Shakespeare in this respect too easy; this is a play in which situations exist to balance one another, not to develop the action. But even when Lyly is committed to showing the development of individual love he does so without involving us in the history of an emotion. Sapho's love (or Alexander's) is conducted inside the static debate framework of Love versus Honour. We do not follow Sapho with any sense of sharing her adventure, for the limits of possibility are already predetermined by the debate and all Sapho can do is illustrate its theoretical dilemmas.

It is this implication in the history behind Julia's disguise that separates most decisively Shakespeare's handling of the love-disguise motif from Lyly's. As in *The Comedy of Errors* and (more certainly) in *The Taming of the Shrew*, we are led here, in *Two Gentlemen*, to see the complexities involved as within ourselves. And again, the desire to explore the pathos of, 'What does it feel like to be mistaken for another?', which runs through these early plays, is accompanied by a treatment of the action as a series of contrasting planes of reality; these are set against one another and seem designed to be reconciled at the end by our clear awareness of what are the more important attitudes and what are the less. Julia's story of how (as Sebastian) she played the part of 'Ariadne passioning for Theseus' perjury and unjust flight' is one of those typically Shakespearian regresses (an actual boy on the stage pretending to be a girl pretending to be a boy pretending to be a girl) which so tease us out of thought that we become aware of the pattern of responses as having to be lived through before it can be comprehended. But this comprehension is not, as with Lyly, one which sets the whole play at a dream-like and diminished distance.

Julia 'plays' at being Sebastian, and remarks, ruefully of her own performance,

> Alas, how love can trifle with itself!

But the combination of involvement and disengagement here is only superficially Lylian. In the disguise scene of *Gallathea* we watch the errors of both nymphs from the outside, for no one in the scene is given the dignity of understanding what is happening. We are involved in an appreciation of the nymphs' tentativeness, but we do not share any single point of view, as we share that of Julia; we see, in *Two Gentlemen*, that a seeming lightness may cover and make tolerable a real heartbreak, and we are not in any doubt, I think, about the different planes of reality which are involved.

These distinctions should not, however, blind us to the fact that *Two Gentlemen* is a play which is much closer to the temper of Lyly's world than are the plays which I have already treated —*Comedy of Errors* and *Taming of the Shrew*. Even if we leave on one side the delighted evocation of female wilfulness (which I shall discuss later) we can see that this is a play which rates elegance as a major virtue, and one may allow that the author is conscious of the glamour of *Euphues* (whose story of two friends is very similar to that of Valentine and Proteus), even if he has not, as yet, made any close study of Lyly's plays (I do not accept T. W. Baldwin's suppositions in this field).[3] But even if Shakespeare has become conscious of Lylian values in this play, he is by no means subdued to imitation, or diverted away from his other, and probably earlier interests. When we look at many elements which are supposed to connect the two play-wrights we are often made conscious of the differences rather than the similarities. T. M. Parrott, in his book on *Shakespearean Comedy* refers to I, i. 70 ff. of *Two Gentlemen* as 'a dialogue between a lover and a page that reads almost like a transcript from one of Lyly's comedies' (p. 114). This is an unfortunate point on which to base a connection for it would seem that the function of the servants in Shakespeare's early comedies is one thing which most clearly differentiates his aims from those of Lyly. As I have said already, Lyly maintains the balance of his form by keeping its various elements in separate compartments. The comedy of Lyly's pages is nearly always to be found in speech with other pages; and the wit of Lyly's lovers is nearly always to be found in dialogue with other lovers. It follows that 'a dialogue between a lover and a page' is only found in Lyly where the 'lover' is himself a clown, is in fact Sir Tophas. In *Two Gentlemen*, as elsewhere in his work, Shakespeare crosses or interlaces his different elements so that they throw light on one another, in terms of character as well as in the (Lylian) terms of plot. In the scene which has been cited by Professor Parrott there is an excellent contrast between the elegance of the letter-writer (Proteus) and the boorishness of the letter-carrier (Speed) which is at the same time a contrast between the giddiness of the lover and the flat-footed stability of the servant's outlook,

> Assured of certain certainties.

Each throws light on the other, and taken together they evoke an ideal of conduct which neither can attain to, but which sets both within a scale of conduct. Shakespeare works constantly through scenes in which there is this kind of contrast; Lyly moves slowly and deliberately from one world (complete in itself) to another (complete in itself), without involving us in comparative evaluations. The greater flexibility of Shakespeare's method is obvious. He shows also a unique capacity to avoid hard and fast distinctions. Shakespeare's plays are built on a schematic framework, as are Lyly's, but it is Shakespeare's way to avoid committing himself too far, and to allow diverse significances to burgeon round the framework of his materials. Thus Lyly's servants have a simple and definitive set of characteristics—quick wit, love of mischief, empty bellies. The servants of *Two Gentlemen* are much more difficult to define. It is usually suggested (and there is much to support the suggestion) that Speed is intended as a page—pert, quick-witted (as his name suggests) and keenly critical, while Launce is seen as a clown, rustic, slow-moving and affectionate (cf. Moth and Costard in *Love's Labour's Lost*). But Shakespeare is not confined by this distinction. When the two servants meet after their separation (in Act II, scene v) their dialogue is presented as between equals; their wit is of the same kind. Launce is a clown when he talks to his dog, and thus serves to define the elegance of Proteus; but Speed has exactly the same function when he is contrasted with Proteus in Act I, scene i. The elusiveness of Shakespeare's art is his own secret.

It is often said that Lyly is Shakespeare's master in the matter of constructing sub-plots, and taught him how to set the boorish against the noble in such a way that one balances the other. I have suggested here that Shakespeare interlaces sub-plot and main plot in a way that is unlike Lyly; but this does not remove the supposition that he learned from Lyly the general art of setting clowns and kings in a complex but harmonious relationship. It must follow, however, from what I have said about parody in Chapter III that the relationship of the two playwrights cannot be a simple master and pupil one, for the general principles were of wide diffusion, and in terms of detail Shakespeare does not follow Lyly until he comes to write *Love's Labour's Lost*; and there, it is certainly true, he copies the history of Armado from that of Tophas in Lyly's *Endimion*. In his earliest plays Shakespeare shows that he is aware of that form of parody wooing which we have already noticed in the sub-plot of *Fulgens and Lucres*, and which Lyly does not use. As the servants in *Fulgens and Lucres* woo in their carnal way the maid of the lady their masters woo with honour, so in *The Comedy of Errors* we find Dromio the servant repeating at a lower level the love-situation of his master, Antipholus of Syracuse. Antipholus finds himself claimed as husband by a lady he has never seen before; his bewilderment and embarrassment are expressed in terms of gentlemanly sensibility, shown clearly by the device of making the chief advocate for his marriage a lady for whom he has conceived a sudden passion, but who claims that she is his sister-in-law. At the end of this assault on Antipholus' sensibility comes a comic parody of it; Dromio rushes in, in full flight from *his* embarrassing experience: 'I am due to a woman—one that claims me, one that haunts me, one that will have me . . . she's the kitchen-wench, and all grease, and I know not what use to put her to but to make a lamp of her and run from her by her own light' (III. ii. 80-96). The dismay of carnality and the dismay of honour are thus set face to face in a way which is more like *Fulgens and Lucres* than anything in Lyly. The physical detail of the servant's discomfiture adds body to the mental discomfiture of the master; what had become, at the higher level, too emotionally involved, is loosened by the farce of the servant; and when the two resolve at the end of the scene to flee from the 'witches' of Ephesus, we have a sense of the two levels coalescing into one mutually reinforced statement about 'transformation' and loss of identity.

In *Two Gentlemen* (Act II, scene ii) we see Proteus saying farewell to his beloved Julia; this is followed immediately by his servant Launce's famous demonstration how he said farewell to his family, everybody weeping but his dog Crab. Here the parody, far more certainly than is the case with *The Comedy of Errors*, throws new light on the preceding episode, and affects our interpretation of its high-strained Petrarchan rhetoric. The Proteus-Julia farewell is an exercise on the silence, apparent insensitivity and genuine suffering of true love:

> what, gone without a word?
> Ay, so true love should do: it cannot speak;
> For truth hath better deeds than words to grace it.

Launce's dog, Crab, takes up the burden of this Stoic *apatheia*:

> Now the dog all this while sheds not a tear, nor speaks a word

and thereby not only makes a comic point of its own, but prepares us for the breakdown of the Petrarchan emotion of his master.

The parallelism and parody in these two episodes function in a way quite different from that of Lyly's sub-plots. The most obvious difference is that in Shakespeare the servant-action clashes with and modifies our response to the main action. The separate world of Lyly's pages does not make this effect. Even in *Endimion*, with the most developed sub-plot, the love which Sir Tophas expresses for Dipsas does not in any way modify the view we take of Endimion's love for Cynthia. The theme of hopeless adoration which is serious in one case and comic in the other only serves to measure the distance which separates the hero from the fool. Lyly assumes without question that the 'true' view is the courtly one enshrined in Cynthia, Alexander, Sapho or even Midas (as he appears at the end of the play). The parallel attitudes may give this an added grace or fill in the background, but they do not modify its 'reality' with suggestions of alternative 'realities'.

In *A Midsummer Night's Dream* and *Love's Labour's Lost* (as I shall suggest below) Shakespeare follows Lyly in developing his action out of parallel instances of behaviour. This would seem an obvious place to look for parody of the upper levels by the lower; but in fact *A Midsummer Night's Dream* shows very little of the kind of parody we have seen in *The Comedy of Errors* and *Two Gentlemen of Verona*. It would look as if the complexity of thematic cross-reference in this play inhibited the simple parody of master by servant which thrives best in a simple two-deck narrative. *A Midsummer Night's Dream* handles the Mechanicals much as Lyly handles his page-plots, keeping them separate from their social superiors till the last act. The parallel use of love-juice to make Titania dote on Bottom and to sort out the errors of the quartet of lovers might seem to show parody in action; but the structure of the work seems to hide rather than promote the parallel, and even when perceived, it does not seem to add anything to either episode. Following Lyly, Shakespeare has abandoned parody.

The same general point could be made about the sub-plot elements in *Love's Labour's Lost*. Here we have a precise link with Lyly, for it is clear that the figure and the history of Armado are derived from those of Sir Tophas in *Endimion*. Armado, like Tophas, is a braggart soldier who abandons war-talk for love-talk. Like him he is accompanied by a page who fools him by being quicker-witted than he is; he makes an unsuitable choice in love, and at the end of the play he shares (at his comic level) the fate of the nobler characters. Shakespeare's imitation, however, hardly involves what I have described as the parody elements in *Endimion* (see above, p. 237 ff.). The function of Armado is more difficult to see schematically than is that of Tophas. His role places him between the rustics and the nobles and he appears sometimes to be attached to one group, sometimes to another; for Shakespeare handles his multiple plots to suggest the variety of social experience at different levels. While Lyly keeps his parallel episodes in separation from one another, and stresses their similarity, Shakespeare interlaces his episodes and stresses the *different* responses which make up a unified though wide-ranging social scene. Shakespeare, in consequence, can work with a much wider range of styles, as he does even in his earliest plays. Lyly may have given Shakespeare an ideal of 'harmonious variety', but the evocation of a whole range of responses by this means represents Shakespeare's own discovery.

These earlier comedies of Shakespeare—*Comedy of Errors, Taming of the Shrew* and *Two Gentlemen*—show a gradual approach to Lyly's kind of love-comedy, but at the same time we can see in them a continuity of interests which are quite unLylian. In none of these plays, moreover, do we see any imitation of Lyly's mode of play construction. Instead, Shakespeare seems to have started with the intrigue plots of Roman and Italian comedy (*Menaechmi* and *I Suppositi*) and to have decorated these with his own devices, though to the Tudor taste, by realistic and romantic additions. When he broke away from this formula, in *Two Gentlemen*, it was to the matter of romance, with a first attempt to dramatize a prose narrative. What I take to be the next two comedies, *Love's Labour's Lost* and *A Midsummer Night's Dream*, are however, completely Lylian in their construction, and so in marked contrast to the preceding plays. What has caused this volte-face? We may suppose, with Professor Mincoff, that Shakespeare had been deliberately abstaining from Lyly's mode of writing, because this was antipathetic to his bourgeois outlook, and then suddenly gave in;[4] or suppose (as I would prefer) that Court Comedy was too little adapted to the theatrical conditions of the public theatre to make immediate acceptance possible; and that, in consequence, *Love's Labour's Lost* and *A Midsummer Night's Dream* mark a change, largely because the occasion of these plays is aristocratic rather than popular. It may be, of course, that Shakespeare only discovered Lyly's plays at this late stage.

These two plays, however, whatever their original occasions, are not to be seen only as Court Comedies; and one of the interests of setting them beside Lyly is to see what he did not adopt and what he changed in effect though he imitated in form. In such an enquiry it is perhaps more convenient to begin with *A Midsummer Night's Dream*. This play very obviously constructs its plot in the manner of Lyly, by balancing a number of self-contained groups, one against the other. As in *Sapho and Phao* we have court ladies, gods, pages and the Sybil, who never talk together; as in *Midas* we have shepherds, nymphs, counsellors, pages and gods maintained in separation from one another; so in *A Midsummer Night's Dream* we have fairies, mechanicals, royal lovers (in the manner of the *Heroides*) and young lovers seeking to outwit their fathers, all kept far more distinct from one another than has been the case in the Shakespeare comedies so far discussed.

Not only so, but the groups are introduced to us in the manner of which Lyly was the great exemplar: one by one the groups are presented, and we hear from each in turn what is to be its intention and outlook for the rest of the play. It would almost seem as if Shakespeare were consciously seeking to rival the virtuousity of his master, for the entries of the various groups can be seen to be based on a single theme of love versus authority, which in two entries (the royal lovers, and the fairies) appears in the relationship of husband and wife, and in two (the young lovers, and Pyramus and Thisbe) in that of children and fathers. It is true that the story of Pyramus and Thisbe is not actually unfolded in the first scene of the Mechanicals, and it can be argued that my supposition is forced here. Against this I would set the point that much of the fun of the scene seems to depend on a knowledge of the story. Notice too that the theme of parental opposition would seem to be clearly in Shakespeare's mind in this scene, for he allots parts for Pyramus' father and Thisbe's mother and father, though these disappear before the actual performance.

As if this were not Lylian enough, Shakespeare further bases his comedy on a clearly exposed debate subject of moonlight versus daylight or imagination versus reason, which all the groups sound out in turn. The very profusion of Lylian motifs in the play might seem to turn it into a cento, were it not that this profusion is in itself unLylian. By putting together the debate methods of the earlier Lylian comedies and what I have called the fugal methods of the later plays Shakespeare's play acquires a density of meaning which Lyly never achieved and probably never aimed at. For, even with all these similarities to Lyly, *A Midsummer Night's Dream* remains obviously in the line of the earlier plays which I have discussed. We may see how Shakespeare imitates Lyly yet remains true to himself by looking again at the fugal structure of the play. For if we look at the pattern of the entries from a slightly different angle, we can see a design in which a frame-plot enfolds a contrasting intrigue, just as in *The Comedy of Errors* or *The Taming of the Shrew*. The fable of Theseus and Hippolyta is essential to the others, but since it is without the modern 'dramatic' virtues—suspense, intrigue, continuity or development—it is easy to regard it simply as a device for introducing and then completing (in the manner of the Aegeon plot, and the Sly plot of *A Shrew*) what from this angle must be treated as the main business of the play—the intrigue of the four lovers. This intrigue is more like 'genuine drama' and is, of course, a simple variation on that basic plot of Greek and Roman New Comedy in which the children are forbidden to marry by their fathers and then find means to evade the order, means which breed alternate promises of success and failure. The Italian Renaissance variants on this plot often included recourse to magic, and the interventions of the fairies can be fitted to this view of the play's structure, though their plot is too developed to provide a 'regular' addition. The mechanicals must remain, of course, at the level of a sub-plot.

This view of the play is attractive if we look at it exclusively from the angle of Shakespeare's development; and it might be said to be fairly standard in modern criticism: 'The most important story from the point of view of the comic idea, and the one to which most space is devoted, is that of the Athenian lovers', writes Sir Edmund Chambers (*Shakespeare, a Survey*, p. 81). This is true enough, if we limit the scope of 'the comic idea' sufficiently, but it ignores the planes of reality on which the various stories operate. The lovers' plot is the longest, but it is also that which is most remote from the idea of rational normality, as is clear enough if we listen to the levels of artifice in the verse. If we feel that the artificial verse of the lovers' plot is the central support of the play's reality then we must suppose that reality is badly supported here. This is presumably the reason why some have looked for another hand to be rapped across the knuckles for these defects.

From the point of view of this book what is interesting in this view of the play is the evidence it provides of Shakespeare's evasiveness in handling the Lylian structure. As the play would seem to have provided entertainment for a courtly occasion and also to have appeared on the public stage, so, in form, it combines some of the aspects of a Lylian court entertainment with

features which can be read in the more purely narrative way of
Shakespeare's earlier plays. This ambiguity in the structure
can be pushed still further. The system of fugal entries is
handled in such a way as to accommodate Shakespeare's other
favourite device of a play within a play, seen at large in *The
Taming of the Shrew* and appearing again and again in his
tendency to cross and complicate his actions. Theseus and
Hippolita have to 'stand aside' to allow the plot of Egeus and
the lovers to be expounded. The first exchanges in the wood are
introduced and observed by Oberon, and the later 'fond
pageant' is watched by both Oberon and the Puck. When the
mechanicals rehearse their play they do so against the background of Titania's bower and to the accompaniment of the
Puck's derisive commentary. The performance of the Pyramus
and Thisbe play is only the fullest example of a tendency
apparent throughout the play to interlace the episodes in a
way unknown to Lyly. Even when Shakespeare does not
implicate his themes in one another, he is prepared to use the
tension of a possible clash as a dramatic device: the tense
proximity of the fairy queen and the mechanicals is preserved
throughout 117 lines till 'the shallowest thickskin of that barren
sort' is fitted with his grossest form and only then are the
opposites allowed to embrace:

> *Titania.* Mine ear is much enamoured of thy note;
> So is mine eye enthralled to thy shape;
> And thy fair virtue's force perforce doth move me,
> On the first view, to say, to swear, I love thee.
>
> (III. i. 126-129)

The short breathless scenes of Demetrius and Lysander, each
pursuing the other (as he thinks), till both are laid together in
sleep, may serve as an image of Shakespeare's art in this plot,
the dizzy skill with which the episodes are kept revolving round
one another, but only touching where the author decides they
should. The feelings of Lyly's gods are never confused or inter-
laced with those of his mortals, and their omniscience is never
shown in free comparison with the seeming knowledge of men.
Shakespeare, on the other hand, shows us gods and men enjoying comparable states of consciousness; Oberon and the Puck
are able to change the loves of human beings, but in them-

selves they are hardly capable (Puck not at all) of these same feelings. This raises naturally the question of the comparative value of these kinds of consciousness, and of their comparative reality. Neither Lyly's gods nor his wise women (Sybil and Mother Bombie) give us any assurance about their feelings; Neptune's expressions of anger (in *Gallathea*), Sybil's of weariness or Endimion's of adoration are powerful in themselves, but it is not the mind behind these speeches that we become conscious of, so much as the appropriateness to the play's structure. Lyly's parallel episodes—Tyterus disguising Gallathea, Melebeus disguising Phillida, Cupid disguising himself—reflect on one another in terms of theme and structure but not in terms of the emotions which Tyterus or Melebeus or Cupid may be supposed to feel; and though the feelings of Phillida and Gallathea are more developed, they do not provide any hint of a scale of emotions which we in the audience are required to sort out for ourselves. And it is just this question of the comparative value or reality of different emotional states that links Shakespeare's episodes most closely and leaves them reverberating in our minds.

I have spoken of Shakespeare allowing a 'narrative reading' of *A Midsummer Night's Dream*; he gives his plot, laid out in episodes though it may be, a continuity and a momentum by arranging that all the actions should all point towards a single event at the end of the play. Lyly's different episodes may illustrate one theme; but this is a static relationship, and gives no drive to the action. *A Midsummer Night's Dream* begins with a forecast:

> Now fair Hippolyta, our nuptial hour
> Draws on apace: four happy days bring in
> Another moon . . .
> Four days will quickly steep themselves in night
> Four nights will quickly dream away the time.

The whole action reflects this opening forecast of day turning to night and night turning to dream, to fill the time before the nuptial ceremony. Theseus commands his Master of the Revels to 'stir up the Athenian youth to merriments', and immediately we have a 'show' of traditional New Comedy themes—the angry Athenian father and the children who are disobedient in

322

their love. In the formality of the verse and the handling here there is even a suggestion that Theseus is being shown a comedy to while away the time. But this is no more than a suggestion; what ties the lovers' plot to the main movement of the play towards Theseus' marriage is the decision that their settlement must be made at the same time as 'the sealing-day betwixt my love and me'. The same method ties in the plot of the mechanicals: their play is designed as an 'interlude before the duke and duchess, on his wedding day at night', and they can be seen as another part of the 'pomp . . . triumph, and . . . revelling' which is decreed for the time-scheme of the play. Finally, the fairies are only in the vicinity of Athens because

> the bouncing Amazon
> . . .
> To Theseus must be wedded, and you come
> To give their bed joy and prosperity.

Their plot, like the others, is pulled towards the same conclusive knot which will tie up all the actions and explain their relationship to one another in the image of reconcilement which Shakespeare makes of marriage.

For marriage is here not only the convenient stopping-place which Lyly uses (for example) in *Gallathea* and *Love's Metamorphosis*, but a human goal of such attractive power that all the plots are given direction and relationship by the impulse and social pressure that it involves (leaving aside the sacramental mystery). But it is rather dangerous to use this as an argument for Shakespeare's development of Lyly's form in this play, for it could be argued that *A Midsummer Night's Dream* is a 'wedding play' and so not strictly comparable. I therefore leave the subject for the moment, and shall return to it again when dealing with *Love's Labour's Lost*, where the same objections do not apply. What cannot be discounted from *A Midsummer Night's Dream*, however, is that the episodic construction undoubtedly derived from Lyly is so handled that the advantages of variousness do not impede the sense of direction and of narrative speed.

The debate theme in *A Midsummer Night's Dream*, though it may imitate similar devices in Lyly, is likewise used in a way which is thoroughly Shakespearian, and obviously carries on from the similar though more rudimentary form in *Two Gentlemen*. This is not to say that *The Comedy of Errors* and *The Taming of the Shrew* are simple in their intellectual interests; but they are not organized as debates; there is no formal statement of opposing intellectual attitudes; the themes arise more casually and more by implication in the handling of the plot. The fault of *Two Gentlemen* is, I take it, that it goes too far in the opposite direction from this, and makes the debate theme too central. The idea of love versus honour is worked out in terms of the two characters, Valentine who sacrifices love for friendship (here, as usually, the concomitant of honour), and Proteus who sacrifices honour to love. This Lylian kind of structure will, however, only work when the characters are as simple as are Lyly's; it is perfectly possible to comprehend the opposition between Sapho and Venus inside the terms of Honour versus Love, for the tendency to become identified with these ideals is the only tendency we notice in these characters. In *Campaspe*, the contrast between Alexander and Apelles is rather more complex but is still not outside the control of the intellectual concept of the magnanimous mind on the one hand and the ordinary will of man on the other. But the debate theme of *Two Gentlemen* is quite incapable of controlling the history of Proteus in whose complex nature will and reason are seen at psychological odds:

> I cannot leave to love, and yet I do;
> But there I leave to love where I should love.
> Julia I lose and Valentine I lose;
> If I keep them I needs must lose myself;
> If I lose them, thus find I by their loss—
> For Valentine, myself, for Julia, Silvia.
> I to myself am dearer than a friend,
> For love is still most precious in itself;
> And Silvia—witness Heaven that made her fair—
> Shows Julia but a swarthy Ethiop.
>
> (II. vi. 17-26)

One of the difficulties of *Two Gentlemen* is that where friendship wins (in Valentine) we see the matter at merely intellectual focus; but where love wins (in Proteus) we have a psychological dimension as well. Proteus acquires not only a stance in the debate, but another quality which breaks the intellectual see-saw under its weight—I mean the quality of knavery.

Knavish actions are performed in Lyly's plays, but knavery is not a quality of any of his persons. Midas is said to be a tyrant, and we see him like another Paris choosing the wrong alternative; but this is merely intellectual error, not knavery in grain. We see Tellus in her jealousy throwing Endimion into a perpetual sleep, and Erisichthon impiously hewing down the sacred tree; but these wrong deeds belong to the intellectual constructions in the plays: jealousy is shown as the opposite of calm constancy, and is a tribute to the *semper eadem* serenity of Cynthia; Erisichthon's impiety exists in a balanced relationship besides Ceres' benignity. Shakespeare, on the other hand, implicates us in the knavery of Proteus by showing the psychological pressures which move him to make his choice, rather than the balance of attitudes which make up the plot. Proteus wishes to seem a gentleman of honour and a course of honour is available to him. But he chooses to enjoy the appearance of honour while triumphing in the reality of double treachery. Here the Shakespearian contrast of appearance and reality is used to reinforce a distinction unknown to Lyly and one which unbalances the overt debate between Love and Honour—a distinction between the man who can heartlessly manipulate the surface of life and the man who is the victim of his own idealism, between the villain and the hero as Shakespeare comes to see it in later plays (Iago and Othello, Claudius and Hamlet, Edmund and Edgar). Though this contrast is only touched upon in *Two Gentlemen* it is still strong enough to make the denouement of the play ludicrously inadequate to the interest.

Miss Bradbrook has remarked that 'in releasing Silvia, Valentine was displaying in transcendant form the courtly virtue of magnanimity, the first and greatest virtue of a gentleman'.[5] This is no doubt historically accurate, and perhaps was Shakespeare's intention. But there can be little doubt that as a display of magnanimity *Two Gentlemen* is less satisfactory than *Campaspe*. For in *Campaspe* the whole organization of the play serves this end; love rears its lovely head in Alexander's court only as a foil to honour, and is discussed only to prepare the way for its rejection. In *Two Gentlemen* the magnanimity of

Valentine cannot swallow up the passion of Proteus, for passion
has been expressed as a reality too psychologically disruptive to
be laid by a calmly rational asseveration: 'I'll love no more'.

Though Shakespeare could find no warrant in Lyly's *plays*
for this presentation of Proteus, he might well have found an
exact image of the sophistry of Proteus, the man who prefers
dishonourable love to honourable friendship, in Euphues, who
deceives Philautus to obtain Lucilla. Just as Proteus is given
soliloquies in which he sets friendship against love and comes
to the villanous conclusion, 'I to myself am dearer than a
friend' (with its reverberations from Richard III and Iago),
so Euphues is given a lengthy soliloquy in which *he* decides to
betray his friend:

> Shall I not then hazard my life to obtain my love? and deceive
> Philautus to receive Lucilla? Yes, Euphues, where love beareth
> sway, friendship can have no show . . . And canst thou, wretch,
> be false to him that is faithful to thee? Shall his courtesy be cause
> of thy cruelty? Wilt thou violate the league of faith, to inherit the
> land of folly? Shall affection be of more force than friendship,
> love than law, lust than loyalty? Knowest thou not that he that
> loseth his honesty hath nothing else to lose?   (I. 209 f.)

There is no episode of this kind in the *Diana* of Montemayor,
the major source of *Two Gentlemen*, and one may justly suspect
that *Euphues* has helped to shape Shakespeare's handling of his
story. But there is an essential difference. In *Two Gentlemen* we
feel the quality of Proteus's villainy because we are shown it
from the point of view of the girl whose innocence he has
betrayed. Love is no longer an emotion that the man describes
to the audience (as in the sonnet-sequence), but an emotional
relationship whose effect, no less than its force, is made dramatic.
Shakespeare has joined the entanglements of Romance—characters loving and betraying one another and evoking the pathos
of human inconstancy—to the debate interest in human
motives and principles; the resultant mixture is unbalanced
from either point of view.

The debate structure in *A Midsummer Night's Dream* avoids
this unbalance. It might be said that Theseus and Hippolyta
'stand for' Reason, and this would not be ludicrously inappropriate, for they are characters of rounded attitudes but not
of any psychological complexity. The play, I would suggest,

deliberately avoids the psychological overloading of *Two Gentlemen:* notice, for example, the lack of any inner debate to accompany Helena's decision to betray her friend (I. ii. 226 ff.). Here Shakespeare, in the manner of, and presumably following the lead of Lyly, makes the plot carry a much larger share of the meaning. It is the whole world of Theseus and Hippolyta, rather than the feelings of either of them, that actualizes the idea of Reason or Daylight—the daylight to which their horns and dogs must awake the dreamers before the latter can find themselves. It is still more difficult to make any single character or group of characters 'stand for' Imagination or Moonlight, and perhaps the attempt of Starveling to impersonate 'Moonshine' in the Pyramus play should be sufficient to warn us against expecting this. The method which Shakespeare uses to convey the quality of Imagination or Moonshine is very remarkable: he has created (single-handed) a whole realm of action whose poetic atmosphere is alone sufficient to characterize the ideas it contains. Moonlight is a quality which suffuses the middle scenes of the play and which (with its attendant associations derived from Maying or Midsummer superstition) is clearly placed on trial in Theseus' great speech about the poet, the lover and the madman. This speech is the crown of the debate, and shows the extent to which it is a genuine debate between equally persuasive possibilities. For there is no need to take Theseus' judgment against imagination as crushingly final unless the play as a whole endorses it; it is, after all, an *ex parte* judgment. It is Theseus himself who says that 'the best in this kind are but shadows; and the worst are no worse if imagination amend them'—that is, in a play it is up to the spectators to create the truth of what they see; and there is no suggestion that this is less true of the play in which Theseus himself appears. What happens in the Athenian woods by moonlight is sufficiently near play (see below) to be able to draw on the same excuse. Certainly the lovers are prepared to make valid the happenings of the night by just this:

> *Dem.*   Are you sure
> That we are awake? It seems to me
> That yet we sleep, we dream. Do not you think
> The duke was here and bid us follow him?
> *Her.* Yea; and my father.

Hel.   And Hippolyta.
Lys. And he did bid us follow to the temple.
Dem. Why, then we are awake; let's follow him;
      And by the way let us recount our dreams.
                                        (IV. i. 189-195)

By being prepared to live the visions that have appeared to
them they make them true; and here the lover's creative
imagination (to be questioned more insistently in *Troilus*) is
allowed its say. Hippolyta in her reply to Theseus's great
speech condemning imagination (a reply too seldom taken into
account) makes something of the same point as the lovers do:
where the imagined facts hang together with inner logic and
consistency, as of a world that could be lived in, then the
imagination may have some claim to truth. The discrimination
here has some aspects in common with that which Coleridge
was later to elaborate between fancy and imagination; the
former is indeed an 'airy nothing', but the latter however
'strange and admirable' can be defended as possessing a kind of
truth. It is not a defence, however, that Shakespeare himself
develops, leaving the debate (as was his wont) between the
opposed views, with the kind of ironic twist that makes Theseus
say

                 I never may believe
            These antique fables

when he himself is just another such 'antique fable'. Moreover
it is Theseus himself who sets the main course of the play
towards 'another moon', and turns time, the natural element
of Reason, into

            a step-dame or a dowager
      Long withering out a young man's revenue.

It can be seen, even from what has been said already, how
closely this debate theme of reason against imagination, daylight against moonlight touches on the larger Shakespearian
distinction of appearance against reality, play against truth,
and so, inside its Lylian form, carried on the dominant interests
of his 'pre-Lylian' Comedy. This especially obvious in the
Mechanicals' preparations for their play, with all the attendant
worry about the lion and how he must indicate to the ladies,
'I am no such thing: I am a man as other men are', and about

'Wall' and 'Moonshine'. As in the preceding plays, the problem
of appearance and reality becomes associated with Ovidian
metamorphosis. We are given a complex pattern of double
disguising: first Bottom plays Pyramus, where the nobility of
the role (the appearance) is lost in the boorishness (reality) of
the player; but Bottom is then translated into the role of an ass
and proceeds to play the accepted lover with so much aplomb
that we are caught once again in the gap between the appearance and the reality. Less obvious is the confusion of play and
truth in the escapades of the lovers. In Act III Helena is being
wooed by both Demetrius and Lysander. The lovers protest
that this is true or real:

> Be certain, nothing truer; 'tis no jest,
>
> (III. ii. 280)

but Helena can only suppose that she should act the part of
the audience at a play ('o excellent!') rather than that of the
participant in a true event. She cannot believe (and in part she
is right—the action is moonlight rather than real) that Demetrius and Lysander *mean* what they say, are not merely acting
out a pageant of love. As elsewhere, we see Shakespeare placing
the levels of appearance and reality one behind the other:
Helena supposes it to be a 'game' (though a bitter one);
Demetrius and Lysander think it is 'real'; Puck and Oberon
see it as a fond pageant, and we in the audience know that it is
all a play. Shakespeare has altered the Lylian effects to something more true to his own vision—a vision of dream and
reality so intermingled that we cannot tell where play ends and
reality begins, and where the debate itself is lost in the uncertainty of knowledge.

The confusion of dream and reality in this play (indicated
by the title) has sometimes been associated with Lyly's court
prologue to *Sapho and Phao*: 'Whatsoever we present, whether it
be tedious (which we fear) or toyish (which we doubt), sweet
or sour, absolute or imperfect, or whatsoever, in all humbleness
we all, and I on knee for all, entreat that your Highness imagine
yourself to be in a deep dream, that staying the conclusion,
in your rising your Majesty vouchsafe but to say, *And so you
awaked.*' The contrast here of reality (the court) against dream
(the play) might seem to run counter to the assumption on

which I have worked—that the theme of appearance and reality is a dominant interest in Shakespeare but not in Lyly. But as I have pointed out above (p. 306 ff.) there is an essential difference. Theseus is *inside* Shakespeare's play, and whether we accept his views or reject them we are working in terms of the reality/unreality of the play itself, not setting the unreality of the play against the reality of the audience.

Professor Mincoff has treated *A Midsummer Night's Dream* as the most fundamentally Lylian of Shakespeare's plays'.[6] It would seem however that *Love's Labour's Lost* is more obviously Lylian, preserving the highest proportion of direct borrowings, with a structure and tone which most clearly reflects that of Lyly, and especially that of Lyly's *Endimion*. In this play, as in *A Midsummer Night's Dream*, I suspect that the closer following of Lyly is due to the author's sense of some special and unusually courtly audience for whom the play is designed. The *recherché* nature of much of the wit in *Love's Labour's Lost*, the absence of any easily followed plot, the collusive nature of much of the laughter at pretension ('you and I know what's what'), all point away from the public theatre towards a more private and highly bred occasion; performance at the Inns of Court has been suggested and the suggestion is very plausible.

Shakespeare is here closer to Lyly than elsewhere in his career, in the balancing of groups of characters, one against the other, reflecting on one another in terms of theme and attitude, and dealing especially with attitudes of love. He also makes it more clear than elsewhere in his drama that he is basing his play on a debate, and is sacrificing plot movement to the static representation of opposed attitudes. Indeed in this respect he goes far beyond Lyly. Even the most static of Lyly's plays—*Sapho and Phao* seems a fair competitor for this position —contains a developing tension between lover and beloved, and a dynamic contest of wills (as between Venus and Sapho). In *Love's Labour's Lost* Shakespeare dares to be far more openly intellectual than this. The king announces a programme which has been chosen for intellectual reasons not circumscribed by character, and Berowne takes the other side and argues it by a logic which, though sophistical, is rigorously pursued.

The debate between love and 'honour' (I. i. 6) which appears at the beginning of the play, may be compared with that in

Campaspe. In Lyly, the debate in Alexander's mind is most explicitly represented by Hephestion's long speech in Act II, scene ii, where the opposing views are balanced as modes of action in a particular situation:

> Remember, Alexander, thou hast a camp to govern, not a chamber; fall not from the armour of Mars to the arms of Venus, from the fiery assaults of war to the maidenly skirmishes of love, from displaying the eagle in thine ensign to set down the sparrow. I sigh, Alexander, that where fortune could not conquer, folly should overcome. But behold all the perfection that may be, in Campaspe: a hair curling by nature, not art, sweet alluring eyes, a fair face made in despight of Venus, and a stately port in disdain of Juno, a wit apt to conceive and quick to answer, a skin as soft as silk and as smooth as jet, a long white hand, a fine little foot; to conclude, all parts answerable to the best part. What of this? Though she have heavenly gifts, virtue and beauty, is she not of earthly mettle, flesh and blood? (II. ii. 57-70)

But in *Love's Labour's Lost* the debate remains fixed at a higher level of abstraction than this. Berowne's opposition is based not on the propriety to the persons involved but rather on a contradiction inherent in the resolve to study rather than experience:

> Study is like the heaven's glorious sun
> That will not be deep-search'd with saucy looks;
> Small have continual plodders ever won
> Save base authority from others' books.
> These earthly godfathers of heaven's lights
> That give a name to every fixed star
> Have no more profit of their shining nights
> Than those that walk and wot not what they are.
> Too much to know is to know nought but fame;
> And every godfather can give a name.
>
> (I. i. 84-93)

Whereas in *Campaspe* most of the episodes (Alexander discussing painting with Apelles or philosophy with Diogenes) illustrate the debate with oppositions of persons, in *Love's Labour's Lost* the episodes of opposition tend not to act out the debate theme of learning against love, but are most often static bouts of wit, which may conceal personal allusions, but whose general effect is certainly that of self-sufficient verbal brilliance.

The balancing of groups of characters here is similar to that in *A Midsummer Night's Dream*, and the general debt may be assumed to be much the same as that discussed in the case of the other play. Once again the groups can be arranged by social status. The King and his lords are matched by the Princess and her ladies at the top of the social scale. Next comes Adriano de Armado (with his page Moth) who hangs on somewhat precariously to the edge of the court circle—'haunting' it as Shakespeare says. Then come those who are learned but not courtly—Holofernes and Nathaniel—and finally, 'neither learned nor courtly', Costard, Jaquenetta, and Constable Antony Dull. These groups are not, however, deployed as in *A Midsummer Night's Dream* and in Lyly to expose the structure of the plot. It is true that the play opens with a survey of the different worlds, as do *Gallathea* and *A Midsummer Night's Dream*, but Act I is really one continuous movement rather than a series of contrasting episodes; the act and scene divisions throughout the play are fairly arbitrary. The nobles debate their vow to prefer learning to experience; then the debate is transferred to the level of ordinary life, in the case of Costard v. Dull, where the lively humanity of Costard makes Berowne's point all over again:

> Necessity will make us all forsworn
> . . . For every man with his affects is born.

Then we move with the prisoner into the custody of Armado, in whom we discover another of the treasons that the 'necessity' of the oath has given rise to: Armado himself is in love and is preparing to use his wit in the service not of honour but of love. Act I thus sets the scene for the defeat of learning by experience. But the human actions and impulses it initiates do not develop regularly throughout the play. The imprisonment of Costard has no real effect, and Armado's love does not modify anything till we come to the end of the play, and then the loose thread is picked up. If we compare the first Act of *Gallathea* or *Endimion* we may see that the parallel instances in *Love's Labour's Lost* do not point to a resolution in terms of plot. The parallel instances are more concerned to build up a range of affectations than to expose contrasting attitudes which will clash in actions (Endimion's love against Tellus' hate). The main conflict of *Love's Labour's Lost* is thus bound to be a psychological one, when the affectation of the oath comes up against the normal human responses which we expect from the people involved. What we find as we read through the play are static exposures of affectation, which ask not so much for a resolution in terms of action, as for a judgment on their wrongness. The greatest space in the play is given over to displays of linguistic folly; these keep the social groupings of the play nicely discriminated. 'The gentles are at their game and we will to our recreation' says Holofernes to Nathaniel; and both 'game' and 'recreation' express the theme through wit rather than action. The linguistic folly, the

> Taffeta phrases, silken terms precise,
> Three-piled hyperboles, spruce affectation,
> Figures pedantical,

also point to a basic movement of the play through affectation to excess, and so to purgation. It is this Jonsonian comic movement (before the letter) that here justifies the balance and groupings of the characters, and this movement is quite unLylian.

The play is concerned, as Lyly's never are, with 'placing' or judging wit and cultivation in terms which are outside these values themselves. The conclusion of the debate is reached when Berowne in his great 'Have at you then, Affection's men at arms' speech 'proves' that the original vow was null and void and that opposition between love and learning does not really exist. But with Shakespeare the end of the debate cannot be the end of the play. To be able to 'prove' the truth is not to become worthy of love. Shakespeare's 'experience' is a larger concept than Lyly's 'honour', less cultivated and self-aware. The play has shown too large and various a range of experience to be concluded by a decision on the debate. The world of affectation that debated and set up the debate has itself to be judged, and purged.

Moreover, wit cannot be used to purge wit. Everyone in the play is mocked by someone else: the four lords most obviously in the scene (IV. iii) where they are discovered sonneting, but also when they mask as a mess of Muscovites, Moth as Prologue; Armado is mocked by the courtiers; Armado, Costard and the learned men are mocked in their pageant of the Nine Worthies; Boyet is mocked by Berowne, and the ladies by Boyet (perhaps we should except the Princess). But for all this witty 'putting down', we are given no very valid reason to prefer one party in the play to another, or to know which values are preferable, till we are given a standard outside wit. This Shakespeare provides by the intervention of Marcade, the news of the French King's death, and the penalties imposed on the witty lords— to use their wit in the world of suffering, sickness and age that has been so carefully excluded from the play itself.

Shakespeare has written a courtly play, a play which exposes to our admiration the brilliant life of a highly civilized community, bent on enjoying itself. We see the lords and ladies of an ideal Renaissance court, whose wit is as great as their breeding and their poise greater than either, able to control and turn with dexterity all the weight of Humanist learning and all the force of masculine violence on the pinpoint of mixed conversation. Shakespeare, like Lyly, centres his picture of Cortegiano-like brilliance on what is also known as courtship —the verbal technique of wooing. The coincidence of meanings inside one word points to the reason why Lyly and Shakespeare do so. As the poise of a civilization can be measured by the freedom it allows to its ladies, so the manners of a culture are at their critical point in the handling of wooing. We have seen a less wittily refined and presumably more realistic handling of this topic in *The Taming of the Shrew* and a more vaguely Romantic version of it in *Two Gentlemen*, but here in *Love's Labour's Lost* we have a much more precise image of a social ideal, which must owe something to Lyly's very successful handling of the same ideal.

For Lyly the delicacy of wooing is mainly a tribute to the sentiment of honour in the wooer, whether he is a great man (like Alexander) or a great lady (like Sapho) or a nymph (like Gallathea); we are given no sense of the clash of powerful personal impulses in Lyly's love dialogues. The witty bantering of lovers is, in fact, less common in Lyly than might be supposed from the comments of those who have discussed his influence. Undeniably there are scenes in which lovers exchange witty prevarications; more common, however, are long speeches in which the lover communes with himself and sets out the arguments for and against love. The reason why Lyly prefers this technique is fairly obvious: he is concerned with the balance of attitudes to love and honour (or other debate oppositions), not with the minds of the people who dispute. The exchanges which Lyly does show—between Apelles and Campaspe (see above, p. 165), between the nymphs and foresters in *Love's Metamorphosis*, or between the two nymphs in *Gallathea* (p. 202 f.) —express tentativeness or else rebarbative wit, but we are not drawn to suppose that these are qualities being deployed by the characters in their struggle to defeat one another. Rather, we suppose that they are qualities which the author has evoked to convey the situation and its general atmosphere.

Shakespeare on the other hand uses his wit-combats to convey self-imposed restraint and rational self-awareness in the face of genuinely felt emotions. Keeping the atmosphere of Lyly's plays and *Euphues*, he has invented people who are emotionally equipped to live in it. He preserves the delicacy and refinement of Lyly's lovers, in situations in which personal feelings emerge and clash with one another. He turns Lyly's indirection of speech into a means by which characters self-consciously advance their suits while seeming to deny them. This combination of wit and emotional involvement is itself more like life than the situations that Lyly himself devises; but we should notice that this renders the world of pure wit less tolerable as an image of such people's lives. It is for this reason that the 'clouding' of the scene when Marcade enters is essential to the balance of *Love's Labour's Lost*. Lyly's court is complete and self-sufficient as a dramatic world, and is capable of absorbing and judging by its own standards all interventions by the less poised and refined. Shakespeare's court, on the other hand, is judged from outside the court, and the courtiers as well as the yokels have to sink to merely contributory roles in a comprehensive picture.

Shakespeare's wit-combats are concerned not only with the virtuosity but also the feelings of the people involved, and this is obvious as early as *The Taming of the Shrew*. In the 'flytings' between Katherine and Petruchio the exchanges wear the guise of wit; but the contest of wits is only the surface to a contest of wills, a contest for supremacy which is no 'play' but involves the whole beings and the whole future of the contestants. Petruchio pretends to find Katherine amiable and this witty 'suppose' allows him to score many telling and amusing points; but the wit is only a means (not an end as in Lyly) and a means to achieve a quite uncourtly and even inelegant end—the unconditional surrender of the woman.

Two Gentlemen of Verona is much more concerned to be elegant than *The Taming of the Shrew*; in the order of writing which I have followed for the early comedies, *Two Gentlemen* is the first to aim at all obviously at the kind of world that Lyly had created; and it is certainly the first comedy whose wit-combats (between man and man as well as between man and woman) express at all the high-bred minds of elegant courtiers and their ladies. It has been said that the opening banter between Valentine and Proteus 'presents two of Lyly's gentlemen in debate', and in so far as the scene aims at an effect of leisured poise and elegance the comparison is a just one. But Shakespeare brings to the fulfilment of this aim resources that he had already displayed and which Lyly never commanded. The only scene in Lyly's drama which is at all comparable is that between Endimion and Eumenides at the beginning of *Endimion*; and a comparison here only shows up the divergent interests of the two dramatists. The wit of the *Endimion* dialogue is the medium in which the action moves; there is no suggestion that the two friends are deploying wit for personal ends, to tease one another as friends will. Lyly's two men are rather the passive vehicles of wit; there is no irony and no fun. In an exchange like

> *End.* My thoughts have no veins, and unless they be let blood, I shall perish.
> *Eum.* But they have vanities, which being reformed, you may be restored, (I. i. 26-8)

the pun on *veins* and *vanities* is only an incidental decoration to a dispute which is larger in its interest than the persons who dispute it and is not characterizing them in its incidental decoration, but only in its expression of intellectual attitudes. The function of wit in Lyly's scene is to provide a background of courtly elegance, against which the noble madness of Endimion's love for the moon can be defined.

The wit of Valentine and Proteus on the other hand is much

336

less functional to the concerns of the plot; it is true that their banter moves lightly round the debate of friendship versus love, but the two friends remain much more detached, much less representative of attitudes than in Lyly, and in consequence they seem more real: we cannot see what they stand for, so we try to be interested in them for themselves. Of course, Lyly can be witty in this detached way, but it is seldom his principal characters who are involved in such wit. Characters who have clearly defined attitudes, like Endimion, Sapho, Alexander, Midas are not given to banter, and the bantering wit of the pages is seldom attached to any personal qualities in the speaker. Scenes of courtly wit appear as separate episodes which define the nature of elegant disengagements; such are the conversations of the court ladies in *Sapho and Phao* (Act I, scene iv) and *Midas* (Act III, scene iii), but in such scenes the names of the persons speaking hardly matter. Shakespeare takes over the stylish wit of Lyly and attaches it, not merely formally, but integrally, to character and to emotion, and in so doing alters the focus with which we see it.

The use of wit to express the matter of courtship can likewise be seen in *Two Gentlemen* as another part of the attempt to acquire the elegance of Lyly. Lyly's work is characteristically concerned with the delighted evocation of female wilfulness from under the veil of maidenly modesty. Again, his means is not that of Shakespeare—the love dialogue—and when he touches on the subject he makes more obvious than Shakespeare does the ultimate origin in Ovid: 'I would wish thee first to be diligent; for that women desire nothing more than to have their servants officious. Be always in sight, but never slothful. Flatter; I mean lie; little things catch light minds, and fancy is a worm that feedeth first upon fennell . . . choose such times to break thy suit as thy lady is pleasant. The wooden horse entered Troy when the soldiers were quaffing. . . .' etc. (*Sapho and Phao*, II. iv. 58-61, 76-8). It is typical that Shakespeare, when he uses this *topos* (as he does in *Two Gentlemen*, Act III, scene i) complicates the Ovidian advice by placing it in the ironic situation of Valentine advising the Duke and so betraying himself. He keeps the Lylian glitter of wit, but adds to it varying levels of attitude and response.

We can see another development of the witty attitude to

female frailty in love in the scene in *Two Gentlemen* in which Julia tears her lover's letter before she will attempt to read it. In *Euphues* we read of gentlewomen who conceal the reality of love beneath the appearance of wit: thus

> Lucilla, although she were contented to hear this desired discourse, yet did she seem to be somewhat displeased. And truly I know not whether it be peculiar to that sex to dissemble with those whom they most desire, or whether by craft they have learned outwardly to loathe that which inwardly they most love; yet wisely did she cast this in her head that if she should yield at the first assault he would think her a light housewife. . . .
>
> (I. 219)

But in *Euphues* (as in Ovid) the glitter of the wit is such that we get no sense of the beating heart beneath the word-play. We are told that Lucilla's long speech of oracular ambiguity in love was 'such sweet meat, such sour sauce, such fair words, such faint promises, such hot love, such cold desire, such certain hope, such sudden change' (I. 224), and we can see that it is so, intellectually, but we are not involved at all in the flux and reflux of feelings that is indicated. In the scene of Julia's letter we are strongly aware of the claim of technique on our attention; but we are also aware that the lady who goes through the traditional motions of coyness has a life outside these. Shakespeare allows his Julia, as Lyly does not his Lucilla, to comment from the point of view of plain distress on the witty subterfuges she has just performed:

> Fie, fie, how wayward is this foolish love,
> That like a testy babe will scratch the nurse
> And presently, all humbled, kiss the rod!
>
> (I. ii. 57-9)

Such glimpses of the heart[7] behind the wit are rare in *Two Gentlemen*, but they exist, and they alter our response.

We might make the same point about that complementary scene in which Silvia persuades Valentine to write a love-letter to an unnamed third person and then refuses to accept it:

> But I will none of them; they are for you
> . . . take it for your labour
> And so good morrow, servant.
>
> (II. i. 116, 122 f.)

338

This is too nearly a trick to be genuinely expressive of feeling, and the crudity of the device is underlined by making Valentine too stupid to understand it, and requiring Speed to explain:

> . . . she hath taught her suitor . . .
> That my master, being scribe, to himself should
> > write the letter.
>
> > > (II. i. 126-9)

It was only gradually that Shakespeare learned to present a lover

> as true as truth's simplicity
> And simpler than the infancy of truth

in a way which distinguished between simplicity and naivety.

A Midsummer Night's Dream is a play without wit-combats. The lovers are not sufficiently poised above their fates to be able to deploy wit, and Theseus—the pattern of manners in the play—is too mighty for the two-way traffic of witty banter.

Love's Labour's Lost on the other hand, as if to right the balance, is a play largely made up of wit-combats. In this play we may see the Lylian impulse to express elegance turning into the Jonsonian effort to criticize elegance, and both involve a world where everything has to be expressed in words before it can be brought into focus. It is by reaching into language that the persons in the play come to define themselves, whether it be Armado with his 'Assist me some extemporal god of rhyme, for I am sure I shall turn sonnet. Devise, wit; write, pen; for I am whole volumes in folio', or Costard's 'O, and the heavens were pleased that thou wert but my bastard, what a joyful father wouldest thou make me!'—spoken of the *bon* Moth (or *mot*).[8]

This verbal focus is very clear in the central love scenes where the ladies control their own fates by possessing the greater freedom, flexibility and sanity of wit. Female delicacy is not what Shakespeare is seeking to evoke here, but rather the female capacity to see through the shams and pretensions which so easily beset the male intelligence; for we are shown this intelligence captivating itself (as well as us) by its power to order and mould language into expressive patterns. The play is based, as I have suggested above, on a debate-theme of learning against experience (the principal experience being love) but the wit-combats can hardly be said to turn on this, for there is an analogous contest going on all the time, in the lords' effort to get away with mere words and the ladies' capacity to turn empty words into traps and flouts. 'They do it but in mocking merriment', says the Princess, 'And mock for mock is only my intent'; the wit of the lords is a double-edged weapon which can be turned back on themselves: 'Not a word with him but a jest', says Maria of Berowne. 'And every jest but a word', adds Boyet. The play invites comparison with *Euphues*, for it, no less than Lyly's book, is an exposure of the insufficiency of wit. Longaville, the first of the votaries to be described, is said to have 'a sharp wit match'd with too blunt a will' (II. i. 49) (that is, his power to mock is matched by purposes which wit itself cannot fulfil), and the same might be said of all the lords. But the 'anatomy of wit' in Shakespeare's play is conducted in terms of words (the index of minds) and not in terms of actions. Matched against the sharp sanity of the ladies, witty words are shown for the inflated currency they are. Wit is not here as in Lyly the necessary language of the work, but is one mode of utterance which can be given a moral relation to others, and the play ends, as *Euphues* could not, with the suggestion of a mode of living in this world which is both elegant and heartfelt. This is, of course, only a suggestion; if we look at the love-wit in *Love's Labour's Lost* simply as a stage in the evolution of Beatrice's wit, we will be oppressively aware of its brittleness and Ovidian inhumanity; but if we compare it with Lyly we may see how far it succeeds in 'placing' wit in the larger context of the good life.

The distance of Shakespeare's concern for language in the play from the verbal world of Lyly is neatly epitomized by the relationship of that scene in which the lords discover one another in love and in 'the numbers that Petrarch flowed in', from its original in *Gallathea*—the scene where the nymphs of Diana discover each other to be under the rule of Cupid. We may begin by noticing that the nymphs are much more the passive victims of their emotions than are the lords. We may see this in the first speech of each episode:

> *Telusa.* How now? what new conceits, what strange contraries breed in thy mind? Is thy Diana become a Venus, thy chaste thoughts turned to wanton looks, thy conquering modesty

to a captive imagination? Beginnest thou with Piralis to die
in the air and live in the fire, to leave the sweet delight of
hunting and to follow the hot desire of love? O Telusa, these
words are unfit for thy sex, being a virgin, but apt for thy
affections, being a lover. And can there in years so young, in
education so precise, in vows so holy, and in a heart so chaste,
enter either a strong desire or a wish or a wavering thought
of love? Can Cupid's brands quench Vesta's flames, and his
feeble shafts headed with feathers, pierce deeper than Diana's
arrows headed with steel? (III. i. 1-12)

Compare now

Berowne. The king he is hunting the deer; I am coursing myself:
they have pitched a toil; I am toiling in a pitch—pitch that
defiles: defile! a foul word. Well, set thee down, sorrow! for so
they say the fool said, and so say I, and I am the fool: well
proved wit! By the Lord, this love is as mad as Ajax: it kills
sheep; it kills me, I a sheep: well proved again o' my side!
I will not love: if I do, hang me; i'faith I will not. O, but her
eye—by this light, but for her eye, I would not love her; yes,
for her two eyes. Well, I do nothing in the world but lie, and
lie in my throat. By heaven, I do love: and it hath taught me
to rhyme, and to be melancholy; and here is part of my rhyme,
and here my melancholy. (IV. iii. 1-13)

Telusa is concerned to describe her situation so that it will fit
in with and enhance the rest of the play; she speaks, in consequence, as if she was outside herself and an objective witness.
Berowne's speech, on the other hand, is not content to describe
love-madness, but tries to express the mind of one who is
infected by it. Telusa sets herself against a clear pattern of
expectations—which reflects the debate structure of the play.
Berowne's comic self-disgust is more complex and more personal: he calls himself a fool, but we are not intended to
believe him.

As the scene progresses we may see that Lyly's concern in
relating the confessions of love to one another is to construct
a sum of addition, so that the different entries will chime
wittily:

Eurota. Ah, would I were no woman!
Ramia. Would Tyterus were no boy!
Telusa. Would Telusa were nobody! (III. i. 108-111)

341

There is no interaction here to differentiate the several passions displayed and described; when they are laid side by side we may say that they add up to a 'definition of love' and that it was this that Lyly was aiming at:

> *Eurota.* . . . I pray thee tell what is love?
> *Ramia.* If myself felt only this infection I would then take upon me the definition, but being incident to so many, I dare not myself describe it. (III. i. 78-81)

Shakespeare's handling of the several discoveries is more like multiplication than addition, a geometrical rather than an arithmetical progression. The first discovery does not fade out when the second one is made, but adds its dimension to each statement of discovery that follows. Shakespeare superimposes his treasons against chastity one on top of the other, where Lyly lays them side by side. The effect in *Love's Labour's Lost* is to build up a depth of perspective on human weakness, comedy behind pathos behind intellectual statement.

This richness of perception and statement is the crux or hinge of the play's movement, and a means of differentiating its mode of judgment from that of Jonson. For Jonson judges his follies by means of rigid principles; but Shakespeare judges his follies against a sense of richer living. It is only when the lords come to see themselves wisely enough to know what fools they have been that they are free to repudiate their original vows and set about winning the ladies, and Shakespeare is free to imagine them in the real world of hospitals and sickness.

In *Gallathea*, on the other hand, the definition or focusing of love which the scene achieves is an isolated point of wit which is given high definition and effectively screened from results by the fact that all the lovers and beloveds are ladies.

If we find in *A Midsummer Night's Dream* and *Love's Labour's Lost* Shakespeare's most Lylian structures, it may be worth while looking forward to a later play which repeats many of these Lylian features, in Shakespeare's mature manner—to *As You Like It*.

As You Like It is a comedy which groups its characters by differentiating their attitudes and balancing these against one another, in the manner of the earlier plays. The balance is here a symmetrical one round the central characters, Rosalind and Orlando; Silvius and Phebe appear on the side of affectation, balancing Touchstone and Audrey, on the side of grossness, while brother Oliver and 'sister' Celia repeat the central situation in a minor key. Moreover, the play is openly based on a debate theme to which all the characters contribute—a theme of affectation versus naturalness once again (as in *Love's Labour's Lost*), but expressed this time in terms of attitudes to court versus country, or pastoral versus rustic life. Much of the action is without intrigue or plot in the ordinary sense; once the action moves to the forest of Arden the characters are used to expose each other's attitudes rather than to forward or retard one another's actions. As in *Love's Labour's Lost*, the play ends with a messenger from outside bringing surprising news; the key changes and the characters disperse, carrying their reconciled virtues to their various destinations.

But the similarity of *As You Like It* to these earlier plays (and especially to *Love's Labour's Lost*) only serves as a starting-point to talk about the difference of effect, and this crucial difference is one that shows Shakespeare taking his farewell of Lyly and going his own way. In *Love's Labour's Lost* the groups are arranged against one another like teams in a game. The members of the teams number off, one after the other, and each repeats (for our delight) the actions of the team-leader. As they move through their figures (like dancers) we experience the pleasure of group activity and the sense of a power greater than any of the individuals, operating through the pattern and forcing one after another into its mould. This resembles the manner of Lyly (in a play like *Love's Metamorphosis*); but even in *Love's Labour's Lost* there is more differentiation between the characters of those who make up the teams than there is in Lyly. When we come to *As You Like It*, however, we find that Shakespeare's power of discriminating between different responses to the same situation has immensely developed, while the power to mark them as repetitions has not been lost; the pattern remains though it is no longer predictable.

Berowne, the most supple intelligence in the earlier play, is able to talk to Holofernes or Costard or Armado as well as to his social equals, but he is not implicated in their responses; it is wit, not emotion, that sparks across the social gap. In *As You*

Like It, on the other hand, we learn that Rosalind *despises* Jaques, *scorns* Phebe, *pities* Silvius—in each case there is emotional involvement. The relationship between Rosalind's love and the other loves in the play is not simply that between a team-leader and the followers (superior skill in play against inferior skill); hers is central, comprehensive and normative, while theirs is marginal and more or less aberrant, and this contrast affects all the repetitions. When, towards the end of the play, the attractive force of love has sorted out the characters into a pattern of couples, we have the apparently stilted old technique of 'numbering down the line':

> *Silvius.* And so am I for Phebe.
> *Phebe.* And I for Ganymede.
> *Orlando.* And I for Rosalind.
> *Rosalind.* And I for no woman.   (V. ii. 78-81)

The formality of this pattern, however, does not strike us, in its context, as something that the author has imposed on his play from the outside. We tend to suppose Rosalind to be responsible for it, using it as part of her scheme to fulfil her own love. It is she who introduces the other characters, and it is she who finally breaks the pattern when it approaches too close to her own tender emotions:

> Pray you, no more of this; 'tis like the howling of Irish wolves against the moon.

We delight in the formality of the final movement of the play towards marriage; the settling towards full close as the couples 'come to the ark' in Act V appears as a tribute to the power of great creating Nature, operating on the group rather than the individual. But coupled to an awareness of the propriety and indeed naturalness of formalism and ritual at this moment is another awareness, that such concords are not achieved without individual goodness and individual effort. Rosalind does more than lead the matrimonial dance; we feel that it is through the triumph of her normative temperament that it is able to take place at all. Certainly there are no giants to be killed, no spells to be broken before Jack can have Jill; but unless we understand the nature of her triumph over the aberrations that confront her, unless we understand, that is, the comprehensive range of her love, there is no sense in the partial histories of

Silvius or Audrey or Oliver. When Hymen enters with Rosalind and Celia it is to be doubted whether Hymen has brought Rosalind (he says he has—but we do not need to believe him) or Rosalind, Hymen. The masque has two presenters—Hymen to speak the general introduction, and Rosalind to settle the details by revealing her true identity to the others—and we may suppose that it is only because she has to head the procession herself that she delegates the general office to Hymen.

The wit-combats of *As You Like It* are as sparkling as those of *Love's Labour's Lost*, but they differ in the extent to which they point back to the characters of the people who speak in them. Affectation of language has given way to affectation of temperament, and verbal brilliance is imputed more clearly to the speaker than to the author.

We have suggested that *Love's Labour's Lost* differs from Lyly in using wit as a medium in which characters realize themselves; if this is so then we can see that *As You Like It* takes Shakespeare much further along the road that leads away from Lyly and towards the modern drama of character. That this was the general direction of Shakespeare's development is generally accepted. What standard judgment goes on to add, however, is less easy to accept: that Shakespeare abandoned 'crude formalism' when he discovered the world of psychological interest. We may grant that Shakespeare vastly exceeds his contemporaries in expressive power, and is, in his power to express individual emotions, as modern as Ibsen or O'Neill; but to centre Shakespeare's achievement on this aspect of his everywhere abundant genius is to fail to see him as an Elizabethan, and in discussing his relationship with his contemporaries this is, of course, fatal. We may speak, if we will, of Lyly's characters as 'flat' and of Shakespeare's characters as 'round', but these novelistic terms tell us nothing of the interaction of plot and character by which flat turns into round, and this is what we need to understand if we are to see Shakespeare growing out of Lyly. Lyly's art is certainly two-dimensional; it shows people going through the motions that the plot and the author give to them; but we may rejoice in the formal treatment of this simple relationship where plot commands and characters obey without any sense that we are being given a narrow view of the world. Indeed so far as an interpretation of the world is concerned, two-dimensional art has some advantages. Take the tradition that we have already glanced at in our discussion of Heywood's *Play of Love* (see above, p. 121 f.). In such a play characters are given their meaning by the plot, as plot is given its expression by the characters. If the plot is 'about' love—that is, an anatomy of love—then the characters must express the gamut of attitudes to love; and this they do by showing and defending the different stances of 'loving-not-loved', 'loved-not-loving', 'both-loved-and-loving', 'neither-loved-nor-loving'. In so far as it goes, such a work is remarkably complete and self-sufficient, and so long as the author can rely on an audience which takes a somewhat specialized view of the human condition for granted, so long will it remain satisfactory. The giving of meaning to characters by placing them in interrelated attitudes round a central motif or interest is obviously a method used by Spenser[9] and it turns up also in Sidney:

> Zelmane . . . inflamed by Philoclea, watched by Gynecia and tired by Basilius . . . was like a horse, desirous to run, and miserably spurred, but so short-reined as he cannot stir forward. Zelmane sought occasion to speak with Philoclea; Basilius with Zelmane; and Gynecia hindered them all. If Philoclea happened to sigh (and sigh she did often) as if that sigh were to be waited on, Zelmane sighed also; whereto Basilius and Gynecia soon made up four parts of sorrow. (*Works*, ed. Feuillerat, I. 95 f.)

Shakespeare, working in the public theatre, could hardly take for granted the same degree of abstraction in the attitudes depicted. He has to rely on realistic detail to make the relevance of his characters obvious to his audience; it is not what his people mean but what they are that has given his drama its perennial popular appeal. Yet (as has been widely recognized in this century) the organization of the plays goes on using the framework of characters-as-attitudes, organized round central dilemmas. To see Shakespeare's characters as 'round' is to see one truth; but the relationship of character to character (Prospero-Ariel-Caliban; Troilus-Cressida-Diomed; Duke-Angelo-Escalus) is often of a brusquely formal kind; and it is at this point that we can see how he grows beyond Lyly. Most obviously, I would say, Shakespeare makes his characters aware of themselves in fulfilling the formal roles that the plot requires;

we sense their power of choice, and the difference of intention from achievement. It is the double focus of these two aspects that gives us the sense of depth in such figures as Rosalind or Viola or Richard II.

Thus the formality of the conclusion in *As You Like It* may be organized on traditional lines:

> *Ros.* [*to Duke*] To you I give myself, for I am yours.
> [*to Orlando*] To you I give myself, for I am yours.
> *Duke S.* If there be truth in sight, you are my daughter.
> *Orl.* If there be truth in sight, you are my Rosalind.
> *Phe.* If sight and shape be true
>   Why then, my love adieu!
> *Ros.* I'll have no father, if you be not he;
>   I'll have no husband, if you be not he;
>   Nor ne'er wed woman, if you be not she.
>
> (V. iv. 110-118)

But we are not required to appreciate the formality for its own sake, since it can be seen as an expression of the heroine's joyful self-awareness and her consequent command over her environment. By seeing the ritual through the mind of one who desires it we are empowered to forget that it is a mode of construction. But it is hardly open to those who wish to see Shakespeare in relation to his contemporaries to ignore the traditional technique which Shakespeare has transformed; and an isolation of the technique brings us back, inevitably, to Lyly.

We have seen Shakespeare experimenting with forms and techniques which have no counterpart in Lyly, and coming into clear contact with the older dramatist only under special circumstances. The movement from Plautine or Ariosto-like intrigue—heartless, fast-moving, bourgeois—to the gracious romantic sanity of *As You Like It* or *Twelfth Night* could no doubt have been accomplished by Shakespeare even if John Lyly had never existed (given Shakespeare's power to humanize or suffuse with sentiment the rigid structures he inherited); but, as Professor Mincoff has remarked, 'even a genius will not break down the wall to enter a room, when there is an already open door waiting for him'.[10] The existence of accomplished dramas dedicated to the image of delicate sentiment and gracious amusement must have made much easier Shakespeare's

passage across the middle ground of his comic development—
that area in which he had to learn the lightening of power by
playfulness [Petruchio into Berowne] and the strengthening of
sentiment by understanding [Valentine into Romeo]. And this
was just where Lyly's 'court comedies' had their virtue.

I have suggested that the two most 'Lylian' of Shakespeare's
plays were devised for courtly occasions. But even if this is true,
it does not mean that they were not played in public as well.
We know that as late as 1605 *Love's Labour's Lost* was looked on
as a model play for the entertainment of royalty,[11] but both
plays have entertained many audiences without courtly background or pretensions. It is Shakespeare's achievement, in
short, to have preserved courtly virtues in a form that makes
them accessible even to democrats, and much of the relationship between Lyly and Shakespeare can be seen in the movement from court comedy to the comedy of courtliness.

Love's Labour's Lost is a play which asks us to admire the
high-polished self-consciousness of court society, and it is a play
which is very close to Lyly's *Endimion*. But the groupings of
characters in *Love's Labour's Lost*, though 'Lylian' in technique,
do not occur in *Endimion*, and in any case produce an effect
which would be inappropriate in a courtier-dramatist. I have
noted above how Shakespeare interlaces his groups while Lyly
keeps his separate; one effect of this in *Love's Labour's Lost* is to
'place' the court in relation to other ways of life; this effect is
crowned by the palinode at the end, which is quite unLylian.
It is in the nature of Lyly's art that the relationship between
the groups should often be implied rather than expressed: the
play pays homage to its social occasion by reserving for the
court circle the full appreciation of its *ethos*. Shakespeare's
usual method is to keep the key to our response in the play
itself, and to this *Love's Labour's Lost* is no real exception, even
though it may have hidden meanings. The King of Navarre
is clearly related to the other nobles; like them he is *inside* the
action. Lyly's Cynthia, on the other hand, stands above the
action open to the other characters in the play; she is presented
on a scale so different from them that dramatic interplay is
impossible.

In this respect, *A Midsummer Night's Dream* is more like Lyly;
the whole play looks up to Theseus and there is no overt

parody or criticism of his actions. But Theseus is not the centre of a court life, and his magnanimity or royalty of nature does not provide the final focus of the play, as does the magnanimity of Alexander or Sapho or Cynthia. Even where Lyly has no royal figure in sight his plays tend to be resolved by some stroke of mercy or compromise from above, as is the case in *Love's Metamorphosis*, *Gallathea* and *The Woman in the Moon*. Shakespearian comedy, on the other hand, normally works forward to a reconciliation at all levels, which is *achieved* rather than *given*.

Shakespeare's interlacing of servants and masters can be seen to work in the same way. Lyly's servants have a different set of values from their masters, but hardly make us revise our attitudes to the masters. The 'realism' of the sub-plots is not seen as a criticism of the 'artificiality' of the courtly scenes, but is presented as another variety of 'style'. But even from the beginning of his career Shakespeare allows his Launce, Speed and Christopher Sly to enrich by their social comment the meaningful artificiality of the worlds above them, and to show the ironies that the courtly life must face up to before we can endorse its claim to represent man at his best.

Lyly's court comedies are not required to justify the activities they flatter; they pay their audience the compliment of, 'Who could doubt, looking around this hall, that the courtly life is a significant and splendid one?' Shakespeare could not make the same facile appeal; and he is obliged to convey the sparkle and virtuosity of life at these levels through the expressed feelings of a participant. Just as in *Love's Labour's Lost* and *A Midsummer Night's Dream* he has built the sovereign into the action, so he justifies the court-game by the vision of one who sees that it is only a game, and yet shares with us the enjoyment of playing in it—Petruchio, Mercutio, Berowne. But such men, if they are to remain admirably masculine, must not convey the attractions too meltingly, and this restricts the warmth of sentiment in the play. Shakespeare's mature resource is to take the great ladies of Lyly's audience and to place them on the stage as Beatrice, Rosalind, Olivia, Viola. The sparkle and glamour of court life is humanized through the minds of those who sense and suffer its promises and privations, its tendency to folly as well as its unique opportunities, and we, whatever our initial assumptions, are able to share their view.

NOTES

I

1. I refer to the supposition that what is to be valued in the age is what points forward to the liberal civility of the late nineteenth century. See H. Butterfield, *The Whig view of history* (1931); cf. L. B. Smith, 'The "taste for the Tudors" since 1940', *Studies in the Renaissance* VII (1960), 167-83.

2. Thus when J. E. Neale says that 'Elizabethan England should be regarded as a revolutionary age' (*Essays in Elizabethan history* (1958), p. 28) he speaks accurately enough of the *tendency*; but he does not describe at all (he is not seeking to) the self-consciousness of the period. But this can hardly be disregarded when we discuss writers and their relation to their background.

3. Perhaps the most uninhibited expression of what the late nineteenth century wanted to see in the Renaissance is given by Vernon Lee in her *Euphorion* (?1882) from which one may quote one sentence: 'For the first time since Antiquity man walks free of all political and intellectual trammels, erect, conscious of his own thoughts, master of his own actions, ready to seek for truth across the ocean like Columbus, or across the heavens like Copernicus' (I. 46 f.). Against this one may set the fact that the Copernican hypothesis was a mathematical accommodation put forward by a pious monk in an effort to 'save the appearances', or one could point to the common view that the discovery of America only revealed the baseness of man's nature. The widely used American college text-book, H. S. Lucas' *The Renaissance and the Reformation* (1934, 1960) is a good current example of these older views.

4. *Miscellaneous Works of Sir Philip Sidney*, ed. W. Gray (1860), p. 22. J. B. Black tells us how 'Euphuism . . . spread like an epidemic' and how Robert Greene 'broke new ground *in the right direction* with his coney-catching tracts' (second edn. p. 293 [my italics]). Legouis calls Euphuism 'a disease of language' (p. 261).

5. See H. Weisinger, 'The Renaissance theory of the reaction against the middle ages as a cause of the Renaissance', *Speculum* XX (1945), 461-67. The Humanist attitude is summed up in Richard Pace's comment that a monkish opponent is 'non theologus sed Scotista' (*De Fructu*, p. 93). Erasmus in the Preface to his New Testament says, 'Let those who like, follow the disputations of the schools, but let him who desires to be instructed rather in piety than in the art of disputation first and above all apply himself to the fountain-head' [the Gospels]. In his Ratio verae theologiae (*Opera Omnia* (1703-06), V. 134) he gives a long list of the unfruitful speculations

and needless subtleties of the schoolmen. This is not to deny, of course, the plain fact that most of the Renaissance attitudes are derived from the middle ages. The change was a change of emphasis. A Renaissance author writes, 'If we enter into the consideration of the nature of bees, how well they are ordered in their hives; if we look into the spinning of the spider's web, if we note the members of a man's body, how well they are ordered, much more ought Reason to persuade and teach us . . .', and so far he writes entirely in a medieval tradition, which might have gone on, '. . . teach us the Infinite Goodness and Wisdom of the Maker of all these'. Actually the passage concludes, 'teach us to range and bring the subjects of a good commonweal into a decent order'—which indicates clearly enough the different focus with which these same things are now seen. Cf. also E. L. Surtz, 'Oxford reformers and scholasticism', S.P. XLVII (1950), 547-56.

6. Lyly speaks of 'these abbey lubbers . . . which laboured till they were cold, ate till they sweat and lay in bed till their bones ached' (I. 250 f.). Abraham Fraunce speaks of ideas, 'not lurking in the obscure headpieces of one or two loitering friars, but manifestly appearing in the monuments and disputations of excellent authors' (*Lawyer's Logic*, p. 2). Ascham speaks of 'idle monks and wanton canons'. For Idleness as the first of the Puritan sins see Louis B. Wright, *Middle class culture in Elizabethan England*, p. 256.

7. 'Discourse on Sedition', printed in John Strype's *Sir John Cheke* (1705), pp. 245, 246.

8. So Erasmus instructs Charles V in his *Institution of a Christian Prince* that 'there is no duty by the performance of which you can more secure the favour of God, than by making yourself a prince useful to the people' (quoted in Seebohm, *The Oxford reformers* [Everyman edn.] p. 233).

9. The locus classicus for this view is Pico della Mirandola's oration *De hominis dignitate*.

10. *Opera Omnia*, X. 1742, quoted in F. Caspari, *Humanism and social order in Tudor England* (1954), p. 39.

11. *English Literature in the Sixteenth Century* (1954), p. 53.

12. The single figure of Ralegh might serve by itself to scotch the idea that the energy of Elizabethan courtiers and seadogs operated so freely because they knew no law of constraint. Ralegh's poetry and still more obviously his *History of the World* show a mind racked by melancholy and a strong sense of the world's vanity.

13. Cf. Legouis, op. cit., p. 377: 'The most direct and original expression of the national genius [is] dramatic. Elsewhere imitation and artifice play a part; aristocratic sentiment or an ephemeral fashion is a check on spontaneity, ruling out whatever is of the people, or colouring style or subject to make it archaic, euphuistic, Arcadian or pastoral'. Cf. H. S. Lucas, op. cit., who tells us that Shakespeare 'grew up without discipline, married at eighteen, . . . a self-made man . . . took an independent attitude toward tradition . . . relied almost entirely upon his own instincts' ([2nd ed., 1960], p. 439).

14. J. F. Danby, *Poets on Fortune's Hill* (1952), p. 71.

15. See Edgar Wind, 'Art and Anarchy', *The Listener*, 1st Dec. 1960, p. 976.

16. This is especially obvious in Legouis' praise of the Elizabethans for their 'rejection of strict rules', that is, because their syntax and their prosody was uncertain (p. 255 ff.).

17. It is odd that C. S. Lewis, *Studies in Words* (1960), though he devotes a chapter to 'wit', does not mention Lyly.

18. See J. E. Neale, *Elizabeth I and her Parliaments, 1584-1601*, pp. 278, 297.

19. E. A. Baker, *History of the Novel*, II. 14: 'The other great obstacle to the advance in the art of fiction—the one indeed which was at the root of all the trouble—was the lack of any definite notion of what a story or novel should be'.

20. Richard Pace, *De Fructu* (1517), p. 72.

21. Cf. Henry Peacham, *The Complete Gentleman* (1634): 'For since all virtue consisteth in action, and no man is born for himself . . . hardly they are to be admitted for noble who (though of never so excellent parts) consume their light, as in a dark lanthorn, in contemplation and a Stoical retiredness.' (1906 edn. p. 2)

22. See the excellent treatment of this point in W. G. Zeeveld, *Foundations of Tudor Policy* (1948).

23. In adopting this spelling of the grammarian's name I have followed the practice outlined in the preface, of choosing the accepted rather than the proper or consistent form. 'Lily' is the form used in D.N.B. and the British Museum Catalogue, and would seem to be an Anglicization of the Latin *Lilius*. From his will it would look as if *Lyly* was the English form used by the grammarian. Feuillerat has used this form consistently for the whole family, but I feel it is too late now to disagree with the accepted works of reference.

24. R. S. Stanier, *History of Magdalen College School* (1940), p. 19.

25. This information, like almost everything else we know about William Lily, comes from the 'elogium' that George Lily, his eldest son, contributed to Paulus Jovius' *Chronicon*.

26. See José Ruysschaert, 'Les manuels de grammaire Latine composés par Pomponio Leto', *Scriptorium* VIII (1954), 98-107.

27. G. B. Parks, *English Travellers to Italy* (1954).

28. See Seebohm, op. cit., pp. 53 f.

29. See L. Bradner and C. A. Lynch, *The Latin epigrams of Sir Thomas More* (1953).

30. Polydore Virgil, *History of England* [Camden Soc. LXXIV], p. 147.

31. On the tangle of parts which make up 'Lily's Grammar' see V. J. Flynn, *Proceedings of the Bibliographical Society of America* XXXVII (1943), 85-113.

32. There is an edition of Stanbridge's and Horman's Vulgaria in E.E.T.S. o.s. 187 (1932).

33. See Ascham, *The Schoolmaster* (ed. Arber), p. 25 f.; cf. Douglas Bush, *The Renaissance and English Humanism* (1939), pp. 60 ff.

34. Quoted in J. H. Lupton's *Life of Colet* (1887), pp. 291 f.

35. A more powerful figure than Ascham expressed the same view: 'There has never been a great revelation of the Word of God unless He has first prepared the way by the rise and prosperity of languages and letters,

as though they were John the Baptists' (Letter of 29th March 1523, in Preserved Smith, *Luther's Correspondence*, II. 176 f.). Cf. More's letter to Bugenhagen, in E. F. Rogers, *Correspondence of Sir Thomas More* (1947), p. 142.

36. See Seebohm, op. cit.

37. Erasmus's description of St. Paul's school is in his epistle to Justus (Jodocus) Jonas (*Opus Epistolarum*, ed. P. S. Allen, IV. 514-27).

38. Quoted in Lupton, op. cit., p. 290.

39. Woodward, op cit., p. 73. cf. D. L. Clark, *John Milton at St Paul's School* (1948), p. 45.

40. E. F. Rogers, *Correspondence of More*, pp. 111-20.

41. *Opus Epistolarum*, I. 508.

42. Lupton, op. cit., pp. 188 ff.

43. It has been suggested that Rightwise's *Dido* was in fact written by Dionysia Lily (see Feuillerat, p. 11).

44. On Paduan Aristotelianism see *Journal of the History of Ideas* I (1940), 131-206, and B. Nardi, *Saggi sull' aristotelismo padovano* (1958).

45. Herrtage, *England in the reign of Henry VIII*, E.E.T.S. e.s. 12 (1871), p. x. Cf. *Letters and Papers of Henry VIII*, VIII, item 581, in which George Lily replies to Starkey's advice that he should study 'philosophy and the books of the old lawyers'.

46. J. S. Phillimore, 'Blessed Thomas More and the arrest of Humanism', *Dublin Review* CLIII (1913), 1-26; cf. Douglas Bush, 'Tudor Humanism and Henry VIII', *University of Toronto Quarterly* VII (1937-38), 162-77.

47. The phrase comes from a letter written to Starkey by Edmund Harvel, dated 18th June 1531 (*Letters and Papers of Henry VIII*, V, item 301), quoted by Zeeveld, op. cit.

48. The three 'Parnassus Plays' have been edited by J. B. Leishman (1949).

49. Cf. Caspari, op. cit., p. 81.

50. Quoted in Huizinger, *Waning of the Middle Ages* (English edn. 1924), p. 71.

51. Cf. R. M. Sargent, *At the court of Queen Elizabeth* (1935), p. 6; Eleanor Rosenberg, *Leicester, patron of letters* (1955), pp. 179, 323 f.

52. C. S. Lewis, *Sixteenth century*, p. 19.

53. See G. Luck, '*Vir facetus*: a Renaissance ideal', S.P. LV (1958), 107-21.

54. Roberto Wiess, *Humanism in England during the fifteenth century* (1941) [second edn. (1957), p. 109].

55. C. R. Thompson, *Translation of Lucian by Erasmus and More* (1940), p. 22.

56. The case of Edmund Spenser may well be cited to show the insufficiency of the generalizations here attempted, for he was not confined to a world of witty irresponsibility by the pressure of Elizabeth's court. On the other hand, Spenser seems to have chosen, deliberately, an old-fashioned mode of writing. His political and religious outlook is as much Edwardian as Elizabethan; and the immediate price he paid for this power to generalize the Tudors was an immediate neglect. It is worth

remembering that in this period *The Shepheards Calendar* seems to have sold better than *The Faerie Queene*.

II

1. See Corpus Christi College (Cambridge) MS. 114, p. 821; the signature is wrongly transcribed in M. R. James' catalogue as 'Lysly'.

2. Feuillerat has collected most of the biographical documents into an Appendix of *Pièces Justicatives* (Appendix A), and I shall cite normally from this collection. George Lily's will is printed on pp. 507-09.

3. Feuillerat, p. 510 f.

4. ibid. 506.

5. ibid. 512.

6. John Strype, *Memorials of Thomas Cranmer* (1812 edn., I. 364).

7. I do not think he should be identified with Parker's amanuensis: 'He [Parker] kept skilled amanuenses in his household, especially Lyly who could counterfeit any antique writing' (Strype, *Matthew Parker* (1821), II. 497 f.). This must be the man referred to in Feuillerat, p. 22, n. 3.

8. Feuillerat, p. 516.

9. ibid. 516.

10. ibid. 504, 513.

11. ibid. 15 f.

12. Bond, II. 35 f.

13. See Peter Lyly's will, in which 'my loving friend Raynolde Wolfe, citizen and stationer of London' is named as an executor (Feuillerat, p. 520), and Cape and Woodruff, *Schola Regia Cantuariensis* (1908), p. 64.

14. Cape and Woodruff, op. cit.; *Registrum Matthaei Parkeri* (1928-33), III. 909.

15. *The Book of the Governor* [Everyman edn.], p. 70.

16. Cape and Woodruff, p. 80.

17. C. W. Boase and A. Clark, *Register of the University of Oxford*, II. ii. (1887), p. 49, n. 4.

18. See J. H. Hexter, 'The education of the aristocracy in the Renaissance', *Journal of Modern History* XXII (1950), 8, and Douglas Bush, *U.T.Q.* VII, 169.

19. See 'Table C' in Boase and Clark, *Register*, II. ii. 414.

20. Bodleian MS. Ashmole 208, quoted in Feuillerat, 274, n. 2.

21. See J. Dover Wilson, *John Lyly* (1905), pp. 133 f. One should add the new evidence printed in *R.E.S.* XXIII (1947), 302-04.

22. See, for example, E. K. Chambers, *Elizabethan Stage*, III. 37.

23. See the letter from the Rev. H. A. Wilson quoted in Bond, I. 11.

24. A Harmony of the Essays, ed. Arber (1895), p. xii.

25. *Works*, ed. Jackson (1619), p. 436, quoted in William Ringler, *Stephen Gosson* (1942), p. 14.

26. For example, *An foeminae sint literis instruendae* (M.A., 1581).
Utrum ludi scenici in bene instituta civitate probandi sunt (M.A., 1584).
An ex optimo academico fiat optimus aulicus (M.A., 1592).

27. op. cit., p. 86, n. 4.

28. See W. N. King, 'John Lyly and Elizabethan rhetoric', *S.P.* LII (1955), 149-61.

29. Feuillerat, p. 522 f.

30. J. Dover Wilson, 'John Lyly's relations by marriage', *M.L.R.* V (1910), 495-97.

31. See, for example, the title-pages of *Greene's farewell to folly*, *Greene's mourning garment*, *Philomela*, etc.

32. Grosart's *Harvey*, II. 128.

33. Feuillerat, 42.

34. Cape and Woodruff, op. cit.

35. See *S.C.* 'April', 38 f.: 'Bring hither . . . gilliflowers / Bring coronations and sops in wine', and compare Bond, II. 134: 'here will be gilliflowers, carnations, sops in wine'.

36. It is usually supposed that the 'passions' of which Lyly speaks in this letter refer to love-sonnets which he had actually composed: 'and seeing you have used me so friendly as to make me acquainted with your passions, I will shortly make you privy to mine, which I would be loth the printer should see.' Bond's wild goose chase for lyrics written by Lyly (see the correspondence in the *Athenaeum* for 1903) derived in part from this belief. But the words do not necessarily imply that such poems are in actual existence, only that such a lover would be expected to write love poems.

37. J. Dover Wilson, 'Euphues and the Prodigal Son', *The Library* X (1909), 337-61.

38. W. N. King, loc. cit.

39. S. L. Woolf, 'A source of *Euphues*', *M.P.* VII (1910), 577-85.

40. I. 198.

41. See L. Sorieri, *Tito e Gisippo in European literature* (1937).

42. 'Before *Euphues*', *Quincy Adams Memorial Studies* (1948), 475-93.

43. ibid. p. 476.

44. *William Shakspere's Five-Act Structure* (1947).

45. Dover Wilson pointed to dramatic elements in *Euphues* in his 1909 article in *The Library*. He is not, however, so concerned with structure as with the idea that an 'old play' lies behind the work as its source: '*The Anatomy of Wit* is to a large extent nothing but an old play cast into narrative form' (352). This seems to the present writer to be an unjustifiably large assumption.

46. R. H. Perkinson, 'The epic in five acts', *S.P.* XLIII (1946), 465-81.

47. See T. F. Crane, *Italian social customs of the sixteenth century* (1920).

48. L. Torretta, 'L'Italofobia di John Lyly', *Giornale storico della letteratura Italiana* CIII (1934), 205-53.

49. See H. Wölfflin, *The principles of art history* (English trans. 1932); cf. below, Cap. III, n. 105.

50. Preface to translation of Guazzo's *Civil Conversation*.

51. waar in vervat zijn bezondere Vermaakelijkheden des Verstants, bestaende in, Aardigheeden, Hof-Reedenen, Quinck-slagen, Sprencken, Vragen, Antwoorden en Brieven.

52. H. M. C. 11th Report (iii), p. 19.

53. Grosart's Harvey, II. 215. Feuillerat (p. 77, n. 3) has a notable caveat, pointing out that Harvey elsewhere uses 'secretary' to mean 'writer'.

54. B. M. Lansdowne MS. 42, item 39, quoted in Feuillerat, 533.

55. Grosart's Harvey, I. 83-5.

56. The best account of this episode is in E. K. Chambers, *Sir Henry Lee* (1936), p. 150 ff.

57. H. M. C. Rutland MSS., I. 150.

58. Feuillerat, p. 540; Malone Society Collections, II. 123.

59. Grosart's Harvey, II. 212.

60. ibid. II. 213.

61. Bodl. MS. Tanner 169, fols. 69v-70, first printed by F. P. Wilson in *M.L.R.* XV (1920), 81 f. Even this testimony may not be as objective as it looks. Thomas Churchyard is mentioned as one of the group with which the letter is concerned. Churchyard had been patronized by Oxford and seems to have lost favour about the time that Lyly was gaining it.

62. See *M.L.R.* VI (1911), 92-94.

63. The evidence for the date is the statement in the second petition (see below, p. 86) that Lyly had been her Majesty's servant for thirteen years. The second petition is dated 1601 in MS. Tanner 169, and this date accords well with hope of forfeitures [from the Essex rebels]. In the first petition, being made her Majesty's servant is associated with being told to aim all his courses at the Revels. On the other hand, the letter to Cecil of 22nd December 1597 (Feuillerat, p. 554 f.) speaks of his endurance 'that these twelve years with unwearied patience have entertained the proroguing of her Majesty's promises'. This would carry the date of the promise back to 1585, which is probable enough in general terms, being immediately after the collapse of the Blackfriars venture. Perhaps the Queen made a general promise at this date, and made it more specific at the later date.

64. *V. C. H. Wilts*, V. 117. Browne Willis (*Notitia Parliamentaria* (1730)) omits Lyly's name from the Hindon list.

65. His name appears only once in Simonds d'Ewes' *Journal . . . of Queen Elizabeth*: in February 1598 he was a member of the committee which discussed a Bill 'for the reformation of abuses in wine casks' (1693 edn., p. 592). He does not appear in Heyward Townshend's *Historical Collections* (1680); the official Journals are missing for these parliaments.

66. See the side note to III. 408, and Bond's note, III. 585.

67. Brie, 'Lyly und Greene', *Englische Studien* XLII (1910), 217-222; cf. Pruvost, *Greene*, p. 315.

68. See the letter by B. M. Wagner in T.L.S., 28th September 1933.

69. In *Queen Elizabeth's Entertainment at Mitcham* (1953) Leslie Hotson has printed two Progress entertainments as 'attributed to John Lyly'. The first was given at the house of Dr Julius Caesar on 12th-13th September 1598. The evidence for attribution to Lyly consists in this case of 'inimitable characteristics' of Lyly's style. Hotson assembles a list of parallels which are not, I fear, much more persuasive than Bond's—including such matters as the use of the word 'limbecks', reference to the clear seeing of an eagle, to the story of Zeuxis and the virgins of Crotona, and the use of the pun

on 'angels'. Hotson does not refer to the letter from Mathew to Caesar quoted below. So far as it goes this may seem to add to the evidence against Lyly, for Mathew's letter, written after the entertainment, seems to imply that Lyly was not known to Caesar. The second entertainment printed by Hotson was given at the Chiswick house of Sir William Russell on 28th-29th July 1602 and it appears in a MS. signed 'John: Lilly' (Finch Hatton MS. 2414). Hotson says that the MS. 'may be in Lyly's own hand'; it may, and equally well it may not. One point would seem to count against it: all the autograph letters assembled by Feuillerat concur in the spelling 'Lyly', and all but one spell the Christian name 'Jhon'. It is true that the Elizabethans did not have modern qualms about spelling, but the isolated inconsistency here can only weaken the case. But even if the document is not autograph it is worth noting that a contemporary thought Lyly a possible author for an entertainment of this kind.

70. See Chambers, *Eliz. Stage*, III. 407, and *Lee*, p. 145. Cf. *M.L.R.* XXX (1935) 52-55.

71. First printed by Austen Warren in *Notes and Queries*, 4th March 1939.

72. Reprinted here (in a modernized version) from the Petyt MSS. by kind permission of the Treasurer and Masters of the Bench of the Honorable Society of the Inner Temple.

73. See the letter to Robert Cecil of 5th February 1602/3 (Feuillerat, pp. 562 f.).

74. Feuillerat, p. 564.

75. Deborah Jones, 'John Lyly at St. Bartholomew's', in *Thomas Lodge and other Elizabethans*, ed. C. J. Sisson (1933), p. 390.

III

1. The best survey of this material is in E. K. Chambers, *The Elizabethan Stage* (hereafter, *E.S.*); see especially I. 17 ff. and appendices A and B (IV. 75 ff.).

2. See R. C. Strong, 'The popular celebration of the accession day of Queen Elizabeth I', *J.W.C.I.* XXI (1958), 86-103.

3. *E.S.*, I. 213.

4. John Stowe, *Survey of London* [Everyman edn.], p. 89.

5. E. K. Chambers, *Medieval Stage*, I. 406 f.

6. *E.S.*, I. 71 f.

7. ibid. I. 73.

8. Note by Edward Buggins, yeoman of the Revels, printed in *E.S.*, III. 21, n. 2.

9. *E.S.*, IV. 87; L. M. Ellison, *Early Romantic Drama at the English court* (1917), p. 79.

10. A. Feuillerat, *Documents of the Revels in the reign of Elizabeth* [Matier-alien, XXI (1908)] (hereafter, *Revels*), p. 145.

11. ibid. p. 191.

12. Ascham, *Works* (ed. Giles), I (i), p. 192.

13. See below, p. 112 f., on her reactions to *Palamon and Arcite*.

14. *Revels*, p. 359.

15. See *Damon and Pithias* (M.S.R.), 1659 f. When Cornishe's Children [of the Chapel Royal] played *Troilus and Pandar* in 1516, Cornishe himself played Calchas [? and a Herald]. *Letters & Papers H8*, II. ii. 1505 f. In 1559 Sebastian Westcott (Master of the Paul's boys), with 'Mr. Heywood' (probably John Heywood the dramatist) and 'Mr Philip' (probably the organist of St Paul's and perhaps the author of *Patient Grissil*) acted with the children (*E.S.*, II. 13). Cf. Sydney Anglo, 'William Cornish', *R.E.S.* X (1959), 347-60.

16. See K. M. Lea, *Italian popular comedy* (1934), I. 12, 252.

17. ibid. II. 362 ff.

18. See Grace Frank, *Medieval French Drama* (1954), p. 182 f.

19. H. N. Hillebrand, *The Child Actors* (1926), p. 28.

20. *E.S.*, II. 11.

21. Warton's *History of English Poetry* (1871 edn.), III. 163.

22. Thomas Heywood, *Apology for Actors* (1612), sig. C3v.

23. John Brinsley, *Ludus Literarius* (ed. Campagnac), p. 174 f.

24. ibid. p. 214.

25. See ibid. p. 213.

26. Charles Hoole, *A new discovery of the old art of teaching school* (ed. Campagnac), p. 142.

27. The whole question of the formality or otherwise of Elizabethan acting is much disputed. The distinction between the boys and the men is not much invoked in this connection; but if we do invoke it we must concede, I suggest, that the boys (given the kind of plays in which they performed and the kind of things they could not do) must have been *more* formal than the men. On the whole question see A. Harbage, 'Elizabethan acting', *P.M.L.A.* LIV (1939), B. L. Joseph, *Elizabethan acting* (1951), M. Rosenberg, 'Men or Marionettes', *P.M.L.A.* LXIX (1954). T. W. Craik, *The Tudor Interlude* (1958), makes a point which has some bearing here. He notes that in both the Coventry plays and in Robert Wilson's *Three Ladies of London* (1584) there is evidence of single roles being split between several actors. In such cases, as he remarks, 'an acting style is wanted which is common to both players' (p. 42); the obvious style to serve in such cases is one of well trained formality.

28. *E.S.*, II. 17, n. 2.

29. ibid. II. 33.

30. See *M.L.R.* XLVII (1952), 49 f. for an early extension of the privilege to Paul's.

31. The song is by John Redford (who was Master at Paul's); it is quoted in C. C. Stopes, *William Hunnis* (1910), p. 151 [Materialien, XXIX].

32. *E.S.*, I. 201, n. 2.

33. See Gregory Smith, *Elizabethan Critical Essays*, II. 210.

34. See below, pp. 168 ff. and 184 ff.

35. There is no evidence to tell us exactly where the playhouse 'in Paul's' was situated. Hillebrand very plausibly supposes that their singing-school (St Gregory's church) was also their theatre.

36. As has been assumed, for example, by T. W. Baldwin, *Five Act Structure*, p. 500.

37. See the figures in *E.S.*, II. 4-6.

38. Ben Jonson, *Cynthia's Revels*, Induction, 194-96.

39. The music is in B.M. Add. MS. 15117 fol. 3.

40. See F. S. Boas, *University Drama in the Tudor Age* (1914), Appendix V.

41. Hillebrand, p. 41; *E.S.*, II. 25. There is evidence in the Revels accounts that the boys' companies were often larger. *Alucius* of 1579 (Chapel Boys) required eighteen pairs of gloves (*Revels*, p. 320); *Scipio Africanus* of the same year (Paul's) required eighteen (ibid. p. 321); the Paul's Boys had eighteen pairs for Twelfth Night 1581 and the Chapel Boys had the same (and also seventeen new suits of apparel) for Shrove Tuesday 1581 (ibid. p. 336).

42. Hillebrand, op. cit., p. 258.

43. The quotation comes from a lost book, *The Children of the Chapel Stripped and Whipped*, cited in Warton, op. cit., IV. 217.

44. See Appendix A.

45. Leslie Hotson, *The First Night of* Twelfth Night (1954), p. 202. On court staging cf. L. B. Campbell, *Scenes and machines on the English stage during the Renaissance* (1923), T. S. Graves, *The court and the London theatres* (1913), Glynne Wickham, *Early English stages* (vol. I, 1959).

46. op cit., p. 24.

47. The staging for these occasions is discussed in Wickham, op. cit., I. 248 and Appendix H, in Hotson, *Shakespeare's wooden O* (1959), p. 161 ff., and in *E.S.*, I. 227. The basic description of the Oxford performance is translated in *P.M.L.A.* XX (1905), 502-28.

48. See *E.S.*, I, 228 and Nichols, *Progresses of James I*, I. 538.

49. Boas, op. cit., p. 100.

50. *E.S.*, I. 228.

51. Bacon, 'Of Masques and Triumphs'.

52. *First Night of* Twelfth Night, p. 91.

53. *Revels*, p. 240, etc.

54. ibid. pp. 204, 266 f., 306, etc.

55. *E.S.*, III. 33.

56. cf. above, p. 82

57. *Revels*, p. 203, mentions 'lathes for the hollow tree' as a property.

58. On the popularity of the chivalric romances see R. S. Crane, *The vogue of the medieval chivalric romance during the English Renaissance* (1919); cf. L. M. Ellison, op. cit.

59. See *Revue Germanique* VII (1911), 421 ff.; the play is discussed in Ellison, op. cit., 77 ff.

60. *Revels*, pp. 303-8.

61. See the series of articles on this topic by Louis B. Wright: *M.P.* XXIV (1927), *J.E.G.P.* XXVI (1927), *Englische Studien* LXIII (1928-29), *Anglia* LII (1928).

62. In what follows I adopt with appropriate slavishness the description in Boas' *University Drama* (chapter V).

63. *Revels*, p. 141.

64. ibid. p. 244.

65. Holinshed's Chronicles (1808 edn.), IV. 508.

66. E. Welsford, *The Court Masque* (1927); R. Brotanek, *Die Englischen Maskenspiele* (1902); P. Reyher, *Les Masques Anglais* (1909).

67. C. R. Baskervill, 'Some evidence for early romantic plays in England', *M.P.* XIV (1916-17), 467.

68. Welsford, op. cit., p. 51; *Medieval stage*, II. 169.

69. Welsford, op. cit., p. 67 ff.

70. Malone Soc. Collections, I (ii). 144 ff.

71. See George and Portia Kernodle, 'Dramatic elements in the medieval tournament', *Speech Monographs* IX (1942), 161-72. Cf. F. H. Cripps-Day, *History of the tournament* (1918). See also Sydney Anglo's review of Wickham, op. cit. in *Renaissance News* XIII (1960), 157-62.

72. 'Of masques and triumphs'.

73. Welsford, op. cit., p. 123.

74. *C.S.P. Ven. 1527-33*, p. 59 f., discussed in Baskervill, *M.P.* XIV, 472 f.

75. *Revels*, p. 141.

76. op. cit., p. 89.

77. See Nichols, *Eliz.*, II. 312 ff.

78. G. Kernodle, *From art to theatre* (1944); cf. his *Speech Monographs* article cited above (n. 71), pp. 166-71. This use of the castle is close to that in earlier plays like *Mary Magdalen* and *The Castle of Perseverance*; we may also compare the storming of Constance Custance's house in *Ralph Roister Doister*.

79. Described in Kernodle, op. cit.; cf. J. J. Mak, *De Rederijkers* (1944).

80. See *Medieval Stage*, I. 80.

81. loc. cit.

82. For example, *An monarchia sit optimus status reipublicae?* (Nichols, I. 185), or *an maior sit scripturae auctoritas quam ecclesiae?* (Nichols, I. 186) of the Queen's visit to Cambridge in 1564; and the *an princeps declarandus esset electione potius quam successione* of her Oxford visit in 1566 (Nichols, I. 238).

83. *Parrott Presentation Volume* (1935), p. 27.

84. *Stephen Gosson* (1942).

85. Sixt Birk, *De vera nobilitate orationes duae . . . tota rei actio in ludi formam redacta* (1538). See the article by A. W. Reed, 'Sixt Birk and Henry Medwall', *R.E.S.* II (1926), 411-15.

86. *Revels*, p. 276.

87. *Book of the Governor* [Everyman edn.], p. 182.

88. H. de Vocht, *De invloed van Erasmus* (1908).

89. See W. A. Neilson, *Origins and sources of the courts of love* (1899), and F. T. Crane, op. cit.

90. *England's Eliza* (1939), p. 140.

91. ibid. p. 213.

92. Edited by J. P. Brawner in *Illinois Studies in Language and Literature* XVIII (1942); cf. my note '*The Wars of Cyrus* and *Tamburlaine*' in *Notes and Queries* for October 1961.

93. Cf. Painter's *Palace of Pleasure*, II. iii.

94. See Ellison, op. cit. *passim*.

95. See Geoffrey Bullough, *Sources*, I. 206.

96. ibid. I, 270.

97. Spenser, *Virgil's Gnat*, 121 ff.

98. Holinshed's Chronicle (1808 edn.), IV. 133.

99. *Life of Sir Philip Sidney* (ed. Nowell Smith), p. 154.

100. See K. O. Myrick, *Sir Philip Sidney* (1935), especially chapters I and VIII.

101. Bond has an excursus on 'Italian influence' which reaches the conclusion that there is little or no evidence of Lyly's knowing or imitating the Italians. Feuillerat reaches much the same conclusion. On the other hand, Miss Violet Jeffrey, in *John Lyly and the Italian Renaissance* (Paris, 1928) has argued at great length for a connection. Not all her evidence, however, is acceptable, and many of her parallels point to an ultimate rather than an immediate connection, between two representatives of a widely diffused European tradition. In the absence of close verbal parallels it seems dangerous to rely on parallel situations, in an art as stereotyped as court entertainment.

102. W. W. Greg, *Pastoral Poetry and Pastoral Drama* (1905), p. 234.

103. See *Medieval stage*, I. 403 ff. On medieval parody in general see Paul Lehmann, *Die Parodie im Mittelalter* (1922) and *Parodistische Texte* (1923).

104. For this point I am indebted to the unpublished book of my friend, the late Francis Klingender, tracing the use and development of animal imagery. MS. Douce 5 in the Bodleian is a good example of the genre, with its apes wearing mitres and copes and engaging in liturgical actions.

105. As noted above, the currency of the term seems to derive from H. Wölfflin. It has been applied to Elizabethan drama by A. P. Rossiter, in his *English Drama* (1950), and by Madeleine Doran, *Endeavours of Art* (1954).

106. Edgar de Bruyne, *L'Esthétique du moyen âge* (1947), p. 130, paraphrasing Migne's *Patrologia Latina* CLXXV, 943 ff. Commenting on the same passage in his *Etudes sur l'esthétique du moyen âge*, de Bruyne remarks, 'Hugues énonce ici à la tête de tous les théologiens qui suivront, le principe métaphysique en vertu duquel se justifie l'infinie variété de l'art mediéval: multipliez les sculptures dans une cathédrale: si belle que soit chacune, elle ne prend toute sa valeur que dans un ensemble innomerable: comment épusier la beauté de l'Infini?'

107. De Bruyne says of poetic descriptions, 'Le poète ne peut sauter aucun détail imposé par la clarté logique' (*Esthétique*, p. 219); and again, 'La *longueur* qui semble aux mediévaux la rançon de la *précision*, elle-même attribut de la *clarté* intellectuelle, n'est donc pas considérée par plusieurs de leurs esthéticiens comme un défaut esthétique' (*Etudes*, II. 48).

108. 'Puisque l'imagination est au service de la raison, ne nous étonnons donc pas de l'extrême variété, de la multiplicité, de l'incohérence des allégories qui suivent dans les œuvres mediévales: *l'unité de l'objet*, en effect, découle non point des images invoquées, mais de la *réalité pensée*' (*Etudes*, II. 336).

109. On the medieval sermon see de Bruyne, *Esthétique*, p. 250, *Etudes*, II. 53 ff., Harry Caplan, *Medieval artes praedicandi* (1934), Etienne Gilson, 'Michel Menot et la technique du sermon mediéval', *Revue d'histoire franciscaine* II (1925), 299-350—reprinted in *Les idées et les lettres* (1932)—and T. M. Charland, *Artes praedicandi* (1936), G. R. Owst, *Preaching in medieval England* (1926).

110. Charland, op. cit., p. 132.

111. Gilson, op. cit., p. 341 quotes ,'magis enim amanda est animarum aedificatio quam sermonis continuatio'.

112. See Rosemary Freeman, *English Emblem Books* (1948), p. 19 ff. for an important consideration of the difference between medieval and Elizabethan allegory.

113. On this topic there is an excellent discussion in Marco Mincoff, *Baroque literature in England* (Sophia, 1947).

114. See C. R. Baskervill, 'Conventional features of *Fulgens and Lucres*', *M.P.* XXIV (1926-27), 419-42.

115. The character of 'Trecatio' in Edwardes' *Palamon and Arcite* about whom Queen Elizabeth remarked, 'God's pity, what a knave it is!' (Boas, p. 103), may be supposed to represent Edwardes' comic addition to the Chaucerian story.

116. W. Creizenach, *English drama in the age of Shakespeare* (1916) speaks of parallel sub-plots in Philips' *Patient Grissil* (1558-61) and the anon. *Esther and Ahasuerus* (*c*. 1580-92). The latter survives only in a mutilated German version (Hertz, *Englische Schauspieler und Englisches Schauspiel* (1903), p. 111) and this would seem to give insecure evidence. In *Patient Grissil* the parallel sub-plot seems notable only by its absence.

117. See Jean Seznec, *La survivance des dieux antiques* (London, 1940).

118. See Edgar Wind, 'Studies in allegorical portraiture, I', *J.W.C.I.* I (1937-38), 138-62, and Frances Yates, 'Elizabeth as Astrea', *J.W.C.I.* X (1947), 27-82.

119. Commentary on Ben Jonson, *Cynthia's Revels* (3 vol. Gifford-Cunningham edn., I. 205).

120. The fullest treatment of these habits is found in Pierre Villey's *Les sources et l'évolution des Essais de Montaigne* (second edn., 1933).

121. See C. S. Lewis, *The allegory of love* (1936) for an account of the tradition.

122. *The Elizabethan sermon* (1940), p. 37 f.

123. *C.S.P. Spanish 1558-67*, p. 375.

124. *Life of Sidney*, p. 156.

125. Grosart's *Daniel*, III. 179.

126. See Frances Yates, op. cit.

127. See E. C. Wilson, *England's Eliza*, for an admirable account of these.

128. 'Elizabethan Chivalry', *J.W.C.I.* XX (1957), 4-25.

129. R. M. Sargent, *At the court of Queen Elizabeth* (1935), tells us the story of Dyer's career. Sargent's interpretations have not, however, obtained universal acceptance; and I have sought to restrict myself to points not contradicted elsewhere.

130. Gilbert Talbot to the Earl of Shrewsbury, 11th May 1573, quoted in Sargent, p. 28.

131. Sidney's Lelius is presumably Sir Henry Lee, and his Philisides would seem to be a self-portrait; but nothing depends on these identifications.

132. I mean 'the plays which they *produced*'; I do not wish to be taken to imply that these men were necessarily the authors of the works their troupes performed. See *M.L.Q.* XII (1951), 134-36 for a useful caveat on this point.

133. *E.S.*, IV. 160.

134. op. cit., p. 281; Mrs I-S. Ewbank points out to me that the transition would be less jarring for those who were used to the tradition of 'Elisa, queen of shepherds all'.

135. loc. cit.

136. *E.S.*, III. 516.

137. *Complaint and Satire* (1956).

IV

1. I should explain at this point that I postpone any consideration of the sub-plots in Lyly's plays until I have concluded my play-by-play survey. See below, p. 229 ff.

2. T. W. Baldwin, *Five-act structure*, p. 500 ff.

3. See Bond, III. 110.

4. J. W. Bennett, 'Oxford and *Endimion*', *P.M.L.A.* LVII (1942), 354-69.

5. E. K. Chambers, *Lee*, p. 283.

6. I am grateful to Mr Bryant for lending me a copy of his paper when it proved to be unobtainable by ordinary methods.

7. P. W. Long, 'The purport of Lyly's *Endimion*', *P.M.L.A.* XXIV (1909), 164-84.

    P. W. Long, 'Lyly's *Endimion*: an addendum', *M.P.* VIII (1910-11), 599-605.

    C. R. Baskervill [Review of Feuillerat], *M.L.N.* XXVII (1912), 147-52.

    B. F. Huppé, 'Allegory of love in Lyly's court comedies', E.L.H. XIV (1947), 93-113.

8. Dover Wilson calls it 'the boldest in conception and the most beautiful in execution of all Lyly's plays' (op. cit., p. 101). The performance in the Taylorian Institution (at Oxford) in 1944 is thus described by C. S. Lewis, 'When I saw *Endimion*, the courtly scenes (not the weak foolery of Sir Tophas) held me delighted for five acts' (*Sixteenth Century*, p. 316).

9. Not only in the *Love's Labour's Lost* instances discussed below but also in the pinching of Corsites by fairies, which is resurrected for Falstaff's benefit in *Merry Wives*.

10. See D. C. Allen, 'Neptune's "Agar" in Lyly's *Gallathea*', *M.L.N.* XLIX (1934), 451 f.

11. *Pastoral Poetry*, p. 231.

12. *England's Eliza*, p. 143.

13. *Pastoral Poetry*, p. 232.

14. Cf. Dryden: 'I writ not always in the proper terms of navigation, land-service, or in the cant of any profession. . . . Virgil has avoided those proprieties, because he writ not to mariners, soldiers, astronomers, gardeners, peasants etc., but to all in general, and in particular to men and ladies of the first quality, who have been better bred than to be too nicely knowing in the terms.' ('Dedication of the Aeneis', Ker, II. 236.)

15. The obvious play to be mentioned as preceding *Campaspe* in the use of prose is Gascoigne's *Supposes*, derived from the verse as well as the prose version of Ariosto's *Suppositi*. Stylistically as well as in terms of plot-construction, *Supposes* is an extremely neat and workmanlike job, but it is without notable refinement. See G. Tillotson, 'The prose of Lyly's comedies', *Essays in criticism and research* (1942), pp. 17-30.

16. See J. E. Bernard, *The prosody of the Tudor interludes* (1939).

V

1. *Menaphon*, ed. G. B. Harrison (1927), p. 19.

2. See René Pruvost, *Matteo Bandello and Elizabethan fiction* (1937), pp. 103-95.

3. R. W. Chambers, *The continuity of English prose* (E.E.T.S., 1932).

4. See *Much Ado*, II. i. 113.

5. J. Swart, 'Lyly and Pettie', *English Studies* XXIII (1941), 18.

6. Both Pruvost (*Greene*, p. 92) and G. Wilson Knight (*R.E.S.* XV (1939), 1-18) have made the comparison with Pope.

7. This book is not recorded in *S.T.C.* There is a copy in the Huntington Library, San Marino.

8. See e.g. F. Landmann, *Der Euphuismus* (1881), C. G. Child, *John Lyly and Euphuism* (1894).

9. See Feuillerat, p. 446 ff.

10. For Aelfric's 'Euphuism' see *M.P.* XXII (1924-25), 353 ff. Cf. J. P. Schneider, *The prose-style of Richard Rolle of Hampole with special reference to its Euphuistic tendencies* (1906).

11. Jonas Barish, 'The prose-style of John Lyly', *E.L.H.* XXIII (1956), 15.

12. See above, n. 6.

13. See above, n. 11.

14. *Wit and rhetoric in the Renaissance* (1937); cf. G. Williamson, *The Senecan Amble* (1951).

15. 'The immediate source of Euphuism', *P.M.L.A.* LIII (1938), 678-86. Cf. John Rainolds, *Oratio in laudem artis poeticae*, ed. Ringler and Allen (1940).

16. We should note here Nashe's statement that Lyly was an 'immoderate' admirer of the preaching of Launcelot Andrewes (cited Bond, I. 60, n. 3).

17. Cf. J. S. Weld, 'Some problems of Euphuistic narrative', *S.P.* XLV (1948), 165-71.

18. Cf. Barish, op. cit., p. 22 f.

19. *Opera omnia* (1703-06) I.

20. See Lauchert, 'Der Einfluss der Physiologus auf Euphuismus', *Englische Studien* XIV (1890), 188-210; Hoehna, *Physiologus in Elizabethan Drama* (1930), 21-32.

21. See Pruvost, *Greene*, p. 64, citing Faral.

22. Such as the *Formularum* of Eucherius (5th century) [*P.L.* 50], the *Allegoriae* of pseudo-Hrabanus Maurus (13th-14th centuries) [*P.L.* 112], the *De Universo* of Hrabanus Maurus (9th century) [*P.L.* 111], etc.

23. See the figure of Castilio Balthazar in Marston's *Antonio and Mellida*.

24. Act IV, scene i (*Plays*, ed. Harvey Wood, II. 113).

25. I am indebted to Mr John Vaughan for pointing out the reference and lending me a photostat.

26. The speech is contained in B.M. Add. MS. 48109 (Yelverton MS. 121).

27. W. G. Crane (op. cit., p. 91) has suggested that the difference between the two styles may be seen as stemming from the difference between Cambridge Ramism and Oxford Aristotelianism.

28. Cf. the third sonnet in Sidney's *Astrophel and Stella*.

29. It may be worth noting the sense of French elegance introduced by new elements in the vocabulary (*charm*, *shock*, etc.).

30. See above, p. 82.

VI

1. Lawrence Babb, *The Elizabethan Malady* (1951), especially chapters VI and VII.

2. The moralization of Ovid's *Metamorphoses* seems to have been standard in Europe at least from the time of the *Ovide Moralisé* (1316-1328) till beyond the date of Sandys' translation (1626) and to have provided a whole iconography of the passions. See M. D. Henkel, *Vorträge der Bibliothek Warburg*, 1926-27, pp. 58-144.

3. See T. W. Baldwin, *Five-act structure* (1947) and *The genetics of Shakspere's plays* (1959). General objections to the methods employed by this author to establish dates may be seen in my review of the latter book (*R.E.S.* 1961).

4. Marco Mincoff, 'Shakespeare and Lyly', *Shakespeare Survey* XIV (1961), 15-24.

5. M. C. Bradbrook, *Shakespeare and Elizabethan Poetry* (1951), p. 151.

6. op. cit, pp. 20-22.

7. The logical conclusion to this difference can be seen if we compare the passage in *Twelfth Night* which is taken from Lyly, with its original in *Gallathea*. In Lyly's play the statement, 'My Father had but one daughter, and therefore I could have no sister' (III. ii. 36) is part of a balanced sequence, in which it must find its partner before it is complete: 'if I had but one [*sister*], my brother must needs have two.' Lyly plays up the wit

of the exchange, by emphasizing the balance, and so plays down the sincerity. Throughout the scene the two nymphs wittily echo one another, but each in fact is speaking to *us*; it is only we in the audience who can know the truth and understand the wit. We appreciate their delicacy in conjecture, as they circle round the possibility that the other 'boy' is really a girl. We appreciate that the situation is bound to call out their characteristics by frustrating their intentions, and we are able to apprehend the whole scene as a structure because of its linear simplicity of organization. But Shakespeare's scene (II. iv) is full of chiaroscuro and complex cross-reference. Viola knows the truth of the whole situation and plays with the idea of reaching a much-desired self-expression without speaking unambiguously. We in the audience know what she really means, while Orsino only grasps the surface appearance. Here the doubleness of expression involves more than a pattern of wit; it evokes Viola's complex relationship of frustration and fulfilment, which is what the page role allows to her, at the same time as it reminds us of her brother, and her aloneness in the world. The equivoque in Shakespeare sets a feeling behind a feeling, in a context of other but related thoughts (the embassy to Olivia). Viola says, 'a woman may die of love', 'I may die of love for you', 'I am alone in the world—but I am not sure even of that', 'melancholy thoughts have no place in a context of business', and no doubt other things as well.

8. The word *Moth* was pronounced *mote* in Elizabethan English (Kökeritz, p. 320). The final consonant was often sounded in French words (see the rhyme in this very play between *Boyet* and *debt* (V. ii. 333 f.); in any case there was the cognate English word, *mot, mott, motte*, with a very similar range of meanings. It seems probable that this is what Costard is referring to when he says to Moth: 'I marvel thy master hath not eaten thee for a word; for thou art not so long by the head as honorificabilitudinitatibus' (V. i. 36 ff.). The play employs French puns elsewhere; the [*env*]*oy*/*goose* puns in III. i have been remarked already (see *M.L.N.* LX) and we probably ought to add the play on *posterior*/*culled* at V. i. 78 f.

9. The case is obviously complicated by the relationship being allegorical as well as formal. But one might say that the method of each book of the *Faerie Queene* is to exhaust the oppositions that are appropriate to that virtue, and sometimes this shows up simply in the formal stances in such groups as Palmer-Guyon-Furor-Occasion-Pyrochles.

10. op. cit., p. 24.

11. See the letter from Cope to Robert Cecil printed in *E.S.*, IV. 139: 'there is no new play that the Queen [Anne of Denmark] hath not seen, but they have revived an old one called *Loves Labore Lost*, which for wit and mirth he says will please her exceedingly'. The letter is dated 1605.

APPENDIX

The Authorship of the Songs in Lyly's Plays

The question of the authenticity of the songs printed in Lyly's plays is one of the three spacious playgrounds opened to scholars by the study of Lyly— the others concern the origin of Euphuism, and the meaning of *Endimion*. It has seemed unnecessarily cumbrous to canvas the arguments for and against the songs inside a chapter devoted to the unity of the plays, and I have chosen to raise the rather special issues involved, here in a separate place.

The natural supposition is that the songs printed in Lyly's plays are by Lyly. Doubt was not cast on this till the advent of modern bibliography, with its scrutiny of the details of the early texts. This revealed that the quarto editions of Lyly lacked the song-texts (except in the anomalous case of *The Woman in the Moon*, where the 'copy' behind the printed text is clearly of a different kind). The songs supposed to be Lyly's are found first in Blount's collected edition of 1632, *Six Court Comedies*, which is otherwise dependent on the preceding quartos. It is clear, moreover, that the plays contained songs from the very beginning, for the songs that Blount supplies are clearly asked for in the quarto texts, either by cues in the speeches or by stage directions. We are faced, in consequence by alternative possibilities, either that Blount in 1632 recovered songs that had been lost for nigh on fifty years, or that he had new songs specially written for the occasion. I say 'specially written' for some at least of the songs are too closely integrated into their contexts to be borrowings from other contexts (e.g. *Gallathea*, IV. ii; *Midas*, III. ii; *Endimion*, III. iii). Neither alternative looks very attractive; we are faced by what W. R. Bowden calls 'the choice . . . between something that occasionally did happen [*songs recovered*] and something that might have happened [*songs specially written*]' (*The English Dramatic Lyric, 1603-42*, p. 308); only a painful sifting of details can tip the balance of judgment one way or another.

But before we consider details, it seems appropriate to make some general points about song-texts in the Elizabethan theatre; for neglect of these has vitiated some arguments in the past. Songs cannot be treated as integral parts of Elizabethan dramatic texts; frequently they got lost; Bowden tells us that over thirty songs are missing from the text of Massinger (p. 87); even when printed, they are often misplaced, and this has led to the plausible suggestion that they were contained not in the prompt-book but on separate sheets, separately available to the actors, as were letters, speeches etc. In the case of troupes of choirboys, such as those who presented Lyly's

Appendix

plays, whose Masters were musicians, and whose song-books must have been an important part of their capital, the effort to guard and preserve songs, evident elsewhere, must have been especially strong. If this was the reason why the early quartos of Lyly's plays do not contain the songs, it would also be a reason for supposing the songs to have been preserved in the music-library of the Paul's boys. In any case, this line of argument ought to make us suspicious of ideas that MSS of the songs which did not contain theatrical corrections of the play-text could not have been 'authentic'.

Effective argument based on authentic details has been the prerogative of those who have wished to deny Lyly's authorship of the songs; the first attack remains the most effective piece of reasoning in the whole field— I refer to W. W. Greg's 1905 essay in the first volume of *M.L.R.* Yet the presuppositions on which this essay rests are hardly tenable today, and much of this Appendix must be taken up with a tedious point-by-point examination of Greg's arguments, together with those of his supporter, J. R. Moore (writing in *P.M.L.A.* for 1927).

The obvious starting-point for a dating of the songs is a sense of the lateness of the style. But 'sense' in this sense can hardly be the basis of an argument, and Greg sought to crystalize his impressions by pointing to words in the songs which *O.E.D.* did not cite from sixteenth century contexts. This is slippery ground, for *O.E.D.* is not designed to supply fine discriminations of date, and even Greg was unable to retain his footing. Warwick Bond, in a subsequent reply, was able to supply what *O.E.D.* had omitted— sixteenth century contexts for the suspect words—and the lexical attack on the authenticity of the songs must be admitted to be a failure.

A far stronger basis of argument is supplied by the appearance of two songs from *Campaspe*—'O for a bowl of fat Canary' and 'What bird so sings, yet so does wail'—the former in the second edition of Middleton's *A Mad World my Masters* (1640), and the latter in Dekker and Ford's *The Sun's Darling* (1624). The appearance of these songs in plays by other men must mean either that Blount lifted them from other contexts to supply gaps in his *Lyly*, or that Dekker (I shall suppose him to be the author of *The Sun's Darling* song) and Middleton used extant Lyly songs to pad out their plays. Greg and Moore have concentrated on the second of the two songs—the late date of the first makes it unimportant as evidence—and have argued that the version in Blount is derivative (*a*) because the text is inferior and incoherent and (*b*) because it is less well integrated into its dramatic context. Here I may quote (side by side) the two texts:

DEKKER (Bowers' text)

What bird so sings, yet so does wail,
'Tis Philomel the Nightingale;
Jugg, Jugg, Jugg, Terue she cries,
And hating earth, to heaven she flies
— Cuckow.
Ha, ha, hark, hark, the Cuckows sing
Cuckow, to welcom in the Spring.

368

Brave prick-song; who is't now we hear!
'Tis the larks silver leer a leer:
Chirup, the Sparrow flies away;
For hee fell too't ere break of day.
Ha, ha, hark, hark, the Cuckows sing
Cuckow, to welcom in the Spring.

BLOUNT (Bond's text)

What Bird so sings, yet so dos wayle?
O t'is the rauish'd Nightingale.
Iug. Iug, Iug, Iug, tereu, shee cryes,
And still her woes at Midnight rise.
Braue prick song! who is't now we heare?
None but the Larke so shrill and cleare;
How at heauens gats she claps her wings,
The Morne not waking till shee sings.
Heark, heark, with what a pretty throat
Poore Robin red-breast tunes his note;
Heark how the iolly Cuckoes sing
Cuckoe, to welcome in the spring,
Cuckoe, to welcome in the spring.

The argument in which Greg compares the texts of these two songs contains many implausibilities and in some places an ignorance of Elizabethan expression which we must attribute to the period rather than the man. He supposes that *prick-song* means choral music and is therefore more appropriate in its Dekker context; in fact, it is conventionally and generally used of the nightingale (leaning her breast against the thorn). In the Dekker version *prick-song* appears isolated between the cuckoo and the lark, for neither of whom it has any propriety. Again, the Dekker line, 'And hating earth, to heaven she flies' bears an obvious relation to lark-lore, but little or none to the nightingale, which is not a soaring bird, either in myth or nature. In both these cases the Dekker lines sound like a confused memory of the Blount ones. Greg also takes the double stanza form of the Dekker version to be a sign of its superiority, but it could equally well be regarded as a simplification of the more complex, *durchkomponiert*, non-stanzaic form in Blount. The twice-repeated 'Cuckoe, to welcome in the spring' need not be regarded as a relic of the stanzaic refrain in the Dekker; twice-repeated refrain-lines in non-stanzaics songs are common enough not to require this hypothesis. Without going outside Shakespeare one can find it in 'Tell me where is fancy bred' and in 'Come thou monarch of the vine'. Greg's further 'presumption that . . . he [Blount's reviser] was influenced by the lark-song in *Cymbeline*, a striking expression from which he appears to have borrowed' (p. 50) seems equally unnecessary. The lines, 'at heauens gats she claps her wings,/The Morne not waking till shee sings', give a unified conceit which by-passes Shakespeare's 'the lark/At heaven's gate sings' though the tradition also includes that. Shakespeare's lark is singing an aubade (like Cloten);

2A

Blount's lark is not only doing this, but also clapping at the gate with her wings. Both give perfectly permissible variations on a tradition sufficiently lengthy and complex to weary Dr Furness (see the note in the New Variorum *Cymbeline*), but variations which need not depend on one another.

For the rest, Greg's vision of a reviser who thought that 'Dekker's grammar was open to criticism, and [who] felt constrained to alter the second [line] in order to obtain a personal consequent to "who"'' (pp. 49-50) sounds more like a picture in a mirror than one in a microscope; the rigour of logic here may be in excess of what the material will bear.

Another line of argument in respect of these two songs has been pressed by J. R. Moore, who finds the context in *The Sun's Darling* to give greater support to the song, and supposes therefore that this is the original context. It is true that the episode in which Dekker uses this song is one which contains much reference to birds. This is not surprising, however; act II is that devoted to Spring 'who first taught birds to sing', and the many references to Spring in the act are likely to be accompanied by a fair number of references to birdsong. There are no detailed connections between the song and the action, and as far as general connections are concerned a song borrowed to fit a context is likely to do as well as does a song written for its context. As far as the question of priority is concerned no help seems to be forthcoming from this line of argument.

A second type of argument followed by Moore would seem to be equally indecisive. He points out that there is some contradiction between stage directions in Blount's *Lyly* and the songs to which they refer, and takes this to be a sign of Blount's distance from the 'authentic copies'. I have already given reasons which may serve to explain the many misplacings of song in Elizabethan dramatic texts; if the 'authentic copies' were on loose sheets, they were very liable to become misplaced. Indeed, the misplacement would seem to be an argument *against* Blount as the man who commissioned the songs. One would expect the man who commissioned songs to be able to fit them into the texts for which he designed them. If he did not understand or notice the incongruence, this may have been because he did not understand the songs which he had turned up.

Moore's last line of argument for Blount as the man responsible for the 1632 songs depends on the manifest absence of some songs even from the 1632 text. He remarks, 'Only those songs called for in the stage directions or in the last speech of a scene . . . [are] recovered' while 'four (or perhaps five) songs called for by the dialogue of the plays (although not specified by the stage directions of the quartos) . . . [are] omitted' (p. 630). His preferred explanation is that 'his [Blount's] "reviser" read the plays too hastily, taking his cues only from obvious stage directions and from the last speech in each scene' (p. 632).

In general this is true; but the evidence is not always easy to assess. Thus *Mother Bombie*, V. iii. 55 ff. (Q. 2 text) reads:

Syn. You know Memphio is very rich and wise, and therefore let us strike the gentle stroke, and sing a catch, sing.
Nas. God morrow, Mistress Bride, and send you a huddle.

We should compare with this an earlier passage in the same scene—V. iii. 22 ff. (also in the Q. 2 text):

> *Bed.* . . . what shall we sing?
> *Syn.* The love-knot, for that's best for a bridal. Sing. God
>   morrow fair bride, and send you joy of your bridal.

It is not immediately obvious in the two passages, as quoted from the Q. 2 text (which was the basis of Blount's *Mother Bombie*), why he supplied a song for the first context and not for the second. Moore's argument can only be sustained if we suppose that the Q. 1 text was read in the search for the missing songs (in Q. 1 [1594] the second *sing* of the first quotation is italicized and so able to be taken as a stage direction), though Q. 2 [1598] was used by Blount to set up his text from. This implies a more complex process in the search for the songs than Moore had allowed, though it does not, in itself, imply that his argument was wrong. But even if we admit that Blount's reviser only responded to certain obvious demands for song in the Quarto texts, it does not follow that a full corpus of the songs did not exist, or was not available. We know that seventeenth-century printers were careless in most respects, and it would be sheer folly to convert their 'did not avail himself of' into 'was not available'. If, as we have supposed, the songs were written on separate sheets, we have a situation of enough difficulty to explain the careless omission of some songs from the less obvious contexts. At least, we have an explanation not notably worse than that which requires the remote hypothesis of songs specially written for a new edition.

Most of the features of the songs that have been described do not require this remote hypothesis, but can be fitted easily into the framework of what seems obvious—that if Blount sought the songs he would look first among the music archives of the Paul's boys. It is worth while noting in this connection that the two plays Blount excluded from his collection were the two over which the Paul's boys had no control—*Love's Metamorphosis*, which seems to have passed to the Chapel boys, and *The Woman in the Moon*, which may not have been written for any of the boys' companies. If the songs lay in the Paul's library, written in separate sheets (or in part-books) then the misplacing when the printer tried to integrate them with the quarto texts, which supplied the rest of his copy, is explicable. The failure to supply all the songs could also fit into this supposition, though not so easily. The reappearance of 'O for a bowl of fat Canary' in Middleton's *A Mad World my Masters*, and in authentic form, could be attached to the fact that Middleton's play was presented by the boys of Paul's. The less authentic form of 'What bird so sings' found in *The Sun's Darling* has been explained (by W. R. Bowden) as a memorial reconstruction, and piracy may be the proper explanation here.

One small point may be thought to support the supposition that Blount had recourse to some music collection for his texts of the songs. *Endimion*, as printed by Blount, differs from the quarto, not only in the insertion of three songs, but also in the addition of a Dumb Show, with the stage direction, 'Music sounds', for which there is no cue in the quarto. Greg notes

Appendix

the Dumb Show, but dismisses it with, 'It is simply the representation of the dream subsequently related by Endimion in V. i.'(p. 51). This is more or less true (the details are not identical), but hardly explains why Blount would take the trouble to *invent* a Dumb Show, hardly (*pace* Greg) a *dernier cri* in 1632, not required by the economy of the play and remarkably ineffective in *reading* (and it is as a reading text that Blount presents the plays). The stage direction 'Music sounds' may help us here. It is, I believe, the only appearance of such a direction in Lyly's plays. This is the only common point which links the Dumb Show with the songs, and if we are to look for a common source for both additions we must look for it first where the music was preserved.

Of course, even proof that Blount had recourse to the music library of the Paul's boys would not require us to believe that the songs he found there were by Lyly. The plays may have been revived and the songs rewritten, for all we know. That this happened to *Endimion* is the conclusion drawn by Mr W. J. Lawrence from one piece of evidence. Thomas Ravenscroft included in his *Brief Discourse* (1614) a 'fairies' dance' which seems to fit the context of the fairies' punishment of Corsites in *Endimion* IV. iii, remarkably well. The quarto stage direction for this runs, 'The fairies dance, and with a song pinch him, and he falleth asleep; they kiss Endimion and depart'; the crucial lines in Ravenscroft run

> Pinch him black
> And pinch him blue
> That seeks to steal a lover true.

This would seem to refer, unequivocally, to the punishment of Corsites, who is pinched for seeking to steal the body of the 'lover true' Endimion from the lunary bank where he lies sleeping.

There is, however, in Blount, another song which corresponds, even more narrowly, to the situation described in the play. Does the Blount song represent the original, and the Ravenscroft belong to a revival? We cannot tell; it only seems to darken the murk of conjecture to have two texts for this one song, lacking any knowledge of the fates of songs in the playhouse, or the process by which fashion affected them.

INDEX